Johann Joseph Fux

Johann Joseph
Fux
and the music
of the
Austro-Italian Baroque

edited by
HARRY WHITE

Scolar Press

Published by
SCOLAR PRESS
Gower House
Croft Road
Aldershot
Hants GU11 3HR
England

Ashgate Publishing Co.
Old Post Road
Brookfield
Vermont 05036
USA

British Library Cataloguing in Publication Data
Johann Joseph Fux and the music of the Austro-Italian Baroque.
　1. Austria. Music
　I. White, Harry
　780.92

ISBN 0-85967-832-6

Printed in Great Britain at the University Press, Cambridge

Contents

Acknowledgements

It is my pleasant duty to record thanks here to a number of people who encouraged the production of this volume from its inception onwards and who helped in various ways to bring it into being. My greatest debt is to Professor Hellmut Federhofer, for his most valuable suggestions in connection with the range of contributions included in this book. Professor Federhofer's unrivalled command of Fux scholarship, together with his own remarkable achievement in this field of study, have greatly enhanced the design and scope of the present volume. I am likewise indebted to Professor Rudolf Schnitzler, whose wise counsel was particularly useful in the matter of Fux's sacred-dramatic music, and who placed his specialized knowledge of the oratorio repertoire at the imperial court in Vienna at my disposal. I should also like to express my gratitude to the contributors to this volume as a whole for various points of information and for assistance above and beyond the essays published here. My thanks are also due to Professor Friedrich Wilhelm Riedel and Dr Gernot Gruber, both of whom expressed keen interest in this project.

I am particularly grateful to Dr Ingeborg Harer and Dr Sophie Kidd, who prepared English versions of the papers by Wolfgang Suppan and Erika Kanduth respectively, and to Seán Lysaght, who translated the introduction to Ingrid Schubert's bibliography.

Finally, I should like to thank Brian Last and Ellen Keeling of Scolar Press, for their expert assistance in the preparation of this volume.

Harry White,
Dublin, 1991

Notes on contributors

Hellmut Federhofer is emeritus professor of musicology at Johannes Gutenberg University in Mainz. His research has been principally concerned with the history and theory of music in Austria. He established the series *Mainzer Studien zur Musikwissenschaft* and *Musik Alter Meister* and was editor of *Acta Musicologica* from 1962 until 1986. His many books, editions and articles are listed in the *Festschriften* published to mark his sixtieth birthday in 1971 (Mainz, Schotts Söhne) and his seventy-fifth birthday in 1986 (Tutzing, H. Schneider, 1988). The author of several studies and editions of the music of Fux, he has been editor-in-chief of the Johann Joseph Fux *Gesamtausgabe* (Graz) from 1955 to 1967 and since 1986.

Rudolf Flotzinger has been professor and head of the department of musicology at Karl-Franzens University, Graz, since 1971. He was co-editor, with Gernot Gruber, of *Musikgeschichte Österreichs* from 1977 until 1979. He has published widely on medieval and eighteenth-century music and is general editor of the series *Grazer Musikwissenschaftliche Arbeiten*, in which his *Fux-Studien* appeared in 1985.

Robert N. Freeman studied musicology at the University of California, Los Angeles. He is currently associate professor of music at the University of California, Santa Barbara. His research includes the history of music at the Austrian abbeys in the eighteenth century, and he is the author of *The Practice of Music at Melk Abbey based upon the Documents, 1681–1826* (Vienna, 1989). In 1979 he published a thematic catalogue of the works of Franz Schneider (1737–1812).

Erika Kanduth has been professor of Romance languages at the University of Vienna since 1973. Her numerous studies of Italian literature include *Wesenzüge der modernen italienischen Erzahlliteratur* (Heidelberg, 1968) and *Cesare Pavese im Rahmen der pessimistischen italienischen Literatur* (Vienna and Stuttgart, 1971). She has prepared various texts for editions of music, among them *La donna forte nella madre de' sette Maccabei* (1976) and *Il trionfo della fede* (1991) for the Fux *Gesamtausgabe*.

Colin Lawson is senior lecturer in music at the University of Sheffield, and the author of a book on the chalumeau. He is professor of classical studies at the Guildhall School of Music and Drama, and principal clarinet of the London Classical Players and The Hanover Band, with which he has toured and recorded extensively.

Josef-Horst Lederer has lectured in the department of musicology at Karl-Franzens University, Graz, since 1972. He was appointed an assistant professor in Graz in 1988, having completed his *Habilitation* there in 1985. His publications include editions of Fux's *Missa brevis solennitatis*, K.5, in 1974 and ten trio-sonatas in 1990 for the *Gesamtausgabe* of the composer's works.

Alfred Mann, professor emeritus on the faculties of Rutgers University and the Eastman School of Music, University of Rochester, published the first modern translations from Fux's *Gradus ad Parnassum* in Germany (1938) and the United States (1943). He also published a critical edition of the original text of the *Gradus* for the Fux *Gesamtausgabe* in 1967. He is the author of *The Study of Fugue* (various editions, 1958 to 1987) and *Theory and Practice* (1987) and has served as editor for volumes of the complete works of Handel, Mozart and Schubert.

Ingrid Schubert lectures in musicology at Karl-Franzens University, Graz, where she completed a doctorate in 1970. Her publications include an edition, with Gösta Neuwirth, of the *Te Deum*, K. 270, for the Fux *Gesamtausgabe* in 1979.

Herbert Seifert received his Ph.D from the University of Vienna with a dissertation on Giovanni Buonaventura Viviani. He is now professor of musicology at Vienna and has published several studies of seventeenth- and early eighteenth-century music. His books include *Die Oper am Wiener Kaiserhof im 17.Jahrhundert* (Tutzing, 1985).

Wolfgang Suppan is professor of musicology and director of the *Institut für Musikethnologie* at the University for music and the performing arts in Graz. His research interests include organology and music for wind instruments. He has edited books on the anthropology of music, on European folk music and a *Lexikon des Blasmusikwesens*. He is general editor of the series *Musik aus der Steiermark* (Freiburg), *Musikethnologie Sammelbände* (Graz) and *Alta musica* (Tutzing).

Rudolf Walter was for many years professor and dean of church music at the State *Hochschule* for music and the performing arts in Stuttgart. Since 1971 he has also been honorary professor of musicology at Johannes Gutenberg University in Mainz.

Harry White lectures in music at University College, Dublin. He completed a doctorate on the oratorios of Fux in 1986 and has edited *Il trionfo della fede* for the Fux *Gesamtausgabe* (1991). Co-editor of *Irish Musical Studies: Musicology in Ireland* (Dublin 1990), he is currently writing a book on the da-capo aria in the sacred-dramatic music of Fux, Handel and Bach.

Introduction

Harry White

The year 1991 marks the 250th anniversary of the death of Johann Joseph Fux, imperial *Kapellmeister* at the court of Charles VI in Vienna from 1715 until his decease. Prior to this appointment, Fux was an important member of the court's retinue of composers, singers and instrumentalists from 1698 onwards, first as court composer and additionally as deputy *Kapellmeister* (from 1711) and *Kapellmeister* to the widow of Joseph I, Wilhelmine Amalia (from 1713).[1] He also held the position of deputy *Kapellmeister* at St Stephen's Cathedral in the city from 1705, and succeeded J. M. Zächer there as principal *Kapellmeister* in 1712, a post he relinquished on his appointment as *Kapellmeister* to Charles VI.

Johann Joseph Fux has long been regarded as the outstanding exponent of the late Austro-Italian Baroque, and his works comprise a monumental and definitive example of music under the demanding patronage of the Holy Roman Empire. That patronage represented a systematic cultivation of music for the express purposes of celebrating the political, cultural and religious stability which the Habsburg dynasty enjoyed in great measure during the reigns of Leopold I, Joseph I and Charles VI, especially in the period 1680–1740. In the music of Fux and that of his colleagues at the imperial court (especially Antonio Caldara, Marc' Antonio Ziani, Francesco Conti and Giuseppe Porsile) the impact of this patronage is abundantly clear. Whether as a composer of festive operas, *serenate*, orchestral and *a-cappella* masses, various kinds of liturgical music, sacred-dramatic works (oratorios) or instrumental music, Fux may be regarded as the great culminator of a specifically Austrian tradition of imperial and Roman Catholic music which both reflected and actively nourished the concept of *auctoritas* so central to the realization and implementation of 'Holy Roman Empire'. Fux's music is imbued with this concept, which equally informs the many secular and sacred-dramatic texts he set, either in terms of imperial celebration or re-affirmation of Roman Catholic doctrine.

Fux's relationship with the imperial court in Vienna ranks in comparative importance with that of Bach and the town council of Leipzig or that of Handel and the rival patrons of Italian opera in London. Fux's music embodies a vital and independent synthesis of socio-political and cultural conditions during the late Baroque which enlarges our sense of the plurality and dissemination of musical styles during the first half of the eighteenth century. If the term 'baroque' appears increasingly under duress as investigations of this plurality intensify, there are nevertheless important factors which Bach, Handel, Fux and Alessandro Scarlatti (for example) share, and which justify the perception of Fux as the primary exponent of a locally defined and developed version of baroque style and structure. Fux's cultivation of the *da-capo* aria, for example, is one outstanding manifestation of his contribution in terms of a formal-dramatic structure which pervades the Baroque as a whole. In short, it is useful to consider two factors in particular in an overall assessment of Fux's music. First, its dependence upon the conditions of imperial patronage which obtained in Vienna; second, its intrinsic relevance to a wider understanding of baroque style in general.

This volume of essays explores the range of Fux's achievement from a number of different perspectives. As Hellmut Federhofer argues in the opening essay, Fux has not yet received the exhaustive scholarly attention enjoyed by his great contemporaries which would determine with exactitude the number, chronology and transmission of his works. Federhofer nevertheless traces the evolution of Fux scholarship from its tentative beginnings, through the seminal investigations of Ludwig Ritter von Köchel, to the work of the present day. While financial restrictions remain to hinder this work, many of the implications of this scholarship, and the lacunae which it has identified, cannot be adequately addressed. The continued publication of Fux's 'complete' works (such as they are known), and the gradual dissemination of his music in performances and recordings, however, have manifestly stimulated a renewal of interest in Fux, particularly since the founding of the Johann Joséph Fux-Gesellschaft in 1955, in which Federhofer himself has played so distinguished a part. When we recall that 1991 is for many people a 'Mozart year' above all else, it is difficult to avoid some contrast between the healthy state of Mozart scholarship (also greatly enabled by Köchel) and the considerable scrutiny of sources which Fux's music still awaits.

Robert Freeman's essay on the music archive at Melk Abbey in Lower Austria partly addresses this question of sources. Freeman speculates as to why Fux's music and that of his pupils should have been so poorly preserved there and provides much valuable information on the whole question of the transmission of baroque music in Austria. In many respects, this (and the sources appended to it) may be regarded as an instructive companion piece to Freeman's similar investigation of Caldara sources which appeared in 1987.[2]

If Fux enjoys a widespread reputation today, it is as the author of the *Gradus ad Parnassum* that he does so, and two essays in this volume consider aspects of this most influential of treatises on composition. Alfred Mann discusses the history of its use by, and influence upon, Haydn, Mozart, Beethoven and Schubert, through the initial agency of Bach and his pupil, Lorenz Mizler. This absorbing *Rezeptionsgeschichte* (and to a lesser extent, that of Fux's *Singfundament*) testifies to Fux's importance quite apart from the inherent interest of his own compositions. Rudolf Flotzinger, by contrast, offers a brief but compelling argument for the 'incompleteness' of the *Gradus* itself, which he adduces from Fux's remarks at the close of the work on his unfulfilled intentions of providing further material, and also from the design of the treatise as a whole.

One of the distinguishing features of late baroque Austrian music in general and of Fux's music in particular is its scoring and instrumentation. Fux's use of the chalumeau, trumpet, trombone and cornett is especially noteworthy in this respect, and both Colin Lawson and Wolfgang Suppan consider the technical and expressive dimensions of this use in their respective essays. Fux's chalumeau and cornett scoring in particular are features by which his *concertante* and *obbligato* textures in dramatic music may be distinguished in the main from those of his (north) German and Italian counterparts.

Instrumental music is also a vital consideration in Josef-Horst Lederer's detailed disclosure of certain of the copyists of Fux's trio-sonatas. Lederer's identification of different copyists (partly indebted to previous work undertaken by Wilhelm Gleissner) allows him to date the trio-sonatas and certain of Fux's vocal works in terms of when these were copied. We may note here in passing that Lederer's investigation invites emulation in the wider context of many of Fux's other works, given that the majority of these were transmitted by means of court copies (as against original manuscripts, few of which survive in Fux's case).

Fux's secular-dramatic works were the subject of an outstanding dissertation by John Henry van der Meer, published in 1961 as *Johann Joseph Fux als Opernkomponist* (Bilthoven). In the present volume, Herbert Seifert has drawn upon this dissertation and also upon his own subsequent research, to provide a cogent survey of Fux's operas and other dramatic works. Seifert's account offers a useful summary of the occasions for which these works were written, their essential structural and stylistic features and the court personnel who participated in their performance.

A somewhat different approach informs the two essays in this volume devoted to Fux's sacred-dramatic works, in the light of Howard Smither's chapter on the Viennese oratorio in his history of the genre, the first volume of which appeared in 1977.[3] Erika Kanduth considers the *internal* dynamics and dramaturgical-poetic principles which inform the libretti of Fux's *sepolcro* oratorios, while the present writer offers an assessment of the historical development of these texts towards a stylistic analysis of Fux's musico-dramatic resources.

Rudolf Walter's essay on the genesis and development of Fux's *Offertorium* settings is also primarily stylistic and analytic in focus. Walter considers the content and liturgical significance of Fux's choice of biblical texts and offers a parallel with Lutheran settings. In his stylistic discussion and in the appendix of works which follows it, Walter discriminates between different styles of biblical setting in terms of the liturgical function of each. Fux thus emerges as a vital figure in the development of baroque style in the context of Roman Catholic liturgical music.

This volume closes with a bibliography of Fux studies, (including a discography, editions of the music and theoretical works, iconographical studies, etc.) which should prove an indispensable source for further Fux scholarship. Ingrid Schubert explains in the introduction to her work that its form and content are greatly indebted to Hellmut Federhofer, whose own bibliographical work on Fux has greatly facilitated subsequent research, including that of the present writer.

The inclusion here of source studies, stylistic analyses, general surveys and more specialised investigations of different aspects of Fux's music and theoretical works, in addition to bibliographical material and an assessment of the present condition of Fux research, is ultimately designed to serve one end. If the present volume stimulates an increase in the performance and research of Fux's works, it will have fulfilled its purpose.

Notes

[1] A summary of Fux's life and works is available in *The New Grove Dictionary of Music and Musicians* (London, 1980), edited by Stanley Sadie. See 'Fux, Johann Joseph', by Hellmut Federhofer, Volume 7, pp. 43–6. See also Federhofer's essay, Chapter 1 in the present volume, which revises some of the biographical material to be found in the *Grove* article.

[2] See Robert Freeman, 'The Caldara manuscripts at Melk Abbey', *Antonio Caldara: Essays on his life and times*, edited by Brian W. Pritchard (Aldershot, 1987), pp. 213–46.

[3] Howard Smither, *A History of the Oratorio* I *The Oratorio in the Baroque Era: Italy, Vienna, Paris* (Chapel Hill, 1977), pp. 365–415.

1 Johann Joseph Fux und die Gegenwart

Hellmut Federhofer

Als Johann Joseph Fux am 13. Februar 1741 im Alter von 81 Jahren seine Augen schloß, wenige Monate nachdem Maria Theresia ihrem Vater Karl VI, auf den Thron gefolgt war, ging eine für Österreich glanzvolle Epoche der Musikgeschichte zu Ende. Sie ist untrennbar mit dem Namen des Hauses Habsburg verbunden. Der Kaiserhof in Wien, an dem auf allen Gebieten der Kultur Persönlichkeiten von Rang wirkten, setzte so wie für andere Künste auch für die geistliche und weltliche Musik allgemein gültige Maßstäbe. Der Höhepunkt dieser als Zeitalter des Barocks in die Literatur eingegangenen Epoche fällt in die unmittelbar den Türkensiegen des mit Fux ungefähr gleichaltrigen Prinzen Eugen folgenden Jahre.

Noch wenige Jahrzehnte zuvor war die abendländische Kultur ernstlich bedroht. Sie hätte eine vom tatsächlichen Geschichtsverlauf völlig abweichende Entwicklung nehmen müssen, wäre es dem Großwesir Kara Mustafa gelungen, im Jahre 1683 Wien und damit die Hauptstadt des Kaiserreiches zu erobern, ähnlich wie rund 200 Jahre vorher Konstantinopel und das byzantinische Kaiserreich den Anstürmen der Osmanen zum Opfer gefallen war. Sowohl für Fux als auch für W.A. Mozart, deren beider Gedenktage in das Jahr 1991 fallen, hätten die politischen und gesellschaftlichen Voraussetzungen für ihre künstlerische Entfaltung gefehlt. Der Höhepunkt ihres Schaffens lag nämlich in Wien. Für Fux, der seit dem Ende des 17. Jahrhunderts ohne Unterbrechung bis zu seinem Ableben drei deutschen Kaisern, nämlich Leopold I., Joseph I. und Karl VI., zunächst als Hofkomponist, dann als Vizehofkapellmeister und schließlich durch über zwei Jahrzehnte als oberster Hofkapellmeister diente, gilt dies in besonderem Maße. Denn in den rund vier Jahrzehnten seines Wirkens am kaiserlichen Hof schuf er – in Entsprechung seiner mit dem Amte verbundenen Pflichten – eine Fülle geistlicher und weltlicher Werke, die ihn als den bedeutendsten österreichischen Komponisten seiner Zeit ausweisen. Als solcher ist er in die Musikgeschichte eingegangen. Ludwig Ritter von Köchel, der seine lebenslangen musikhistorischen Forschungen auf Fux und Mozart konzentrierte, verzeichnet in seiner auch heute noch grundlegenden dokumentarischen Fux-Biographie über 400 Nummern, von denen sich allerdings etliche auf ein und dieselben Werke in verschiedener Überlieferung oder Bearbeitung beziehen.[1] Einen heutigen wissenschaftlichen Erfordernissen entsprechenden thematischen Katalog, der auch die nach Köchel erfolgten Funde sowie alle mittlerweile notwendig gewordenen Berichtigungen berücksichtigen müßte, gibt es bisher nicht. Als Vorbild für einen solchen könnte Köchels Mozart-Werkverzeichnis dienen, dessen Neuauflage derzeit geplant wird. Trotz großer Quellenverluste, die fast durchwegs einer älteren Zeit, nicht den Folgen des Zweiten Weltkriegs anzulasten sind, und des Fehlens fast aller Autographen – einschließlich von Skizzen und Entwürfen – ist noch immer ein imponierender Werkbestand vorhanden. Den größten Teil hiervon verwahrt in Handschriften von Wiener Hofkapellkopisten, die im Auftrag von Fux arbeiteten, die ehemalige Hofbibliothek und heutige Österreichische Nationalbibliothek Wien. Gleich J.S. Bach sind zu Lebzeiten von Fux nur ganz wenige Werke im Druck erschienen, nämlich der dem damaligen König und späteren Kaiser Joseph I. gewidmete *Concentus musico-instrumentalis* (Nürnberg, 1701, Felsecker), die Oper *Elisa* (Amsterdam, 1719, Roger) und das berühmte Kontrapunktlehrbuch *Gradus ad Parnassum* (Wien, 1725, van Ghelen).

Der Nachruhm von Fux gründet sich vor allem auf dieses in lateinischer Sprache abgefaßte und auf Kosten Kaiser Karls VI. gedruckte Werk, das noch im 18. Jahrhundert Übersetzungen in die deutsche, französische, italienische und englische Sprache gefunden hat. Von ihnen ist die deutsche Übersetzung durch Lorenz Christoph Mizler, einen Schüler von J.S. Bach, die wichtigste und wertvollste. Sie bezeugt indirekt das Interesse, das Bach selbst für dieses Werk hegte – ein Exemplar der lateinischen Originalausgabe befand sich in seiner Bibliothek – und sie sorgte neben dieser für weite Verbreitung im gesamten deutschen Sprachraum. Sein theoretisches Vermächtnis nahmen J. Haydn, W.A. Mozart und L. van Beethoven auf. Einflußreiche Theoretiker knüpften an seine Lehre an, so daß sie bis in die Gegenwart lebendig geblieben ist.

Was aber bedeutet ihr sein umfangreiches kompositorisches Oeuvre? Oder anders gefragt: was könnte es ihr bedeuten? Es ist zwar unrichtig, daß nach seinem Ableben sein Schaffen der Vergangenheit anheimgefallen wäre. Aber eine ungebrochene, bis in das 19. Jahrhundert reichende Tradition betrifft nur einen schmalen, dem stylus antiquus verpflichteten Teil seiner geistlichen Komposition, der hauptsächlich im klösterlichen Bereich fortlebte. Während Werke von J.S. Bach in Leipzig durch Johann Gottfried Schicht und in Berlin durch Carl Friedrich Fasch und Carl Friedrich Zelter kontinuierlich gepflegt wurden, was F. Mendelssohn Bartholdy zur Wiederaufführung der *Matthäus-Passion* im Jahre 1829 inspirierte, lebte Fux nur als Theoretiker und Schöpfer der Kaiser Karl VI. gewidmeten *Missa canonica* im Gedächtnis fort. Seine Instrumentalmessen, Vespern und Litaneien, seine zahlreichen Solo-Motetten und Antiphonen, Arien und Duette aus Oratorien und Opern samt seiner Instrumentalmusik blieben dagegen weitgehend unbeachtet. Erst Köchel korrigierte das einseitig gewordene Fux-Bild. Dank seiner Forschungen im Wiener Hofkapellarchiv konnte er neben allen unbestrittenen Verdiensten des

Komponisten um die Bewahrung des stylus antiquus zugleich dessen Bedeutung für Pflege und Verbreitung des *stylus modernus* überzeugend nachweisen. Die rund 25 noch erhaltenen Oratorien, Sepolcri und Opern von Fux brauchen einen Vergleich mit den Oratorien und Opern von G.F. Händel nicht zu scheuen. Dennoch hatte Köchels Werk keine unmittelbare Auswirkung auf die Praxis. Ihr stand die glückliche Situation, in der sich Österreich als Musikland im 18. und 19. Jahrhundert befand, im Weg. Die Meisterwerke der Wiener Klassik erfuhren in Kopien und Drucken weiteste Verbreitung. Sie setzten neue Maßstäbe und verdrängten ungewollt älteres Musikgut, das daher dem gesellschaftlichen Bewußtsein rasch entschwand. Andere Länder erlebten in dieser Zeit keine derartigen Höhepunkte ihrer Musikentwicklung, so daß sich Altes neben Neuem leichter behaupten konnte. Beispielsweise riß in England die Pflege des Händel-Oratoriums niemals ab, sie wurde vielmehr zum nationalen Prestige, so daß in den Jahren 1787–1797 Samuel Arnold, Organist der Westminsterabtei, eine 36-bändige Händel-Ausgabe veranstalten konnte. In Österreich wirkte sich eine durch die Romantik geförderte Rückbesinnung auf das Erbe der Vergangenheit erst verhältnismäßig spät in der Praxis aus. Der Cäcilianismus war nur an älterer *a-cappella*-Musik interessiert. An neuzeitlicher instrumentaler Kirchenmusik bestand nicht der geringste Mangel. Es mag daher verständlich erscheinen, daß erst am Ende des 19. Jahrhunderts Instrumentalmessen von Fux im Druck zugänglich wurden. Zwei von ihnen, K 28 und E 113, eröffneten – zusammen mit der bereits erwähnten *Missa canonica*, K 7 und einer weiteren *a-cappella*-Messe, K 29 – die von Guido Adler 1894 begründete Reihe der *Denkmäler der Tonkunst in Österreich*. Dort veröffentlichte 1910 Egon Wellesz die berühmte Festoper *Costanza e fortezza* (1723). Es folgte 1916 ein Neudruck des *Concentus musico-instrumentalis* (1701). Jedoch erschien es unmöglich, eine auch nur repräsentative Auswahl seiner Werke im Rahmen dieser für das gesamte musikalische Erbe der Habsburgermonarchie bestimmten Denkmälerreihe zu veröffentlichen. Daher blieb auch weiterhin die Kenntnis seiner Werke beschränkt. Während 1851 mit der ersten großen Bach-Ausgabe begonnen werden konnte, ja selbst die erste Gesamtausgabe der Werke von H. Schütz bereits 1885 zu erscheinen begann, konnte erst die 1955 gegründete J.-J.-Fux-Gesellschaft (Graz) den Plan einer Gesamtausgabe, der zwar bereits früher bestand, dessen Ausführung durch den Zweiten Weltkrieg jedoch vereitelt worden war, ernstlich ins Auge fassen. Es stellte sich nämlich heraus, daß das von Köchel mitgeteilte Quellenmaterial, das sich hauptsächlich auf die Bestände der Österreichischen Nationalbibliothek Wien, ferner einiger österreichischer Klosterbibliotheken und des Nachlasses von Jan Dismas Zelenka in Dresden erstreckte, zahlreicher Ergänzungen bedürftig war. Nach den Aufsehen erregenden Funden von Andreas Liess in Prag[2] ließen systematische Nachforschungen die weite Verbreitung der Fux-Werke im Habsburgerreich, vor allem in Böhmen und Mähren, erkennen.[3] Erst dadurch war die Voraussetzung für eine der Wissenschaft und Praxis dienende Gesamtausgabe geschaffen.

Obwohl diese seit 1959 erscheint und umfangreichere Werke gesondert, kleinere dagegen in Einzelbänden zusammengefaßt-veröffentlicht werden, liegen bisher erst 16 Bände im Druck vor. Das schleppende Erscheinen beruht vornehmlich auf einem finanziellen Problem. Als österreichisches Forschungsunternehmen wird diese Veröffentlichung nicht – wie jene der Musiker-Gesamtausgaben in der Bundesrepublik Deutschland – von der Konferenz der Akademien der Wissenschaften, vertreten durch die Akademie der Wissenschaften und Literatur in Mainz, gefördert, sondern ist fast ausschließlich auf Subventionen seitens der Steiermärkischen Landesregierung in Graz angewiesen, die derzeit ungleich höhere Summen für den in seiner kulturellen Bedeutung propagandistisch überbewerteten 'Steirischen Herbst' als für den größten Komponisten ihres Landes aufbringt. Die Gesamtausgabe konnte daher vorläufig nur einen Bruchteil des erhaltenen Werkbestandes der Wissenschaft und Praxis zur Verfügung stellen. Der Schaden liegt auf beiden Seiten. Obwohl seit Ende des Zweiten Weltkrieges bemerkenswerte Forschungsergebnisse vorgelegt werden konnten, muß eine heutigen wissenschaftlichen Ansprüchen genügende Fux-Biographie, die Leben und Werk gleichermaßen umschließen und Köchels Werk ersetzen sollte, so lange ein Desiderat der Forschung bleiben, als die Gesamtausgabe über ihr Anfangsstadium nicht hinausgelangt ist. Bleibt doch zu bedenken, daß mit Ausnahme der Oratorien und Opern – infolge Verlusts der meisten Autographe – von den sonstigen Werken fast keine Partituren, sondern nur noch Stimmen vorhanden sind, die erst spartiert werden müssen. Auch Echtheitsprobleme harren noch der Lösung, gibt es doch noch andere Träger gleichen Namens, wie Vinzenz Fux im 17. und Peter Fux am Ende des 18. Jahrhunderts, ohne daß die Quellen stets die Vornamen der Autoren angeben, so daß Zweifel über die Urheberschaft entstehen können. Aber auch Verwechslungen mit anderen Komponisten lassen sich mehrfach nachweisen, ohne daß eine eindeutige Zuschreibung bisher möglich war. Als bemerkenswertes Beispiel sei auf die Triosonate K 330 hingewiesen, die Erich Schenk nach einer Quelle in Kremsmünster als Werk von J. J. Fux, dagegen Günter Haußwald nach einer Vorlage in Dresden als Komposition von G.Ph. Telemann veröffentlichten, während Rudolf Flotzinger nachweisen konnte, daß dieses Werk von keinem der beiden Meister stammt, da die Kremsmünsterer Quelle bereits vor 1675 entstanden sein muß.[4]

Den bisherigen Ausführungen zufolge ist es verständlich, daß die Fux-Forschung – anknüpfend an Köchel und Adler – von Wien aus ihren Ausgang nahm. Im Umkreis der Wiener Adler-Schule entstanden die ersten größeren Studien, wie von Heinrich Rietsch, Viktor Halpern, Franz Brenn und Egon Wellesz. Diese Arbeiten werden in der dem vorliegenden Band beigefügten Bibliographie von Ingrid Schubert angeführt. Auch A. Liess, der nach 1930 die Fux-Forschung tatkräftig vorantrieb und die Editionsleitung der damals bereits geplanten Gesamtausgabe übernehmen sollte, gehört als Adler-Schüler dem genannten Kreis an. Mit dem Aufblühen der Musikwissenschaft nach dem Zweiten Weltkrieg und dem zunehmenden Interesse der Praxis an der Musik vor und zur Zeit von J.S. Bach begannen auch ausländische Forscher sich mit dem Werk von Fux näher zu beschäftigen. Insbesondere ist auf das dreibändige Werk von John Henry van der Meer,

J.J. Fux als Opernkomponist (Bilthoven, 1961) hinzuweisen, in dem erstmals einer von Fux durch drei Jahrzehnte gepflegten Gattung eine umfangreiche Monographie gewidmet worden ist: Detaillierte Analyse gipfelt in einer systematischen Darstellung von Operntext, Inszenierung, Instrumentaleinleitung, Rezitativ, Nummerntypus, Arien- und Ensemble-form, Chor, Ballett, Orchester und musikalischer Oratorie. Die Publikation ist auch für die Praxis von Belang, da der dritte Band mit über 90 Notenbeispielen vollständige Arien mitenthält. Der unfreiwilligen Emi-gration von E. Wellesz ist die erste, in englischer Sprache erschienene Buchveröffentlichung über Fux zu verdanken, die – trotz ihrer Kürze – bestens geeignet ist, 'to introduce Fux to English readers and more generally to put his case again with music examples that will give some idea of the wide range of forms he mastered'.[5] Das 25-jährige Bestehen der Fux-Gesellschaft bot Anlaß zu einer kritischen Übersicht der im Zeitraum 1955–1980 veröffentlichten Studien, die sich gänzlich oder teilweise mit des Meisters Leben und Werk befassen.[6] Nachdem es 1949 Anton Kern gelungen war, Fux 1680/81 als 'grammatista' am Jesuitengymnasium in Graz und 1681 auch als 'musicus' in dem ebenfalls von Jesuiten geleiteten Ferdinandeum nachzuweisen,[7] wodurch erstmals Licht in das Dunkel seiner ersten 36 Lebensjahre fiel, konnte ihn 1976 Siegfried Hofmann von August 1685 bis Ende 1688 als Organisten an der St Moritzkirche und zugleich als 'philosophiae studiosus' und danach als 'I[uris] U[triusque] studiosus' in Ingolstadt eruieren, an deren Jesuitenuniversität er aber bereits Ende 1683 als 'logica studiosus' Aufnahme fand, wie R. Flotzinger feststellte.[8] Weiterhin unbekannt bleibt jedoch, was Fux veranlaßte, sein in Graz begonnenes Studium in Ingolstadt fortzusetzen, durch wessen Vermittlung und auf welchem Weg er von Ingolstadt zu einem bisher noch nicht identifizierten ungarischen Bischof – vermutlich Leopold Graf Kollonitz (Kollonitsch; 1631–1707) – gelangte, bei dem Kaiser Leopold I. zu seinem besonderen Wohlgefallen Fuxsche Meßkompositionen hörte. Infolgedessen ist es möglich, daß er nur dank kaiserlicher Fürsprache Schottenorganist in Wien wurde, bevor er 1698 unter Verzicht auf den üblichen Instanzenweg vom Kaiser zum Hofkomponisten ernannt wurde. Auch die Frage nach seinen Lehrern ist noch unbeantwortet, so daß die Biographie seiner ersten Lebenshälfte nach wie vor erhebliche Lücken aufweist. Daß Fux über eine akademische Bildung verfügte, läßt sich bereits aus seinen lateinischen Sprachkenntnissen schließen, derer er sich im *Gradus ad Parnassum* in gewandter Weise bediente. Sichergestellt ist aber nunmehr, daß er sich bereits in jungen Jahren diese Bildung erworben hatte.

Läßt die biographische Forschung noch auf mancherlei Überraschungen hoffen, so dürfte die hauptsächlich im Jahrzehnt 1950–1960 erfolgte planmäßige Erfassung von Köchel und Liess noch unbekannten Quellen in in- und ausländischen Bibliotheken sowie Archiven insofern zu einem gewissen Abschluß gelangt sein, als bedeutsame Neufunde kaum mehr zu erwarten sind, falls der musikalische Nachlaß von Fux tatsächlich als verloren gelten muß, was zu befürchten ist. Immerhin ließ sich das durch Köchel und Liess aufgelistete Oeuvre inzwischen um über 100 unbekannte Kompositionen und zahlreiche bisher unbekannte Abschriften bereits bekannter Werke erweitern.[9] In diesem Zusammenhang können den bereits erfolgten Berichtigungen von K (Köchel)-, L (Liess)- und E (Ergänzungs)-Nummern mittlerweile bekanntgewordene Korrekturen hinzugefügt werden: Zweifel an der Echtheit des heute verschollenen *Graduale Ex Sion*, K 138 (die einzige Stimmabschrift befand sich im Stift Göttweig) erscheinen unbegründet, da das von Köchel mitgeteilte Incipit mit dem Anfang einer untextierten Fuge aus dem *Gradus ad Parnassum* (Wien, 1725, p.215 ff.) übereinstimmt. Vermutlich wurde sie von anderer Hand bearbeitet und mit einem passenden Text versehen, um sie in dieser Gestalt der Praxis zugänglich zu machen. Hingegen wurde *Ave maris stella*, L 51 bereits von Alfred Dörffel als Werk von Felice Anerio im vierstimmigen *a-cappella*-Satz veröffentlicht,[10] so daß die erst im 19. Jahrhundert erfolgten Zuschreibungen an Fux, aber auch an Georg Albrechtsberger, hinfällig werden. Ulrich A. Tegtmeyer, Leiter des 'ensemble >johann joseph fux<', dem beide Berichtigungen zu verdanken sind, stellte ferner fest, daß die in einem handschriftlichen Traktat (Sign. I B 10) des Wiener Minoritenklosters überlieferten fünf zweistimmigen Kontrapunktbeispiele mit der Überschrift 'A D(omine) J.J. Fux Exempla dissonantiarum ligatarum et non ligatarum'[11] aus dem *Musico prattico*[12] von Giovanni Maria Bononcini stammen, der sein Werk Leopold I. gewidmet hat. Die Abfolge der Beispiele stimmt ebenfalls in beiden Quellen überein. Möglicherweise verwendete sie Fux im Unterricht, so daß sie in der genannten Handschrift, deren größerer Teil eine Abschrift ausgewählter Stellen aus der *Musurgia universalis* (Rom 1650, liber V) von Athanasius Kircher – jedoch ohne Namensnennung – enthält, fälschlicherweise ihm zugeschrieben wurden. Aus dem Werkbestand von Fux sind ferner die Oratorien *Santa Geltrude*, E 59 und *Ismaele*, E 60 zu streichen, die zwar in Wiener Partiturabschriften (Meiningen, Staatliche Museen) ihm zugeschrieben werden, aber den 1694, vier Jahre vor Fux zum Hofkomponisten ernannten Carlo Agostino Badia zum Verfasser haben.[13] Erst kürzlich konnte festgestellt werden, daß die Motette *Caro mea vere est* für zwei Soprane mit Generalbaß K 164 nicht von Fux, sondern von Antonio Caldara stammt.[14] Sie ist in dessen *Motetti a due, a tre voci*, op. 4, Bologna, 1715, enthalten und bereits von Eusebius Mandyczewski in den *DTÖ*, Bd.26 (1906) nach diesem Druck und einer zeitgenössischen Partitur-Abschrift veröffentlicht worden. Daß die einzige bekannte Kopie, die dieses Werk unter dem Namen von Fux überliefert, aus dem Bestand der Wiener Hofkapelle stammt, ist sonderbar. Die Fehlzuschreibung dürfte darauf zurückzuführen sein, daß diese Abschrift erst nach dem Tod von Caldara (+ 1736) und Fux (+ 1741) angefertigt worden ist, wie die Aufführungsdaten (9. Februar 1742 bis 12. März 1744) auf dem Umschlag erkennen lassen.

An Buchpublikationen sind – neben den beiden von van der Meer und Wellesz – zwei für die Fux-Forschung wichtige Veröffentlichungen hervorzuheben: Friedrich Wilhelm Riedel weist anhand einschlägiger Musikalienbestände sowie Materialen zur Zeremonial- und Gottesdienstordnung Funktion, stilistische Zuordnung und Aufführungsorte der Kirchenmusik am Hof Kaiser Karls VI. nach, in deren Repertoire das Oeuvre von Fux eine dominierende Stellung eingenommen hat, während Walter

Gleißner – gestützt auf Riedels Forschungsergebnisse – den zahlreichen Vespern und Vesperteilen eine monographische Darstellung widmet.[15] Dabei finden die dem liturgisch-höfischen Zeremoniell entsprechende Differenzierung nach Vesper-Typen hinsichtlich Stil, Besetzung, Umfang und zyklischer Anlage ebenso Berücksichtigung wie Tonalität, Satztechnik, Textbehandlung, musikalisch-rhetorische Figuren, Themenbildung, Rhythmus und Mensur als Gestaltungs- und Ordnungsfaktoren. Wenngleich die Unterscheidung der zahlreichen Kopistenhände, die an der Herstellung der Abschriften für den Wiener Kaiserhof arbeiteten, nur in größerem Zusammenhang zu einem endgültigen Ergebnis hinsichtlich der Datierung führen kann, so leistet Gleißners Studie aus dem Blickwinkel der Materialien zur Vesperkomposition eine wichtige Vorarbeit zur Lösung dieses Problems. Einzeluntersuchungen von Othmar Wessely und dem Verfasser selbst behandeln die Beurteilung von Fux durch Musiktheoretiker, wie Johann Mattheson, Francesco Antonio Vallotti, Lorenz Christoph Mizler, während der Nachweis musikgeschichtlicher und stilistischer Beziehungen zwischen Fux und Bach F.W. Riedel und Christoph Wolff zu verdanken ist.[16] Daß die Literatur über den *Gradus ad Parnassum* bereits einen beachtlichen Umfang angenommen hat, kann angesichts seiner Bedeutung für die Zukunft nicht wundernehmen. Mehr noch als das Verhältnis zur zeitgenössischen Musiktheorie beansprucht der Einfluß dieses Werkes auf J. Haydn, W.A. Mozart und L.van Beethoven besonderes Interesse. Ihm kommen Neudrucke sowohl des Originaldruckes (Wien, 1725; repr. 1966 und 1967) als auch von Mizlers deutscher Übersetzung (Leipzig, 1742; repr. 1974) entgegen. J. Haydn ließ dem in seinem Besitz befindlichen lateinisch abgefaßten Exemplar, das im Zweiten Weltkrieg verbrannte, eine sorgfältige Kommentierung angedeihen,[17] die glücklicherweise abschriftlich in drei Exemplaren überliefert ist. Die älteste und zuverlässigste Übertragung, die vielleicht noch zu Haydns Lebzeiten erfolgte, befindet sich in der Bibliothek des Smith College, Northampton, Massachusetts. Eine weitere fertigte Carl Ferdinand Pohl an. Diese befindet sich im Archiv der Gesellschaft der Musikfreunde, Wien. Eusebius Mandyczewski fertigte offenbar eine Kopie von Pohls Übertragung in einem Gradus-Exemplar aus dem Besitz von Gustav Nottebohm an. Mandyczewski schenkte es dem angesehenen österreichischen Organisten Josef Labor, wie dem Vermerk auf der Rückseite des Vorsatzblattes zu entnehmen ist. 'Für meinen lieben Freund/J. Labor/mit Haydn's Notizen versehen./Wien Dezemb.1887./Eusebius.' Seit 1988 befindet sich dieses Exemplar in meinem Besitz. Durch Haydns Vermittlung übte Fuxens Werk einen maßgeblichen Einfluß auf W.A. Mozart aus. In den Attwoodstudien, dem bedeutendsten Dokument der Kompositionslehre zur Zeit der Wiener Klassik, greift Mozart ebenso auf das Artensystem des *Gradus ad Parnassum* zurück, wie in den erst jüngst veröffentlichten Aufzeichnungen von Mozarts Theorie- und Kompositionsunterricht für Barbara Ployer und Franz Jakob Freystädtler.[18] Hinsichtlich Beethoven wies bereits G. Nottebohm auf die bedeutende Rolle hin, die das Werk in dessen Unterricht spielte, sowohl in seiner Unterweisung durch J. Haydn und G. Albrechtsberger, als auch in jener Erzherzogs Rudolph durch Beethoven als

Lehrer.[19] Nunmehr liegt seit kurzem eine umfassende Dokumentation aus der Feder von Alfred Mann über Aufnahme und Verarbeitung von Fuxens didaktischem Erbe in Studium und Lehre der drei Meister der Wiener Klassik vor.[20] Wer Heinrich Schenkers Lehre von der Einheit zwischen strengem und freiem Satz zustimmt, dem dürfte die Bedeutung, welche Haydn, Mozart und Beethoven dem *Gradus ad Parnassum* beimaßen, kaum rätselhaft erscheinen. Wie sehr selbst vordergründig das Artensystem die Komposition im Zeitalter der Klassik beeinflussen konnte, wies erstmals Warren Kirkendale an Beethovens op.133 überzeugend nach.[21]

Die erwähnte Publikation von A. Mann fällt bereits in das Jahrzehnt 1980–1990. Dieser Zeitraum konnte im oben zitierten Forschungsbericht nicht mehr berücksichtigt werden. Mittlerweile sind zwei größere, in Buchform erschienene Arbeiten an erster Stelle anzuführen. Sie betreffen Biographie, Echtheitsprobleme, Instrumentenkundliches und Aufführungspraxis. R. Flotzinger faßt in seinen *Fux-Studien* drei ursprünglich als Jahresgaben der J.-J.-Fux-Gesellschaft einzeln erschienene Veröffentlichungen zusammen: Die erste 'Die Anfänge der Johann Joseph Fux-Forschung im Zeichen des österreichischen Patriotismus' vereint Belege aus der Zeit vor Köchel; sie sind deshalb bemerkenswert, weil deren Verfasser, wie Ernst Ludwig Gerber, Franz Sales Kandler, Aloys Fuchs und Simon Molitor offenbar etliche Köchel unbekannte und mittlerweile teils verschollene Quellen noch zur Verfügung standen.[22] Dennoch bleibt Köchels Verdienst ungeschmälert, erstmals methodisch auf Originaldokumente und Archivalien zu rekurrieren. Der zweite Beitrag 'Johann Joseph Fux auf dem Weg von Hirtenfeld nach Wien' enthält sowohl eine Fülle von Kommentaren und Vermutungen im Anschluß an die bisherigen spärlichen Funde zur Biographie als auch den überzeugenden Nachweis, daß Fux bereits während seiner Ingolstädter Zeit als Komponist mit kleineren geistlichen Werken hervorgetreten ist, die leider verschollen sind. Die dritte Untersuchung 'Vinzenz Fux' klärt die Herkunft dieses zwar ebenfalls aus der Steiermark (Weißkirchen) gebürtigen, mit J.J. Fux offensichtlich jedoch nicht verwandten Komponisten des 17. Jahrhunderts auf und bietet ein Werkverzeichnis mit Incipits samt Berichtigungen von Fehlzuschreibungen an J.J. Fux, die Köchel infolge Namensgleichheit – bei fehlendem Vornamen in den überlieferten Quellen – unterlaufen sind. Allerdings erweist sich das *Graduale Ex Sion*, K 138 nicht als Werk von Vinzenz Fux, sondern als Bearbeitung einer textlosen Fuge aus dem *Gradus ad Parnassum*, wie bereits vermerkt wurde. Die kontroverse Beurteilung etlicher Fakten und die Zurückweisung von Hypothesen, die sich an erstere knüpfen, durch Herbert Seifert beweisen, wie sehr gerade die Biographie, aber auch Echtheitsfragen noch zahlreiche Rätsel aufgeben.[23] Seifert macht ferner auf eine bisher unbekannte Darbietung mit Instrumentalmusik von Fux am Hof im Jahr 1698 und auf einen fraglosen Lesefehler Köchels aufmerksam: einwandfrei steht nunmehr fest, daß Fux seit dem 1. Oktober 1711 – nicht erst seit 1713 – als Nachfolger von Marc Antonio Ziani das Amt des Vizehofkapellmeisters bekleidet hat, was auch mit dessen Ernennung zum Hofkapellmeister am 1. Januar 1712 bestens übereinstimmt.

Dem zweiten in Buchform erschienenen Werk liegt ein 1985 in Graz stattgefundenes Symposium 'Die Bedeutung der Blasinstrumente im Schaffen von Johann Joseph Fux' zugrunde, das 'Fachkollegen, die zu den besten Kennern des barocken Bläsermusizierens und der barocken Blasinstrumente in Europa und in den USA zählen', bestritten haben. Die für Wissenschaft und Praxis gleich wertvollen Referate, die Seifert mit seinem Köchel vielfach ergänzenden und berichtigenden Beitrag 'Die Bläser der kaiserlichen Hofkapelle zur Zeit von J.J. Fux' eröffnet, sind zwei Jahre später unter einem etwas geänderten Titel,[24] fast gleichzeitig mit einer ähnlichen, nicht minder wichtigen Sammelpublikation über Zeit, Leben und Werk von A. Caldara,[25] erschienen. Beide Veröffentlichungen berühren sich thematisch vielfach und ergänzen einander. Erstmals wird Klarheit über die Fux und Caldara zur Verfügung gestandenen Instrumentalisten, ihre z. T. vielseitige Verwendung und ihr Instrumentarium gewonnen, wodurch unsere Kenntnis der damaligen Aufführungspraxis wesentlich erweitert wird. Diesem Themenkreis schließt sich die Frage nach der Stimmung an. Es kann als erwiesen gelten, daß sich Fux für die gleichschwebende Temperatur entschied, gleich wie Jean Philippe Rameau sich letztlich ebenfalls zu ihr bekannte.[26]

Erst im Druck befindet sich eine von H. White verfaßte Monographie über die Fux-Oratorien. Nach den Opern (J.H. van der Meer) und Vespern (W. Gleißner) wird mit ihr eine weitere bedeutende Werkgattung mit einer Gesamtdarstellung bedacht.[27] Als praktisches Ergebnis dieser Arbeit ist die Veröffentlichung des Oratoriums *Il trionfo della fede*, K 294 (1716) anzusehen, das – entgegen Köchel – unmittelbar vor dem Oratorium *Il fonte della salute*, K 293 entstanden ist.

Anläßlich des 58. Bachfestes der Neuen Bachgesellschaft fand 1983 in Graz ein Symposium statt, auf welchem – anknüpfend an Forschungsergebnisse von F.W. Riedel und Chr. Wolff – das Verhältnis Fux-Bach aus der Sicht der Theorie, Kompositionspraxis, Stilistik und Semantik in Einzelvorträgen von Alfred Mann, Wolfgang Suppan, Othmar Wessely und dem Verfasser erneut Behandlung fand.[28] In den Symposiumsbericht wurde auch eine Kurzfassung von R. Flotzingers bereits erwähntem Beitrag über Fuxens Weg von Hirtenfeld nach Wien aufgenommen.

Anzuführen sind einige kleinere Veröffentlichungen, wie von Karl Batz, Flotzinger, Roswitha Karpf, Riedel und dem Verfasser.[29] Sie betreffen das ungetrübte Verhältnis zwischen Theorie und Praxis von Fux, die Beurteilung des *Gradus ad Parnassum* durch H. Schenker, den französischen Einfluß in der Klaviermusik von Fux, die *Missa Sanctissimae Trinitatis*, E 113, die – nach Flotzinger – ursprünglich eine Marienmesse war, und die Bedeutung der ihr vorangestellten Solmisationssilben als thematische Substanz des Werkes,[30] die Erbhuldigungsreise Kaiser Karls VI. nach Innerösterreich (1728), an der zwar Fux nicht teilnahm – wie R. Karpf anhand einer erstmals veröffentlichten vollständigen Namensliste des den Kaiser begleitenden Hofmusikpersonals nachweist – von dem jedoch zahlreiche Werke, u. a. die Kammeroper *Orfeo ed Euridice*, K 309 am Geburtstag des Kaisers (1 Oktober 1728), bei dieser Gelegenheit zur Wiedergabe gelangten, Riedel teilt die betreffenden Köchel-Nummern mit.

Das Erscheinen der Gesamtausgabe, von der bis 1980 13 Bände vorlagen, geriet im letzten Jahrzehnt ins Stocken, scheint aber für das nächste Jahrzehnt gesichert zu sein. Nach 1980 erschienen:

Serie I. Messen und Requiem
Bd 4: *Missa gratiarum actionis*, K 27 (Wolfgang Fürlinger) 1981.
Bd·5: *Requiem*, K 55 (Klaus Winkler) 1990.

Serie II. Litaneien, Vespern, Kompletorien, Te Deum
Bd 3: *Laudate Dominum*- und *Magnificat*-Kompositionen (Walter Gleißner) 1990.

Serie VI. Instrumentalmusik
Bd 3: 10 Triosonaten (Joseph-Horst Lederer) 1990.

In Herstellung oder Bearbeitung befinden sich folgende Werke:
Serie I. Messen und Requiem
Bd 6: *Requiem*, K 51–K 53 (Klaus Winkler).
Bd 7: *Missa humilitatis*, K 17 (Helmut Federhofer-Rosemary Moravec).

Serie III. Kleinere Kirchenmusikwerke
Bd 2: Motetten und Antiphonen für 2 Soprane und Instrumentalbegleitung (Jürgen Neubacher).
Bd 3: Motetten für 4 Stimmen mit Instrumentalbegleitung (Rudolf Walter).

Serie IV. Oratorien
Bd 3: *Il trionfo della fede*, K 294 (Harry White).

Serie V. Opern
Bd 3: *Il mese di marzo consecrato a marte*, K 306 (Renate Groth).

Serie VII. Theoretische und pädagogische Werke
Bd 2: *Singfundament* (Eva Badura-Skoda–Alfred Mann).

Außerhalb der Gesamtausgabe edierte W. Fürlinger folgende Messen von Fux:
Missa Dies mei sicut umbra, K 12, Altötting, Coppenrath, 1985.
Missa matutina, K 20, Augsburg, Böhm, 1979.
Missa Sancti Antonii, K 32, Augsburg, Böhm, 1978.
Missa velociter currit, K 43, Altötting, Coppenrath, 1979.
Missa, K 46, Stuttgart, Hänssler, 1973.

Ferner erschien ein Facsimiledruck der Oper
Orfeo ed Euridice, K 309 (1715) nach der Partitur in der Österreichischen Nationalbibliothek Wien (MS 17231), mit einer Einleitung von Howard Mayer Brown, New York-London, 1978 (= *Italian Opera 1640-1770*, A Garland Series).

Bearbeitungen edierte W. Suppan unter dem Titel *Johann Joseph Fux (1660-1741) für Blasinstrumente, for winds, pour instruments à vent, in Verbindung mit der Johann-Joseph-Fux-Gesellschaft*, Graz, H. 1ff., Freiburg o. J. Zweck dieser Reihe ist es, Instrumentalwerke von Fux modernen Bläserensembles in Partitur und Stimmen zur Verfügung zu stellen. Die bisher erschienenen 5 Hefte enthalten Bearbeitungen von Werken aus dem *Concentus musico-instrumentalis*.

Mehr noch als die Wissenschaft ist die Praxis vom Fehlen einer zum Abschluß gebrachten oder zumindest fortgeschrittenen Gesamtausgabe betroffen. Häufiger werden lediglich einzelne Nummern aus dem *Concentus musico-instrumentalis*, der – wie erwähnt – bereits 1916 einen Neudruck erfuhr, und die wenigen erhalten gebliebenen Werke für Tasteninstrumente zu Gehör gebracht.[31] Der Praxis fehlen vor allem die zahlreichen, noch unveröffentlichten Triosonaten in der Originalbesetzung sowie Solomotetten für ein und mehrere Stimmen. Aber, bedarf die Praxis ihrer tatsächlich? Gibt es nicht bereits genügend Neudrucke älterer Musik und sollte sie nicht eher der Neuen Musik eine Chance zu ihrer Verbreitung geben anstatt versunkenes Kulturgut ins Hörbewußtstein zurückzurufen? Eine derartige Frage stellt sich prinzipiell jeder älteren Musik und betrifft zugleich Sinn und Zweck staatlicher Förderung von Gesamtausgaben, einschließlich jener der Werke von Arnold Schönberg. Sie läßt sich nicht mit Phrasen, wie kulturelle Verpflichtung, Erbe der Vergangenheit, historisches Bewußtsein und ähnlichen Formulierungen, die eine Alibifunktion bei Fest- und Gedenkreden ausüben, sondern nur pragmatisch überzeugend beantworten, nämlich als Beantwortung der Frage: besteht ein Bedarf für eine jahrhundertealte Musik, die zu einer Zeit mit völlig anderen Gesellschaftsordnungen und Wertvorstellungen entstand?

Frühere Epochen gingen wenig pietätvoll mit der jeweils älteren Musik um, sofern sie nicht, wie der gregorianische Choral aus kirchlich-religiösen Motiven dem stilistischen Wandel weitgehend entzogen war. Jedes Zeitalter orientierte sich, ohne von Skrupeln der Reflexion geplagt zu sein, am jeweils erreichten Niveau der Musikkultur, deren Überlegenheit gegenüber früheren Entwicklungsstufen nicht in Zweifel stand. In den jeweils zeitgenössischen Werken schien das Kunstschöne am idealsten verkörpert zu sein. Vorangegangenes wurde als Vorstufe zur eigenen Entwicklungshöhe betrachtet und fiel der Vergessenheit anheim. Gewiß läuft die Entwicklung in den bildenden Künsten dazu parallel, aber mit anderen Folgeerscheinungen. Ältere Bauwerke, die man gerne durch Neubauten ersetzt haben wollte, ließen sich meist nur mit größeren Unkosten, jedenfalls nicht so leicht zerstören wie veraltete Musikalien vernichten. In welchem Umfang dies tatsächlich erfolgte, mag man daraus ersehen, daß gedruckte Musikalien aus der Zeit vor 1800, z. T. auch noch aus späteren Dezennien, im allgemeinen wesentlich seltener als alte Bücher geworden sind, mag es sich um theologische, juristische, naturwissenschaftliche oder medizinische Veröffentlichungen handeln. Selbst bei Auflagen mit mehreren hundert Exemplaren blieben oft nur wenige oder überhaupt keine erhalten. Der bereits erwähnte *Concentus musico-instrumentalis* von

Fux läßt sich beispielsweise nur in einem einzigen Exemplar (Berlin, Deutsche Staatsbibliothek), die Oper *Elisa* in nur mehr acht Exemplaren nachweisen.[32] Zudem gelangte überhaupt nur ein Bruchteil von Kompositionen zum Druck. Um so leichter fielen handgeschriebene Musikalien der Vernichtung anheim, sobald sie keine praktische Verwendung mehr fanden. Der maßgebliche Grund für das Ausmaß der Verluste liegt im raschen Veralten von Musik früherer Jahrhunderte, und zwar als Folge eines ununterbrochenen stilistischen Wandels. In dem Maß jedoch, in dem die Selbstgewißheit kultureller Überlegenheit über vorangegangene Entwicklungsstufen verschwand, verwandelte sich allmählich das zunächst nur antiquarische Interesse für die musikalische Vergangenheit in ein ästhetisches Verständnis oder doch in das Bemühen um ein solches älterer Musik. Bereits in der Romantik begann – trotz aller Meisterleistungen, die sie hervorbrachte – die gleichsam nachtwandlerische Sicherheit künstlerischen Gestaltens zu schwinden. F. Schubert litt unter der Größe Beethovens und wollte sich noch in seinem Sterbejahr dem Kontrapunktunterricht bei Simon Sechter unterwerfen. Im Bemühen, in der Vergangenheit einen Halt zu finden, sah sich der Künstler bald durch die Musikforschung unterstützt, was die lebenslange Freundschaft von J. Brahms mit Philipp Spitta, dem hervorragenden Bachforscher und -biographen sowie Herausgeber der Werke von H. Schütz erklärt. Unmittelbar aus der Kunstentwicklung der beiden letzten Jahrhunderte läßt sich die Renaissance alter Musik begreifen. Sie ist der Gegenwartskultur nicht aufgepfropft.

In diesem Zusammenhang darf die Entfremdung, die zwischen der Neuen Musik, als dodekaphone, serielle und aleatorische Verfahren sie zu beherrschen begannen, und dem Musikpublikum eingetreten ist, nicht verschwiegen werden. Anstelle einer langgehegten Hoffnung, daß sich diese Kluft schließen könnte, ist die Einsicht der Unvereinbarkeit zwischen dem ästhetischen Anspruch des Neuen, das eine bestimmte musiksoziologische Richtung zum Gewissen unserer Zeit hypostasieren wollte, und der Erwartung des Hörers getreten. Die heutige Musikszene erlebt keine erbitterten Richtungskämpfe mehr, die noch am Jahrhundertbeginn zu lauten Protesten im Konzertsaal führten. Eine Art Waffenstillstand ist vielmehr eingetreten, indem – nach dem Vorbild einer parlamentarischen Demokratie – mehreren ästhetischen Wahrheiten ein Existenzrecht zugebilligt wird. Massenmedien und öffentliches Konzertleben spiegeln dieses in der Musikgeschichte gänzlich neue Phänomen in seiner gesellschaftsbezogenen Wirklichkeit getreu wider. Es ist hier nicht der Ort, dafür eine Erklärung zu suchen. Aber es wäre unredlich, die Kluft, welche die heutige musikkulturelle Szene von jener früherer Zeiten trennt, zu verschweigen. Vor rund 100 Jahren wurden J. Brahms, A. Bruckner, A. Dvořák, J. Strauss, P. I. Tschaikowsky oder G. Verdi – alle Genannten weilten damals unter den Lebenden – enthusiastisch gefeiert, und ihre Werke immer wieder aufgeführt. Diese fanden im Original oder in Klavierauszügen und zahlreichen Transcriptionen breiten Einlaß in die Hausmusik. Ihren Erfolg schmälerte auch die Zukunft nicht, so daß die Namen ihrer Schöpfer im Gedächtnis späterer Geschlechter bis auf den heutigen Tag fortleben. Welcher Komponist der Gegenwart könnte sich an

Ansehen, Erfolg und Bedeutung ihnen an die Seite setzen? Ein Vakuum ist vielmehr eingetreten, und es darf bezweifelt werden, daß der konstatierte Gegenwartstrend einer 'Vorwärts nach Zurück-Mentalität', die 'unbestreitbar an Boden' gewinnt,[33] in der Lage sein wird, ein neues Kunstzeitalter mit Werken im Rang einer entschwundenen Hochkunst einzuleiten.

Diese scheinbar vom Thema abschweifenden Überlegungen erschienen als notwendig, um dem gegen die Pflege älterer Musik mehrfach erhobenen Vorwurf des Konservativismus und der Regression des Hörens zu begegnen. Es ist falsch, den Hörer schelten zu wollen, weil er sich aus unbewohnbar gewordenen Musiklandschaften in bewohnbare musikalische Lebensräume zurückzieht. Auch im alltäglichen Leben verhält sich der Mensch nicht anders. In solchem Zusammenhang müssen die heutigen großen Musiker-Gesamtausgaben gesehen werden. Sie sind keine philiströse Liebhaberei oder eine Kulturheuchelei, sondern eine Notwendigkeit, die sich aus der kulturellen Situation der Gegenwart zwangsläufig ergibt. Für den Umstand, daß das opus von Fux bisher an diesen Unternehmungen nur am Rand beteiligt war, gibt es keine sachlichen Begründungen. Die Werke der Architektur und bildenden Kunst seiner großen Zeitgenossen, hervorgehoben seien der um etwa vier Jahre ältere Johann Bernhard Fischer von Erlach – gleich Fux ein gebürtiger Steiermärker – Johann Lukas Hildebrand und Georg Raphael Donner, die neben ihm in Wien wirkten, sind allgemein bekannt. Sie zählen, wie das Belvedere, das Prinz Eugen sich erbauen ließ, die Karlskirche, das Schwarzenberg-Palais oder das Schloß Schönbrunn zu Wiens Sehenswürdigkeiten. An Bedeutung steht Fux diesen Künstlernamen nicht nach, nur hat es seine Kunst wesentlich schwerer, ins allgemeine Bewußtsein zu treten, da sie auf die klangliche Realisierung eines heute erst teilweise zugänglichen Notentextes angewiesen ist.

Als eine vom ästhetischen Konsens zwischen Komponist und Hörer getragene Kunst zeugt sie vom Selbstverständnis einer Zeit, die alles Besondere in einem Allgemeinen begründet fand. Die Normen eines vom Wechsel der Kulturformen unabhängigen Systems erblickte Fux – mit Giovanni Pierluigi Palestrina als verehrungswürdigem Vorbild – im *stylus antiquus*, der nur scheinbar einen Gegensatz zum *stylus modernus* seiner Zeit darstellt. Die bereits von älteren Theoretikern, wie Christoph Bernhard mittels der Figurenlehre dargestellte Einheit von altem und neuem Stil, der sich satztechnisch auf jenen gründet und ebenfalls einem geregelten Konsonanz-Dissonanz-Verhältnis unterliegt, stand auch für Fux fest. Der *stylus modernus*, dem er sich auf dem Gebiet der geistlichen und weltlichen Musik mit demselben Eifer widmete wie er den stylus antiquus bewahrte und praktizierte, setzte diesen nicht außer Kraft, sondern bewahrte seine fundamentalen Stimmführungselemente in prolongierter Gestalt auf der Grundlage des Generalbasses. Dieses Bekenntnis sprach Fux nicht nur als Komponist, sondern auch als Theoretiker aus, wenn er das Fundament jeder Komposition in einer auf göttlicher Setzung beruhenden Naturordnung erblickte. L. Chr. Mizler gab diese Überzeugung in seiner Vorrede zur Übersetzung des *Gradus ad Parnassum* mit den Worten wieder: 'Der Grund der Setzkunst bleibet unverrückt, es mag sich der

Geschmack ändern wie er will.'[34] Auf solcher Einsicht gründet die nur scheinbar widersprüchliche stilistische Vielfalt seiner Werke. Sie sind in ihrem bisher noch nicht voll erkannten Umfang ein überzeugendes Beispiel für das harmonische Verhältnis zwischen Altem und Neuem, zwischen Tradition und Fortschritt. Auch in den anspruchsvollsten Arien seiner Oratorien und Opern, in denen die besten zeitgenössischen Gesangssolisten mitwirkten, bildeten der Konsonanz-Dissonanzgegensatz und seine im *stylus antiquus* verankerten Prinzipien in ihrer überzeitlichen Bindung die musiksprachliche Grundlage aller noch so kühnen Ausdrucksgestaltung.

Fux teilt in gewisser Weise das Schicksal von J. Haydn in zweierlei Hinsicht: Beiden wurde im Gegensatz zu Mozart das Glück zuteil, große Kenner und Liebhaber, die z. T. selbst kompositorisch hervortraten, als Mäzene ihrer Kunst zu finden. Diese waren zugleich ihre Dienstherren. Haydn fand sie in den Fürsten von Esterhazy, Fux in drei aufeinanderfolgenden habsburgischen Kaisern. Ohne sie wäre beider Meister künstlerische Entwicklung anders verlaufen. Beiden Komponisten gemeinsam ist aber auch die Tatsache, daß bis heute keine vollständige Ausgabe ihrer Werke vorliegt. Jene Haydns ist allerdings weit fortgeschritten. Rund 70 Bände liegen bereits vor. Die Gesamtausgabe wird vom Joseph-Haydn-Institut Köln vorzüglich betreut. Zudem fand Haydn in Anthony van Hoboken einen modernen Mäzen, dem auch ein dreibändiger thematischer Katalog von nahezu 2.000 Seiten zu verdanken ist, nach welchem die Haydn-Werke heute zitiert werden. Derartiger Vorteile kann sich Fux dagegen nicht rühmen. Weder liegt ein der Publikation Hobokens vergleichbarer thematischer Katalog vor, noch ist die Gesamtausgabe seines Oeuvre institutionell verankert, ihr Erscheinen infolgedessen finanziell nur ungenügend abgesichert. Es fehlt ein moderner Mäzen, der mit jener Liebe seine Werke förderte, die ihnen neben allem Repräsentationsbedürfnis, das sie zu befriedigen hatten, vom Haus Habsburg entgegengebracht wurde. Ein solcher wäre nicht nur des Dankes seitens der Wissenschaft und Praxis, sondern auch aller Musikliebhaber sicher, denen die österreichische Musikkultur der Vergangenheit lebendige Gegenwart bedeutet.

Die zweihundertfünfzigste Wiederkehr des Todestages von Fux dürfte der geeignete Anlaß dazu sein, mit derartigen Überlegungen und Wünschen für ein gutes Gelingen der Gesamtausgabe vorliegenden Band zu eröffnen.

Anmerkungen

[1] Ludwig von Köchel, *Johann Josef Fux* (Wien, 1872/R. 1988).

[2] Andreas Liess, *J.J. Fux, ein steirischer Meister des Barock, nebst Verzeichnis neuer Werkfunde* (Wien, 1947).

[3] Hellmut Federhofer, 'Unbekannte Kirchenmusik von J.J. Fux', *Kirchenmusikalisches Jahrbuch* 43 (1959), S.113ff.; ders. und Friedrich Wilhelm Riedel, 'Quellenkundliche Beiträge zur J.J. Fux-Forschung' *Archiv für Musikwissenschaft* 21 (1964), S.111ff.

[4] Rudolf Flotzinger, *Fux-Studien* (Graz, 1985) (= *Grazer musikwissenschaftliche Arbeiten* 6), S.90f.

[5] Egon Wellesz, *Fux* (London, 1965), S.X.

[6] Federhofer, '25 Jahre Johann Joseph Fux-Forschung' *Acta musicologica* 52 (1980), S.155ff.

[7] Anton Kern, 'J.J. Fux. Neue biographische Forschungen' *Musica orans* 3, 1 (Wien–Graz, 1950), S.8.

[8] Siegfried Hofmann, 'Die Ingolstädter Jahre des späteren Wiener Hofkapellmeisters J.J. Fux', *Ingolstädter Heimatblätter* 39, 1 (1976), S.1f.; Flotzinger, op. cit., S.44.

[9] Vgl. die in Anm. 3 angeführten Quellen.

[10] *Musica sacra* Bd. 1. Lateinische Texte. Sammlung berühmter Kirchenchöre, hrsg. von Alfred Dörffel, Nr. 3 (Leipzig, o. J.).

[11] Veröffentlicht von Federhofer, 'Drei handschriftliche Quellen zur Musiktheorie in Österreich um 1700', *Musa-Mens-Musici, Gedenkschrift Walther Vetter* (Leipzig, 1969), S.148ff.

[12] (Bologna, 1673), S.64–68.

[13] Rudolf Schnitzler, *The Baroque Oratorio at the Imperial Court in Vienna. A Critical Catalogue of Sources* (Publikationen des Instituts für Österreichische Musikdokumentation 16). Im Druck. Die beiden genannten Oratorien werden auch in den Artikeln C.A. Badia (Eva Halfar in MGG; L.E. Bennett in *The New Grove Dictionary of Music and Musicians*, hrsg. von Stanley Sadie) (London, 1980) erwähnt.

[14] Freundliche Mitteilung des Geschäftsführers der J.-J.-Fux-Gesellschaft, Herrn Oberbibliothekar Dr. Harald Bogner, Graz. Vgl. *Köchel*, op. cit., Beil. X, S.74.

[15] Riedel, *Kirchenmusik am Hof Karls VI. (1711–1740). Untersuchungen zum Verhältnis von Zeremoniell und musikalischem Stil im Barockzeitalter* (München–Salzburg, 1977) (*Studien zur Landes- und Sozialgeschichte der Musik* 1); Walter Gleißner, *Die Vespern von J. J. Fux. Ein Beitrag zur Geschichte der Vespervertonung* (Glattbach, 1982).

[16] Vgl. Federhofer, '25 Jahre Johann Joseph Fux-Forschung' *Acta musicologica* 52 (1980) S.168ff.

[17] Vgl. die betreffenden Studien von Alfred Mann, ferner jene von Denis Arnold und Susanne Wollenberg in der 'Fux-Bibliographie' von Ingrid Schubert sowie Federhofer, op. cit., S.188ff. und den Artikel 'Fux' in *The New Grove Dictionary of Music and Musicians*, hrsg. von Stanley Sadie (London, 1980), Bd.6, S.43–6.

[18] *Thomas Attwoods Theorie- und Kompositionsstudien bei Mozart*. Vorgelegt von Erich Hertzmann (+) und Cecil B. Oldman, fertiggestellt von Daniel Heartz und Alfred Mann (Kassel [etc.] 1965) (W.A. Mozart, *Neue Ausgabe sämtlicher Werke* X/30/1). *Barbara Ployers und Franz Jakob Freystädlers Theorie- und Kompositionsstudium bei Mozart*. Vorgelegt von H. Federhofer und A. Mann (Kassel [etc.], 1989) (W.A. Mozart op. cit., X/30/2).

[19] Gustav Nottebohm, *Beethoveniana* (Leipzig und Winterthur, 1872), S.177ff. *Beethovens Abschrift von zwei Fugen aus dem Gradus ad Parnassum*, S.179f. und S.213 auf vier zehnzeiligen Seiten (zwei Einzelblätter) in Querformat bei Henrici, Versteigerung CXLII-Ludwig van Beethoven, *Manuscripte-Briefe-Urkunden* (Berlin, 1928) S.1. Dazu wird vermerkt: 'Die mit besonderer Sorgfalt verfertigten Abschriften sind 1809 entstanden und offenbar durch den Unterricht, den der Meister dem Erzherzog Rudolf erteilte, veranlaßt worden.' Vgl. auch Otto E. Albrecht, 'Beethoven Autographs in the United States', *Beiträge zur Beethoven-Bibliography*, hrsg. von Kurt Dorfmüller (München, 1978) S.10.

[20] Alfred Mann, *Theory and Practice. The Great Composer as Student and Teacher* (New York–London, 1987).

[21] Warren Kirkendale, 'The "Great Fugue" Op. 133: Beethoven's "Art of Fugue" ', *Acta musicologica* 35 (1963), S.14ff.

[22] Rätselhaft bleibt die Nachricht Molitors über einen angeblichen Druck von 36 Trios von Fux (Amsterdam 1700): 'Merkwürdig ist, daß dieser große Mann in dem lezten Dezenium des 17. Jahrh: nebst seinen 36 Trios für 2 Violin und Baß:/welche 1700 in Amsterdam im Stich erschienen sind:/auch das berühmte Requiem im Jahre 1697 zur Leichenfeier der Erzherzogin Eleonora verwittibten Königin von Polen und Herzogin von Lothringen geschrieben hat, aus welchen Compositionen – die ich größtentheils besize – so klar zu entnehmen ist, daß die ihm in der Kunst um 25 Jahre später nachgefolgten Deutschen Heroen: Händel und Seb. Bach, wie auch der so hochgefeierte Pergolesi, unsern braven Fux sich zum Muster und Vorbild genommen haben.' Simon Molitor, 'Materialien zur Geschichte der k.k. Hofmusik', Mus. Hs. 30369, B1. 34, Österreichische Nationalbibliothek Wien, Musiksammlung. Von dem angeführten Druck fehlt jede Spur. Rudolf A. Rasch (Utrecht) teilt freundlicherweise mit, daß dieser in Rogers ziemlich vollständigen Katalogen aus der Zeit um 1700 nicht nachweisbar ist und möglicherweise eine Verwechslung mit Arcangelo Corelli vorliegt.

[23] Herbert Seifert, 'Zur neuesten Fux-Forschung, Kritik und Beiträge', *Studien zur Musikwissenschaft* 38 (1988), S.35ff.

[24] *Johann Joseph Fux und die barocke Bläsertradition.* Kongreßbericht Graz, hrsg. von Bernhard Habla (Tutzing, 1987) (*Alta Musica* 9).

[25] *Antonio Caldara: Essays on his life and times.* Hrsg. von Brian W. Pritchard (Aldershot, 1987). Vgl. dazu auch meine Besprechung *Die Musikforschung* 42 (1989), S.88ff.

[26] Federhofer, 'Johann Joseph Fux und die gleichschwebende Temperatur', *Die Musikforschung* 41 (1988), S.9ff.

[27] Harry White, 'The Oratorios of J.J. Fux', unveröffentlichte Diss., Univ. of Dublin 1986. Vgl. ferner ders., 'Erhaltene Quellen der Oratorien von J.J. Fux', *Kirchenmusikalisches Jahrbuch* 67 (1983), S.123f.

[28] *Johann Sebastian Bach und Johann Joseph Fux.* Bericht über das Symposium anläßlich des 58. Bachfestes der Neuen Bachgesellschaft 24.–29 Mai 1983 in Graz. Hrsg. von Johann Trummer und Rudolf Flotzinger (Kassel [etc.], 1985).

[29] Karl Batz, 'Zwei Meister des musikalischen Barock im Umfeld der Universität zu Ingolstadt', *Ingolstädter Heimatblätter* 45, Nr. 16 (1980), S.21f.; Federhofer, 'J.J. Fux – Choral styles and the *Gradus ad Parnassum*', *American Choral Review* 24 (1982) (= *Festschrift für A. Mann u. d. T. From Schütz to Schubert*), S.14ff.; ders., 'Fux's *Gradus ad Parnassum* as viewed by Heinrich Schenker', *Music Theory Spectrum* 4 (1982), S.66ff.; R. Flotzinger, 'SOL-DO-MI-RE-DO. Ein subjectum und seine (Be)Deutung', *Studien zur Musikwissenschaft* 33 (1982), S.13ff.; ders., 'Fux und Graz', Programmheft des 58. Bachfestes der Neuen Bachgesellschaft 24.–29 Mai 1983 Graz, S.77ff.; Roswitha Karpf, 'Die ganze Welt ist Bühne', *Historisches Jahrbuch der Stadt Graz* 15 (1984), S.53ff.; F.W. Riedel, 'Die Musik bei der Erbhuldigungsreise Kaiser Karls nach Innerösterreich 1728', *Florilegium musicologicum, Hellmut Federhofer zum 75. Geburtstag*, hrsg. von Christoph Hellmut Mahling (Tutzing, 1988) (= *Mainzer Studien zur Musikwissenschaft* 21), S.275ff.

[30] Dazu vgl. Seifert, 'Zur neuesten Fux-Forschung' op. cit., S.49ff.

[31] Ohne Anspruch auf Vollständigkeit folgen in alphabetischer Reihenfolge Namen zeitgenössischer Interpreten, die sich dem Werk von Fux in besonderer Weise widmeten, sowie Hinweise auf Aufführungen umfangreicherer Kompositionen:

Paul Angerer/Wien; René Clemencic, Leiter des Clemencic Consort/Wien; Wolfgang Fürlinger, zugleich Herausgeber und Bearbeiter von Fux-Werken/Linz; Nikolaus Harnoncourt/St Georgen im Attergau; Josef Hofer, Leiter des J.J. Fuxchores/Stubenberg (Steiermark); Bernhard Klebel/Wien; Hans-Martin Linde/Basel; Eduard Melkus/Wien; Thomas Reuber, Leiter der Capella Piccola/Neuss (Rhein); Bernhard Sieberer/Innsbruck; Ulrich Andreas Tegtmeyer, Leiter des 'ensemble >johann joseph fux< '/Hildesheim; Otto Ulf, Leiter der Ambraser Schloßkonzerte und der Woche der alten Musik in Innsbruck/ Innsbruck.

An größeren Werken gelangten zur Aufführung:

Das Oratorium *La fede sacrilega*, K 291 in Graz (Stephanieensaal, 1960), anläßlich des 300. Geburtstages von Fux, und in Wien (Konzerthaus) durch P. Angerer, der mit dem Südwestdeutschen Kammerorchester und seinem 'Concilium Musicum' auch Instrumentalmusik von Fux an zahlreichen Orten, wie Wien, Köln, Stuttgart, Karlsruhe, Neapel in rund 30 Konzerten und Rundfunksendungen zur Aufführung brachte.

Die Oper *Psiche*, K 313 gelangte in Wien (Albertina, 1970), Graz (Rundfunk, 1971/72), Innsbruck, Brno (CSSR) und bei den Brühler Schloßkonzerten (bei Köln) unter Leitung von E. Melkus zur Aufführung. Er brachte auf zahlreichen Tourneen, die ihn nach Deutschland, Italien, in die USA und nach Mexiko führten, immer wieder auch Instrumentalwerke von Fux zu Gehör und widmete ihnen eine Schallplatte (Amadeo).

Anläßlich des 1983 in Graz stattgefundenen 58. Bachfestes der Neuen Bachgesellschaft führten Solisten und Orchester der Hochschule für Musik und darstellende Kunst in Graz das *Te Deum*, K 270 auf; vorangegangen waren von J.S. Bach, die Ouverture Nr. 2 h-moll BWV 1067 und das Konzert für 2 Violinen d-moll BWV 1043. Höhepunkte der letzten Jahre bildeten die Festaufführung der großen Oper *Angelica vincitrice di Alcina*, K 310 unter Leitung von Nikša Bareza anläßlich der Wiedereröffnung des Grazer Opernhauses 1985; die Wiedergabe der Oper *Pulcheria*, K 303 durch H.-M. Linde im Tiroler Landestheater 1986; der Oper *Orfeo ed Euridice*, K 309 durch das Ensemble London Baroque in Wien 1987; der Festmesse, K 45 durch B. Sieberer im Rahmen des Europasommers 1987 in der Stiftskirche Fiecht/Tirol; des Requiems, K 51–54 unter Leitung von R. Clemencic in Wien (Brahmssaal) 1988 und des Oratoriums *La fede sacrilega*, K 291 durch Th. Reuber in Neuss sowie als 7. Kempener Klosterkonzert mit Förderung des Kultusministers von Nordrhein-Westfalen 1989. Die von Publikum und Presse beifällig aufgenommene Wiedergabe wurde durch eine Einspielung festgehalten, die im Handel erhältlich ist. Abweichend von der üblichen Konzertpraxis versucht der evangelische Theologe und Organist U.A. Tegtmeyer als Leiter des seit Beginn der 70er Jahre bestehenden 'ensemble >johann joseph fux<', mit rund 12 Musikern den Grundriß einer gottesdienstähnlichen Struktur durch geistliche Musik im Sinn ökumenischer Bestrebungen abzubilden und damit Fuxens geistliches Werk seiner ursprünglichen Bestimmung wieder anzunähern. Bereits seit vielen Jahren bilden im Gottesdienst an der Kirche der Barmherzigen Brüder in Linz (Österreich) Messen von Fux einen Kernpunkt liturgischen Wirkens unter Leitung von W. Fürlinger. (Alle diese Angaben beruhen auf persönlichen Mitteilungen an den Verfasser und auf Konzertberichten).

[32] RISM A/I/3; A/I/11, Einzeldrucke vor 1800 (Kassel [etc.], 1972), S.130f.; (1986), S.491.

[33] Reinhard Kannonier, *Bruchlinien in der Geschichte der modernen Kunstmusik* (Wien–Köln–Graz, 1987) (= *Kulturstudien* 8), S.253.

[34] J.J. Fux, *Gradus ad Parnassum*, deutsche Ausgabe von L. Ch. Mizler, Vorrede des Übersetzers, Blatt 2[v].

2 The Fux tradition and the mystery of the music archive at Melk Abbey

Robert N. Freeman

The concept of an eighteenth-century musical *Reichsstil*, or imperial style, emanating from Vienna and disseminating at least in a northwesterly direction from the Habsburg's capital throughout Europe, was put forward over a quarter of a century ago by F.W. Riedel.[1] Since then bits and pieces of evidence have gradually come forward, such as the recently published copy by J.S. Bach of Francesco Conti's *Languet anima mea*,[2] to support the thesis that the transmission of music in a good part of eighteenth-century Europe travelled in directions that not only corresponded to the geo-political outlines of the sprawling Austrian Empire as it existed at that time, but even trespassed them.

The Benedictine abbey of Melk in Lower Austria stood like a janitor at the western doorstep of the centre of this empire. Because of many factors, not the least of which was its location at the intersection of the old imperial highway and the Danube waterway, marking the end of the first-day's post route some eighty kilometres west of the capital, one would expect its role in the dissemination of the imperial style to be primary. It is the intent here, therefore, to study this role and to provide a companion piece to an earlier investigation dealing with Antonio Caldara's manuscripts located at Melk.[3] An attempt will be made to examine the surviving musical sources at Melk not only for Fux, but also for his pupils Franz Tuma and Georg Christoph Wagenseil, and by so doing put the Fux tradition at the abbey into a somewhat larger framework. Naturally the same powerful economic, historical and political ties that were found to bond Caldara's music to Melk must have also been at work on that of Fux and his school.

The exchanges of personnel between the Viennese Hofkapelle and the abbey's musical organizations, which have been traced back to the sixteenth century,[4] continued in Fux's time, as is well-established by the survival of part of the correspondence between Abbot Berthold Dietmayr and Emperor Charles VI. A document of 1719 refers to a 'Musical Impost', a financial expenditure designed to support the renewal of a four-year 'Pauschhandlung' or exchange, presumably between the court chapel and the abbey's *alumnat.*[5] That Fux himself thought highly of musicians with Melk backgrounds is made clear in the Kapellmeister's evaluations of his lead trombonist, Leopold Christian (1669–1730), son of Johann Jacob Christian, the abbey's *Thurnermeister* from 1663–1673.[6] On one occasion (1724) he described Christian as 'der erste Virtuos in der Welt in disem Instrument.'[7] Fux had probably become familiar with the performance forces available at Melk early on in his career, since he was very likely present at the abbey to direct the production of his Latin school drama, *Neo-Exoriens phosphorus*, given there in celebration of Dietmayr's investiture, July 1701[8]. Later, one of his pupils, Franz Tuma, was commissioned to collaborate in the composition of another theatrical work, the operetta *Martis und Irene Verbindung*, performed at Melk in 1736, about which more will be said later on.

This solid documentary evidence of direct contacts between Fux (and at least one of his pupils) and Melk, however, contrasts sharply with the situation of musical sources for him at the abbey. A recent search through Melk's music archive in quest of his compositions produced information about only twelve works that are or were at one time or another located there and that can be even remotely brought into association with his name. These are listed in Appendix I at the end of this chapter. Moreover, upon closer scrutiny this number must be reduced even further to only three surviving works of uncontested authenticity: a voice method and two church sonatas (App. I A8, B3–4). All of the rest must be classified as either doubtful (App. I A3–5), spurious (App. I A6–7, B1–2), lost (App. I A2) or a bowdlerized nineteenth-century edition (App. I A1). Of the three authentic works, the Melk copy of the 'Fuchsische Solmisation', or what has become known in the literature as the *Singfundament*, raises the most interesting questions.

J. J. Fux: *Singfundament*

The *Singfundament* is thought to have been composed by Fux during his years as deputy and first *Kapellmeister* at St Stephen's Cathedral in Vienna, 1705–15. Until recently it has been attributed to the composer on the basis of several eighteenth-century MS copies – three located in the archive of the Gesellschaft der Musikfreunde in Vienna, two of which were thought at one time or another to be autographs, and two others in a private collection.[9] To these can be added still other sources located in Vienna and Budapest that have been newly uncovered by Alfred Mann and Eva Badura-Skoda in the process of preparing the work for the Fux collected edition. Although it belongs to a long line of pedagogical texts that ultimately may be traced to the German translation of Carissimi's *Ars cantandi*, the *Wegweiser* published in Augsburg, 1689,[10] the *Singfundament* is perhaps exceptional in that it had such an unusually long history of influence and practical use, extending late into the nineteenth century.[11] Othmar Wessely has shown how a violin method was derived from the work around 1830,[12] and near the end of the century Julius Stockhausen incorporated many of Fux's exercises into his *Gesangsmethode* published in Leipzig in 1884.

Because it lacks the explanatory theoretical text found in the Viennese sources, the Melk copy of the *Singfundament* (App. I A8) has been considered to be a fragment of secondary importance. Since it was first described by Andreas Liess in 1948,[13] it has been believed to have been compiled by Haydn's pupil, Robert Kimmerling, and the years of his tenure as music director at Melk, 1761–77, have been accepted as the date of the manuscript's origins.[14] Liess' description of the source, however, was faulty in many significant details. Ignoring the several different scripts and the positioning of lines, he interpreted the title page to read 'Fuchsische 49 Solmisationen', implying that the exercises contained therein were merely an 'Auszug' confined to that number for either alto or soprano. In fact the manuscript, which consists of sixteen oblong bifolia strung together, comprises two groups totalling sixty-two exercises, and all are scored for two sopranos. Their consecutive numbering together with the terminal colophons appearing on folios 11 and 16 indicate that the source, unto itself, has always remained intact. The complete information on the title page reads:

49. / Die Fuchsische + Solmisation. Egregium opus. / Nº 1056 V. [Bottom of page:] C. M. / 1827. [Lower right-hand corner:] P Robert Kimerling / mp / Regent chori / in Melk. [See Plate 1]

This is rendered in three different hands that can be identified as belonging to:

a Robert Kimmerling: 'Die Fuchsische + Solmisation. Egregium opus.; 'P Robert Kimerling / mp / Regent chori / in Melk.'
b Rupert Helm (1748–1826): '49.' The cipher refers to the numbering in one of Helm's thematic catalogues, the extensive 'Gesang- und Schlag-stücke', compiled around 1820[15] and is, therefore, unrelated to the number of exercises contained in the manuscript.
c Amand Polster, music director at Melk, 1825–1828: 'Nº 1056 V.'; 'C[hori]. M[ellicensis]. / 1827.' Represents the current archival siglum and the year it was assigned to the MS by Polster.

In the best tradition of the Benedictines, Fux's method was, in other words, cared for and transmitted from one music director to the next over a period of three-quarters of a century. But none of these three individuals was responsible for copying the music itself, which was written in still another, fourth hand, that of Joseph Weiss, organist at the abbey from 1729 until 1759. The identification of his calligraphy for the first time in 1987[16] made it possible to trace a number of copies of compositions by Caldara and others, including a church sonata by Fux (App. I B4), prepared by Weiss for Melk, and thereby establish his pre-eminent role in perpetuating the imperial court church style at the abbey at mid-century. This copy of the *Singfundament* serves only to confirm the earlier findings.

Weiss copied the *Singfundament* onto manuscript paper of a type that

Plate 1. Title page of Fux's *Singfundament* (App. I A8), copied Joseph Weiss. (A–M: V 1056). *Reproduced with permission*

remained in use at Melk at least up to *c.* 1757–63. Its watermark closely resembles one found in performance materials located at Melk for works composed by J.G. Albrechtsberger: the autograph parts to his oratorio, *Christo Kreutz Erfindung*, the score of which was written originally in Raab in 1757, but whose parts were probably used for a performance at Melk in the years 1757–59 when Albrechtsberger returned to the vicinity of the abbey to take up his new position as organist at Maria Taferl; and his offertory *Precatus est Moyses*, composed at Melk in 1763 (see Plates 2–3)[17]. Such long periods of use were not unusual since it is known that large quantities of paper were purchased by the abbey at one time and then kept for many years.[18] This new information places the dating of the Melk copy of the *Singfundament* somewhat earlier than has heretofore been considered – near the end of the period 1729–59 rather than 1761–77.

Although Badura-Skoda was unable to inspect the Melk copy in the course of her initial investigation of the sources for the *Singfundament* in 1953, she rightly suspected that it was related to one of the Viennese manuscripts.[19] Indeed the musical text of the individual duets closely follows in most cases the variants found in one of the Viennese MSS (A–Wgm 1317). Weiss' copy has in common with the other sources the overall grouping of the exercises into a *cantus durus-mollis* division, but its interior arrangement has a character of its own, the actual sequence of the duets corresponding only partly with the Viennese sources. Weiss followed a strict metric organization in arranging each division: those duets in common time (C) were followed by exercises in triple simple meters (3/2, 3/4) with compound patterns (6/4, 6/8, 12/8) placed at the end.

Until the newly discovered copies of the *Singfundament* are evaluated, it remains to be seen just where the Melk MS stands in relationship to other sources. It undoubtedly will occupy an important place if only because of Weiss' Viennese origins, his significant activity as a copyist of the music of Fux and Caldara and his collaboration with Fux's pupil Franz Tuma.

Franz Tuma: Prologue to *Martis und Irene Verbindung*

The number of works preserved at Melk by Franz Tuma, the pupil thought to reflect the more conservative side of Fux's teachings, is likewise small – three Masses, two Miserere, one church sonata and newly discovered vocal fragments to an operetta – only seven works in all (see Appendix II). With the bulk of it representing church music, this selection is, nevertheless, typical for the composer, whose reputation rested primarily with his liturgical works. Tuma's Masses (App. II A1–3) very likely still formed part of the core performance repertory at Melk during the administration of music director Rupert Helm (1778–1787). The parts carry old catalogue sigla and style designations ('ordin[är]:') that seem to correspond to the division of styles in Helm's inventory of 1787 where 'ordinär' and 'Messen mit mehreren Instrumenten' are differentiated.[20] These classifications in turn can be traced to those established by Fux and Killian Reinhardt ('mediocre', 'solenne', etc.) for the Viennese court chapel some sixty years

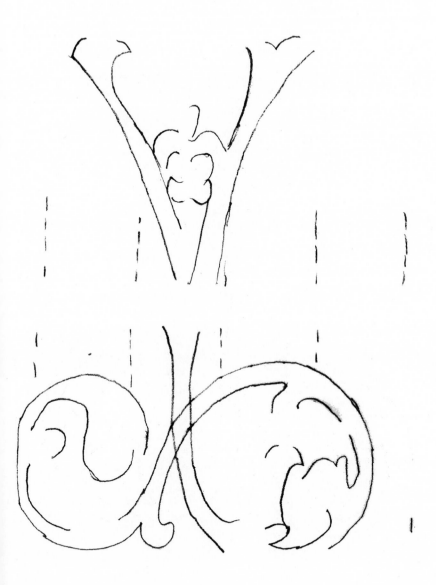

Plate 2. Watermark contained in paper used for Fux's *Singfundament* (App. I A8).

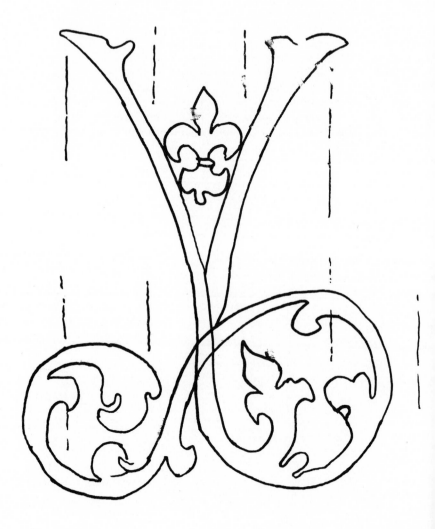

Plate 3. Watermark contained in paper used at Melk Abbey, *c.* 1757–63.

earlier.[21] Our attention, however, is drawn not so much to these compositions as it is to the non-liturgical items, which are truly unique. For example, the Melk copy of the church sonata (App. II B1), entitled '*Sinfonia à 3*' and scored for two violins, violone and organ (with figures), turns out to be the only known source for this work.[22] It is possible, therefore, that it was composed specifically for the abbey where it was performed in 1746.

Since 1960, when its MS libretto was first described,[23] it has been known that Tuma collaborated with the Melk organist J. Weiss in the composition of a German operetta, *Martis und Irene Verbindung*, performed at the abbey in 1736. The work was originally intended to celebrate the marriage of Maria Theresa and Francis of Lorraine that had taken place in Vienna on February 12 that year, but the first performance at Melk had to be postponed on account of a serious illness that befell Abbot Dietmayr. The text was very likely composed by Father Martin Kropf, professor of rhetoric of the cloister school, who was described in 1736 as the 'Herr Commicus', the usual term used to refer to the house poet or librettist.[24] At the bottom of the title-page (see Plate 4) one learns that this was:

> an operetta conceived by Melk artisans, and that part that is addressed to His Excellency [Abbot Dietmayr] is set to music by the virtuoso Herr Francisco Tuma. The main work, however, [is set] by Herr Joseph Weiss, organist at the exempt cloister of Melk, and composed in the year 1736.

Tuma, in other words, was responsible for providing music for the prologue, which comprises just nine of the thirty-eight pages of the libretto. The circumstances that brought the two composers together in this particular collaborative effort are unknown, but when one considers the relationship between other composers, such as that of teacher–pupil between Caldara and Reutter represented in their *collaborazione* – the operas *La forza dell'amicizia* (1728) and *La pazienza di Socrate* (1731) – one may speculate that some kind of similar connection between Tuma and Weiss could have already existed (perhaps a common teacher in Fux?)

The significance of this work, which has not received much attention heretofore, is twofold. It is the only known dramatic attempt by the composer, and it occupies an important place in the eighteenth-century theatrical repertory at the Austrian cloisters. Produced at Melk considerably earlier than those recorded at Seitenstetten (*c.* 1750), Kremsmünster (1758) or Linz (1763) and not to be imitated there again until 1764,[25] *Martis und Irene* is perhaps the earliest known example of an independently performed German stage work at an Upper or Lower Austrian monastery.

The music to this historically important operetta was long thought to be lost. In 1989, however, in the course of preparing material for this article, it was possible to uncover fragments of three vocal parts belonging to the work's prologue uncatalogued in the abbey's music archive (App. II A6). The fragments add information to that found in the libretto regarding the roles and identity of the cast: the part of 'Austria', a tenor, performed by Mathias Muthentaller, a musician and clerk employed at Melk from 1719 until his death in 1742; 'Fama' (Justice), a soprano sung by the abbey's well-paid (150 florins annually) professional 'discantist' (= falsettist), Friderich

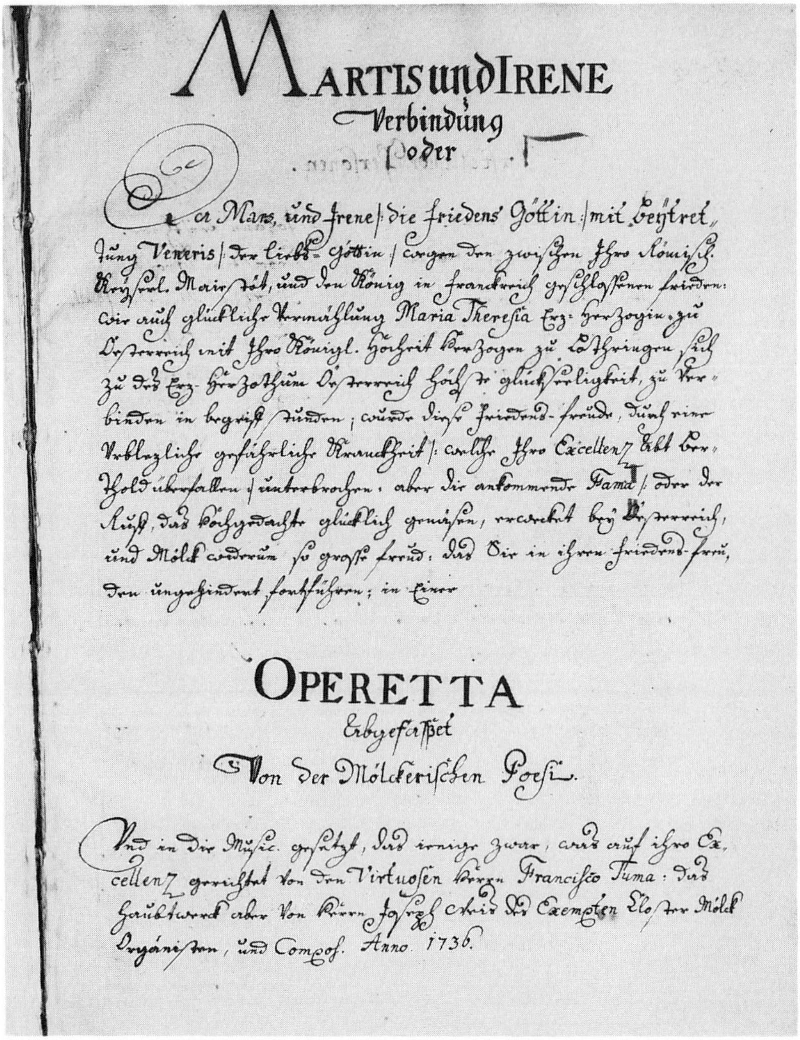

Plate 4. Title page of the libretto for *Martis und Irene Verbindung* (App. II A6), 1736. (Melk, Stiftsarchiv, 15. Gymnasium, Karton 2.). *Reproduced with permission*

Zöhrer, engaged at Melk from 1727 until 1743, when he moved to Vienna; 'Mellicium oder Mölck' (Melk), designated tenor in the libretto, but a bass in the parts, performed by Sebastian Kropf, a relative (brother?) of the librettist; and the role of 'Fluss Melk' (River Melk), designated bass in the libretto, but an alto in the parts, assigned to Thadeus Deiber, a choirboy.

Unfortunately, what is left of the music does not allow any portion of the score to be fully reconstructed, but by combining the fragments with the libretto, the general plan and some of the details of the prologue, referred to as an 'applausus' in the text, can be laid out (see Table 1).

Table 1   *Martis und Irene Verbindung:* layout of Tuma's prologue

Item Text Incipit Key/Meter (Design)	Role (voice)
[Recitativ] 1. Aria 'Klaget, ihr Kinder Österreichs'	Austria Austria (T)
Recitativ 2. Aria 'Ach Unbestand'	Austria Austria (T)
Recitativ	Melk/Fluss Melk
3. Aria [duet] 'So verändert sich das Glück!' F/C (Strophic)	Melk/Fluss Melk (AB)[a]
Recitativ	Fama/Austria
4. Aria 'Auf bestürztes Mölck'	Fama (S)
Recitativ	Fama/Melk
5. Chorus [Trio] & Recitativ 'Brich an gewünschter Tag' G/3/4 (ABA')	Austria/Melk/ Fluss Melk (ATB)
[Recitativ] 6. Schlusschor 'Wann Österreich die Friedensposaunen erhebt' A/C (Da capo)	Melk Tutti (SATB)

[a] See Plate 5

It is evident, even from this rough outline, that Tuma must have had considerable technique and imagination when it came to setting a dramatic text.[26] The traditional sequence of recitative and solo aria was balanced and broken up by the inclusion and distribution of an equal number of ensembles – a duet, a trio and final chorus. Further variety was assured by the wide range of scorings, formal designs (strophic, da capo, ABA') and keys (F, G, A). Tuma made use of the technique of having an ensemble interrupted by recitative (No. 5 'Brich an gewünschter Tag'), an effective musical-theatrical device used on occasion by Handel. The fragment of the duet illustrated in Plate 5, as brief as it is, displays a bold style of solo vocal writing. The concerto-like rhythms (𝅘𝅥𝅮𝅘𝅥𝅮), syncopations, and disjunct intervals alternating with colorature must have presented a challenge even for the. most talented of Melk's choirboys.

Georg Christoph Wagenseil: *Sinfonia-Sestetto*

The sources at Melk for Wagenseil, one of Fux's prize pupils, are almost as scanty as they are for his teacher and for Tuma. Only eleven works preserved at the abbey can be attributed to him (see Appendix III), a small number, but one representative, nevertheless, of most areas of his compositional activity: sacred music, chamber and orchestral works; only his music for the theatre is lacking. Here, too, one encounters valuable and informative sources. The lone church composition, the Latin aria, 'Eja gentes plausus dato' for bass solo, chorus and orchestra (App. III A1), was acquired by Melk in 1780 according to the information entered by Adam Krieg into his thematic catalogue of 1821.[27] This late date is curious, because it is believed that Wagenseil composed most of his church music early in his career, before 1745. Melk's acquisition of this composition was related to a general resurgence of interest in older court chapel music in the late 1770s–1780s.[28] Two other works, the symphonies in G and A (App. III B2, 4), came into the Melk collection through Karl Gegenbauer (d. 1791), a celebrated violinist in the employ of the bishop of St Pölten, who also owned a large collection of solo violin sonatas and concertos by Franz Benda, some of which were acquired by Melk in 1785.[29] Perhaps because its original wrapper, which served as a title page, was found separated from its parts, the Melk copy of the flute concerto in G (App. III B8) has escaped the notice of Wagenseil scholars. It not only provides a second source to the only one previously known to exist in Karlsruhe (Badische Landesbibliothek), but because of its Austrian provenance it probably supersedes the German copy in importance.

As small as this repertory is, it is evident that Wagenseil's music was appreciated at Melk, where it enjoyed a long history of performance. One of the three surviving keyboard concertos (App. III B6–7, 9) still had a place in the performance repertory of Robert Stipa, the abbey's virtuoso fortepianist active until 1850.

Among the more interesting and, from the standpoint of classification and performance practice, perhaps most controversial of these works is the Melk copy of Wagenseil's so-called sextet (App. III B5), a work long known only from a Viennese source, a set of manuscript parts formerly belonging to the imperial court archive entitled 'Sestetto', dating from the 1760s.[30] Although it has never been published, the composition has gained some attention in the literature because of its unusual scoring (four violins, viola and 'cello), and because it specifically calls for 'violoncello' it has been noted as 'the only potentially "true" string sextet' in mid-century Viennese

Plate 5. Fragment, alto part for *Martis und Irene Verbindung* (App. II A6), prologue no. 3. (A–M: VI Fragmente, fliegende Blätter, udgl.) *Reproduced with permission*

chamber repertory.[31]

J. Kucaba seems to have been the first to take notice of the source at Melk, which he classified as a 'non-symphony'[32] in spite of the fact that the work was known at the abbey from the beginning as a 'sinfonia'. It was designated as such by Rupert Helm in one of the several thematic catalogues prepared by him between 1790–1820[33] and by Adam Krieg in the fourth *Abteilung* (orchestral music) of his catalogue begun in 1821. Both Helm and Krieg had access to the original title page on the wrapper that was presumably among those disposed of in the 1930s. The parts themselves, which have the Viennese 'violoncello' replaced by 'Basso' ('Violone' in Krieg's catalogue and on the modern wrapper), were prepared on the same paper as that used for the abbey's copy of the *Singfundament* by Fux (see Plate 3). The copy must date, therefore, not later than 1757–63, earlier perhaps than the Viennese source.

The term 'sinfonia' may not have been used at Melk as haphazardly as it apparently was in Viennese chamber music before 1750.[34] At Melk there seems to have been a desire for fuller or at least louder orchestral scorings, as can be observed in other works by Wagenseil acquired by the abbey. Rupert Helm added parts for clarini to the keyboard concerto in C (App. III B7), and Wagenseil's symphonies at Melk, known elsewhere usually or only with oboes, have these instruments replaced by clarini or horns (App. III B1, 3).[35]

A comparison of the Viennese and Melk sets of parts for what might be therefore more accurately referred to as the *Sinfonia-Sestetto* indicates that these sources were probably not copied from one another. Besides the significant differences in general features, such as the title (*sinfonia* vs. *sestetto*) and scoring (basso/violone vs. 'cello), the parts at Melk are consistent in their omission of the modifier 'moderato' in the tempo indication of the first-movement fugue. The Melk source is practically devoid of the signs of articulation (staccatos) and ornamentation found in abundance in the Viennese parts, but, as was seen in the case of Caldara's manuscripts, the absence of such signs was typical of copies of Viennese works prepared at the abbey.[36] It seems likely, therefore, that the Melk source was copied from some unknown third source, and this very well may have been one in the form of a score.[37]

A study of the textual variants found between the two sets of parts produces some interesting results. Except for a very small number of minor rhythmic oversights all of the variants in the Melk parts can be interpreted as having been made as deliberate 'improvements' over the Viennese or third source from which they were copied. For instance the initial chord with its open fifth in the first movement may have sounded too archaic for Melk ears and was reorchestrated (see Examples 1a–b). Several other examples of these 'improvements' are found in the slow middle movement. Suspensions were removed apparently in order to eliminate dissonances that may have been deemed too harsh such as those in measures 10–13 in the first violins to avoid major and minor seconds being formed with the second violins and at measure 16 in the third violin to avoid a g-sharp-g diminished octave with the violas (see Examples 2a–b).

Example 1a. G.C. Wagenseil, Sinfonia-Sestetto (App. III B5), opening of the first movement based on the Viennese parts.

Example 1b. The same excerpt based on Melk parts.

Example 2a. G.C. Wagenseil, Sinfonia-Sestetto (App. III B5), Fuga, mm 10–16 based on the Viennese parts.

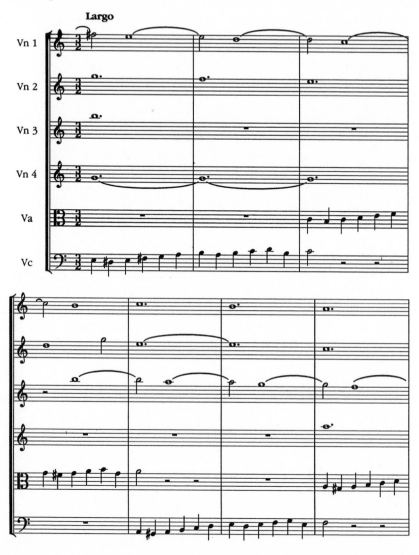

Notwithstanding the title, scoring and fast–slow–fast sequence of movements of the Melk source, the work itself, when viewed from the standpoint of the character of its movements, has more to do with Wagenseil's church sonatas than with his symphonies. A fast, brief toccata-like section introduces a 73-measure double fugue in A major, the coda of which is derived from the introduction, a rarity in the repertory of mid-century fugues, but a feature found in at least one other example by Wagenseil, in his church sonata in c minor (WV 450).[38] There follows a solemn

Example 2b. The same excerpt based on the Melk parts.

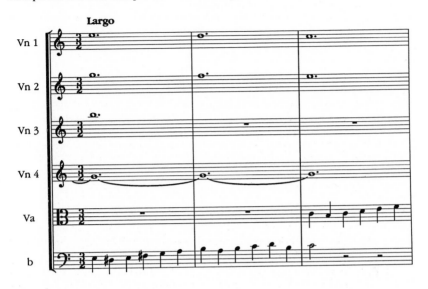

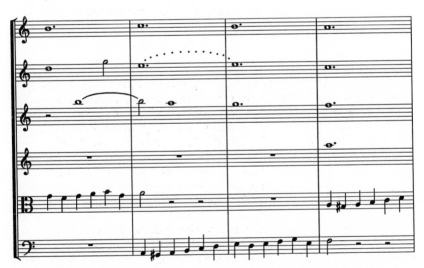

movement in the parallel minor marked *Largo*, a tempo seldom found in
the symphonies. The austerity of these movements is relieved only by a
concluding quick dance more in the style of a *bourrée* rather than the typical
Tempo di menuet of the early symphonic finales. All of these movements
are pronouncedly baroque in character and technique, and one wants to
place the date of this composition in the 1740s along with Wagenseil's
other church sonatas.[39]

The sources of the *Sinfonia-Sestetto* present, therefore, not so much a

Table 2   *Holdings of Fux, Tuma, Wagenseil and Caldara in selected Lower and Upper Austrian monastic collections*

Institution	Fux	Tuma	Wagenseil	Caldara
Göttweig[a]	30	40	44	96
Herzogenburg[b]	57	98	19	126
Kremsmünster[c]	55	20	26	53
Melk	3	7	11	33

[a] Based upon entries contained in *Der Göttweiger thematische Katalog von 1830*, edited by Friedrich Wilhelm Riedel, 2 vols (Munich, 1979) (*Studien zur Landes- und Sozialgeschichte der Musik*, 2/3).
[b] Based upon entries contained in *Catalogus Selectiorum Musicalium Chori Ducumburgensis quibus accedunt. Instrumenta musica Diarium Cantus Figuralis aliarumq[ue] functionum Musicae totius Anni. Index Generalis Catalogi Conscripti Anno 1751* MS (A–H) 2 vols.
[c] Totals according to Altman Kellner *Musikgeschichte des Stiftes Kremsmünster* (Kassel, 1956) pp.350, 355.

problem in determining the work's genre, but rather they may point to a specific example of a Lower Austrian orchestral performance of a Viennese chamber work. They reflect the duality of performance practice that existed in regards to the eighteenth-century sonata[40] and other genres, a duality that persisted at Melk through the first quarter of the following century, as one of the subtitles in Adam Krieg's catalogue testifies: 'Chamber music for the entire orchestra' ('Kammer=Musik für das ganze Orchester').[41]

In conclusion

By way of summary it can be said of the preceding brief survey that, in spite of contacts with the abbey proven for at least two of its composers, the Fux 'school' is represented by a disappointingly small number of works at Melk. If one adds to the three surviving authentic compositions by Fux those by his students Tuma (7) and Wagenseil (11), a combined total of only slightly more than twenty works is reached, hardly much evidence in support of Melk's role in disseminating the *Reichsstil*. This modest repertory, never-theless, was found to contain several items of special value, either because of their rarity, early dating or relevance to eighteenth-century performance practices.

The oddity of this particular source situation can be readily seen from Table 2, a comparison of the Fux–Tuma–Wagenseil and Caldara holdings at Melk with those presently or formerly belonging to collections at other Lower and Upper Austrian monasteries. The figures clearly show how exceptionally poor Melk ultimately became as a reservoir for sources of the very tradition that it was pledged to preserve by virtue of its eleventh-century margravial endowment.

The discrepancy arising out of documented contacts between Viennese composers and Melk on the one hand and the poverty of corresponding musical sources surviving at the abbey on the other is by no means one confined to Fux and his school. It applies also to identifiable 'house' composers active at Melk contemporaneously with Fux. For example,

Table 3   *Melk organists, 1684-1812*

Name	Dates of Employment	Works at A-M
F. Schneider	1 Jan. 1766 – 5 Feb. 1812	178[a]
J.G. Albrechtsberger	1 April 1759 – 6 Aug. 1765	121[b]
J. Weiss	15 Dec. 1729 – 13 Feb. 1759	50[c]
G.H. Freitag	Jan. 1721 – 14 Nov. 1729	1
I. Debouchier	May 1716 – Dec. 1720	
J.C. Gerersdorfer	1 Dec. 1696 – 29 Dec. 1715	
M. Gläsl	15 Mar. 1695 – Oct. 1696	
J. Wagner	1 Jan. 1693 – 15 Mar. 1695	
M. Egenhofer, A. Baumgartner	Sept. – Dec. 1692	[1?]
J. Mercklin	Jan. – Aug. 1692	
J.C. Weichlein	Jan. 1686 – 1 Aug. 1691	
J. Zillich	1684 – 20 Nov. 1686	

[a] Robert N. Freeman, *Franz Schneider (1737-1812), A Thematic Catalogue of His Works* (New York, 1979).
[b] See the listing of his works in Robert N. Freeman, 'The Practice of Musik at Melk Monastery in the Eighteenth Century' (Ph.D., diss. University of California, Los Angeles, 1971) Appendix C. 2.
[c] Includes twenty-five copies made by him of works by other composers; see Robert N. Freeman, 'The Caldara Manuscripts at Melk Abbey' in Pritchard, op. cit., p. 229f.

documentary sources indicate that the most prolific composer at the abbey during Fux's period was the music director Father Albert Baumgartner (1677–1730). During his lifetime he was referred to as Melk's 'Compositor musices' and upon his death he was remembered by his brothers for 'his works, [which] were considered very useful not only by us, but also by others.'[42] Although his church music can be traced at other locations (incipits for nine works are contained in a thematic catalogue of 1751 at Herzogenburg and two others survive at Göttweig), only a single work, a *Salve Regina* attributed to a 'P. Albertus', is preserved at Melk (III 59). Furthermore, Baumgartner is known to have composed scores for at least four theatrical works produced at the abbey between 1709–28, but not a trace of the music for them has survived there.

A similar situation exists for a number of Melk organists, who, among their many other duties, were expected to provide the abbey with original musical compositions, even though they were not specifically called upon to do so in their contract that survives at Melk dating from the period of Fux (1693).[43] Because the organists were usually lay employees, the force of the Melk documents can be brought to bear here, allowing this problem to be approached from a somewhat different perspective. From them, particularly from the abbey's financial account books, it is possible to reconstruct the succession of organists employed by Melk from 1684 through 1812 with never more than an occasional three- or four-month gap. When one adds to this list the number of extant works based upon music-archival evidence, the details can be illustrated as shown in Table 3. Taking into account the fact that the total number of surviving works by these composers must have been affected to some degree by factors such as their length of employment and individual productivity, the table shows that there was a dramatic and almost total disappearance of music composed by organists employed before 1729.

Such data illustrate the enigmatic circumstances that have long shrouded the music archive at Melk, circumstances that collectively make up what might be referred to as its mystery – that is the fact that so much music from the first half of the eighteenth century, and, for that matter, from all the earlier periods of the abbey's past has vanished without explanation. Clearly, some kind of calamity must have befallen this collection, but its nature, cause and date of occurrence have yet to be determined. Three events, any one of which may have been responsible for triggering the loss of the music, have been proposed:[44]

1. The 'lack of proper supervision' over the collection during the years the abbey's school was transferred to St Pölten, 1787–1811; an explanation first put forward by Maximilian Stadler.[45]
2. The great fire that engulfed part of the abbey on 10 August 1738.
3. The intense building activity during the period of the abbey's reconstruction under Abbot Dietmayr, particularly during the years 1730–44, when the rooms of the music director and the dormitories of the choirboys were relocated.

The foregoing investigation of the Fux tradition at Melk sheds at least a glimmer of light on this puzzle. For one thing, the dated works by Tuma, notably the church sonata performed in 1746 and especially the fragments to the operetta produced in 1736 (App. II B1, A6), can be combined with what has already been identified as the earliest eighteenth-century Mass preserved at Melk, one by Georg Zechner dated 1735 (A–M: I 48), to help narrow down the time of the mysterious disaster to the middle of the 1730s. This new evidence of music surviving both the transfer of the school in 1787 and the fire of 1738 tends to weigh against these as possible causes of the tragedy and lends support to the remaining thesis that the archive was disrupted during the earlier period of reconstruction. It would be an irony, nevertheless, if the creative activities, which produced the magnifcent baroque monument that is so much admired today, might very well also have led to the obliteration of much of the abbey's baroque musical heritage.

Notes

[1] 'Der "Reichsstil" in der deutschen Musikgeschichte des 18. Jahrhunderts', *Bericht über den Internationalen Musikwissenschaftlichen Kongreß Kassel 1962*, edited by Georg Reichert and Martin Just (Kassel, 1963) pp.34–36.

[2] *Stuttgarter Bach-Ausgaben*, series C, supplement: Durch Johann Sebastian Bach überlieferte Werke, edited by Yoshitake Kobayashi (Stuttgart, c.1982); the work can be added to the well-known copy by Bach of Caldara's *Magnificat*, edited by Christoph Wolff (Kassel, 1969).

[3] Robert N. Freeman, 'The Caldara Manuscripts at Melk Abbey' in *Antonio Caldara: Essays on his life and times*, edited by Brian W. Pritchard (Aldershot, 1987) pp.[214]–46.

[4] Robert N. Freeman, *The Practice of Music at Melk Abbey Based Upon the Documents, 1681-1826* (Vienna, 1989) (*Österreichische Akademie der Wissenschaften, phil.-hist. Klasse, Sitzungsberichte* 548 = *Veröffentlichungen der Kommission für Musikforschung* 23) p.64.

[5] ibid., doc. n.7194. For another interpretation of this document, see *Jakob Prandtauer und sein Kunstkreis*, edited by Rupert Feuchtmüller (Vienna, 1960) p.118, no.44.

[6] Freeman, op. cit., [*The Practice*], p. 106; Herwig Knaus, *Die Musiker im Archivbestand des kaiserlichen Obersthofmeisteramtes (1637-1705)* (Vienna, 1968) (*Österreichische Akademie der Wissenschaften, phil.-hist. Klasse, Sitzungsberichte* 264/1 = *Veröffentlichungen der Kommission für Musikforschung*, 10) v.2, p.38.

[7] Ludwig Ritter von Köchel, *Johann Josef Fux, Hofkompositor und Hofkapellmeister der Kaiser Leopold I., Josef I. und Karl VI. von 1698 bis 1740* (Vienna, 1872) Beil. VI, p.102.

[8] Only the printed text survives. See Friedrich W. Riedel, 'Abt Berthold Dietmay von Melk und der kaiserliche Hofkapellmeister Johann Joseph Fux', *Unsere Heimat* 36 (1965) pp.59ff.; idem, ' "Neo-Exoriens Phosphorus", ein unbekanntes musik-dramatisches Werk von Johann Joseph Fux', *Die Musikforschung*, 18 (1965) pp. 291–3; Freeman, op. cit. [*The Practice*], Appendix B, OW 5.

[9] A-Wgm: 1317-8, 712; A-Wwessely. See Andreas Liess, 'Fux, Johann Joseph', *Die Musik in Geschichte und Gegenwart*, hrsg.von Friedrich Blume, (Kassel, Basel, 1967), vol. 4 col. 1167 and Eva Badura, 'Beiträge zur Geschichte des Musikunterrichtes im 16., 17. und 18. Jahrhundert' (D.Phil., diss. University of Innsbruck, 1953) p.74.

[10] A specimen of the print is preserved in A-Wn: SA. 71. F6.

[11] See Hellmut Federhofer, 'Johann Joseph Fux als Musiktheoretiker' in *Hans Albrecht in Memoriam* (Kassel, 1962) pp.109–10.

[12] Othmar Wessely, 'Johann Joseph Fuxens "Singfundament" als Violinschule', *Vierzig Jahre Steirischer Tonkünstlerbund* (Graz, 1967) pp. 1–(9).

[13] Andreas Liess, *Johann Joseph Fux, Ein steirischer Meister des Barock* (Vienna, 1948) p.85.

[14] Wessely, art. cit., p.2, n.6.

[15] Alexander Weinmann, *Handschriftliche thematische Kataloge aus dem Benediktinerstift Melk* (Vienna, 1984) (*Tabulae Musicae Austriacae*, 10) Kat. IVd, T. 55, p.130 = Schlagstück no. 49.

[16] See Freeman, 'The Caldara Manuscripts at Melk Abbey' in Pritchard, op. cit., pp.218; Plate 1 for a facsimile, 229f.

[17] See Dorothea Schröder, *Die geistlichen Vokalkompositionen Johann Georg Albrechtsbergers* (Hamburg, 1987) (*Hamburger Beiträge zur Musikwissenschaft*, 34) v. 2, p.333, K.2 ('Jaurini [= Györ/Raab] 1757') and p.137, C.I.12 ('Comp. 1763 Mellicii.').

[18] For examples see Robert N. Freeman, *Franz Schneider (1737-1812), A Thematic Catalogue of His Works* (New York, 1979) pp.225-6.

[19] Although for the wrong reasons, having been misled by Liess' faulty description of the scoring; see Badura, op. cit., p.80.

[20] Robert N. Freeman, 'Zwei Melker Musikkataloge aus der zweiten Hälfte des 18. Jahrhunderts', *Die Musikforschung* 23 (1970) p.176.

[21] Friedrich W. Riedel, *Kirchenmusik am Hofe Karls VI. (1711-1740)* (Munich, 1977) 67ff.

[22] Herbert Vogg, 'Franz Tuma (1704-1774) als Instrumentalkomponist, nebst Beiträgen zur Wiener Musikgeschichte des 18. Jahrhunderts: Die Hofkapelle der Kaiserinwitwe Elisabeth Christine' (D.Phil., diss. University of Vienna, 1951) v. 3, no. B I 9.

[23] Feuchtmüller, op. cit., pp. 245-6, no. 452.

[24] Robert N. Freeman, *The Practice of Music at Melk Abbey Based Upon the Documents, 1681-1826* (Vienna, 1989) doc. n. 7365.

[25] ibid., p. 269ff.

[26] For a synopsis of the plot, see ibid.

[27] *CATALOG, aller auf dem Stifts=Chore von Melk vorhandenen Musikalien. Verfasst im Jahr 1821* A-M, MS, 5 parts in 4 vols.

[28] See Freeman, op. cit. [*The Practice*], p.299.

[29] ibid., p.292f.

[30] A-Wn: s.m. 3746; the dating according to James Webster, 'Violoncello and Double Bass in the Chamber Music of Haydn and his Viennese Contemporaries, 1750-1780', *Journal of the American Musicological Society* XXIX (1976) p.424.

[31] James Webster, 'Towards a History of Viennese Chamber Music in the Early Classical Period', *Journal of the American Musicological Society* XXVII (1974) p.223 n.50. I plan to submit a modern edition of the score to Musikhaus Doblinger, Vienna, for publication.

[32] *Georg Christoph Wagenseil*, edited by John Kucaba in *The Symphony 1720-1840*, Series B, III, Barry S. Brook, editor-in-chief (New York, 1981) p.1, N:A1. The Melk copy was unknown to Scholz-Michelitsch; see her *Das Orchester- und Kammermusikwerk von Georg Christoph Wagenseil: Thematischer Katalog* (Vienna, 1972) WV 487.

[33] Weinmann, op. cit., Kat. VII (T. 68), p.160, with incorrect call number.

[34] Webster, op. cit., p.227.

[35] Oboes may have been a perennial problem at Melk. As late as 1827 clarinets had to substitute for oboes in a performance of Beethoven's third piano concerto, op. 37; see Robert N. Freeman, 'New Sources for Beethoven's Piano Concerto Cadenzas from Melk Abbey', *Beethoven Forum* (in press).

[36] Freeman, 'The Caldara Manuscripts at Melk Abbey' in Pritchard, op. cit. p.217.

[37] This is suggested by the nature of an error in the fugue where at measure 52 the third violin part briefly incorporates music of the fourth violin, as if the copyist's eye had momentarily dropped down a line in a score.

[38] Warren Kirkendale, *Fugue and Fugato in Rococo and Classical Chamber Music* 2nd ed. revised and expanded, trans. by Margaret Bent and the author (Durham, NC, 1979) p.51. The fugal movement of the *Sinfonia-Sestetto* should be added to the ten fugues by Wagenseil catalogued by Kirkendale (p.282).

[39] ibid., p.8.

[40] ibid., pp.42ff.

[41] Krieg, op. cit., v.2, IV. Abtheilung.

[42] Freeman, op. cit. [*The Practice*], doc. n.7303.

[43] ibid., doc. n.6931.

[44] ibid., p. 26f.

[45] *Abbé Maximilian Stadler, seine Materialien zur Geschichte der Musik unter den österreich-ischen Regenten,* edited by Karl Wagner (Kassel, [1974]) (*Schriftenreihe der Internatio-nalen Stiftung Mozarteum,* 6; *Publikationen des Instituts für Musikwissenschaft der Universität Salzburg,* 7) p.149.

Appendices:

Thematic listings of the compositions associated with J.J. Fux, F. Tuma and G.C. Wagenseil at Melk Abbey

All of the works listed below are MSS unless otherwise indicated. Abbreviated tempos are spelled out, and original clefs are modernized. Abbreviations for voices and instruments are used according to *The New Grove Dictionary of Music and Musicians*, edited by Stanley Sadie (London, 1980). 'Reference(s)' are to catalogues and modern editions. The following bibliographical abbreviations are used:

Freeman = Robert N. Freeman, *The Practice of Music at Melk Abbey Based upon the Documents, 1681-1826* (Vienna, 1989) (*Österreichischen Akademie der Wissenschaften, phil.-hist. Klasse, Sitzungsberichte* 548 = *Veröffentlichungen der Kommission für Musikforschung*, 23), Appendix B.

Krieg = [Adam Krieg] *CATALOG, aller auf dem Stifts=Chore von Melk vorhandenen Musikalien. Verfasst im Jahr 1821* [ff.] A–M, MS, 5 parts in 4 vols.

Kucaba = *Georg Christoph Wagenseil,* edited by John Kucaba in *The Symphony 1720-1840*. Series B, III. Barry S. Brook, editor-in-chief (New York, 1981).

KV = Ludwig Ritter von Köchel, *Johann Josef Fux, Hofkompositor und Hofkapellmeister der Kaiser Leopold I., Josef I. und Karl VI. von 1698 bis 1740* (Vienna, 1872).

Liess = Andreas Liess, *Johann Joseph Fux, Ein steirischer Meister des Barock* (Vienna, 1948).

Peschek = Alfred Peschek, 'Die Messen von Franz Tuma (1704–1774)' (D.Phil., diss. University of Vienna, 1956), 3 vols.

Reichert = Georg Reichert, 'Zur Geschichte der Wiener Messenkomposition in der ersten Hälfte des 18. Jahrhunderts' (D.Phil., diss. University of Vienna, 1935).

Riedel = *Der Göttweiger thematische Katalog von 1830*, edited by Friedrich Wilhelm Riedel (Munich, 1979) 2 vols. (*Studien zur Landes- und Sozialgeschichte der Musik*, 2/3).

Schröder = Dorothea Schröder, *Die geistlichen Vokalkompositionen Johann Georg Albrechtsbergers*, 2 vols. (Hamburg, 1987) (*Hamburger Beiträge zur Musikwissenschaft*, 34).

Vogg = Herbert Vogg, 'Franz Tuma (1704–1774) als Instrumentalkomponist, nebst Beiträgen zur Wiener Musikgeschichte des 18. Jahrhunderts: Die Hofkapelle der Kaiserinwitwe Elisabeth Christine' (D.Phil., diss. University of Vienna, 1951), 3 vols.

Weinmann = Alexander Weinmann, *Handschriftliche thematische Kataloge aus dem Benediktinerstift Melk* (Vienna, 1984) (*Tabulae Musicae Austriacae*, 10).

Weiss. = Andreas Weissenbäck, 'Thematisches Verzeichnis der Kirchenkompositionen von Johann Georg Albrechtsberger', *Jahrbuch des Stiftes Klosterneuburg* VI (1914) 1–160.

WV = Helga Michelitsch, *Das Klavierwerk von Georg Christoph Wagenseil, Thematischer Katalog* (Vienna, 1966); Helga Scholz-Michelitsch, *Das Orchester- und Kammermusikwerk von Georg Christoph Wagenseil, Thematischer Katalog* (Vienna, 1972) (*Tabulae Musicae Austriacae*, 3).

Appendix I

J.J. Fux (authentic compositions indicated with an asterisk [*])

A. *Vocal*

1. Mass

A–M: VI 2644.

score: pr.'(Klosterneuburger Messe)' ed. V. Goller, *Meisterwerke Kirchlicher Tonkunst in Österreich* I (Vienna–Leipzig, 1914)

Reference: ed. *Fux-GA*, Ser. I Bd. 2 (as 'Missa Lachrymantes Virgines')

2. Mass [missing]

A–M: I 337.

References: Krieg, entered 1835; KV 50

3. Antiphon: Magnus Dominus [doubtful]

A–M: II 553 (attributed Johann Fuchs).
parts: SATB, 2 vn, va, vc, 2 cl, 2 hn, org, vle
References: Krieg ('Joan: Fuchs'), entered 1836; Liess, p.85 (Ferdinand
             Fuchs)

4. Antiphon: Asperges me [doubtful]

A–M: III 240 (anonymous attribution).

parts: SATTB
copyist: J.G. Albrechtsberger
References: KV 204,6; Riedel 2516 (attributed [Adam] Fux); ed. *DTÖ*
             Jhg. II/1, Bd. 3, p.86

5. Antiphon: Vidi aquam [doubtful]

A-M: III 243 (anonymous attribution).

parts: SATB, vn, 2 trbn, timp, org
copyists: unidentified, eighteenth century; trbn, org, 19th century
References: Liess 52; (with sources attributed to J.G. Albrechtsberger):
              Weiss. 272; Riedel 2501; Schröder F. II.4

6. Hymn: Pange lingua [spurious]

A-M: VI 496a.

score: pr., no. 2 of 'Vier Tantum Ergo', ed. J.E. Habert, *Beilage zur
              Zeitschrift für Kath. Kirchenmusik* (Gmunden, 1883)

References: KV 279,4; Riedel 2428 (with text 'Nobis datus nobis
              natus'); ed. *DTÖ* Jhg. III, Bd. 5, p.17 (with correct
              attribution to Johann Stadlmayr)

7. Hymn: Tantum ergo [spurious]

A-M: VI 496b.

score: pr., no. 3 of 'Vier Tantum Ergo', ed. J.E. Habert, *Beilage zur
              Zeitschrift für Kath. Kirchenmusik* (Gmunden, 1883)

References: KV 269; Riedel 2491; ed. *DTÖ* Jhg. III, Bd. 5, p.18 (with
              correct attribution to Johann Stadlmayr)

*8. Die Fuchische Solmisation. Egregium opus

A–M: V 1056.

> score: [SS]
> copyists: J. Weiss; R. Kimmerling (superscript)
> References: Liess, p.85; Weinmann 117 (T.55) (as missing)

B. *Instrumental*

1. Variazioni a tre Soggetii per due Violini [spurious]

A–M: V 1057.

> parts: 2 vn, pr. Traeg no. 15 (with correct attribution to Peter Fux)
> Reference: Weinmann 101 (T. 44) (with misattribution '[Johann Joseph] Fux')

2. Duetto für 2 Flöten [spurious]

A–M: VI 475.

> parts: 2 fl
> copyist: 'Fux pria / 837.' (title page)
> note: cryptogram on 'Flauto 2da', fol. 2: 'Laurenz Fux in Maria Taferl'

*3. Sonata

A–M: V 1058.

parts: headed: 'Sonata.' 'Violino 1 ^{mo}:', 'Violino 2 ^{do}:', 'Violoncello
               Conc:', 'Organo.', 'Violone Conc:'
copyist: unidentified, mid-eighteenth century
References: Krieg, entered 1827; KV 384

*4. Sonata

A–M: V 1059.

parts: 'Violino P ^{mo}:', 'Violino 2 ^{do}:', 'Organo'
copyist: J. Weiss
note: modern wrapper carries attribution 'J.P. Fux'
References: Krieg ('Jos. Fux'), entered 1827; Liess 53

Appendix II

F. Tuma

A. *Vocal*

1. Mass

A–M: I 11.
parts: headed: 'N⁰ i.' 'Canto', 'Alto', 'Tenore', 'Passo', 'Alto
            Trombone', 'Tenore Trombone', 'Organo', 'Violone'
copyist: unidentified, third quarter eighteenth century
References: Reichert 50; Vogg A I 25

2. Mass

A–M: I 9.
parts: headed: 'No° 2 ordin:' 'Canto', 'Alto', 'Tenore', 'Passo', 'Alto
               Trombone', 'Tenore Trombone', 'Organo', 'Violone'
copyist: as for I 11 above
References: Reichert 40; Vogg A I 38; Peschek A5

3. Mass

A–M: I 10.
parts: headed: 'N.° 24 ordin:' 'Canto', 'Alto', 'Tenore', 'Passo',
               'Violino', 'Alto Trombone', 'Tenore Trombone',
               'Organo', 'Violone'
copyists: R. Helm? (vn 1); others as for I 11
References: Reichert 60; Vogg A I 51; Peschek B3

4. Miserere

A–M: III 55.

parts: 'Soprano Conc:', 'Alto Conc:', 'Tenore Conc', 'Passo Conc',
'Violino I ^{mo}' , 'Violino Secondo', 'Alto Viola', 'Trombone 1.
Conc:', 'Trombone 2 ^{do} Rip:', 'Organo', 'Violone'
copyist: unidentified (Melk), *c.* 1778–80
Reference: Vogg A II 26

5. Miserere

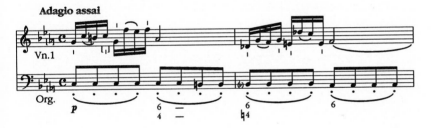

A–M: III 56.

parts: 'Canto', 'Alto', 'Tenore', 'Passo', 'Violino I ^{mo}' (2 copies),
'Violino 2 ^{do}', 'Alto Viola', 'Trombone 1 ^{mo}', 'Trombone
2 ^{do}', 'Organo', 'Violone'
copyist: as for III 55 above
Reference: Vogg A II 25

6. Prologue to Operetta: *Martis und Irene Verbindung* (fragments)

A–M: VI Fragmente, fliegende Blätter, udgl.

    parts: 'Fluss Melk alto' (single leaf, nos 3, 5), 'Tenore' (1 bifolium, nos 5–6), 'Chorus Tenore' (single leaf, no. 5), 'Basso' (2 leaves, nos 5–6)

    copyist: J. Weiss (some captions)

    Reference: Freeman OW 17

B. Instrumental

1. Church sonata

A–M: V 1087.

    parts: 'Violino Primo.', 'Violino Secondo.', 'Organo.', 'Violone.' Organ headed: 'Franz [?] 746 / Sinfonia à 3 / Violino Primo. / Violino Secondo. / con / Basso. è Violone. / Del Sig.ᶠ Fran.ᶜᵒ Thuma.'

    copyist: unidentified (Melk), eighteenth century

    Reference: Vogg B I 9

Appendix III

G.C. Wagenseil

A. Vocal

1. Aria

A–M: II 110.

parts: 'Basso Conc.^{to}' (3 copies), 'Canto Ripⁱⁱ' (2 copies), 'Alto Ripⁱⁱ' (2 copies), 'Tenore Ripⁱⁱ' (2 copies), 'Basso', 'Violino 1mo' (2 copies), 'Violino 2do', 'Clarino 1mo', 'Clarino 2do', 'Tympani', 'Organo', 'Violone'

note: vocal parts contain three different texts

copyist: unidentified (Melk), eighteenth century

Reference: Krieg, '1780. / De Dedicatione Eccl. / De Scto v. Sancta. / De Tempora. Beata / De Resurrectione.'

B. *Instrumental*

1. Symphony

A-M: IV 40.

parts: headed: 'Symphonia.' / 'Violino Primo', 'Violino Secundo',
            'Alto Viola', 'Clarino Primo Ex C:', 'Clarino Secundo Ex
            C:', 'Tympano Ex C:', 'Basso', 'Violone'
copyist: unidentified, eighteenth century
References: WV 358 (oboes in place of clarini); Kucaba C7; ed. idem,
            Garland, 1981 (B III 8) based on A-M source with facs. of
            vn 1; Weinmann 158 (T.68) (as missing)

2. Symphony

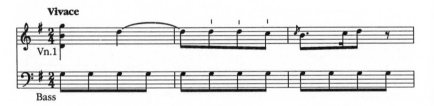

A-M: V 859.

parts: 'Violino Primo:', 'Violino Secondo:', 'Basso:' Bass headed:
            'Sinfonia Ex g: / a 3. / Con / Violino Primo / Violino
            Secondo / e/ Passo. / Ex Rebus Caroli Gegenbauer / Del
            Sigl. Christoph: Wagenseill'
copyist: unidentified, eighteenth century
References: WV 411; Kucaba G1; ed. idem, Garland, 1981 (B III 6)
            (based on A-M source)

3. Symphony

A–M: IV 38.

parts: 'Violino Primo', 'Violino Secondo', 'Viola', 'Cornu^{imo} Ex C',
'Cornu 2do in C', 'Basso'

copyist: F. Schneider?, *c.*1765

References: WV 418 (oboes in place of horns); Kucaba G6; Weinmann
158 (T. 68) as missing; ed. A. Copland (Vienna, 1971)
(oboes in place of horns)

4. Symphony

A–M: V 860.

parts: 'Violino Primo', 'Violino 2do:' 'Basso.' Bass headed: 'N3. /
Symphonia / a/ Tre / con / Violino Primo: / Violino
2do: / è / Basso: / Ex Rebus Caroli Gegenbauer / Del
Sigl: Christoph: Wagenseill'

copyist: unidentified, eighteenth century

References: WV 423; Kucaba A11

5. Symphony-Sextet (= church sonata)

A–M: IV 39.

parts: 'Violino Primo', 'Violino 2$\frac{do}{=}$', 'Violino 3$\frac{tio}{=}$', 'Violino 4$\frac{to}{=}$',
             'Viola', 'Basso.'
copyist: unidentified (Melk), c.1757–63
References: Krieg, 'Sinfonia'; WV 487 (as 'Sestetto'); Kucaba N:A1;
             Weinmann 158 (T. 68) (as 'Sinfonia' with incorrect call
             number)

6. Concerto

A–M: V 861.

parts: 'Cembalo', 'Violino Primo', 'Violino Secondo', 'Basso.' Bass
             headed: 'Concerto ex C. / per il Cembalo / Due Violini /
             e Basso. / Del Sigre Wagenseil.'
copyists: R. Helm? (title page and captions); others as for IV 39
             above
References: WV 267 = 232 Concerto; Weinmann 188 (T. 56); ed. W.
             Upmayer (Vieweg, 1936)

7. Concerto

A–M: V 858.

parts: [keyboard], 'Violino Primo', 'Violino 2do.', 'Clarino Primo', 'Basso.' Keyboard headed: 'Concert / Pour le Clavessin / avec / Deux Violons / Par Monsieur / Christoffe Wagenseil'
copyists: R. Helm (clarino primo, basso), *c*.1775; others as for IV 39 above
References: WV 266 = 231 Concerto (with variant, m. 1, b. 3 = [musical figure] Weinmann 130 (T. 55)

8. Concerto

A–M: VI 2767b (anonymous attribution).
parts: 'Traverso', 'Violino Primo', 'Violino Secondo:', 'Passo'
copyist: unidentified, eighteenth century
note: wrapper with title page 'Del Sigl: Cristofforo Wagenseil.' found uncatalogued
References: WV 347; ed. H. Kölbel (Zurich, 1967)

9. Concerto

A–M: V 862.

parts: 'Clavi Cembalo.', 'Violino Primo', 'Violino Secondo', 'Basso.
             Bass headed: 'Concerto / per il / Clavi Cembalo / Con /
             Violino Primo / Violino Secondo / ed / Basso / di Signor
             / Wagenseil'

copyists: R. Helm (some captions); parts as for IV 39 above

References: WV 332 = 244 Concerto; Weinmann 118 (T. 56)

10. Divertimento

A–M: V 147.

part: cembalo headed: 'Divertimento / a/ Cembalo, / Del Sigr:
             Cristoforo / Wagenseil'

copyist: c.1760–70 (according to WV)

Reference: WV 63

3 Johann Joseph Fux's theoretical writings: a classical legacy

Alfred Mann

> You will readily see, dear Friend of the Muse, that I have given but little consideration to the theoretical part of this treatise, to its practical part, however, a great deal; for this was by far the greater need (action being the very test of excellence).[1]

With these words Johann Joseph Fux introduces his *Gradus ad Parnassum* to the reader. The work was instantly famous, and its fame was founded in the author's reputation as a composer and conductor, rather than that of a theorist. Fux's triple position as court composer, imperial chapel master, and chapel master at St Stephen's Cathedral marked a new era in which the leadership of Viennese music passed from Italian to German hands; he became the *Wiener Altmeister*. Yet the model he represented to Viennese Classicism shone forth through his pedagogy.

The significance of the *Gradus ad Parnassum* having been realized at its appearance, the book was sold out within a year. Its Latin text had assured an international distribution and the demand for its availability in modern language was voiced in the most prominent circles. Georg Philipp Telemann had announced his intention to issue a German translation (a plan that did not come to fruition), and Johann Mattheson hailed the news in an 'Ode upon seeing the announcement of the translation of Fux's Graduum ad Parnassum in the Catalogue des Oeuvres en Musique de M. Telemann'.[2]

It was evidently Johann Sebastian Bach who was the first to recognize that what was needed was a translation based on thorough discussion of the work's methodical and philosophical foundations, and we must attribute to the influence of Bach, whose personal copy of the *Gradus* has been preserved, that his pupil Lorenz Christoph Mizler took up the challenge. Mizler, a student of theology, law and natural sciences, had entered the University of Leipzig in 1731 and, like many of the young Leipzig scholars, had also taken up private studies with Bach. He became a lecturer at the University in 1736 and began to work on his translation of the *Gradus* in the same year. Its publication, in 1742, coincided with his last semester of teaching duties at the University, which was entirely devoted to lectures on Fux's work. In 1738 he established the Society of Musical Sciences to which Bach was elected in 1747.

We must distinguish here between two approaches to Fux's writing. Mizler, the humanist, was concerned with the issue of re-introducing music as an academic discipline. Bach, the composer, approaching the final phase of a supreme creative career, was concerned with artistic horizons fully perceptible only to himself: Fux's work aided him in his growing preoccupation with the *stile antico* which led to a decisive metamorphosis of the style of his later years.[3]

Mizler's own achievement remains ambivalent. In the Leipzig *Neue Zeitungen von gelehrten Sachen* there appeared on 17 August 1742 the following announcement of his translation:

> So far as the German edition is concerned, it offers a more usable text than the Latin, not only because Herr Mizler has presented it in a clear German version, whereas the Latin version is at places obscure and unintelligible, but because he has improved upon it here and there and added many helpful annotations.[4]

In his introduction Mizler assumes a modest attitude about justifying these changes and additions:

> Hr. Fux has by no means said everything that might be said about such things. . . . The beginner must not be frightened with tomes of all too great a size, so that their eagerness to learn will not be impeded.

> It is precisely for this reason that I have not added more commentary than seemed highly needed. Otherwise Fux's work would no longer remain his.

Nevertheless, he challenged the very basis of his author's teaching by renouncing the system of church modes. This is done with some uneasiness. His footnote regarding the modes extends over eight pages, on which no more than two or three lines per page are allotted to the original text. It is the polemic argument of Johann Mattheson, published in the latter's *Critica Musica* (II, 1724-25) with which Mizler sees himself obliged to take issue. While he defends Fux's stand against that of Mattheson, he fails to understand it, for he dismisses the system of modes as having no place in the circle of fifths.

Similar is his attitude with regard to the classification of intervals. He rejects Fux's explanation of the dual nature of the fourth, as he does Fux's definition of the third as an imperfect consonance. In the view of his time it is the fourth that stands invariably as imperfect consonance, though it may require resolution, whereas the third takes its place among the perfect consonances. The latter point leads Mizler's arguments into new contradictions, for the rule against parallel progressions of perfect consonances, which he translates faithfully from the original text, obviously does not apply to the third.

Like that of his student, the writing of Bach's son exhibits an equivocal attitude toward Fux's authority. Asked by Johann Nicolaus Forkel, in connection with the latter's plan for a Bach biography, concerning the teaching of his father, C.P.E. Bach wrote in his letter of 19 January 1775: 'In composition he started his pupils right in with what was practical, and omitted all the *dry species* of counterpoint that are given in Fux and others.' Yet in the same letter he lists Fux as the first among Bach's contemporaries whom 'in his last years he esteemed highly'.[5]

The incongruities disappear a generation later. It took the vision of another composer of foremost stature to recognize that the value of Fux's work was founded in the exposition of timeless principles rather than arbitrary rules. With the work of Haydn, his own studies and his influence as a teacher, Fux's *Gradus* assumed its role as a classical legacy. Unlike Gottlieb Muffat, Johann Dismas Zelenka, Franz Tuma and Georg Christoph Wagenseil, who were Fux's direct students, Hadyn experienced the impact of his teaching from a certain distance. The venerable *Kapellmeister* was still living when Haydn became a choirboy in the court chapel, and he was doubtless instructed from the pages of Fux's *Singfundament* (as was Schubert in later years). Fux's contrapuntal instruction, however, did not take on significance in Haydn's studies until 1750 when, with the help of a generous loan from a friend, and liberated from daily chores that had earned him his living after an abrupt dismissal from the court chapel (in which his voice could no longer serve), he set up meagre housekeeping in a small Viennese attic room. There, free to work, and having even acquired a 'worm-eaten clavier', as the Haydn biographer Georg August Griesinger reports, he 'envied no king his lot'.

We are rather well informed about the period of Haydn's concentrated study that now began. As well as the *Biographische Notizen über Joseph Haydn* (1809) by Griesinger, Royal Councillor to the Saxon Legation, who was introduced to Haydn by the publisher Gottfried Härtel, we have the *Biographische Nachrichten von Joseph Haydn* (1810) by Albert Christoph Dies, a writer and artist who taught at the Imperial Royal Academy and eventually became gallery director to Prince Esterházy. The accounts by both authors, who also conferred with one another, were prepared on the basis of regularly scheduled conversations with Haydn, arranged for the expressly stated purpose of collecting biographical information; the book by Dies is even divided into thirty 'visits' whose dates are carefully noted.[6]

Dies writes:

> Haydn was pleased to see the improvement in his situation. What lay closest to his heart, though, was to . . . enable himself through a serious study of theory to bring order . . . into the outpourings of his soul. He decided to buy a good book. But what?[7]

Dies rightly surmises that Haydn left the choice to chance, but he is doubtless in error when he notes 'the bookseller named the writings of Carl Philip Emanuel Bach as the newest and best',[8] for C.P.E. Bach's famous *Versuch* was not published until three years later. As is documented by Griesinger, the decisive influence of C.P.E. Bach's work exerted upon Haydn emanated from Bach's keyboard sonatas which had appeared in the early 1740s, and he quotes Haydn as saying: 'I did not come away from my clavier till I had played through them, and whoever knows me thoroughly must discover that I owe a great deal to Emanuel Bach.'[9] Both Griesinger and Dies confirm that C.P.E. Bach, in later years, acknowledged Haydn's professed debt with pleasure.

Dies is even farther afield when he mentions Johann Philipp Kirnberger's work, published in the 1770s (*Die Kunst des reinen Satzes*) in connection with Haydn's early studies. Haydn's commentary on Kirnberger's writing is preserved – but as entered in his copy of Fux's *Gradus.* It becomes clear from Griesinger's report that it was the latter which proved to be Haydn's find when he 'decided to buy a good book'. He mentions, in fact, that Haydn found two works: Johann Mattheson's *Der vollkommene Kapellmeister* (1739) and Fux's *Gradus ad Parnassum*, and he says of the latter that it was 'a book he still in his old age praised as a classic and of which he kept a hard-used copy'; he continues:

> With tireless exertion Haydn sought to comprehend Fux's theory. He worked his way through the whole method, did the exercises, put them by for several weeks, then looked them over again and polished them until he thought he had got them right.[10]

Haydn's concentrated study of the work was to signify the decisive role it assumed in the rise of the Viennese Classical style, and it is through Haydn's own commentary, entered in well-nigh overwhelming detail in the 'hard-used copy', that we can fathom the remarkable phase into which the history of Fux's work now entered. This priceless document, preserved in later years at the Esterházy library, fell victim to the flames of the Second World War.[11] But the Haydn biographer Carl Ferdinand Pohl, in foresight dictated by scrupulous scholarship, had entered Haydn's annotations into another copy of the original edition, which now forms part of the collection owned by the Gesellschaft der Musikfreunde, Vienna. It is not the only one duplicating Haydn's marginalia, for in recent years Dr Richard Sherr, a young scholar at Smith College, Northampton, Massachusetts, discovered a similar transcription of Haydn's remarks in a copy of the original edition extant in the holdings of the College's library. A comparison of the two sources shows that the latter must considerably antedate Pohl's transcription, that it suggests a more accurate reading, and that it may well go back to Haydn's immediate circle. Haydn evidently lent out his annotated copy for the purposes of study. Although we can no longer trace the course of his innumerable entries over the years by means of changes in the master's own handwriting, a development which must have spanned a lengthy period of time lies readily before us.[12]

In his discussion of Haydn's works, Paul Henry Lang has persuasively stated that the composer, in approaching his fortieth year, encountered the 'crisis in his artistic career'. Lang observes that in his quartets Op. 20

> the sure and steady stylistic development comes to a halt . . . for their composer is at the crossroads and experiencing the same romantic upheaval that agitated Goethe before he was able to master his own self to reach his resolute, transfigured classicism. Arrived at this point, Haydn realized that a major element was missing in his style, the absence of which prevented the final integration of his idiom and form. . . . Haydn realized that what was needed was a more judicious part writing which in turn impelled him to a reinstatement of

polyphony in musical construction. This, we might say, represented the final and decisive step toward the achievement of the classical ideal of instrumental style.[13]

What happened in Haydn's work during the decade of the 1770s is reflected a decade later in his pedagogical influence, which markedly increased during the 1780s.[14] It had a unique bearing upon the artistic association of Haydn and Mozart and there are unmistakable indications that Mozart's extensive use of Fux's work must be ascribed to the fact that Haydn's annotated copy of the *Gradus* had gone through Mozart's hands.[15] One of Haydn's students, C.F. Magnus, compiled, apparently from the composer's dictation, an abstract of his counterpoint instruction, which summarizes Fux's rules.[16] It is preserved only in fragmentary form, but evidently several such abstracts were used by the students of Haydn, among them Beethoven, whose complete *Einleitung zur Fuxischen Lehre vom Kontrapunkt* has been preserved.[17]

Haydn's and Mozart's interpretations of Fux's teaching, although so obviously interrelated, differ in some characteristic details. At the crucial time in the evolution of his own style, Haydn returned to the work he knew so well, and, in some of his most significant annotations, expressed the manner in which he had first approached it. Having grown up in the imperial chapel, where Fux's singing instruction was still alive, he had quite naturally accepted and absorbed the letter and spirit of Fux's manual. But he had done so with a critical approach. He had found, and corrected, a multitude of printer's errors in the text and, with the thoroughness that was typical of him, had emended mistakes even in Fux's Errata listing.

This conscientious procedure was now also applied to the didactic examples from Fux's *Gradus*. Haydn's vigilance was alert especially where the printer's flaw interfered with essential matters, such as the formation of the cambiata figure and the logic of thematic entrances (see Examples 1 and 2).

That the corrected formation of the melodic line was intended is apparent in the latter case from the original notation of the preceding measure, which is placed at the end of a line and followed by a small 'direct' or guide indicating that the note *d* is to appear at the beginning of the next line – we

Example 1

Example 2

Example 3

are dealing with an obvious misprint that had apparently gone unnoticed until Haydn discovered it.

But Haydn carried his careful revision beyond such matters. He absorbed the principles presented by Fux so thoroughly that he reached a point where he found himself correcting not only the printer but the master himself. An example that is particularly impressive occurs in a three-part fugue; it is the change of a single note with which he transformed a merely accompanimental passage into a thematic entrance, completing a second exposition according to Fux's own structural model as given at the beginning of his discussion of fugue (Example 3).

Mozart, at the outset farther removed from Fux's work, and having been trained in childhood as an instrumentalist rather than as a singer, found his way to the *Gradus* much later. There is no evidence that he was acquainted with the work before the Vienna years in which the lively exchange with Haydn began. In a notebook dated 1784 and devoted to the instruction of Barbara Ployer, the student for whom Mozart's piano concertos K 449 and K 453 from the same year were written, we find Mozart's first references to Fux's text and method. But they form only a fragmentary addition to a course of instruction otherwise quite differently designed. Mozart changed this design in time to conform to that followed in Haydn's teaching, though it goes without saying that their marked individuality remains clear in the preserved documents.

What sparked Mozart's intense interest in Fux's teaching was the work with another student, the young English composer Thomas Attwood, which began in 1785. Attwood's evident talent and his brilliant performance at court had prompted the Prince of Wales, two years earlier, to send the eighteen-year-old to Italy for study. Yet Attwood's work under the guidance of two Neapolitan composers, Felipe Cinque and Gaetano Latilla, apparently left the young composer dissatisfied. 'Perceiving the decline of the Italian school and foreseeing the ascendancy of that of Germany, he proceeded to Vienna and immediately became a pupil of Mozart.'[18]

Some of the composition exercises Attwood had written in Naples have been preserved.[19] It is likely that it was after looking through these that Mozart decided on an initial review of the principles of four-part harmony (a review which was completed in less than two months). But following this, the need for more conscious linear training having become all too apparent, Mozart took the student back to the beginning of two-part counterpoint and devoted more than half a year to thorough studies according to the species of Fux's *Gradus*.

Mozart followed the design and detail of Fux's work with utter conscientiousness, yet adding liberal annotations variously written in Italian and English. His attitude in dealing with Fux's text presents a highly interesting blend, for it is as intense as it is relaxed. He draws from the pages of the *Gradus* every bit of didactic benefit imaginable, and there is much that he copies and translates note for note and word for word. But he also calmly changes Fux's examples, not in the sense of meticulous proofing or correcting, but rather in that of expressing a different point of view. This becomes noticeable above all in the introduction to three-part writing, for in quoting Fux's examples on the Dorian cantus firmus in the first species of three-part counterpoint he immediately establishes clearer tonal functions (Example 4) and a more pronounced sense of modulation (Example 5).

Example 4

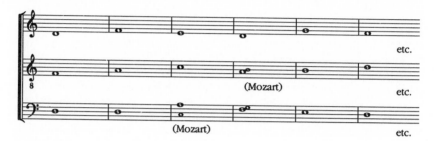

Example 5

Fux had cast his work in the time-honoured guise of the didactic dialogue, a dialogue in which the role of the teacher was represented by Palestrina – Aloysius – and the role of the student – Josephus – by himself. This is, of course, to be understood neither in the meaning of a direct lineage nor in that of modern source study and style criticism. Palestrina's name stood here as a symbol for the *stile antico*, the classical style of vocal polyphony. The authors Fux actually quotes, and whose treatises his writing involves, are such seventeenth-century writers as Angelo Berardi and Giovanni Maria Bononcini, theorists who had remained guardians of the Palestrina heritage.

It is somewhat in the manner in which Fux made himself the disciple of Palestrina that Haydn and Mozart made themselves disciples of Fux and the doctrine preserved in his *Gradus*. And as Fux had done, they interpreted the model of the mentor in the spirit of a later era. For in spite of his scrupulous observance of Fux's text, Haydn, like Mozart, widens its boundaries when it comes to the practical application of the contrapuntal species.

We spoke of the individuality of the two great Viennese masters, of which we are constantly reminded by details as they absorb Fux's work. In his watchful annotations, Haydn, like Fux, uses the Latin language and he carefully weighs the interpretation of technical principles in comments such as 'male juxta alios Authores' ('bad according to other writers') or 'transit' (i.e., 'it may pass'). Mozart's rather different temperament comes to the fore in such delightful asides as his choice of the word *schiocagine* – the noisy slamming down of trumps in a card game – in correcting one of Barbara Ployer's mistakes: 'Ho l'onore di dirle che lei hà fatto la schiocagine (da par Suo) di far Due ottave' ('I have the honour to inform you of a bit of claptrap (on your part) in writing two octaves'). And in an example where Attwood confuses the soprano and alto clefs he bluntly notes 'you are an ass'. Yet with their varying copious commentary they equally refine Fux's contrapuntal rules.

In the half-note motion of the second species of counterpoint, the problem of the interrupted succession of octaves and fifths arises. Fux rejects the sequence of downbeat octaves merely separated by the recurring skip of a third, but he condones similar passages if the skip becomes that of a fourth or of a larger interval. In the *Elementarbuch*, Haydn adopts the rule in examples marked 'bene' and 'male', but he adds a passage that might represent an acceptable compromise (marked 'Leidlicher', i.e., 'more passable'; see Example 6).

Example 6

Mozart departs from the rule in a very general sense, as is indicated by a remark Attwood entered, evidently after Mozart's wording, in his annotations for the third species of counterpoint: 'If in ye preceding bar there is an octave on whatever part of it, & in the following the first Note of it is an octave 'tis all ways as bad as two octaves.' Here, however, we have added documentation that states the matter more categorically. A few months before the conclusion of Attwood's studies, a young composer from Salzburg, Mozart's hometown, had also taken up counterpoint studies with Mozart. Like Attwood, gifted though inexperienced, Franz Jakob Freystädtler received a course of instruction from Mozart that in part overlaps with the Attwood studies and in part tends toward new directions. At the introduction of the second counterpoint species, Freystädtler, probably again from Mozart's dictation, notes a brief summary of points to be observed, to which Mozart adds the remark 'No skip can compensate for octaves or fifths.'[20]

In the rhythmic pattern of the third contrapuntal species, four notes against one, the classical orientation moves farther away from the given model, because chordal and sequential formations of the melodic line – eschewed in the *stile antico* – assume a more natural role. The *nota cambiata* – typical as a formula of melodic design in the works of Renaissance masters, though first codified in Fux's *Gradus* – is fully explained in Haydn's *Elementarbuch*, whereas Mozart makes no mention of it, although he absorbs it – somewhat in the manner of a style exercise – in his own writing (Fantasy and Fugue K 394).

Yet how seriously the classical masters responded to the challenge of integrating the linear element in the extended melodic line is demonstrated by a counterpoint Mozart wrote for Attwood on a fragment from one of Fux's cantus firmi (Example 7) or by Haydn's correction in one of Beethoven's exercises (Example 8).

Example 7

Example 8

Conversely, it is the purely chordal element that claimed their interest in contrapuntal strictness when it came to the discussion of the fourth species and its study of proper dissonance resolution in the syncopated melody. The problem is a dual one, for the contrapuntist must be concerned with a full harmonic sonority in both the suspension and resolution of the chord. Fux had called attention to the issue (*Gradus*, pp.132ff.), but his solution is a radical one: he recommends abandoning the consistency of the species that requires sustaining an unvarying motion in whole notes for all parts placed against the syncopated one (see Example 9).

Haydn and Mozart explore the matter more thoroughly; in fact Haydn's most extensive corrections in Beethoven's exercises are devoted to the fourth species in four-part counterpoint, where the problem reaches its most complex constellations. Though not expressed in verbal commentary, a new rule is formulated in these corrections: the resolution must involve chords in root position; hence a six-four chord suspension leading to a sixth chord becomes unacceptable (Example 10).

Example 9

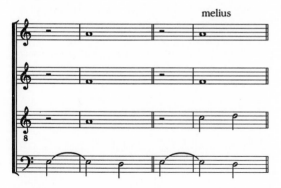

Example 10

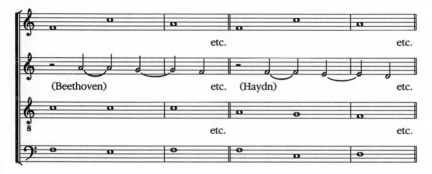

He carries similar emendations into his review of Beethoven's exercises in the fifth contrapuntal species, and how heartily Mozart concurred with his view can be gathered from a remark in Freystädtler's exercises: 'The 4 is disgusting' (Example 11).[21]

It is typical of the orientation of the Viennese masters that a liberal attitude towards Fux's text goes hand in hand with increased strictness in interpretation. Beethoven's annotations in his studies and in his *Einleitung zur Fuxischen Lehre vom Kontrapunkt* contain detailed commentary on the

Example 11

matter of hidden parallels. He quotes a particular example from the *Gradus* on which Fux himself had presented critical comment in the dialogue of his text. Having marked a first instance of hidden fifths with the letter A and the second with the letter B (see Example 12), Fux lets the student offer a question about the first; the teacher answers by calling attention to the second, saying that such passages 'need not be considered faulty because of the difficulty of the species'.

Example 12

Beethoven remarks: 'The second progression, at B, would never be excusable for my ear.'[22]

Beethoven's involvement with Fux's work represents a new phase in the history of the *Gradus*. Introduced to the study of modal species counterpoint through the instruction he received from Haydn, he later abandoned it, but this departure was followed by a decided return. Beethoven's studies with Haydn have been subject to much misunderstanding because the Romantic age tended to stress the younger composer's impatience rather than his consuming interest. The situation was further confused by the fact that Beethoven changed teachers and took up studies with Johann Georg Albrechtsberger. One is apt to forget that the immediate reason was Haydn's departure for his second stay in England (a journey on which Beethoven was originally meant to accompany Haydn), and that Albrechtsberger was Haydn's close friend, to whom he had probably sent his student.

Albrechtsberger, the most prominent didactic figure of his time, held as *Kapellmeister* at St Stephen's the office Fux himself had once occupied, and his great predecessor had remained his 'oracle'.[23] But he modified Fux's contrapuntal teaching by reducing it to the modern scales of major and minor. Thus he took Beethoven through the entire study of counterpoint once again from a different point of view. It is all the more significant that Beethoven, preparing in later years a course of instruction for his patron and friend, the Archduke Rudolph, reverted to the text and orientation of Fux's instruction, copying large portions of the *Gradus* verbatim and reinstating Fux's teaching on the basis of the church modes.

The same tendency emerges from the later phases of Mozart's teaching. Next to those of Fux he had given Attwood a number of additional *cantus firmi*, especially when a phase of work proved to be particularly difficult. In Freystädtler's instruction he widened the group of assigned *cantus firmi* methodically, doubling the number of his freely-designed *cantus firmi* in the Ionian and Aeolian modes in a conscious gesture towards the study of tonal counterpoint that was subsequently codified in Albrechtsberger's teaching. But from Freystädtler he also demanded a more extensive review of entire groups of exercises, and the more drawn out the process became, the more he limited the scope of assignments, reverting eventually to Fux's own cantus firmi in the six authentic modes alone.

With a touch of contrapuntal virtuosity, this return seems playfully announced by Mozart's sketching a two-part example in which he places above one of his own *cantus firmi* one of Fux's as a seconed species counterpoint (the *cantus firmus* he had also used in giving Attwood an example for the third species, see Example 13 and cf. Example 7).

Example 13

etc.

With the Freystädtler studies and Beethoven's course of instruction designed for Archduke Rudolph, the classical interpretation of Fux's contrapuntal teaching comes to an end. Albrechtsberger *Gründliche Anweisung zur Komposition* appeared in 1790, and Schubert's contrapuntal training under Antonio Salieri, imperial chapel master (also an office once held by Fux), were based entirely on Albrechtsberger's method, without specific reference to the *Gradus*. Nevertheless Fux's work reappears in Schubert's studies with copies made from some of the examples contained in Fux's *Singfundament*.

This work, compiled for the vocal instruction of his young choristers about twenty years before the publication of Fux's *Gradus*, is in fact closely connected with the latter; its training in solmization elucidates the melodic principles of the contrapuntist and its exercises – most of them small two-part motets to be sung on solmization syllables – anticipate the studies in imitation with which the student of the *Gradus* is taught to commence the study of fugue. It is interesting that the examples in Schubert's possession were adapted as violin duets, and among the numerous versions of the *Singfundament* is a violin method that formed part of the library of Antonio Polzelli, a violinist in Haydn's Esterházy orchestra: Fux's vocal training continued to serve as a basis of composition for voices as well as instruments.

The concept of classical legacy dominates the history of the *Singfundament* as it does that of the *Gradus*, for in this case we do not even have an original source. The work has come down to us only in numerous copies; each generation of followers – first Fux's own assistants and, in time, later arrangers – fashioned the work anew, and in printed versions of the nineteenth century the *Singfundament* began to take its place in modern vocal pedagogy.

It was the period in which new counterpoint manuals, initiated, by Heinrich Bellermann's *Der Contrapunkt* (Berlin 1862), restored the modal teaching of Fux, also in more or less direct adaptations of his text. In the twentieth century, Fux's study of counterpoint and his study of fugue entered the classroom in newly edited translations.[24] Yet neither Fux's *Singfundament* nor his *Gradus* ever became, in fact, 'theoretical' in the sense of the word's conventional didactic connotation; true to their author's intention, they remained practical in the sense of 'the very test of excellence'.

Notes

[1] Caeterum facile advertes dilecte Philomuse, hoc Tractatu, speculativae parti perparum: activae vero, utpote magis necessariae (virtutis enim laus omnis in actione consistit) plus operae me dedisse. *Gradus ad Parnassum*, Praefatio ad Lectorum, facsimile edition in *Johann Joseph Fux, Sämtliche Werke*, (Graz, 1967), Series VII, vol. 1.

[2] *Grosse General-Bass-Schule* (Hamburg, 1731), p.172.

[3] See Christoph Wolff, *Der Stile Antico in der Musik Johann Sebastian Bachs* (Wiesbaden, 1968).

[4] Quoted in Franz Wöhlke, 'Lorenz Christoph Mizler. Ein Beitrag zur musikalischen Gelehrtengeschichte des 18. Jahrhunderts', *Berliner Studien zur Musikwissenschaft*, edited by Arnold Schering (Würzburg, 1940), Cf. Christoph Wolff, op. cit., p.28.

[5] *The Bach Reader*, edited by Hans T. David and Arthur Mendel (New York, 1947, 1966), p.279.

[6] The two works were re-issued in a modern English edition, *Joseph Haydn, Eighteenth-Century Gentleman and Genius*, by Vernon Gotwals (Madison, Wisconsin, 1963). Griesinger's remarks, mentioned above (and, as the author states, often rendering Haydn's own words) appear on p.10 in the edition by Gotwals, and are, like subsequent quotations, given from his English text.

[7] ibid., p. 95.

[8] ibid.

[9] ibid., p.12.

[10] ibid., p.10.

[11] Letter (dated 17 November 1964) from the director of the Esterházy Archives, Dr Johann Hárich to the author.

[12] Cf. the author's 'Haydn as Student and Critic of Fux', *Studies in Eighteenth-Century Music. A Tribute to Karl Geiringer on his Seventieth Birthday* (London, 1970), pp.323ff.

[13] *Music in Western Civilization* (New York, 1941), p.629.

[14] Cf. Horst Walter, 'On Haydn's Pupils', *Haydn Studies*, edited by Jens Peter Larsen, Howard Serwer and James Webster (New York, 1981), pp.62ff.

[15] See the author's 'Zur Kontrapunktlehre Haydns und Mozarts,' *Mozart-Jahrbuch 1978-79*, pp.195ff.

[16] *Elementarbuch der verschiednen Gattungen des Contrapuncts aus den grösseren Werken des Kappm. Fux, von Joseph Haydn zusammengezogen* (1789), edited, with English translation, by Alfred Mann in *The Music Forum*, vol. III, (New York, 1973), pp.197ff.

[17] Published in Gustav Nottebohm, *Beethoveniana* (Leipzig, 1872), pp.154ff.

[18] This perceptive summary statement appeared in the obituary for Attwood published by William Ayrton, director of the London Philharmonic Society (*Gentleman's Magazine*, May 1838; cf. C.B. Oldman's prefatory essay for 'Thomas Attwoods Theorie- und Kompositionsstudien bei Mozart', *Neue Mozart-Ausgabe*, Series X, vol. 30/1, p.XIII).

[19] See the Appendix of *Neue Mozart-Ausgabe*, Series X, vol. 30/1.

[20] 'Kein Sprung kann Oktaven oder Quinten aufheben', see 'Barbara Ployers und Franz Jakob Freystädtlers Theorie- und Kompositionsstudien bei Mozart', *Neue Mozart-Ausgabe*, Series X, vol. 30/2, p.8.

[21] 'Die 4 ist abscheulich.' The censured measure contains again the resolution of a six-four chord into a sixth chord. The comment, appearing in Freystädtler's hand, doubtless records Mozart's own wording.

[22] See Nottebohm, op. cit., p.181.

[23] Ignaz Ritter von Seyfried, Beethoven's fellow student under Albrechtsberger, in his edition of *J.S. Albrechtsbergers Sämtliche Schriften* (second edition, Vienna, 1837), preface, p.VIII.

[24] The author's editions *Die Lehre vom Kontrapunkt* (Celle, 1938, 1951), *Steps to Parnassus: The Study of Counterpoint* (New York, 1943; London 1944; reissued New York and Toronto, 1965); *The Study of Fugue* (New Brunswick, NJ, 1958; London, 1959; New York and Toronto, 1965; Westport, Ct, 1981; New York, 1987).

4 Zur Unvollständigkeit und denkbaren Anlage der *Gradus* von Fux

Rudolf Flotzinger

Daß die *Gradus ad parnassum* von. J. J. Fux, (Wien, 1725) eines der wirkungsvollsten musikalischen Lehrbücher darstellen[1] und in gewissen Modifizierungen bis in unser Jahrhundert aktuell blieben, ist unbestritten. Diskussionen, ob man sie nur als Kontrapunkt-, als Theorie- oder gar Satz- und Kompositionslehre verstehen könne, gibt es hingegen immer wieder.[2] Zu den Gründen hiefür gehören zweifellos Nachwirkungen unvollständiger Bearbeitungen oder Informationen, schlicht: Vorurteile. Ein weiterer mag auch in der Disposition des Werkes selbst liegen. Einer der wohl besten Kenner hat darauf hingewiesen, daß man neben der äußeren Gliederung in zwei Bücher (*libri*) einen vierteiligen Gesamtplan erkennen könne: dem ersten Buch entspreche dem Umfang nach (nämlich etwa 40 Druckseiten) das erweiterte Schlußkapitel des zweiten Buches, dazwischen lägen die zwei Hauptteile mit je etwa 100 Seiten.[3] So plausibel dies erscheinen mag, sieht es doch darüber hinweg, daß Fux selbst sein Werk als unvollständig bezeichnet hat: In den letzten Zeilen entschuldigt er sich, daß ihn seine Krankheit hindere, sein Werk (das er laut *Praefatio* schon vor vielen Jahren begonnen hatte) zu Ende zu führen. Er stellt daher eine weitere Schrift zur vielstimmigen Komposition (*tractatum de plurimum vocum Compositione*) in Aussicht, tröstet aber gleichzeitig, daß dem, der den vierstimmigen Satz beherrsche, der Weg zum Komponieren mit größerer Stimmenanzahl bereits offen läge; mit anderen Worten: sein Werk sei zwar nicht ganz vollständig, aber hinreichend. Dies mag Anregung genug sein, die Disposition näher zu analysieren und nach etwaigen weiteren Bruchstellen zu suchen.

Daß Fux tatsächlich eine möglichst vollständige Kompositionslehre vorlegen wollte, sagt er nicht nur im Vorwort eindeutig (womit sich solche Diskussionen eigentlich erübrigen müßten), ist nicht nur sowohl dem Titel *Gradus ad parnassum* (Schritte zur Vollendung) als auch dem Frontispiz (die Krönung dessen, der die vielen mühsamen Stufen nach oben hinter sich gebracht hat, durch Apoll selbst darstellend) hinreichend zu entnehmen, sondern wird v.a. im Inhalt und nicht zuletzt im Aufbau des Werkes deutlich.

Wollte man nachträglich ein Inhaltsverzeichnis des ersten Buches anlegen, würde sich bis inclusive Kapitel 22 (*Caput XXII*) keine Schwierigkeit ergeben und zeigen, daß jene jeweils etwa eine halbe bis maximal viereinhalb Seiten lang sind. Das letzte Kapitel *De hodierno musicae systemate* trägt sodann, abweichend von den vorhergehenden, keine Numerierung mehr, sondern die Bezeichnung *Caput postremum*; darüber hinaus ist es mit etwa 8 Druckseiten wesentlich länger als die übrigen. Noch auffälliger ist jedoch die Tatsache, daß es im Folgenden weitere Überschriften gibt, die keine Numerierung mehr tragen und auch nicht als Unterteilungen eines geschlossenen Kapitels verstanden werden können: *De Unisono* (S. 36), *De Secunda* (S.36), *Consonantiae sunt* (S.41), *Motus rectus, contrarius, obliquus* (S.41), *Regula prima, secunda, tertia, quarta* (S.42); bei der Abhandlung der übrigen Intervalle S.37ff. fehlen die entsprechenden Überschriften. Stellte man die zusammengehörigen Abschnitte unter eine gemeinsame Überschrift und numerierte diese wie bisher, ergäbe sich folgende Einteilung:

Caput XXIII	*De hodierno musicae systemate*	S. 35
XXIV	*De intervallis*	36
XXV	*De motu*	41

Damit wären auch die Proportionen wiederum annähernd die gleichen wie bisher, Caput XXIV wäre mit fünfeinhalb Seiten nur geringfügig länger als das längste bisherige. Daß diese nachträgliche, konsequent erscheinende Ergänzung am Schluß dieses Buches angebracht erscheint (ähnlich wie die Unvollständigkeit des Gesamtwerkes am Ende des zweiten Buches, wie gesagt, offen ausgesprochen ist), dürfte kein Zufall sein und sollte aufhorchen lassen.

Ein weiteres Argument für die vorgeschlagene Einteilung könnte man schließlich daraus ableiten, daß das zweite Buch zunächst mit regelmäßig je 5 Lektionen beginnen und somit die 25(= 5 × 5) Kapitel des ersten nicht ganz zufällig gewählt erscheinen. Schließlich bleibt noch darauf hinzuweisen, daß das erste Buch eine bloße Darstellung der Grundlagen durch den Lehrer beinhaltete, während das zweite, da der Schüler aufgrund seiner bisherigen und ständig zunehmenden Kenntnisse bereits 'mitreden' kann, in Dialog-Form gehalten ist. Dieser Unterschied kann neben der von Fux in der *Praefatio* erwähnten Unterscheidung zwischen *musica speculativa* und *activa* als weiteres, formales Argument für die Gliederung in zwei ungleich lange 'Bücher' angesehen werden.

Die Einteilung des zweiten Buches erfolgt zunächst nicht mehr nach Kapiteln, sondern in *Exercitia* (Übungen). Nach einem einführenden Gespräch, in dem man eine Analogie zur *Praefatio* vor dem ersten Buch sehen kann, folgen die besagten je 5 Lektionen zum zweistimmigen (*Exercitium I*), dreistimmigen (*Exercitium II*) und vierstimmigen (*Exercitium III*) Kontrapunkt gemäß den bekannten Fuxschen 'Gattungen'

(Note gegen Note, Halbe gegen Ganze, Viertel gegen Ganze, Ligaturen, gemischt). Dieses Prinzip scheint mit der *lectio unica* des *Exercitium IV De imitatione* neuerlich durchbrochen, hingegen hat die fünfte Übung 7 statt wie bisher 5 Lektionen. Es leuchtet zwar ein, daß die neuen Inhalte *Imitation* und *Fuge* jeweils als *Excercitia* auch eigene Überschriften bekommen (letztere mit den Lektionen: *in genere, duarum, trium, quatuor partium*), doch scheint auch dieses Prinzip in den Lektionen 5–7, die den speziellen Kontrapunkt zum Gegenstand haben (*De Contrapuncto duplici, De contrapuncto duplici cum translatione in decimam, De contrapuncto duplici in duodecima*) wieder durchbrochen. Außerdem folgen dann neuerlich einzelne weitere Überschriften, die z.T. nach Inhalt und Umfang den bisherigen als gleichrangig angesehen werden können: *Contrapunctum in duodecima duarum partium* (S.194), *Paradigma contrapuncti in duodecima, in tricinium vertibile, adjuncto contrapuncto in decima* (S.196), *Fuga tribus subjectis instructa* (S.215), *De Figura variationis & anticipationis* (S.217), *De Modis* (S.221), *Modi transpositi* (S.222), *Octavae harmonice divise & Modi inde oriundi* (S.226), *De variis fugarum subjectis* (S.231), *De Gustu* (S.239), *De stylo ecclesiastico* (S.242), *De stylo a capella* (S.243), *De stylo mixto* (S.273), *De stylo recitativo* (S.274). Daß hier jegliches Strukturierungsprinzip aufgegeben wurde, ist unbestreitbar und auch nie anders gesehen worden (A. Manns vierter Abschnitt beginnt allerdings mitten in dieser Folge). Dadurch war offensichtlich sogar der Drucker irritiert worden: von Seite 193 bis 219 ließ er den Kolumnentitel gleich (er erwähnt also z.B. Fuge, Variation und Antizipation nicht), erst ab *De Modis* S.221 paßte er diese wieder dem Inhalt an. Geht man ähnlich vor wie oben beim ersten Buch, ergibt sich zunächst folgende, wiederum recht konsequent erscheinende Neu-Numerierung der *Exercitia IV* und *V*. Bis dorthin hätte dann das zweite Buch, wie das erste, 5 × 5 Teile:

IV	wird	IV, 1 *De imitatione*	S. 140
V,	1	IV, 2 *De fugis in genere*	143
V,	2	IV, 3 *De fuga duarum partium*	146
V,	3	IV, 4 *De trium partium fugis*	154
V,	4	IV, 5 *De fugis quatuor partium*	168
V,	5	V, 1 *De contrapuncto duplici*	174
V,	6	V, 2 *De contrapuncto duplici in decima*	184
V,	7	V, 3 *De contrapuncto duplici in duodecima*	193
		V, 4 *De fuga tribus subjectis instructa*	215
		V, 5 *De figura variationis & anticipationis*	217

Aus inhaltlichen und methodischen Gründen muß man mit dem Folgenden (und nicht erst mit *De gustu* S.239 wie A. Mann) jedenfalls den Beginn eines neuen Abschnittes, aus diesen und aus formalistischen Gründen könnte man sogar den eines dritten Buches annehmen: das erste würde dann von den allgemeinen Grundlagen handeln, das zweite von den satztechnischen Fertigkeiten und das dritte von der Komposition im eigentlichen Sinn, d.h. die *musica activa* wäre ihrerseits noch einmal zweigeteilt. Nur im zweiten Buch (resp. ersten Teil des zweiten Buches) macht der Schüler systematische Übungen, im ersten und dritten überwiegt die Belehrung durch den Meister. Als Ordnungsprinzip würden daher, trotz der fortgeführten Dialog-Anlage, nun wieder 'Kapitel' naheliegen. Unter der Annahme einer S.238 wiederum nur irrtümlich fehlenden, also zu ergänzenden Überschrift *Vom Tempus* und unter Bezugnahme auf die erwähnten Kolumnentitel[4] ergeben sich 10 solcher Kapitel:

Caput I	*De Modis*	S.221
II	*Modi transpositi*	222
III	*Octavae harmonice divisae*	226
IV	*De variis fugarum subjectis*	231
V	*De tempore*	238
VI	*De gustu*	239
VII	*De stylo ecclesiastico*	242
VIII	*De stylo a capella*	243
IX	*De stylo mixto*	273
X	*De stylo recitativo*	274

Mit Cap.VI beginnt (hierin ist A. Mann jedenfalls zuzustimmen) deutlich ein neuer inhaltlicher Zusammenhang,[5] man könnte diese 10 Kapitel also u.U. auch als 2 mit je 5 Unterkapiteln (entsprechend den Lektionen der Übungen) auffassen. Nur ein Abschnitt (*VIII De stylo a capella*) fällt mit 31 Druckseiten umfangmäßig aus dem Rahmen, doch scheint dies durch ein zentrales Anliegen Fuxens hinreichend gerechtfertigt.

Unvollständigkeit, d.h. Unabgeschlossenheit von Fuxens Manuskript zu dem Zeitpunkt, da es zum Drucker ging, und in das dieser nur wenig eingriff, ist auch noch an einer anderen Stelle und in anderer Weise sichtbar: In den Abschnitten *De Fuga duarum* und *trium partium* (nach unserer Zählung, IV, 3 und 4) sowie im Abschnitt *De Modis* bringt Fux je sechs Beispiele (in den Tonarten: D, E, F, G, A, C), für die vierstimmige Fuge (Ex.IV, 5) bietet er aber nur drei (in D, E, und F). Wiederum handelt es sich dabei um eine Stelle, die nach unserer Deutung als Ende eines größeren Abschnittes anzusehen ist. Als diejenige, wo der als fehlend deklarierte Abschnitt über das vielstimmige Komponieren eingefügt hätte werden können, kommt sie jedoch kaum in Frage. Daß dies nicht dort, wo er erwähnt ist, nämlich einfach als *Kapitel XI* möglich wäre, versteht sich ja von selbst, doch sind weitere Spekulationen darüber müßig. Hingegen wäre zu fragen, ob diese Erwähnung nicht überhaupt nur stellvertretend für weiteres stehen sollte, das Fux ursprünglich geplant hatte.

Nun ist eine grundsätzliche Überlegung angebracht, ob sich aus den gemachten Erfahrungen, insbesondere der offensichtlich große Bedeutung besitzenden Zahl 5 weiteres ableiten ließe.[6] So verlockend dies auch scheinen mag, sollte man diese Möglichkeit jedenfalls nicht über-strapazieren: Die Zahl 5 ist durch die je 5 Gattungen von Proportionen (Caput IV–VIII des ersten Buches) und Kontrapunkten (Ex.I–III des zweiten Buches) grundgelegt und könnte von daher bestenfalls in spieleri-scher Form auf weitere Momente ausstrahlen. Beweiskraft wird man ihr kaum zusprechen können. Fakten aber sind, daß Fux selbst von Unvoll-ständigkeit spricht, daß solche auch darüber hinaus erkennbar ist und die Redaktion des Buches nicht zu Ende geführt wurde. Ansonsten kommen wir über Plausibilität und Annahmen nicht hinaus.

Bleibt noch die Frage, warum Fux sein Manuskript unvollständig aus den Händen gab und mit der Veröffentlichung nicht noch etwas zuwartete. Wiederum gibt er fürs erste hiezu selbst einen Hinweis: Er war bettlägrig und zweifelte, ob ihm Gott noch 'Leben und Gesundheit' für die Vollendung geben würde. Dazu könnte aber auch noch ein anderes Moment (um nicht von einem psychischen Druck zu sprechen) gekommen sein: Mit gutem Recht kann das Fuxsche Werk als eine Parallele zu Johann Bernhard Fischer von Erlachs *Entwurff Einer Historischen Architectur* (Wien, 1721) und zur *Historia metallica seu numismatica* des Carl Gustav Heraeus (Nürnberg, 1721) angesehen werden: Alle drei Werke sind Kaiser Karl VI. gewidmet; Architektur, Numismatik und Musik sind die zentralen imperialen und seine persönlichen Interessen gewesen. Selbst wenn es nicht von vornherein von den drei Autoren, die einander ohne jeden Zweifel gut gekannt haben,[7] so geplant gewesen sein sollte: spätestens das Erscheinen der beiden anderen Bücher (im gleichen Jahr 1721, aber an verschiedenen Orten) mußte Fux motivieren, sein eigenes, an dem er seit Jahren arbeitete, endlich herauszubringen. An der Endredaktion im Zuge der Drucklegung dürfte ihn dann die Krankheit, an der er ebenfalls schon längere Zeit litt (Gicht), gehindert haben. Seine Pläne blieben einigermaßen erkennbar und es ist auch richtig, daß das Vorliegende trotz des fehlenden 'letzten Schliffs' seinen Zweck erfüllte.

Anmerkungen

[1] Um Inhalt und Geist des Werkes gerechter zu werden, wäre es vorteilhaft, die Bezeichnung *Gradus* nicht, wie allgemein üblich, als Singular aufzufassen.

[2] Vgl. Hellmut Federhofer, '25 Jahre Johann Joseph Fux-Forschung', *Acta musicologica* 52 (1980), S.188–94.

[3] Alfred Mann, '*Gradus ad parnassum* ', *Johann Joseph Fux, Sämtliche Werke*, Serie VII Bd. 1 (Graz, 1967) S.VIII.

[4] Diese führte gewöhnlich der Drucker ein oder schlug sie wenigstens dem Autor vor, die Interpretation kann daher nicht nur als nachträglich-willkürlich abgetan werden.

[5] Es sei neuerlich auf A. Mann verwiesen.

[6] Denn daß die Zahlensymbolik und -mystik auch bei Fux eine gewisse Rolle spielen kann, ist inzwischen bekannt; s. Gösta Neuwirth, 'Symbol und Form (des Te Deum K 270)', *Johann Joseph Fux, Sämtliche Werke*, Serie II Bd. 2 (Graz, 1979) S.X–XV.

[7] Fischer v. Erlach stammte bekanntlich wie Fux aus der Steiermark, Heraeus hat an dessen Publikation auch redaktionell mitgearbeitet.

5 The Chalumeau in the works of Fux

Colin Lawson

Although single-reed instruments found a place in Vienna throughout the eighteenth century, research into the history of the clarinet has naturally focused largely upon the decade from 1781, which witnessed the fruitful relationship of Mozart with the virtuoso Anton Stadler. The few surviving instruments from this time indeed testify to the pre-eminence of Viennese manufacturers, with specifications which encourage richness of sound and homogeneity of tone in both registers. A particular feature is their evenness of scale in the lowest part of the compass, a speciality of Stadler's playing which was espoused enthusiastically in Mozart's works. In 1785 the Viennese aesthetician Daniel Schubart characterized the clarinet as over-flowing with love, whilst praising its indescribable sweetness of expression.[1] In addition to the new type of idiomatic clarinet writing inspired by the Mozart–Stadler collaboration, there is other evidence of a more highly evolved playing style in Vienna, for example in Haydn's clarinet parts in the *Creation*, which show a considerable advance by comparison with his relatively cautious approach to the instrument in the London symphonies.

Like so many components of the Classical style, the development of advanced clarinet writing had its origins in the music written one or two generations earlier, notably in the music of Fux and his contemporaries. Indeed, the chalumeau, a single-reed instrument closely related to the clarinet, was used in Vienna from 1706 until at least the 1770s. Only subsequently was its role as a fundamental-register instrument subsumed by the clarinet, the name chalumeau being simply transferred to its bottom register. This development was a source of regret to at least one writer; Schubart claimed that the chalumeau had 'such an interesting, individual sound that the whole world of music would sustain a grievous loss if the instrument ever became obsolete'.[2] Though by this time its career was already at an end, the survival of the chalumeau alongside the clarinet throughout much of the eighteenth century and the rich though little-known repertory it inspired testify to its importance in the history of orchestral colouring.

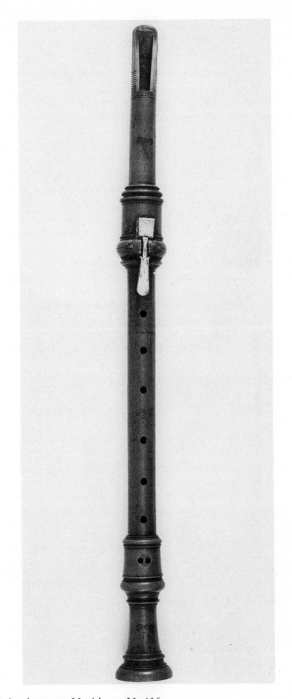

Bayerisches Nationalmuseum, Munich, no. Mu 136

Even in Schubart's day, there was some confusion about the origins of the chalumeau. Referring to it simply as 'die Schalmey' (a term normally reserved in German for double-reed instruments), he stated that it was a small clarinet and most probably the forerunner of the modern oboe, claiming that it gave rise to the invention of both oboe and clarinet but was superseded by the flute on account of its ineffectiveness from a distance. However, Schubart's range of sixteen notes and his citation of repertoire by Telemann and Gluck confirms the real identity of his instrument. During the whole of the nineteenth century the chalumeau barely warranted discussion at all; Köchel again translated the term to 'Schalmei' in his biographical text, though he must have been aware of the original nomenclature from the scores and documents he studied.[3] Whilst attempting no actual definition, he listed the chalumeau together with violetta and German flute as instruments which were relatively new and probably played by non-specialists. At the beginning of the twentieth century Wellesz greatly added to the knowledge of chalumeau repertoire in his series of articles on Viennese opera and oratorio, which cited examples by a variety of composers.[4] The first real definition of the instrument was provided in Kroll's 1932 article 'Das Chalumeau', which contained a handful of repertoire items, including Fux's *Giunone Placata*.[5] Uncertainty persisted, however; in 1939 Carse still considered that chalumeau parts were written for the clarinet in its earliest form, describing it as 'this will o' the wisp amongst wind instruments'.[6] Even generally reliable literature, such as Rendall's book on the clarinet (1954), has subsequently tended to confuse the identity of surviving chalumeaux and clarinets, thus somewhat clouding the issue.[7] Becker's specialist article from 1970 was an important milestone, whose information has been amplified and refined by later writers.[8] A vigorous exchange of views on the subject of chalumeau and clarinet, published in the journal *Early Music* as recently as 1986, clearly indicates that even now the controversy surrounding the instrument has not yet been totally extinguished.[9]

Relatively few chalumeaux survive, and so an understanding of the instrument must be gained from its music and from information in theoretical works. A definition of the chalumeau first appeared in *Gabinetto Armonico* by Filippo Bonanni, printed in Rome in 1722. Other important information concerning its origins and relationship with the clarinet is found in *Historische Nachricht von den Nürnbergischen Mathematicis und Künstlern* (Nuremberg, 1730) by J.G. Doppelmayr. From this source derives the attribution of the invention of the clarinet to Johann Christoph Denner, who is also credited with the improvement of the chalumeau. However, the most comprehensive definition of the chalumeau is to be found in *Museum Musicum* (Schwäbische Hall, 1732) by J.F.B.C. Majer, in a paragraph which also occurs in the *Musikalisches Lexicon* (Leipzig, 1732) by J.G. Walther:

> Chalumeau, plural Chalumeaux (Fr). Fistula postorita (Latin). A shawm or shepherd's pipe made for the most part of cane called *calamus*. Besides this meaning, it is the chanter found on a bagpipe. Furthermore, it denotes a small wind instrument with 7 holes and a range of f″ to a″. Also, a small wind

instrument made of boxwood, with 7 holes, two brass keys near the mouthpiece, and an additional twinned hole near the bottom, playing from f' to a" or b" flat, possibly even to b" natural or c'". (p.153)

Of these four definitions, the first two reflect the generic use of the term prior to the end of the seventeenth century, when no single-reed instrument had yet found its way into art-music. It may be noted that Pierre Trichet in *Traité des instruments de musique* (c.1740) describes the practice of separating the chanter (chalumeau) from the bagpipe and playing it separately, with improved musical effect. The third instrument, effectively a keyless chalumeau, led a somewhat shadowy existence, possibly as a musical toy or novelty, as Baines has suggested.[10] Bonanni also has a definition of this instrument, under the term 'Scialumò'. A later description of this keyless type is found under the entry 'chalumeau' (from 1753) in the *Encyclopédie* of Diderot and d'Alembert, where it is stated that the body of the instrument is of boxwood, but now with a reed of a new material – cane; in addition there is a twinned hole at the bottom of the instrument.[11] Somewhat disparagingly, the writer describes the sound as disagreeable and savage, except when produced by an expert. The instrument is said to be already no longer in use in France; in fact, the presence of the chalumeau there is scarcely documented at all in other sources.

It is the fourth definition by Walther and Majer that represents the two-keyed instrument which appeared in art-music throughout the century. Bonanni listed it as 'calandrone', making a comparison with the recorder in terms of playing technique. The few chalumeaux which survive (in Stockholm and Munich) indicate that this sophisticated version was distinguished by more than merely the two keys which formed a bridge to the (scarcely available) upper register. Comparison of the chalumeau by J.C. Denner with the *Encyclopédie* illustrations, for example, reveals Denner's instrument as much more highly evolved, and closely modelled on the recorder. That such a development should take place is not surprising, for this was an age of experimentation, in which attempts were made to marry various types of instruments. Composers of the early eighteenth century, such as Fux and his contemporaries, were increasingly fascinated by new colour and dynamic intensity. A symptom of this was the demise of the recorder, which was overwhelmed by the new orchestral palette. In 1713 Mattheson wrote of its bland and fawning quality, which bored players and listeners alike.[12] Eventually, of course, it was replaced in the orchestra by the flute, but meanwhile it directly inspired the design of the chalumeau.

Majer (though not Walther) adds a second paragraph, which supplies other significant information:

> Besides soprano and alto (or quart) chalumeaux, one also has tenor and bass chalumeaux, some at French pitch and some at German pitch. They are very hard to play, in particular because of the difficult embouchure. The fingerings correspond for the most part to those of the recorder, but their range extends not much over an octave. Because of this, it is considered unnecessary to report on these in greater detail here, especially since if one can play recorders, one can also play the instruments presented here. (p.32)

Though Majer does not give precise ranges for the consort, musical sources indicate a range of an eleventh (and in the case of the top size a twelfth) upwards from f′, c′, f and c respectively; his chalumeaux were thus equivalent in length to sopranino, descant, treble and tenor recorders, sounding an octave lower due to the acoustical properties of the cylindrical stopped pipe. Of the four sizes it was the soprano which was cultivated almost exclusively in Vienna. Whilst Bonanni's comments on the sound of the chalumeau as 'raucous and rather unpleasant' apparently do refer to the keyed type, uncomplimentary remarks from elsewhere perhaps reflect the role of the more rustic keyless type. For example, Walther in his *Praecepta der Musicalischen Composition* of 1708 writes that 'The chalumeau (Fr.) is a small wind instrument, which sounds like a man singing through his teeth (p.43).' Mattheson, in *Das neu-eröffnete Orchester* of 1713, is yet more damning; 'The so-called chalumeaux may be permitted to perform their somewhat howling symphony of an evening, perhaps in June or July and from a distance, but never in January during a serenade on the water (p.272). Given the clearly defined role of the chalumeau as a tone-colour associated with pastoral contexts in orchestrations of great delicacy, it seems logical to conclude that there were instruments and players whose quality varied widely. Knowledge of the chalumeau is bound to remain incomplete until further specimens emerge to supplement the half dozen or so currently known to survive.

The history of the chalumeau before its arrival in Vienna pre-1706 consists of several isolated sources, but also important documentation of a link between the Denner family and Göttweig Abbey, located some forty miles west of the city on the Danube. The earliest evidence yet uncovered is an invoice list dated 1687 in which 'Ein Chor Chalimo von 4. stücken' was purchased from Nuremberg for the Duke of Römhild-Sachsen.[13] It seems possible that these were built by J.C. Denner, whose stamp appears on a 'Basset-Blockflöte' in the Bachhaus collection in Eisenach. Archival documents record that Denner's son Jacob later supplied chalumeaux to Nuremberg (1710) in addition to Göttweig (c.1720). The instrument's French name reflects the pervasive influence of Parisian makers such as the Hottetterre family, and in 1696 J.C. Denner and the woodwind maker Johann Schell petitioned the Nuremberg city council to be recognized as master craftsmen, and to be granted permission to make for sale the 'French musical instruments . . . which were invented about twelve years ago in France'. Only the recorder and oboe are specifically mentioned in this document, but the chalumeau was probably another of these instruments, whose origins might then be dated c.1684.[14] This espousal of the chalumeau and other instruments originating in France reflects the tendency of contemporary German society to copy slavishly French fashions of all kinds, whether in language, clothes, food, furniture, dances or music.[15] Meanwhile, the earliest evidence of the chalumeau in Germany is contained in an anonymous collection inscribed 'Hannover 1690' and entitled 'XIIe Concert Charivari ou nopce de village a 4 Violon, 2 Chalumeaux 3 Pollissons et un Tambour les Viollons en Vielle'.[16] Furthermore, the autobiographical account which Telemann submitted for inclusion in Mattheson's *Grundlage einer Ehrenpforte* (Hamburg, 1740) notes the chalumeau as one of the many instruments played by him whilst at Hildesheim from 1697 until 1701, where he established contact with French musicians at the court of Brunswick. From 1708 dates an order from Duke Dernath of Schleswig Holstein for four 'Chalimou-Partien' from Jacob Denner (though no chalumeaux by him are known today). A similar order in 1710 from Duke von Gronsfeld in Nuremberg has the earliest reference to 'clarinette', along with families of oboes, recorders and chalumeaux. The bill from Göttweig c.1720 similarly includes a family of 'premieur' and 'second' *chalimou* with two 'basson' (but no clarinet); it has been suggested by comparison with prices of the remaining instruments that they were Majer's soprano, alto and bass respectively, a hypothesis which the nature of the Viennese repertory might tend to support.[17]

Some reference to the clarinet is appropriate to a discussion of Viennese chalumeau repertory, not only to differentiate it from the chalumeau, but because it was in fact also known in Vienna during the first two decades of the eighteenth century. Immediately recognizable from its bell, which replaced the recorder footjoint of the chalumeau, the clarinet also had a thumb key-hole moved further towards the top of the instrument with a smaller tone hole and register tube. Mouthpiece dimensions were a further feature designed to assist production of the upper register, which with its trumpet-like effect was at first the characteristic part of the clarinet's range. The relative ineffectiveness of the lower register at first ensured the survival of the chalumeau, whose role as a flexible woodwind instrument (though of limited range) was quite different, notwithstanding the superficial physical similarity of the two instruments. Their relative roles are neatly summarized in a passage from *Musicus Autodidaktos* (Erfurt, 1738), by J.T. Eisel, who commented that the usual clef for the clarinet was the treble and that then it was treated like a trumpet, whilst sometimes soprano and alto clefs occurred, when it was handled like a chalumeau. Significantly, this differentiation is quite apparent in the music of composers who wrote for both instruments, such as Caldara, Graupner, Handel, Molter and Telemann. The clarinet manifestly post-dated the chalumeau, though it must have been developed before 1707, the year of J.C. Denner's death; a surviving three-keyed instrument in Berkeley bearing his stamp has recently been convincingly authenticated.[18] However, surviving repertory for both instruments points unmistakably to the greater popularity of the chalumeau throughout the first half of the century.

The chalumeau repertory comprises two distinct schools of writing. North Germans such as Telemann and Graupner seem to have had a preference for the lower members of the family, used individually in consort fashion. Though somewhat outmoded, this technique at least overcomes the limitations imposed by the restricted available range. In Vienna, however, a preference for pairs of soprano chalumeaux or for the combination of soprano chalumeau and flute anticipates the use of woodwind in the Classical orchestra. The opera house was a natural environment for the introduction of novel tone-colours, and the chalumeau became a regular *obbligato* instrument there until the death of Caldara in

1736; it continued to be used on an occasional basis until the 1770s. Certain other musical cities show the influence of the Viennese chalumeau, notably Venice (birthplace of Caldara), where Vivaldi wrote an *obbligato* for soprano 'salmoè ' in the oratorio *Juditha Triumphans* of 1716. As early as 1706 the German oboist Ludwig Erdmann was appointed professor of 'Salamuri/Salamoni' (= chalumeau) at the Pietà. Of German cities, Dresden apparently followed the Viennese liking for the soprano chalumeau, as shown by its inclusion in a quartet sonata (undated) by Hasse and its use as a virtuoso solo instrument in a concerto (*c*.1727–34) by Fasch. Less surprisingly, it is also found in an aria in the opera *L'Origine di Jaromeritz in Moravia* (1730) by František Václav Mīča of Jaroměřice in Southern Moravia. Mīča is known to have studied works by composers such as Caldara, whilst operas by Conti were performed in his home city early in the century.[19]

A list of Viennese composers known to have used the chalumeau during the first third of the century includes Ariosti, the brothers Bononcini, Caldara, Conti, Fux, the Emperor Joseph I, Porsile, Reutter and Camilla di Rossi. The tradition was then continued on a more sporadic basis by Bonno, Dittersdorf, Gassmann, Gluck, Hoffmeister, Pichl, Starzer and Werner, among whose work are some important instrumental pieces. In opera the chalumeau typically appeared in just one or two scenes, generally of a pastoral or amorous nature, anticipating the differentiation of clarinet from oboe whose most celebrated illustration is Mozart's *Così fan Tutte*. The chalumeau was often coupled with such delicate colours as the flute, recorder, viola d'amore, viola da gamba or theorbo in scenes of tender, languid emotion. During the period 1710 to 1721 the court orchestral personnel rose from sixty-one to seventy-two, of whom nine were woodwind players. Of the five oboists, at least two played the chalumeau, as is evident from surviving references supplied by Fux which are quoted by Köchel: 'Joseph Lorber, court oboist . . . this applicant is a very fine virtuoso . . . not only on this instrument, but also on the German flute and chalumeau (3.8.1718).' 'André Wittmann, oboist . . . this applicant is the most outstanding virtuoso I have heard, on the oboe and also the chalumeau (21.4.1721).' [20] This proves beyond question that in the opera orchestra the oboists simply transferred to flute or chalumeau when required. Examples in *La Decima Fatica d'Ercole* (1710) and *Dafne in Lauro* (1714), where flute, chalumeaux and two oboes are required together, testify to the presence of at least four upper woodwind players in performances of these works.

The earliest known Viennese opera with chalumeau is *Endimione* by Giovanni Bononcini, written in 1706. The following year an amusing vignette occurs in Silvio Stampiglia's libretto *L'Etearco*, set to music for the Vienna Carnival by Bononcini. In Act III scene 9, the following exchange takes place between two comic characters: Delbo – 'Vuò cercare/Di trovare/ E i Fagotti, ed Oboè ' (I'll try to find both bassoons and oboes); Binda – 'Piacerebbe ancora a me,/Che vi fossero i Scialmò.' (I'd like there to be chalumeaux as well.) This suggests that the chalumeau was at this time an attractive novelty, to be distinguished from traditional woodwinds such as bassoon and oboe.[21] Shortly afterwards, Fux included chalumeaux in *Julo*

Ascanio (1708), the first of nine chamber operas written for special occasions which use the instrument. It was thus apparently excluded only from the large-scale operas, appearing consistently in shorter pieces (for an orchestra of 18 to 24 players) until 1725. A single larger-scale exception is the 'Componimento per Musica' *Gli Ossequi della Notte*, written for the name-day of the Empress in 1709 and scored for a larger orchestra of 48 or 49 players.[22] The actual contexts with chalumeau, comprising expressions of intimate and delicate sentiments, suggest a quickly established orchestral role for what became a favourite *obbligato* tone-colour. In terms of both quantity and quality Fux was its most important Viennese patron, exploring a greater variety of key- and time-signatures in his music for the instrument than his contemporaries. The only idiom not espoused by him was the elaborate *obbligato* with written-out ornamentation characteristic of native Italians such as Bonno and Porsile, and found also in the aria 'Tutto in pianto' which Joseph I contributed to Ziani's *Chilonida* of 1709. For the soprano chalumeau the keys of F and B flat were most comfortable and idiomatic, and it is therefore somewhat surprising that Fux avoids F altogether, though he does have some numbers in B flat. Throughout the Viennese repertory minor keys often coincide with the presence of the chalumeau, and Fux has several *obbligati* in C minor, together with others in D and G minors. Most unusual is his use in four out of eleven operatic numbers of the key of G major, which other composers for the instrument seem to have avoided because of the cross-fingerings it implies. Indeed, as late as the 1780s, Mozart recommended to his pupil Thomas Attwood that for the clarinet the (written) keys of C and F were to be strictly adhered to. For Fux, dramatic contexts were always a consideration, though sometimes also the overriding suitability of tonality for the other instruments involved. A parallel later in the century is Mozart's use of the C clarinet when such a choice was dictated by the necessity to treat companion instruments sympathetically.

Of the numbers in G major the tenor aria 'Su'l mortal che stanco giace' from *Gli Ossequi della Notte* has an accompaniment of 'chalimeaux', violins (without oboes) and four viole da gamba. Since chalumeau and viola da gamba are heard together elsewhere in C minor (in *Il Mese di Marzo*), the dramatic considerations manifestly prevail here, involving the chalumeau in the accidentals f' sharp (playable via the twinned bottom hole), a' sharp, c'' sharp, f'' sharp (all cross-fingered), and most awkwardly g' sharp (half-holed unless another twin hole were provided). Other numbers in G combine chalumeau with the flute, to which this tonality was especially well suited. In the essentially diatonic opening pastoral chorus of *Dafne in Lauro*, this duo partnership replaces oboes between chorus lines and in the middle (duet) section. Chalumeau and flute also colour the G major aria 'Va prigioniero quell' Augelletto' and the opening 13-bar *sinfonia* which is included in the *da capo*.[23] Especially notable is the characteristic use of the chalumeau to double the soprano voice, with parallel thirds and sixths in the flute contributing to the pastoral flavour. In addition to the accidentals listed above, the middle section also demands a cross-fingered d'' sharp from the chalumeau. The aria 'Si, ch'egli è amor, che dorme in molli piume' from *Psyche* adds unison violins to a similar texture. This example, and the aria 'Io di Lete su la sponda' from *Orfeo* (which is scored with full strings and is in the more idiomatic chalumeau key of D minor) well illustrate the gentle dramatic contexts which suggested such colouration. The sensuous love duet 'Si, mio ben, si mio diletto' from *Diana Placata* (Example 1), illustrates a category of some historical importance, since it directly anticipates the role of the clarinet in the opera orchestra in such scenes. Use of flute rather than second chalumeau provides a lower available compass, but with a blend of colour which is none the less homogeneous; indeed, Fux apparently avoided multiple chalumeau combinations after the composition of *Julo Ascanio* in 1708, and it seems that works by other composers (such as the Bononcinis and Camilla di Rossi) which feature two or three chalumeaux all date from no later than this time.

From the same year, *Pulcheria* contains an aria 'Senza un poco di tormento' with chalumeau and recorder, a surprisingly rare combination in

Example 1

........nostro petto fede ugual e ugual costanza.

the repertoire as a whole. The *obbligato* parts are simple but do contain an early example of c''' at the upper end of the chalumeau range. This must have been overblown from f' ; the few surviving specimens confirm the presence of one or two notes in the upper register, though it is remarkable that composers in general took advantage of this only when writing for the soprano size, since one might have expected a partial second register to be more readily available on larger instruments. The note c''' also features in the elaborate *obbligato* to the aria 'Qual il sol in prato o in riva' from *La Decima Fatica d'Ercole*, whose melancholy flavour is enhanced by means of an equally prominent solo theorbo.[24] Examination of Viennese contexts with chalumeau reveals an overwhelming preference for slow tempi, often qualified by markings such as 'Affettuoso'. Exceptional therefore is the stylised Gavotte 'Tutto il bel vorrei raccolto' from *Giunone Placata*, the only operatic example of a *solo* chalumeau *obbligato* by Fux; his choice of instrument was again inspired by the amorous subject-matter.[25]

An overwhelming sweetness of sound is suggested by all these numbers, and it is therefore a particular matter for regret that no actual soprano chalumeaux survive. A close but ambiguous contender is the small instrument in Munich's *Bayerisches Nationalmuseum* (Mu 137), though its pitch and range do not quite correspond with what one might expect from a soprano chalumeau. Nor is its mouthpiece original, fitting uneasily into the main part of the instrument, having a radically smaller bore and being constructed of different material (probably a fruitwood rather than boxwood). The integral footjoint with the one-piece main section suggests a more primitive instrument than Denner's, though the placement of the two keys on the body of the instrument rather than the mouthpiece/barrel probably indicates a later date. The traditional attribution to Stuehnwal is somewhat fanciful, the maker's mark barely readable as (?) 'STV. . .H. . .A. . .X'.[26] Yet more controversial is the identity of the bass chalumeau. The only composer outside Vienna known to have used this size was Christoph Graupner, and it is clear from his music that he intended an instrument equivalent in length to the tenor recorder (with a range of c to f'). Graupner notates both tenor and bass chalumeaux an octave lower than actual sound, in the bass clef. This corresponds to Mozart's notation of the lowest register of both basset horn and basset clarinet later in the century. In the tenor chalumeau parts of three concertos, RV 555, 558 and 579, Vivaldi follows the same practice. Somewhat more controversial is Fux's 'basson' (which forms part of a concertino group with two soprano chalumeaux) in the aria 'Il vincere superbi, e a' vinti il perdonar' from *Julo Ascanio*. Clearly differentiated from the bassoon ('fagotto') found else-where, the 'basson' is actually identified as a chalumeau in other contexts; in the overture to Ariosti's *Marte Placato* occurs the marking 'basso chalamaux senza cembalo', whilst the aria by Joseph I already cited has a continuo of 'basson di chalumeaux e contrabasso, senza cembalo'. Further examples occur in the operas of the Bononcinis. (It may be noted in passing that the cues 'Bassone solo' and 'Grande Bassone solo' in the bass part of the Turin score of Vivaldi's concerto RV 576 refer to the bassoon and are not relevant to the present discussion; in the Dresden repertoire, of which this work formed part, 'bassono' was indeed the standard term for the bassoon.)

Fux's trio of chalumeaux forms an obvious counterpart to the popular double-reed combination of oboes and bassoon. The question arises as to whether, by analogy with other chalumeau sources, the bass part should sound an octave higher. In general this is feasible musically, though resulting in a far more closely-knit texture than is evident in trio combinations for other instruments. Arguing against such an interpretation are the relative prices of Jacob Denner's various chalumeaux in the Nuremberg and Göttweig documents. At Nuremberg in 1710 a 'chalimou' cost three florins, an 'alt-chalimou' five florins, and a 'chalimou basson' fourteen florins. The bill for Göttweig (*c.*1720) shows an even greater differential, with respective prices of two florins thirty Kreutzer, five and fifteen florins per instrument; these represent reductions from a previously submitted estimate of three, seven and eighteen florins. This estimate has the instruments tabulated in choirs of oboes, chalumeaux and flutes, the middle heading being 'I Chor Chalimou mit 6 Stiñen' and then (as with the oboes but not the flutes) French nomenclature – three Primieur Chalimou, one Second Chalimou, two Basson. As already noted, Majer's second size was known as either alt- or quart-chalumeau, the latter term implying a relationship similar to that of treble and descant recorders. Though popular in Germany, this instrument has not yet been traced in Viennese sources. There is, however, at least one bassoon-shaped specimen which has recently been identified as a genuine bass chalumeau, capable of playing Viennese bass parts at pitch.[27] Bearing the mark 'W. Kress', it survives in the Museum Carolino Augusteum at Salzburg (no. 8/1), catalogued as a 'sordun'. Nothing is known of Kress, except that a basset-flute by him is extant in Brunswick, together with oboes in Copenhagen, Linz and Munich; these all appear to originate from the early eighteenth century. His (?)bass chalumeau is made in the form of a dulzian, in one piece with two parallel bores which double back, and with a short bell at the top. A small wood insert at the beginning of the bore is presumably intended to hold a curved or bent crook. With nine finger holes and five brass keys mounted on saddles, the instrument's range is B′ flat to b flat. The bore is cylindrical (which would argue against a double-reed generator) with a diameter/ length ratio similar to early basset horns. Van der Meer has identified the instrument as the earliest bass clarinet, whilst believing that it was played as a bass chalumeau.[28] Three other unstamped single-reed instruments, from collections in Berlin, Brussels and Lugano, find a place in Rendall's discussions of the early bass clarinet.[29] The three-keyed Lugano instrument was built with a long, straight wooden tube and a downward pointing bell, its superior workmanship and construction arguing a date of origin some considerable time after the death of Fux. The Brussels specimen was made from a plank of wood covered in leather, with the bore running along one side of it and the thumb hole opening directly on to it. Seven finger holes enter on the upper surface, at oblique angles as on the wing-joint of the bassoon. The body of the instrument resembles a narrow triangle with blunted apex and is fitted with a brass crook and upturned widely flared bell. The longest of the three keys produces the lowest note e and its twelfth b′, the others are placed at the top of the instrument as on the chalumeau, though the position of the thumb key-hole indicates that it was intended to produce an upper register. In terms of chalumeau history, the Brussels specimen (perhaps from *c*.1750) is nowadays of particular interest as a more sophisticated version of the Berlin instrument which perished in the Second World War. This had only one key for its lowest pitch and was designed to play only in its lowest register. With no indication of the maker or even country of origin of either the Berlin or Brussels instrument, there is of course no definite reason to link either of them with the Viennese repertoire, even though this is the only music which might require this size of instrument.

In view of the operatic contexts including chalumeau, it is scarcely surprising that the instrument finds an occasional role in Fux's oratorios, though here it is virtually the only soprano *obbligato* wind instrument, deeper colours such as trombones or bassoons assuming considerable prominence. The combination of chalumeau and trombone found in several of the oratorio arias was first indicated by Van der Meer in his reference to *Il fonte della salute, aperto dalla grazia nel calvario*.[30] Here the expressive C minor aria 'Vede che il Redentor' illustrates a contrapuntal technique of writing for these instruments together in *stile antico*. In the introductory material there is free use of imitative points which make a special expressive feature of suspended dissonance on the main beat of the bar. A closely related idiom (though with the addition of strings) occurs in the C minor duet 'O beate l'alme umane', from *La Cena del Signore*. The sensuous vocal writing for the two protagonists, 'Un Anima Contemplativa' and 'Lo Spirito Profetico', was clearly inspired by the text (which continues '. . . cui per cibo un Dio rimane pegno eterno del suo amor'), a context which is characteristically suggestive of chalumeau colouring. On the other hand, the central section contains a reference to the trembling of the Angels as they behold the Creator, a typical inspiration for a trombone *obbligato*. In *Il*

testamento di nostro Signor Gesù Cristo sul Calvario the same duo colours
the C minor duet for the Virgin ('Venite o rei mortali e qui dolenti del
vostro Redentore . . .') and the Angel Gabriel ('Venite Angioli tutti e qui
dolenti del vostro Creator . . .'), though in this instance the voices are also
written in *stile antico* for dramatic reasons. In all three of these numbers the
continuo is marked 'senza l'organo', which brings the wind solos into
greater relief.

More overtly operatic is the G major aria 'Sonno amato deh vieni a miei
lumi' in *Il disfacimento di Sisara*, sung by the eponymous General and
accompanied by *pianissimo* violins in thirds and sixths alternating with
chalumeau and flute above a continuo with bassoons but without harpsichord. Of the four oratorio numbers with *solo* chalumeau *obbligato*, the
most poignant dramatically is perhaps the B flat aria 'L'odio non parla in
me', sung by Herodias in *La fede sacrilega nella morte del Precursor S
Giovanni Battista*. Just prior to the dénoument, she claims in this seemingly
tender aria (with chalumeau largely in thirds with the voice) that she speaks
not out of hatred of the prophet, but from fear for her beloved. Illustrative
of other scenes of great delicacy is an *obbligato* of touching simplicity in the
penultimate number of *La donna forte nella madre de' sette Maccabei*,
Maccabea's D minor aria 'Cari pegni, figli amati'. The exceptionally large-
scale C minor aria 'Aveva ancor bambino quel labro suo Divino' sung by the
Virgin in *La deposizione dalla croce di Gesù Cristo Salvator Nostro* contains
Fux's final chalumeau *obbligato*, and is unusual both for its faster speed
indication 'Tempo giusto' and for its continuo group, which exceptionally is
not reduced in any way. In general, the subject matter of oratorio texts
provided dramatic moments in which the chalumeau was entirely appropriate, and in terms of the history of single reeds it seems a matter for special
regret that the type of contemplative context illustrated in Example 2, from
Fux's *Cristo nell' orto*, became the province of oboe and oboe d'amore in the
cantatas and Passions of Bach. At present the only tenuous link between
Bach's family and the chalumeau is the existence of a cantata *obbligato* by
his Meiningen uncle Johann Ludwig Bach.[31]

Another area of study which invites further research is the role of the
clarinet in Vienna during Fux's lifetime. Two references point to an early
interest in the instrument; indeed, with the exception of Vivaldi's *Juditha
Triumphans* of 1716, they indicate the earliest known orchestral usage.
Francesco Conti, who included chalumeaux in operas and cantatas, wrote for
'Clarinette in D' in at least one version of his popular comic opera *Don
Chisciotte in Sierra Morena* of 1719, where the trumpet-like writing occurs
at the beginning of the overture.[32] Caldara included two C clarinets in the
score of *Ifigenia in Aulide* (1718), perhaps having encountered them in
Venice. A *sinfonia*, aria and chorus in Act I scene 2 has parts for 'Clarinetti'
paired with trumpets and timpani. The triadic material is easily playable on
two-keyed clarinets, whilst their association with trumpets reflects a patent
similarity of tone-colour. Caldara's use of the chalumeau in opera and
oratorio occurred afterwards, nicely proving the differently perceived roles
of the two instruments. The court orchestral personnel identified by Köchel
lists no specialist clarinettists before the Stadler brothers in 1787, implying

Example 2

that in the early part of the century, visiting artists or versatile resident wind players must have been involved. In Germany, repertory with clarinet was similarly scarce; Telemann included a clarinet in a single Whitsun cantata of 1721 and then only in a serenata of 1728, whose overall instrumentation also includes chalumeaux.[33]

If the era before the mid-1730s was the golden period of the chalumeau, Graupner in Darmstadt effectively extended its life by including it in over eighty cantatas and in eighteen instrumental pieces written between 1734 and 1753. After that an enthusiasm for the chalumeau by a generation of composers in Vienna after the death of Fux ensured a further prolongation of its life by at least twenty years, heralded by Gluck's *Orfeo* (1762) and *Alceste* (1767). No evidence of a revival of the chalumeau between Bonno's *Eleazaro* (1739) and these works has yet been reported, so the direct inspiration for Gluck's choice of colour must at present remain a matter for speculation. A glance at Köchel's list of players reveals the survival into old age of court oboists who must have known the instrument and perhaps inspired pupils to show an interest in it. André Wittmann took up his position in 1721 and died in 1767 at the age of 98, whilst Daniel Franz Hartmann was appointed the same year, retired in 1760, and died at the age of 81 in 1772. Works from the 1770s with chalumeau parts include Starzer's ballet *Roger et Bradamante* (1771) and Gassmann's opera *I Rovinati* (1772). The first appearance in Vienna of the clarinettist brothers, Anton and Johann Stadler, was in 1773, but around this time divertimenti with chalumeau were still being composed by Dittersdorf, Gassmann and Pichl. Above all, the concerto by Hoffmeister (b. 1754) testifies to the availability of an able player even at this late stage. Equally fascinating historically is the 'Musica da Cammera molto particulare fatta e presentata alla Regina di Moscovia' by Starzer, which is scored for two chalumeaux or flutes, five trumpets and timpani. The composer worked in St Petersburg from 1760 until 1768, and not long afterwards Leopold Mozart copied out all five numbers, specifying flutes for the upper parts. He added arrangements of three numbers by Gluck and the eight movements were subsequently attributed to Mozart (*fils*) as K 187 (later 159c); their correct identity was revealed only in 1937.[34] However, Starzer's music did directly inspire Mozart's own identically scored Divertimento K 188 (240b). In this work flutes are again specified; however, this entire episode offers more than a suggestion that Mozart was at least aware of Fux's favourite *obbligato* instrument, if only as a curiosity.

Notes

[1] C.F.D. Schubart, *Ideen zu einer Aesthetik der Tonkunst* (Vienna, 1806), p.320.

[2] ibid., p.326.

[3] L.R. von Köchel, *Johann Joseph Fux* (Vienna, 1872), p.226.

[4] E. Wellesz, 'Die Opern und Oratorien in Wien von 1660–1708', *Studien zur Musikwissenschaft* VI (1919), pp.5–138.

[5] O. Kroll, 'Das Chalumeau', *Zeitschrift für Musikwissenschaft* XV (1932), pp.374–8.

[6] A. Carse, *Musical Wind Instruments*, (London, 1939), pp.149–50.

[7] F.G. Rendall, *The Clarinet*, 3rd edn, rev. P. Bate (London, 1971), plates 1a and 1b.

[8] H. Becker, 'Das Chalumeau im 18 Jahrhundert', *Festgabe für Heinrich Husmann* (Munich, 1970), pp.23–46. See also C. Lawson, *The Chalumeau in Eighteenth-Century Music* (Ann Arbor, 1981); C. Lawson, 'chalumeau', *The New Grove Dictionary of Musical Instruments* (London 1984), vol. I, pp.327–9.

[9] C. Karp, 'The early history of the clarinet and chalumeau' and A. Rice and C. Lawson, 'The clarinet and chalumeau revisited', *Early Music* 14/4 (1986), pp.545–55.

[10] A. Baines, *European and American Musical Instruments* (London, 1966), p.112.

[11] 'Chalumeau', *Encyclopédie, ou Dictionnaire raisonné des sciences, des arts et des métiers*, ed., D. Diderot and J.L. d'Alembert (Paris etc., 1751–65), vol. 3, p.40.

[12] J. Mattheson, *Das neu-eröffnete Orchester* (Hamburg 1713), p.271.

[13] H. Heyde, *Historische Musikinstrumente im Bachhaus Eisenach* (Eisenach, 1976), p.193.

[14] E. Nickel, *Der Holzblasinstrumentenbau in der Freien Reichsstadt Nürnberg* (Nüremberg, 1971), p.207.

[15] A. Fauchier-Magnan, *The Small German Courts in the Eighteenth Century*, translated by M. Savill, (London, 1980), pp.26–9.

[16] H.O. Koch. *Sonderformen der Blasinstruments in der deutschen Musik vom späten 17. bis zur Mitte des 18. Jahrhunderts* (Diss., Heidelberg, 1980), p.223.

[17] H. Fitzpatrick, 'Jacob Denner's Woodwinds for Göttweig Abbey', *Galpin Society Journal* 21 (1968), pp.81–7.

[18] T.E. Hoeprich, 'A Three-Key Clarinet by J.C. Denner', *Galpin Society Journal* 34 (1981), pp.21–32.

[19] J. Pohanka, Dějiny české hudby v příkladech (Prague 1958), no. 122.

[20] Köchel, op. cit., pp.384, 389.

[21] I am grateful to Michael Talbot for this reference.

[22] J.H. van der Meer, *Johann Joseph Fux als Opernkomponist* (Bilthoven, 1961), vol.I, p.204.

[23] ibid., vol. III, pp.41–3.

[24] The introduction is reproduced in C. Lawson, *The Chalumeau in Eighteenth-Century Music* (Ann Arbor, 1981) p.44.

[25] ibid., p.42.

[26] See A. Rice, *The Baroque Clarinet* (forthcoming). The instrument is illustrated in Lawson, op. cit., plate 1.

[27] K. Birsak, *Die Holzblasinstrumente im Salzburger Museum Carolino Augusteum* (Salzburg, 1973), p.31.

[28] J.H. van der Meer, 'Besprechungen von Kurt Birsak, *Die Holzblasinstrumente im Salzburger Museum Carolino Augusteum*', *Die Musikforschung* 30 (1977), pp.248-9.

[29] Rendall, *The Clarinet*, 3rd edn, rev. P. Bate (London, 1971), pp.139-40: the Brussels instrument is illustrated in his plate 7a.

[30] Van der Meer, *Johann Joseph Fux als Opernkomponist* (Bilthoven, 1961) vol. I, p.184. The aria is illustrated at length in Lawson, op. cit., pp.45-6.

[31] Lawson, op.cit., p.148.

[32] Illustrated in the article 'Conti' in *Die Musik in Geschichte und Gegenwart*, II (1952), cols 1641-2.

[33] C. Lawson, 'Telemann and the Chalumeau', *Early Music* 9/3 (1981), p.316.

[34] E.F. Schmid, 'Gluck-Starzer-Mozart', *Zeitschrift für Musik* 104 (1937), pp.1198-1209.

6 The use of wind instruments (excluding Chalumeau) in Fux's Music

Wolfgang Suppan

To a greater extent, perhaps, than is the case today, composers in the past have habitually tailored their work to meet the needs of their immediate environment and the ability and potential of the singers and instrumentalists at their disposal. During the lifetime of Johann Joseph Fux (1660–1741), such considerations were materially affected by the development of a major–minor system of tonality and the division of the octave into twelve equal semitones. One notable result of this development was the disparity between keyboard and stringed instruments on one side and wind instruments on the other. Although Fux supported the use of equal temperament at least from 1725, as Hellmut Federhofer has recently argued,[1] his writing for wind instruments was undoubtedly affected by the technical difficulties imposed by this system.

Woodwinds, overblowing at the octave or the twelfth, and brass instruments bound to the series of overtones, could only meet the demands of equal temperament in a restricted manner: in the case of woodwind instruments, the use of bores and key mechanisms facilitated a wider range of pitches than had previously been available (the same improvements in part enlarged the use of brass instruments), and the addition of other features such as the hermaphroditic form of the cornett and the development of slides and crooks gradually led to the availability of lower fundamental tones and additional overtones. Valves were to be invented only in the decades after 1800.

A survey of the use of woodwinds and brass in the works of Fux must initially clarify the limitations of such instruments. Second, the question of the technical development of these instruments and the actual ability of the players needs to be addressed. A third consideration is the extent to which the use of such instruments was conditioned by the court ceremonies and liturgical or quasi-liturgical services in which they participated. The whole question of the relationship between court ceremony (secular and sacred) and music has a bearing on the use of winds at the imperial court.

> As a symbolic representation of imperial dignity, ceremony expressed both a
> general sense of religious significance and meaning in Vienna and a particular
> sense of the emperor's own extraordinary musicality and his religious ambition –
> just as it was used in Rome to express the sacred dignity of the pope. Our
> knowledge of such ceremony and its meaning allows us to understand the
> purpose of a transmitted work. We can additionally perceive that a particular
> style [of music] corresponds to a specific ceremonial function.[2]

Between 1695 and 1740, the musical retinue of the court chapel in Vienna
(the *Hofmusikkapelle*) included a total of twenty-eight trumpeters (of
which about ten were in simultaneous employment), twenty oboists
(between six to eight of whom were simultaneously employed), five cornett
players (between two and three in simultaneous employment), eleven
trombonists (of which between four and five were simultaneously
employed), nine bassoonists (between four to five simultaneously
employed) and two horn players (both employed from *c.*1710 onwards;
after 1720 only one of them was engaged).[3] Among the oboists there were
six musicians who also played other double-reed instruments in addition to
the recorder, transverse flute and chalumeau. Three of the bassoonists were
similarly versatile, and one of the timpani players was also known likewise
to change instruments.

This range of instruments suggests that secular and sacred festive music
at court was dominated by the sound of trumpets and trombones. The
trombone in particular was considered by Fux to be especially appropriate
in church;[4] the slide trombone was in effect the only brass instrument of the
period wholly able to meet the demands of an expanded tonal range. Fux
saw to it that the *Hofmusikkapelle* was equipped with the best available
players of this instrument. In 1712 he described one of them, Leopold
Christian the elder, as a 'virtuoso singulare'[5], of the younger Christian he
reported that he did not have in his charge any other comparable musician[6];
in 1721 he remarked of the same player that 'such a virtuoso had not been
available in the past and would not perhaps be found in the future'.[7] Much
of the soloistic trombone writing in Fux's oratorios must be regarded as the
result of having such players at the composer's disposal.

It was a measure of the self-esteem of the imperial court in Vienna, which
regarded itself as the foremost such assembly in the western world, that it
sought to attract not only the finest available *Kapellmeister* but also to
employ the ablest musicians and to purchase the most technically advanced
instruments for the sustenance of its musical life.[8] Apart from players
attached to the *Hofmusikkapelle*, there were other musicians in the service
of various relatives of the imperial family: six oboists taught by Pierre de
Laboussiere, for example, were called from Berlin in 1700 to serve in the
household of the Archduke Charles in Vienna. The court itself also drew
upon the services of military wind and bugle players. From 1700 onwards,
Joseph I, then King of Rome, had four oboists and one bassoonist who were
predominantly of French extraction. In 1713, the Emperor Charles VI sent
a *Hautbois-Banda* of seven players to Barcelona in order to accompany the

Empress from there to Vienna with a customary *Bekanntmachungsschall* (i.e., music to herald her arrival in the capital). It is interesting to note however that none of these players was taken into the service of the court chapel, with the exception of Johann Franz Fasser, who was said to be 'incomparably better' than his six colleagues.

As early as 1698, the teacher of Charles VI, Pater Ignaz Lovina, reported in his diary that the new court composer Fux had written instrumental music for the feast of Saint Joseph (19 March) scored for four flutes, two oboes, bassoons, violins, two 'cellos and four lutes. It is not until 1730, however, that we find the first mention of 'wind music' (*Harmonie*) in connection with the royal *Tafelmusik*, in a report issued by Fux on the availability of musicians: 'Although four oboists are in the service of the court music, one or other of them is frequently indisposed. The wind music is as a consequence often incomplete.' [9] This term *Harmonie*, from which the description '*Kaiserliche Harmoniemusik*' used during the reign of Joseph II is derived, designates the functional music performed at court especially during the second half of the eighteenth century.

A report of the performance of Giovanni Bononcini's *L'Euleo festeggiante nel Ritorno d'Allesandro Magno dall'Indie* on the lake of the Favorita garden in 1699, published in Frankfurt, gives evidence of the total number of musicians assembled in imperial service at Vienna *c*.1700. Approximately 150 musicians are said to have taken part. On an engraving included in the published libretto at least 110 instrumentalists in two sections are discernible, among them more than 50 wind players. [10]

Joseph I, who reigned briefly at Vienna from 1705 until 1711, is credited with having had a particular liking for modern wind instruments, especially as he himself appears to have played the flute. [11] In spite of this, neither the recorder nor the flute was a standard instrument in Fux's orchestral ensemble. Only in some of his larger works does Fux make use of the flute's tone-colour, and no flautists were registered as members of the *Hofmusikkapelle* – the instrument was played by oboists when required. Nevertheless, the conventional semantic association between love (especially the pain of love) and the flute does obtain in some of Fux's dramatic works. (This association is more usually registered in Fux's music by means of the chalumeau, to which the flute played second part.) The flute sounds in *Orfeo ed Euridice* (1715) when the divine singer (Orpheus) stands helplessly on the banks of the river Lethe and in *Psiche* (1720), when Psyche finds herself alone in a rocky wilderness, deserted as a punishment by 'Love' for having asked much too indiscreet a question and in *Pulcheria* (1708), when the text speaks of love and pain as belonging together. On only one occasion, in the opera *Le Nozze di Aurora* (1722), does Fux employ a pair of flutes, in the pastoral aria 'L'arte di ben amar'.

The *sinfonia* for flute, oboe and continuo in Fux's *Concentus musico-instrumentalis* of 1701 has been cited by Ernst Kubitschek as an outstanding and comparatively rare example of Fux's non-dramatic writing for the instrument. [12] In general, one must agree with John Henry van der Meer's conclusion that the sound produced by flautists in Vienna 'never had the light, piercing, penetrating or alternatively shallow characteristics produced by players of the Berlin school, but that on the contrary, it must have been smooth and pleasing'.[13]

Oboes and bassoons were essential components of Fux's orchestra. Leading French exponents of the oboe taught the first and successive generations of Viennese oboists. Gunther Joppig discerns three distinct ways in which this instrument is used in the *Serenade à 8* for two trumpets, two oboes and basson, two violins, an oboe and *basso continuo* from Fux's *Concentus*. In the six movements which make up the *Serenade*, the oboe is deployed as follows:

1 *Marche*:   both oboes paired in *concertante* style at the outset, then *colla parte* with the violin parts.
2 *Gigue*:   *colla parte* with the violin parts.
3 *Menuett*:   *colla parte* with the violin parts.
4 *Aria*:   *colla parte* with the violin parts.
5 *Ouverture*:   *colla parte* with the violin parts.
6 *Menuett*:   *colla parte* with the violin parts, but with a Trio for oboes and bassoon only, in which all three instruments are soloistically deployed.[14]

Of the three usages (*concertante, colla parte* and soloistic), the second one clearly predominates. We may infer from Fux's music generally that oboes and bassoons usually double the outer string parts. If oboes are not to be used, as in certain sections of the *madrigal* choruses of the oratorios, Fux indicates their absence by the use of pause marks.[15] *Senza oboi* markings in the *concertino* sections of Fux's music arise when violinistic passages are unsuitable for the instrument. There are, nevertheless, many demanding oboe passages which clearly reflect the remarkable players whom Fux had at his disposal, such as André Wittmann, of whom the composer observed that he was 'an oboe and chalumeau virtuoso such as I have never before heard' (1721). Fux described Joseph Lorber in similar terms as an oboist who was 'a virtuoso not only of this instrument, but also of the *Flute allemande* and the chalumeau' (1717).[16] The natural versatility of such players was enhanced by the fact that similar fingerings were shared by the oboe, flute, bassoon and chalumeau. Only the technique of embouchure had to be altered.[17]

The principal task of the bassoon was to perform the figured bass *colla parte* with 'cello, viola da gamba, violone, harpsichord or organ. Rhythmical differences between bassoon and string parts in the articulation of such bass lines originate in the fact that in the masses and oratorios of Fux the bassoon tends to follow the vocal bass part (and thus the rhythm of the text setting) whereas the string writing is instrumentally conceived. Beyond this function, the bassoon also participates as a solo or *concertante* instrument in Fux's music and especially in the secular and sacred-dramatic works. In *Julo Ascanio* (1708) and *Orfeo ed Euridice*, Fux includes arias in which a pair of bassoons participate in *concertante* style against the vocal part. Plutone's aria in *Orfeo*, 'Per regnar con più di Gloria', features imitative (contrapuntal) writing for the instrument in addition to demanding parallel passages and gestural figures (a fanfare motive) which materially affect the projection and meaning of the text. A similar degree of virtuosity characterizes the bassoon *obbligato* which accompanies Nicodemo's aria (the last such number in the work) 'Se pura più nel core' in the *parte seconda* of the *sepolcro* oratorio *La deposizione dalla Croce di Gesù Cristo Salvator nostro* (1728). The *serenata Gli Ossequi della notte* also includes an aria for 'Night' ('Gli Spazi del Mondo') which is scored for bassoon and 'cello.

The range of these bassoon parts is from E to e'. Thus it extends to two octaves, including semitones. These latter are more distant from the fundamental scale of the instrument with F as the fundamental tone than those bassoons which have fork fingerings for B flat and E flat. Manuscript parts show high alterations such as f sharp, c sharp, g sharp, and c' sharp, for which the proper bassoon keys were made in the eighteenth century.[18]

Although Johann Mattheson stated in 1713 and again in 1739 that 'cornetts and trombones have now completely disappeared from churches, at least the local ones'[19], both instruments were prominent in South Germany and Austria during the first decades of the eighteenth century. This is true of Fux's music in particular, in which the cornett plays a vital role. It was regarded as an essential feature of the instrumentation employed for 'ordinari' music written in the so-called *stylus mediocris* of the period.[20] The usual instrumentation for such church music included four *ripieno*-wind instruments, with cornett, two trombones and bassoons, in addition to the ordinary *basso* grouping of cello, violone and organ. In much of his solemn church music also, Fux retained the wind *ripieno* with cornett: of 290 church music compositions catalogued by Köchel, 107 call for this instrument in unison with the soprano (vocal) part and with the violin and *violino piccolo* (*violetta*) which partake in the *tutti* sections. Nevertheless, as Markus Spielman observes, 'the complete exclusion of the cornett in [Fux's] opera[s], which forms a sharp contrast to its frequent use in church music, shows Fux to be a progressive composer, no longer bound to certain traditions, who avoids any kind of conservatism.'[21]

In those compositions which represent the display of imperial splendour, Fux makes use of the brilliant sound of trumpets and trombones in several real parts which marks so indelibly the *sinfonie* and choruses of the operas; the clarino parts of his arias, on the other hand 'in which he develops an almost breathtaking virtuosity and exploits the high pitch of the instrument in a spectacular manner', demonstrate in detail the composer's delight in (textural) experiment.[22] In the introductory *sinfonie* of the large-scale operas, which are all scored for trumpets and timpani (according to the number of trumpets required during the course of the work), the use of *concertante* style in the two trumpet groupings would appear to be a characteristic feature. The ceremonial style of the court trumpeter's art is incorporated within Fux's music in the *canzona* design of the *sinfonie* (in part). The resulting 'stereophonic' effect is an essential element of Fux's festive operas. This is true of *Angelica vincitrice di Alcina* (1716), *Elisa* (1719) and *Costanza e Fortezza* (1723). Egon Wellesz remarked on this feature of Fux's style in his brief study of the composer, published in 1965:

This antiphonal style goes back . . . to the great Venetians; it derived from the two niches for the choirs and their organ in San Marco. Indeed, at first hearing, the fanfares of the first movement of the *sinfonia* in *Costanza e Fortezza* remind us of those in Monteverdi's Vespers, but the string section in bars 4–6 produces a stronger contrast than any we might find in a work of the Old Venetian school. This string section leads to G major; but in bar 7 Fux brings the piece back to C major by abruptly turning the tonic G into the dominant of C major . . . . Indeed, there is nothing stiff or old-fashioned in the score, and there is no indication from the music that Fux was getting old.[23] (See example 1.)

In Fux's large-scale operas the differentiated use of trumpets in the choral movements is remarkable and to some extent is derived from the tradition of brass scoring established by Antonio Cesti's *Il Pomo d'Oro*, given in Vienna in 1637. Three kinds of chorus predominate in Fux's operas: warlike settings in which the trumpets interject with stylized signals; choruses of

Example 1

praise and worship in which the trumpet scoring is applied in a manner not at all typical of other movements; and choruses of rejoicing which as a rule are intended to accompany the dance, as in the final chorus of *Angelica* and the *Licenza* which closes *Le Nozze di Aurora* (1722), which contains a minuet-like chorus scored for two trumpets, strings and continuo.

The predominant affection always determines the scoring and instrumentation in the arias of these large-scale works. Diana's aria in *Le Nozze di Aurora* in praise of the hunt is appropriately scored for horns and strings, that of Gloria in *Enea negli Elisi* (1731) features a trumpet *obbligato*, the only such instrument to be used soloistically throughout the arias of this opera.[24]

Detlef Altenburg argues that the importance of *Enea* lies not merely in its increased proportions and elaborate scoring and stage presentation (including special machinery and spectacular effects), but also in the increased virtuosity of the trumpet in the work's single *obbligato* aria. *La Corona d'Arianna*, written and performed some five years before *Enea* in 1726, also manifests the importance and dramatic sensitivity of Fux's trumpet scoring. The one *obbligato* aria scored other than for strings and/ or continuo is Bacco's proclamation that his 'famous trumpet should no longer express victory in war', 'Più non empia mie trombe famose/la vittoria con fiato guerriero'. Altenburg continues:

> Bacco is not here the brave warrior or the glorious victor – the loss of the trumpet idiom in both vocal and clarino sections make this clear. Instead, the splendid military victor speaks as a lover. Fux responds to this textual development with an unprecedented degree of virtuosity in the trumpet writing. The first half of the A-section contains (instrumental) melismas that would do credit to a singer; in the second half of this section, Fux leads the trumpet to the extremes of the clarino register, namely, to the twentieth natural tone. From that point (beginning with the twenty-first natural tone), Fux requires the trumpet part to trill in tenths with the singer descending to the twelfth natural tone[25]. (See example 2.)

Example 2

(As far as major–minor tonality applies, the unsteadiness of the third and seventh pitches of the major key become clear when in the trumpet parts of this period the eleventh natural tone is alternately designated as 'f' and 'f' sharp, as in the A-section of this aria. The seventh natural tone is however rarely required, as in the B-section of this number.)[26]

It is no longer considered surprising that the first collection of church music *Messa, Magnificat et Jubilate a 7 chori conc. con le trombe* by Giovanni Valentini was published not in Venice, Bologna or Rome but in Vienna.[27] The Viennese tradition of *Missa solemnis* with trumpets and timpani most certainly developed independently of Italianate precedents. For the most part, this tradition derived from the demanding repertoire of the court trumpeters (the purity of which was modified for the purposes of artificial presentation). In Fux's masses K5, K26, K38 and L4, we find trumpet scoring in four real parts; the mass K2 features such scoring in five parts. The other masses with instrumental accompaniment feature two trumpets (with timpani) and two trombones or, alternatively, two trumpets, cornetts (*cornetto*) and two trombones. The festal masses and *Te Deum* settings reflect the degree of solemnity and occasion in their scoring, which frequently includes trumpets and timpani. The *Te Deum* setting K 270, scored for SATB, two trumpets, timpani, two violins, viola, *ripieno* cornett, two trombones, bassoon, cello, violone and organ, calls for a

Toccata di trombe between verses nineteen and twenty, without providing music for this movement. In this instance, it is understood that the trumpeters would improvise according to well-established patterns, as they frequently had done at state ceremonies and during court festivities.[28]

The use of trumpets in Fux's *serenate* is restricted by comparison with their use in the large-scale operas. Fux either wholly dispensed with trumpets in his smaller secular-dramatic works or called for one or two trumpet parts. Examples of his sparse but effective deployment of this instrument in the arias of his *serenate* may be found in *Julo Ascanio* and *Pulcheria* (1708). The first aria assigned to Teucro in the former opera, 'Vola, vola già di lido in lido' and the aria 'Quanto in campore armato andrai' from *Pulcheria* both vividly illustrate how Fux uses the trumpet in support of the basic affection of the texts in question.

Fux's use of the trombone is generally confined to sacred music. The instrument is to be found in the masses, requiems, vespers, litanies and psalms and in six of the ten wholly extant oratorios. Moreover, it is included in some of the composer's purely instrumental compositions. There is no evidence for its use in Fux's secular-dramatic music. Fux notates the trombone part in alto, tenor or bass clef. It is used as a bass instrument in various *sonate a tre* and in sacred works scored for three trombones; it accompanies the middle voice, *colla parte* (alto and/or tenor) in sacred works and it functions as an *obbligato* instrument, as in the sonata E 68 and in certain arias with trombone scoring in the oratorios. The *Alma Redemptoris* setting K 186, scored for soprano solo and trombone, two violins, bassoon, cello and violone, indicates the degree of proficiency which Fux expected from the instrument. The excerpts shown in Example 3, from the introductory *sonatine* and the setting itself, graphically demonstrate the virtuoso nature of Fux's trombone writing (in *obbligato* terms) and the extent to which the instrument emulates the coloratura style of the vocal writing:[29]

Example 3

Sonatina, bars 14-28

Bars 40-46 & 128-130

Fux's use of the trombone in his *sepolcro* oratorios, destined for performance during Holy Week (Tuesday or Good Friday), is an especially important feature of his wind scoring. The sound of the instrument would appear to be closely identified with the concept of 'suffering and death' in the oratorios, and it is employed as an *obbligato* instrument generally towards the close of the work in question. Klaus Winkler puts the matter as follows:

> The special instrumentation [trombone *obbligato*] seems to be closely connected with the solution of conflict or with the central message of the text, for accompaniment by strings in four parts otherwise predominates. This thesis may be supported by some similarities between the [trombone] arias: 1. All arias are in slow and solemn tempo. 2. All arias are in 3/4 time, with the exception of 'Da Cristo, ch'è si pio' which is in 6/8. 3. Four of the six arias are composed in c-Dorian; the aria 'Dal Limbo' is in B-flat major, the duet 'Chi ti conosce' in B-flat

[Lydian/Major] respectively. Several different trombone scorings may be distinguished among these numbers: vocal part and trombone [with continuo]; vocal part, chalumeau and trombone [with continuo]; vocal part(s), chalumeau, trombone and strings [including continuo] and vocal parts, trombone and strings.[30]

Only two horn players are listed in the registers of the *Hofmusikkapelle* during Fux's tenure at court. In his opera *Elisa*, however, Fux calls for eight trumpeters, two pairs of timpani and four horns (in addition to *colla parte* oboes). 'Hearing these horns and the chorus of the hunters we seem to be listening to a Romantic opera', Egon Wellesz observed in 1965.[31] We can only conclude that military (bugle) players were added to the usual opera orchestra to cope with the kind of exchange shown in Example 4. Fux's comparatively scant attention to the instrument is explained by the fact that the horn was not yet fully developed in this period. Herbert Heyde elaborated on this point in 1987:

> The first part of the eighteenth century may be characterised as an epoch of transition in horn playing, in which old traditions and new tendencies overlap. Apart from the actual protagonists of the French horn there were also people who objected to the sound of horns in the orchestra, as for example Lady Mary (Wortley) Montagu, who mocked at the *deafening noise* of the horns, having attended an opera in Vienna in 1716. This was a period when several types of horn co-existed and competed with each other. The narrow-bore instruments of the period are the older type in the development of the instrument whereas those derived from the Parforce type of horn are younger. Fritz Piersig observed in 1927 the progressive importance of Vienna in the construction and design of the instrument.[32]

We might add that Fux required the F-horn as early as 1706.[33] In the Moravian museum in Brno (ČSSR) a 'pastorella' for SATB, strings and organ and *tuba pastoricia* attributed to Fux is to be found. Hans Oskar Koch describes this latter instrument as a shepherd's horn.[34]

Example 4

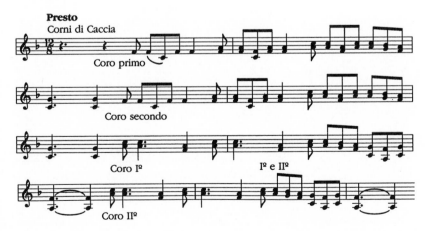

Given the enormous popularity of wind ensembles and the repertoire associated with them today, it is worthwhile to advert to the possibility of reviving interest in Fux's music by means of such ensembles. Fux's music of course can be revived by means of 'authentic' performance on original instruments, but there is also a case to be made for the arrangement of his music for contemporary forces. (The integration of early music in the nineteenth century by means of modern instruments is an instructive precedent.) We know that Fux's music has endured and survived such instrumental alteration in the past. At *Schloss Námest* (Hungary), where Duke Heinrich Wilhelm Haugwitz (1770–1842) maintained a well-equipped orchestral ensemble from 1804 onwards, a copy of Fux's *Missa Corporis Christi* (K 10) is preserved. This copy replaces the original (1713) clarino parts with oboes and clarinets in C and substitutes a flute for the original cornett part.[35] In 1967, Charles Rutherford suggested the possibility of arranging instrumental music by Fux for contemporary wind ensembles.[36] But Fux remains to be discovered by the current renaissance of 'Baroque brass' music, and thus far he has not come to the attention of leading exponents such as the Philip Jones Brass Ensemble. To redress this situation,[37] since 1987 I have been editing a series of 'Fux for Winds' which comprises arrangements from the *Concentus musico-instrumentalis* and other instrumental music for wind ensembles and orchestral groups.

Notes

[1] Hellmut Federhofer, 'Fux und die gleichschwebende Temperatur', *Die Musikforschung* 41 (1988), pp.9–15.

[2] Hellmut Federhofer, '25 Jahre Johann Joseph Fux-Forschung', *Acta musicologica* 52 (1980), pp.155–94, 171.

[3] See Herbert Seifert, 'Die Bläser der Kaiserlichen Hofkapelle zur Zeit von J. J. Fux', *Alta Musica* 9 (1987), pp.19–23.

[4] See Ludwig Ritter von Köchel, *Johann Joseph Fux* (Vienna, 1872, repr. Hildesheim, 1988), p.403.

[5] ibid. p.253ff.

[6] ibid., p.380. Fux made this observation in 1715, and reiterated his high estimation of the trombonist in 1726 and 1727 (see also pp.408 and 410).

[7] ibid., p.389: 'Wan nun dieser Supplicant ein solcher Virtuos ist, dergleichen weder in vergangenen Zeiten, weder vielleicht in zukünfftigen keiner sich finden würd.' Köchel also records (p.403) a testimonial by the composer dated 6 July 1724, in which he refers to

Christian as 'the first virtuoso of this instrument in the world'. (The testimonial/petition in question concerns Christian's son.)

[8] This explains why baroque music composed for the court in Vienna differs considerably in its artistic demands from the *Spielmusiken* of lesser courts. Cf. the music composed by Telemann for Bayreuth, Gotha, Eisenach and Weimar. For further discussion on this point see the present writer's 'Johann Joseph Fux (1660–1741)', *Musica Pannonica* 1, in press.

[9] For the original text and source of this report, see the present writer's 'Harmoniemusik', *Festschrift für Walter Salmen* (Innsbruck, 1991), in press.

[10] See *Relatio historica* 1699–1700 (Frankfurt am Main, 1700), p.9 and *Theatrum Europaeum*, 15 (Frankfurt am Main, 1707), p.547.

[11] See Köchel, *Fux*, p.62.

[12] See Ernst Kubitschek, 'Block- und Querflöte im Umkreis von Johann Joseph Fux – Versuch einer Übersicht', *Alta Musica* 9 (1987), pp.99–119.

[13] John Henry van der Meer, *Johann Joseph Fux als Opernkomponist* (Bilthoven, 1961), vol. I, p.178.

[14] Gunther Joppig, 'Die hohen Holzblasinstrumente (Chalumeau und Oboe) im Schaffen von Johann Joseph Fux', *Alta Musica* 9 (1987), pp.67–87.

[15] The use of oboes is not *always* clear, however, from the manuscript sources of Fux's oratorios in particular.

[16] See *Köchel*, op.cit. p.389.

[17] Joppig, art.cit. pp.68–70.

[18] See Michael Nagy, 'Holzblasinstrumente der tiefen Lage im Schaffen von Johann Joseph Fux', *Alta Musica* 9 (1987), pp.89–98.

[19] See Markus Spielmann, 'Der Zink im Instrumentarium des süddeutsch-österreichischen Raumes', *Alta Musica* 9 (1987), p.121.

[20] See Friedrich W. Riedel, *Kirchenmusik am Hofe Karls VI (1711–1740)* (Munich–Salzburg, 1977), p.146ff.

[21] Spielmann, art.cit., p.141. The cornett does not feature in Fux's oratorios.

[22] Detlef Altenburg, 'Instrumentation im Zeichen des Hofzeremoniells. Bemerkungen zur Verwendung der Trompete im Schaffen von Johann Joseph Fux', *Alta Musica* 9 (1987), pp.157–68; p.168.

[23] Egon Wellesz, *Fux* (London, 1965), p.48. The music example which follows is taken directly from this volume.

[24] See also the survey of Fux's operas by Herbert Seifert, Chapter 8 in the present volume.

[25] Altenburg, art.cit., p.163. The example which follows is taken directly from this article.

[26] There are other demanding sections in the trumpet part of Gloria's aria in *Enea* in which not only the twenty-second natural tone is required on several occasions but also the tenth natural tone (as e^2 flat). Altenburg (ibid., p.164) observes that 'in view of such trumpet parts the virtuoso trumpet concertos of Reutter, Richter and Johann Michael Haydn (which are feared because of their extremely high pitch by players today, even with the benefit of valved instruments), appear in a different light'.

[27] See Riedel, op.cit., p.173.

[28] Köchel, op.cit., Beilage X, p.108, notes that the scoring, design and scope of this setting indicate that it was intended only for great feasts.

[29] ibid., Beilage X, p.81, observes that in the *sonatine* and while accompanying the singer the trombonist is expected to show unusual proficiency.

[30] Klaus Winkler, 'Die Bedeutung der Posaune im Schaffen von Johann Joseph Fux', *Alta*

Musica 9 (1987), pp.177–99; p.185.

[31] Wellesz, op.cit., p.45. The music example is taken directly from this volume.

[32] Herbert Heyde, 'Blasinstrumente und Bläser der Dresdner Hofkapelle in der Zeit des Fux-Schülers Johann Dismas Zelenka', *Alta Musica* 9 (1987), pp.39–65; p.59.

[33] See Horace Fitzpatrick, *The Horn and Horn-Playing in the Austro-Bohemian Tradition from 1680 to 1830* (London, 1970), p.60.

[34] Hans Oskar Koch, *Sonderformen der Blasinstrumente in der deutschen Musik vom späten 17. bis zur Mitte des 18. Jahrhunderts* (Diss., Heidelberg, 1980), p.162.

[35] See Johann Joseph Fux, *Missa Corporis Christi* (1715), K. 10, edited by Hellmut Federhofer (Graz, 1959). Series I, volume 1, *Johann Joseph Fux, Sämtliche Werke.*

[36] See Charles Leonard Rutherford, *The Instrumental Music of Johann Joseph Fux* (Diss., Colorado State College, 1967).

[37] Published by Verlag Schulz, Freiburg im Breisgau.

7 Zur Datierung der Triosonaten und anderer Werke von Fux

Josef-Horst Lederer

Untersucht man die aus der Hofkapelle stammenden und in der Musiksammlung der Österreichischen Nationalbibliothek aufbewahrten Abschriften Fux'scher Werke in Hinblick auf ihre Kopisten, fällt auf, daß nahezu alle Triosonaten sowie zahlreiche andere Kompositionen dieses Meisters in Primärkopien von ein und derselben Schreiberhand vorliegen. Da aufgrund dieser großen (von keinem anderen 'Notisten' auch nur annähernd erreichten) Anzahl von Abschriften im dahinterstehenden Kopisten zweifellos Fuxens Hauptschreiber zu sehen ist und derselbe nach wie vor (s. u.) als anonym gelten muß, soll in vorliegendem Beitrag der Versuch unternommen werden, dessen 'Inkognito' zu lüften und die damit verbundenen Konsequenzen für die Werkdatierung bei Fux aufzuzeigen, wobei bezüglich letzterer darüber hinaus auch noch Überlegungen anderer Natur anzustellen sein werden. Erleichtert wird dieses Bemühen dadurch, daß bereits Walter Gleißner das Kopistenproblem bei Fux im Rahmen seiner Arbeit über dessen Vespern in verdienstvoller Weise in Angriff genommen hat[1] und dabei zu bemerkenswerten, Anregung und gleichzeitig auch Basis zu vorliegender Untersuchung gebenden Resultaten gelangte, wenngleich gerade in der Frage nach jenem Schreiber, der die meisten Abschriften der Vespern anfertigte – und hinter diesem steckt nach dem Schriftduktus ja auch der gesuchte Hauptkopist des Wiener Hofkapellmeisters – keine befriedigende Antwort gefunden werden konnte.[2] Und letzteres ist es auch, was schließlich nochmals (und nicht nur auf die Vespern bezogen) zu fragen berechtigt, welcher von den wenigen, diesbezüglich zur Wahl stehenden Kopisten der Hofkapelle (HK), wie Anton Salcki, Andreas Amiller, Andreas Abendt, aber auch Kielian Reinhardt,[3] Fuxens bevorzugter Schreiber gewesen sein könnte. Da es keine direkten Beweise gibt, also keine Schriftzeugnisse vorliegen, die eine zweifelsfreie Zuordnung erlauben, und auch keiner dieser Schreiber seine Arbeiten signiert hat, kann eine Lösung des Problems nur auf indirektem Wege erfolgen: d.h., es ist zu untersuchen, inwiefern sich die Zeitspanne, in welche die überlieferten Abschriften jenes Hauptkopisten von Fux (vorläufig mit X bezeichnet) fallen, mit Lebensdaten, Anstellungszeitraum und Beschäftigungsart in der Hofkapelle, oder mit sonstigen, die genannten vier Persönlichkeiten betreffenden Fakten jeweils in Einklang oder nicht in Einklang bringen läßt. Zumal dabei naturgemäß die frühesten und spätesten Belege für die Hand von X von entscheidender Bedeutung sind, ist es vorerst einmal notwendig, dieselben aufzulisten, um im Anschluß daran anhand einer Gegenüberstellung bzw. eines Vergleichs mit den einzelnen Kopisten eine Entscheidung zu treffen.

Die frühesten Schriftzeugnisse für den Kopisten X^4 datieren vermutlich bereits aus einer Zeit, in der noch Johann Heinrich Schmelzer Vice- bzw. Hofkapellmeister war. Es sind dies eine Abschrift von dessen Sepolcro *Die Stärke der Liebe* (1677) sowie Kopien von Antonio Draghis Sepolcri *Le trè chiodi* (1678; s. Abb. 1) und *Il titolo posto sù la croce di Christo* (1679; s. Abb. 2), bei denen zumindest Noten und Generalbaßbezifferung (also der Worttext ausgenommen) mit hoher Wahrscheinlichkeit auf eine Autorschaft von X als Schreiber schließen lassen. Vor und nach Draghis Antritt als Hofkapellmeister – und hier wie in der Folge bestehen keinerlei Zweifel mehr – kopierte X für denselben die Oper *Temistocle in Persia* (1681; s. Abb. 3) sowie das Sepolcro *La vita nella morte* (1688)[5]. Unter Marc' Antonio Ziani als Hofkapellmeister schrieb X u.a. dessen *Confitebor* (HK 17410) und *Dixit et Laudate Pueri* (HK 17427) – alle vor 1715, dem Todesjahr Zianis.

Bei Fux fallen die frühesten gesicherten Belege (für X) in dessen Zeit als *Compositore* (1698–1711) – und zwar die Triosonate K 368 = K 362 (s. Abb. 4a und 4b),[6] das Oratorium *La fede sacrilega nella morte del Precursor S.Giov.Battista* (K 291) und die Oper *Pulcheria* (K 303; s. Abb. 5), beide 1708. Die spätesten Quellen (dies gilt für X auch im allgemeinen) stammen aus den Jahren 1726–29. Was die zahlreichen, innerhalb dieser Zeitspanne von rund 20 Jahren liegenden (jedoch nur soweit erforderlich hier angeführten) Abschriften von Fux' Kompositionen durch X betrifft, sei in besonderer Weise darauf hingewiesen, daß letzterer auch eine Stimmen-Kopie des *Te Deum* K 270 (s. Abb. 6a und 6b) angefertigt hat, was in Hinblick auf deren exakte Datierbarkeit mit dem Jahre 1723 ein wichtiges Kriterium für die Entscheidung in eingangs gestellter Frage darstellen wird. Nach 1729 – und dies betrifft sowohl Fux als auch andere Komponisten aus der HK – lassen sich von X angefertigte Abschriften, welche die Annahme einer Entstehung später als zu diesem Zeitpunkt erlauben würden, nicht mehr nachweisen.[7] Zu dieser Feststellung berechtigt die Durchführung zahlreicher, mit jeweils negativem Resultat erfolgter 'Stichproben'.

Bei den nunmehr vorzustellenden, oben genannten Persönlichkeiten soll jener Schreiber an der Spitze stehen, dem (wie bereits in Fn. 2 erwähnt) schon eimal 'die Ehre widerfahren' ist, mit X (zumindest als Hauptkopist der Vespern von Fux) in Verbindung gebracht zu werden.

Anton Salcki (Salchi) wurde 1649 geboren und starb am 1. Oktober 1722 in Wien.[8] Laut einer vom damaligen Hofkapellmeister Antonio Draghi befürworteten Eingabe im Obersthofmeisteramt vom 12.4.1682 wird er in diesem Jahr offiziell als Violinist, Violaspieler und Kopist an der HK angestellt.[9] In einer weiteren Eingabe vom 8.6.1687 berichtet Draghi, daß Salcki 'alle Compositionen deß Capellmeister[s] mit höchster müehe zu

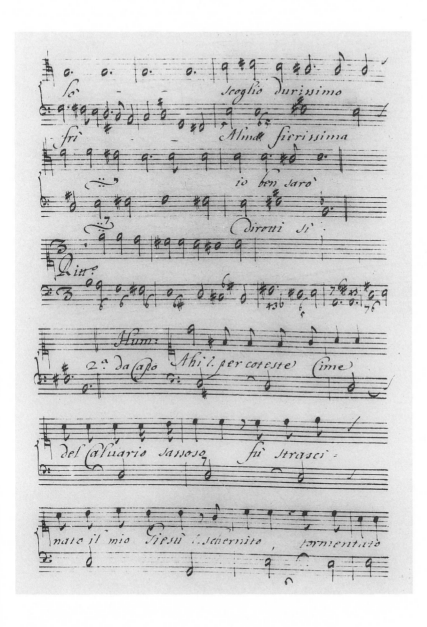

Abb. 1 Schriftprobe aus Antonio Draghis Sepolcro *Le trè chiodi* (1678)

Plate 1. Handwriting sample from Antonio Draghi's Sepolcro, *Le trè Chiodi* (1678)

Abb. 2 Schriftprobe aus Antonio Draghis Sepolcro *Il titolo posto sù la croce di Christo* (1679)

Plate 2. Handwriting sample from Antonio Draghi's Sepolcro, *Il titolo posto sù la croce di Christo* (1679)

Abb. 3 Beginn des 2. Aktes aus A. Draghis Oper *Temistocle in Persia* (1681). [Die dritte und fünfte Textzeile stammt von anderer Hand]

Plate 3. Beginning of the second act of Draghi's opera, *Temistocle in Persia* (1681) (The third and fifth lines of text belong to another hand.)

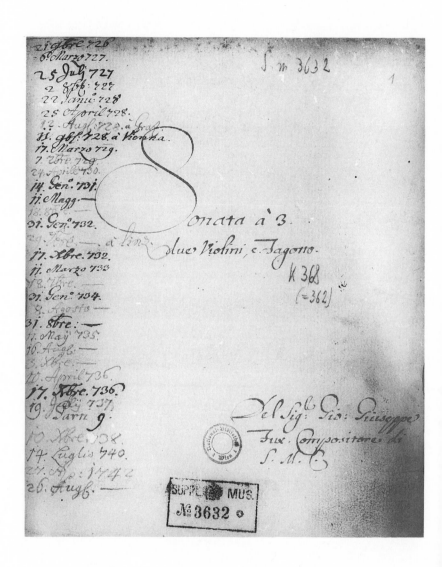

Abb. 4a. Titelblatt der *Sonata à tre* K 368 = K 362 (vor 1711)

Plate 4a. Title page of the *Sonata à tre*, K.368 = K.362 (before 1711)

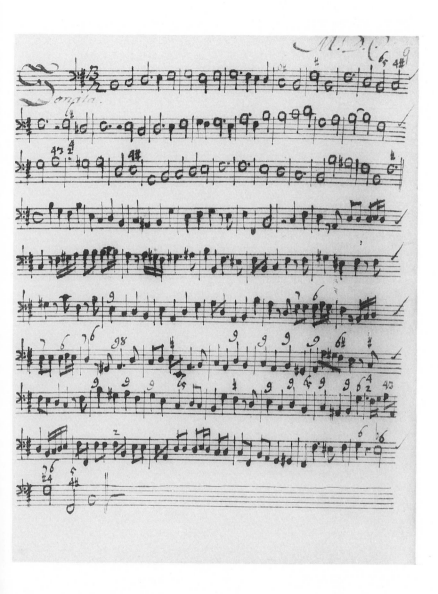

Abb. 4b. Aus derselben Sonate: M.D.C.-Stimme

Plate 4b. From the same sonata: the M(aestro) D.(i) C.(appella) part

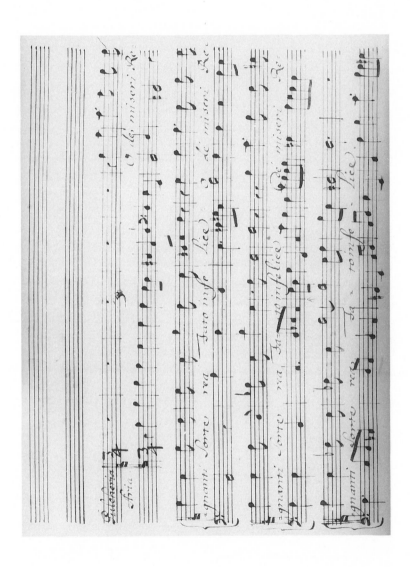

Abb. 5. Schriftprobe aus der Oper *Pulcheria* K 303 (1708)

Plate 5. Handwriting sample from the opera *Pulcheria*, K303 (1708)

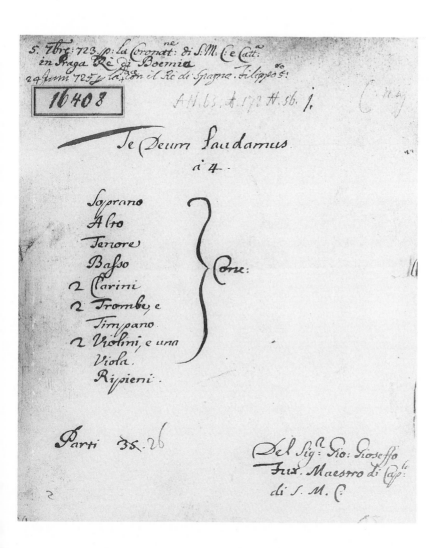

Abb. 6a. Titelblatt des *Te Deum* K 270 (1723)

Plate 6a. Title-page of the *Te Deum*, K 270 (1723)

Abb. 6b. Aus demselben Werk: Beginn der Sopranstimme

Plate 6b. From the same work: beginning of the soprano part

ständen schreiben müsße',[10] was auch aus einer neuerlichen Eingabe vom 28.8.1698[11] hervorgeht und darauf schließen läßt, daß Salcki damals Hauptkopist des Hofkapellmeisters gewesen ist. Mit 1. Oktober 1711 erfolgt seine Pensionierung als Musiker, wobei aber anzunehmen ist, daß er als Kopist fallweise noch weiter tätig war.[12] Nach seinem Ableben kommt seine Witwe Barbara mit Datum vom 6. März 1723 um die 'gewändliche genaden pension' ein, was von Fux ob der 40jährigen Tätigkeit Salckis sehr befürwortet wird.[13] Sein Testament – ausschließlich kurrent abgefaßt, was einen Schriftvergleich mit dem lateinisch geschriebenen Text in Abschriften von Fux'schen Vokalkompositionen durch X nicht zuläßt – ist mit 26. Sept. 1722 datiert und wird im Archiv der Stadt Wien (4707/722) aufbewahrt.

Andreas Amiller, der zweite oben angeführte Kopist, wurde 1681 geboren und starb 69jährig am 27. Oktober 1750 in Wien.[14] Zuvor 'vielle iahre in der Kay. Amalischen Capellen alss würklicher Tenor' beschäftigt,[15] bewirbt er sich in einer Eingabe vom 22. Dez. 1722 um die Nachfolge der durch den Tod Salckis frei gewordenen Kopistenstelle, wobei aus Fuxens Stellungnahme[16] dazu hervorgeht, daß Amiller dem Salcki schon 'in dass eylffte iahr [also ab 1711] in Copirn Beyhilff geleistet' hat. Dem Ansuchen Amillers wird stattgegeben, doch überträgt man ihm damals nur die Kapell-, nicht aber die Theatral-Kopiatur.[17] Letztere bekommt Andreas Johann Ziss (1692–1755). Beide, Amiller und Ziss, werden 1729 in dieser Funktion bestätigt.[18] Amiller wird 1729 noch zusätzlich – als Nachfolger des in diesem Jahr verstorbenen Kilian Reinhardt (s. u.) – zum 'Concert-dispensator' ernannt.[19]

Andreas Abendt, der dritte Schreiber, wurde 1656 geboren und verstarb 73jährig am 3. Dez. 1729 in Wien.[20] Er tritt mit Beginn des Jahres 1677 als Kopist in die kaiserliche Hofkapelle ein, und zwar auf Empfehlung des damaligen Vicekapellmeisters Schmelzer, der bezugnehmend auf Abendts Ansuchen um Anstellung in dieser Funktion darauf hinweist, daß dieser 'auch Zeithero [also bereits vor 1677] beym Notirn und ballett-geign Das seinige gethan hat'.[21] Was seine offizielle Anstellung als Geiger in der HK betrifft, gibt Köchel[22] zwar das Jahre 1686 an, doch muß dieselbe gleichfalls 1677 erfolgt sein, da es in einer Eingabe Abendts um Gehaltserhöhung vom 12. April 1682 heißt, daß er sich bereits 'fünf iahre mit abschreibung der Musicalischen Stucke, und dem Violin gebrauchen' habe lassen.[23] In Zusammenhang mit zahlreichen weiteren Eingaben bis zum Jahre 1705 – es geht immer wieder um Gehaltserhöhungen – kann Abendt stets großes Lob ernten, wobei des öfteren in besonderer Weise hervorgehoben wird, daß er zwei Dienste gleichzeitig (nämlich als Kopist und Violinist) zu versehen habe.[24] Bei Fux findet Abendt (im Gegensatz zu Salcki und Reinhardt) in den von Köchel (Fux, Beil. VI, S.376ff.) vorgelegten Zeugnissen keine Erwähnung, was umso mehr zu bedauern ist, als aufgrund des (bekanntlichen) Fehlens der Bestände des kaiserl. Obersthofmeisteramts nach 1705 von ihm nichts weiter in Erfahrung zu bringen ist. Letztmals wird Abendt im 'Verzeichnuß der Kay[n] Music Ende Septemb. 1729' als 'hohen Alters impotens'[25] genannt. Aus seinem Testament (Archiv der Stadt Wien 5122/729) geht hervor, daß er eine Tochter Maria Anna (verh. Lenz) hatte, seine

Frau Katharina Barbara hieß und bei der Abfassung von dessen letzter Verfügung 'alß erbettener Zeüg' der bekannte HK-Posaunist Leopold Christian fungierte.[26] Genanntes Testament ist überwiegend in Kurrentschrift abgefaßt, läßt aber dennoch (wenngleich in nur sehr eingeschränktem Maße) einen Vergleich mit der Hand von X zu (s. u.).

Über **Killian Reinhardt**, kaiserlicher Partausteiler, 'musicalischer Concertmeister' und Vater einer ganzen Generation von hervorragenden Musikern, ist relativ viel bekannt,[27] sodaß hier nur zur Sprache kommen soll, was seine in vorliegendem Zusammenhang von Interesse erscheinenden Aktivitäten in der Hofkapelle betrifft. 1653 geboren und 76jährig am 25. März 1729 (also im selben Jahr wie Abendt!) in Wien verstorben, erfolgt im Jahre 1683 unter Leopold I. seine Ernennung zum *dispensatore de'concerti* – und zwar unter der Bedingung, daß er sich auch 'obligir[en] müste, die alte[n] compositiones der Capelle widerumb abzuschreiben, welches sehr nothwendig, und sonst[en] viele 100.fl. Kosten dörffte'.[28] Da er in der diesbezüglichen Eingabe vom 4. Februar bereits als 'Notist' bezeichnet wird, muß er schon vor diesem Zeitpunkt für die Hofkapelle kopiert haben, und man verlangte von ihm praktisch nur die Fortführung einer schon zuvor (inoffiziell?) ausgeübten Tätigkeit neben der neuen Aufgabe. 1699 darf er sich 'sogenannter musicalischer Concertmeister' nennen, 1727 schreibt er für Karl VI. die 'Rubriche Generali', ein kaligraphisches Zeremonial, in dem die kirchenmusikalischen Funktionen der HK für das ganze Jahr zusammengestellt werden, wozu er aufgrund seiner Erfahrung und langjährigen Tätigkeit in der HK wohl besser als jeder andere geeignet gewesen sein dürfte. Aus letzterem Grunde hatte man ihn ja schon zuvor – bei Regierungsantritt Karls VI. – in die Kommission zur Neubildung der Hofmusik berufen. Fux hat ihn offensichtlich geschätzt, da er dessen Verdienste anläßlich eines Ansuchens (15.4.1728) um eine Gnadenpension für Frau und Kinder würdigt.[29]

Gilt es nun bei diesen vier musikalisch Bediensteten der Hofkapelle abzuwägen, welcher von ihnen als Hauptkopist Fuxens (X) in Frage kommt, wäre das jeweilige 'für und wider' wie folgt darzulegen bzw. zu begründen.

Johann Anton Salcki wurde offiziell erst 1682 an der HK angestellt (dürfte dort zuvor aber schon inoffiziell als Kopist gearbeitet haben), die frühesten Zeugnisse für X fallen aber bereits in die Jahre 1677–81: es ist äußerst unwahrscheinlich, daß man eine so umfangreiche Komposition wie z.B. Draghis Oper *Temistocle in Persia* (1681) einem 'Anfänger' bzw. 'Aushilfskopisten' anvertraut hat. Salcki ging in einer Zeit in Pension (1711), da X gerade am aktivsten gewesen sein dürfte. Und schließlich das wichtigste: er starb 1722 – die Hand von X läßt sich aber auch noch später mit etlichen Neukopien wie z.B. mit dem *Te Deum* K 270 aus dem Jahre 1723 (s. Abb. 6a und. 6b) nachweisen. Salcki ist demnach auszuscheiden!

Andreas Amiller wurde 1681 geboren, also in jenem Jahr, in dem X die Abschrift von Draghis *Temistocle in Persia* anfertigte, womit sich jede weitere Argumentation erübrigt und auch er ausgeschieden werden kann.

Kilian Reinhardt wurde 1683 (also noch später als Salcki) als Partausteiler mit der zusätzlichen Bedingung angestellt, 'alte compositiones der Capelle widerumb abzuschreiben', was wohl nur bedeuten kann, daß er nicht Neukopien anzufertigen, sondern lediglich älteres (lädiertes?) Notenmaterial neu ('widerumb') zu schreiben oder (bei Bedarf) zu vervielfältigen hatte. Allerdings mag ernsthaft bezweifelt werden, daß er in dieser Funktion nach 1683 überhaupt je nennenswert zum Einsatz kam, da in allen weiteren, bei Knaus[30] noch angeführten Eingaben nie mehr von einer Kopistentätigkeit Reinhardts die Rede ist und derselbe nur noch als 'dispensatore de'concerti' bzw. als 'musicalischer Concertmeister' genannt wird. Wäre es später tatsächlich auch noch zu einer (zusätzlichen) Tätigkeit als Notenschreiber gekommen, so hätte Reinhardt, der in jedem seiner Ansuchen beim Obersthofmeisteramt seine Arbeitsüberlastung hervorstrich (um dadurch zum mehr Gehalt zu kommen bzw. die Beistellung eines Gehilfen zu erwirken), sicherlich nicht versäumt, ein zusätzliches 'Druckmittel' dieser Art einzusetzen, d.h. gebührend darauf hinzuweisen. Und auch Fux hätte bei seiner Befürwortung genannten Ansuchens eine allfällige Kopiertätigkeit Reinhardts namhaft gemacht, was jedoch nicht geschah – sehr wohl aber bei einer ähnlichen Eingabe für die Witwe Salckis (s. o.) der Fall gewesen ist. Schließlich – und dies dürfte wohl am meisten ins Gewicht fallen – läßt sich Reinhardts Schriftduktus, wie er in den *Rubriche Generali* (s. Abb. 7) vorliegt, nicht in Übereinstimmung bringen mit jenem des Kopisten X, den (Wort-)Text in dessen Abschriften vokaler Werke Fuxens betreffend. Auch er kann demnach mit gutem Grund ausgeschlossen werden.

Bleibt schließlich noch der von allen vier Kopisten am längsten in der Hofkapelle dienende Andreas Abendt: er ist der einzige, der mit dem offiziellen Anstellungsjahr 1677 als Schreiber der oben genannten Werke von Schmelzer und Draghi vor 1682 bzw. 1683 (den Anstellungsjahren von Salcki und Reinhardt) in Frage kommt, er stirbt aber auch zu einem Zeitpunkt (1729), ab welchem (wie erwähnt) Abschriften von X nur noch mit erneuerten und von anderer Hand beschriebenen Umschlägen bzw. Titelblättern (also keine Neukopien) vorliegen, auf welche Weise von ihm genau jener Zeitraum (1677–1729) abgedeckt wird,[31] in den die Aktivitäten des Kopisten X fallen. Kommt noch hinzu, daß die (wenngleich) wenigen in Lateinschrift abgefaßten Textpassagen in seinem an sich kurrent geschriebenen Testament bestimmte auffällige Charakteristika (u.a. z.B. die Großbuchstaben *A, J* und *T* oder die Verschlingung der Buchstaben *C* und h als *Ch*; s. Abb. 8a und 8b und vgl. damit z.B. Abb. 12) aufweisen, die typisch für den (Wort-)Text in Abschriften von X sind,[32] womit insgesamt – eine weitere Persönlichkeit bietet sich diesbezüglich nicht an – keine Zweifel mehr bestehen, daß sich hinter Fuxens, bisher 'namenlosen' ersten Kopisten Andreas Abendt verbirgt.[33]

Kann demnach (wenngleich auf indirektem Wege) eines der vordringlichsten Probleme im Gesamtkomplex der Kopistenfrage bei Fux als gelöst betrachtet werden, sind in weiterer Folge die daraus resultierenden Konsequenzen für die jeweilige Entstehungszeit davon betroffener Werke des Hofkapellmeisters aufzuzeigen,[34] wobei gleichzeitig (wie eingangs angekündigt) auch andere, für die Datierung Fux'scher Werke gleichfalls neue Aspekte eröffnende Beobachtungen eingebracht bzw. zur Diskussion

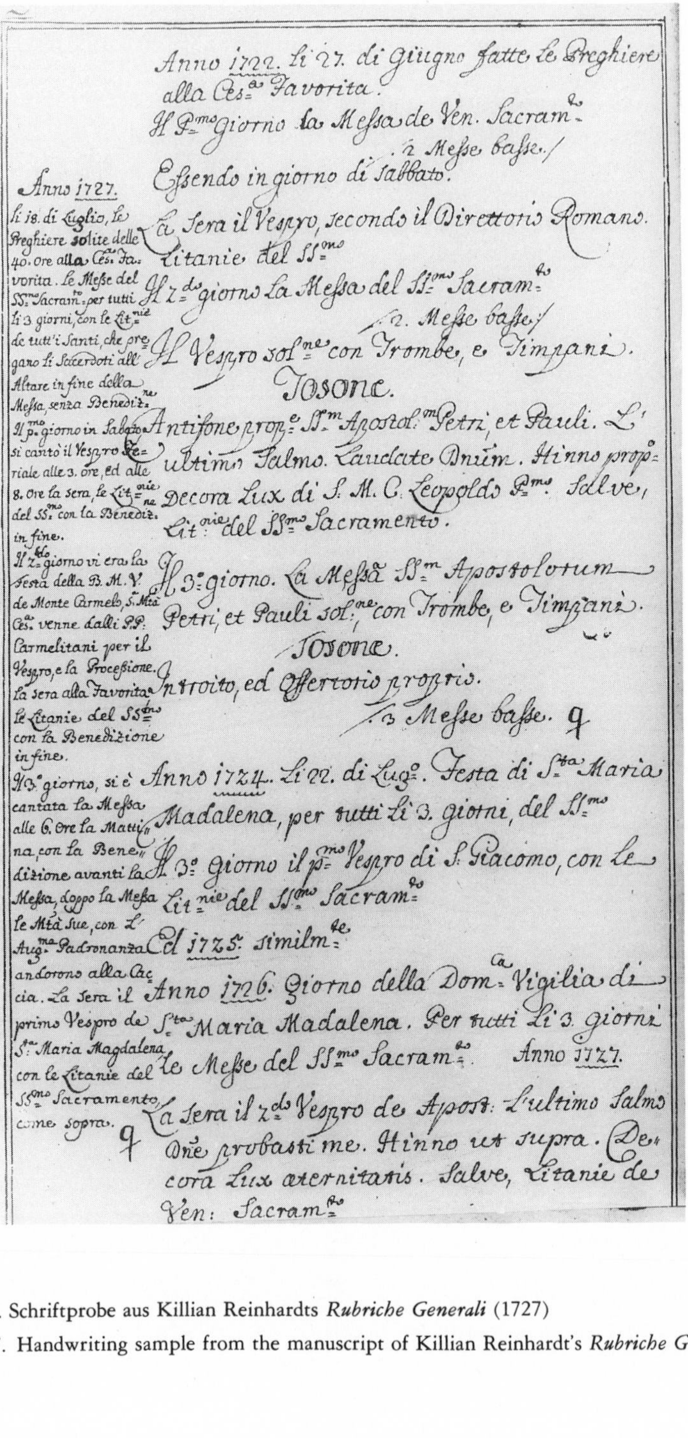
Anno 1722. Li 27. di Giugno fatte le Preghiere alla Ces.a Favorita.
Il P.mo giorno la Messa de Ven. Sacram.to
2 Messe basse.
Essendo in giorno di Sabbato.
La Sera il Vespro, secondo il Direttorio Romano.
Litanie del SS.mo
Il 2.do giorno la Messa del SS.mo Sacram.to
2. Messe basse.
Il Vespro sol.ne con Trombe, e Timpani.
Tosone.
Antifone prop.e SS.m Apostol.m Petri, et Pauli. L'ultimo Salmo. Laudate Dnum. Hinno propo. Decora Lux di S. M. C. Leopoldo P.mo Salve, Lit.nie del SS.mo Sacramento.
Il 3.o giorno. La Messa SS.m Apostolorum Petri, et Pauli sol.ne con Trombe, e Timpani.
Tosone.
Introito, ed Offertorio proprio.
3 Messe basse. 9
Anno 1724. Li 22. di Lug.o Festa di S.ta Maria Madalena, per tutti Li 3. giorni, del SS.mo
Il 3.o giorno il P.mo Vespro di S. Giacomo, con le Lit.nie del SS.mo Sacram.to
Ed 1725. simil.te
Anno 1726. Giorno della Dom.ca Vigilia di S.ta Maria Madalena. Per tutti Li 3. giorni le Messe del SS.mo Sacram.to Anno 1727.
La sera il 2.do Vespro de Apost. L'ultimo Salmo Dne probasti me. Hinno ut supra. Decora Lux aeternitatis. Salve, Litanie de Ven. Sacram.to

Anno 1727. Li 18. di Luglio, le Preghiere solite delle 40. ore alla Ces. Favorita. le Messe del SS.mo Sacram.to per tutti li 3 giorni, con le Lit.nie de tutti i Santi, che pregano li Sacerdoti all'Altare in fine della Messa, senza Benediz.ne
Il p.mo giorno in Sabbato si cantò il Vespro feriale alle 3. ore, ed alle 8. ore la sera, le Lit.nie del SS.mo con la Benediz.ne in fine.
Il 2.do giorno vi era la Festa della B. M. V. de Monte Carmelo, S. M.tà Ces.a venne dalli P.P. Carmelitani per il Vespro, e la Procesione. La sera alla Favorita le Litanie del SS.mo con la Benedizione in fine.
Il 3.o giorno, si è cantata la Messa alle 6. ore la Mattina, con la Benedizione avanti la Messa, doppo la Messa le M.tà Sue, con L'Aug.ma Padronanza andorono alla Caccia. La sera il primo Vespro de S.ta Maria Magdalena con le Litanie del SS.mo Sacramento come sopra. 9

Abb. 7. Schriftprobe aus Killian Reinhardts *Rubriche Generali* (1727)

Plate 7. Handwriting sample from the manuscript of Killian Reinhardt's *Rubriche Generali* (1727)

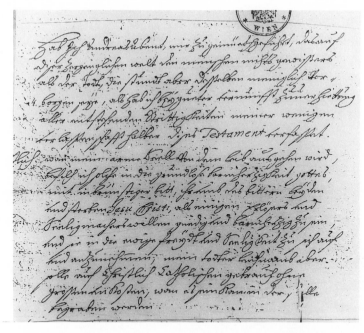

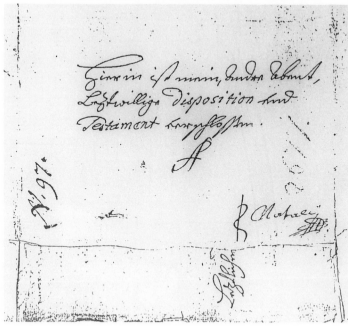

Abb. 8a. u.b. Schriftproben aus dem Testament von Andreas Abendt

Plates 8a and 8b. Handwriting samples from the will of Andreas Abendt

Abb. 9. Schriftprobe aus der Sonata à tre K 387: Schluß der Fagott-Stimme
Plate 9. Handwriting sample from the *Sonata à tre*, K.387. End of the bassoon part

gestellt werden sollen. Die am meisten aufgeführte und auch nahezu ausschließlich durch die Feder Abendts in Form von Primärquellen überlieferte Werkgruppe der Triosonaten möge dabei an den Beginn gestellt werden.

Für die Triosonaten bedeutet dies vorerst einmal, daß von denselben alle von Abendt (alias X) verfertigten, aus der HK stammenden und entweder in der ÖNB oder an einem anderen Ort überlieferten (Stimmen-) Abschriften, deren Aufführungsvermerke erst nach dem Tode dieses Kopisten (also nach dem Dez. 1729) einsetzten, vor diesen Zeitpunkt zu datieren sind. Für die nachstehenden 17 Sonaten liegt somit mit dem Jahre 1729 ein sicherer *terminus ante quem* vor, wobei es sich hier – da Abendt in der Regel auch jeweils das Titelblatt selbst geschrieben hat – naturgemäß nicht um Abschriften mit originalen, sondern erneuerten, ja z.T. nochmals erneuerten Umschlägen handelt:

K 339[35] aufgef. von:	1737–47	12[Anzahl der Aufführungen]
K 351	1747–53	2[nür dis Sonata I]
K 379 = K 361	1732–51	10
K 371	1734–42	21
K 374	1733–47	34
K 376	1730–52	6
K 377	1731–37	6
K 378	1731–47	38
K 379	1732–51	10
K 380	1732–42	32
K 381	1732–46	31
K 382	1735–47	26
K 384	1749	2
K 385	1749–53	5
K 386	1738–44	8
K 387	1739–53	25 (s. Abb. 9)
K 388	1747–52	6

Eine weitere Gruppe von 8 Triosonaten – gleichfalls aus der Hand von Abendt (was hier aber nur von sekundärer Bedeutung ist) – fällt dadurch auf, daß die jeweils ersten Aufführungsvermerke auf den Umschlägen der (Stimmen-)Abschriften in den knappen Zeitraum von drei Monaten, nämlich von November 1726 bis Jänner 1727, fallen. Auf den ersten Blick könnte dieser Umstand vielleicht zur Annahme verleiten, Fux habe in dieser kurzen Zeit 8 *Sonate à tre* komponiert, doch erübrigen sich sofort alle diesbezüglichen Spekulationen, wenn sich bei näherer Untersuchung herausstellt, daß noch 24 weitere Abschriften Fux'scher Kompositionen (sowohl von Abendt als auch von anderen Kopisten, und verschiedenste Werkgattungen betreffend) den Beginn ihrer Aufführungsvermerke ähnlich komprimiert auf die Zeitspanne von Oktober 1726 bis Juli 1727 verteilen Denn: fällt die Schaffung von 8 Triosonaten in so kurzer Zeit schon kaum mehr in den Bereich des Vorstellbaren, so ist völlig undenkbar, daß Fux innerhalb von 8 Monaten insgesamt 32 Werke – darunter umfangreiche Messen, Magnificat, Motetten, etc. – komponiert hat, was demnach nur bedeuten kann, daß diese alle wesentlich früher entstanden sein müssen-, deren jeweils an erster Stelle stehende Aufführungsdaten nicht auch gleichzeitig die Entstehungszeit der Werke signalisieren. Bereits Köchel[36] war dieser Sachverhalt aufgefallen und er hat ihn auch sofort richtig dahingehend interpretiert, daß dahinter nur eine mehr oder weniger simultane Erneuerung der Umschläge bzw. Titelblätter des Notenmaterials stecken könne. Man muß also damals (höchstwahrscheinlich ab Herbst 1726), wohl im Rahmen einer (Archiv-)Revision und zweifellos recht rigoros, mit Aufführungsvermerken vollgeschriebene bzw. stark lädierte Umschläge durch neue ersetzt haben, wobei diese 'Restaurierungs-kampagne' auch nicht nur die Werke des Hofkapellmeisters sondern auch jene anderer Komponisten der HK betroffen haben dürfte, zumal etliche Beispiele darauf hinweisen.[37] Und daß man damals wirklich 'rigoros' vorgegangen sein muß, also nicht (wie sonst üblich) erst aus gegebenem Anlaß einer Aufführung einen unbrauchbar gewordenen Umschlag auswechselte, darauf deutet auch die Existenz von Abschriften mit erneuerten Umschlägen ohne Aufführungsdaten hin:[38] Mit diesem Merkmal behaftete Werke – vormals fraglos häufig gespielt, was die Abnützungsspuren (besonders K 257) nur allzu deutlich zeigen – kamen eben (aus welchen Gründen auch immer) nach dem Zeitpunkt der Umschlagserneuerung überhaupt nicht mehr zur Aufführung-, im Gegensatz zu jenen anderen Kompositionen (mit erneuerten Umschlägen), die entweder sofort bzw. relativ bald (1726/27) oder erst nach und nach (bis in die Jahre 1728/29 hinein) wieder erklangen.

Verantwortlich für diese Neuordnung bzw. Revision des Archivs der HK dürften damals in erster Linie wohl der bereits genannte Concert-dispensator Kilian Reinhardt sowie der ihm zu dieser Zeit beigestellte Gehilfe Andreas Amiller gewesen sein, doch scheint sich auch Andreas Abendt daran beteiligt zu haben: Denn Abendt, der (wie erwähnt) auch die Titelblätter seiner Abschriften stets selbst schrieb, hat hier offensichtlich den Ehrgeiz gehabt, bei seinen eigenen Abschriften auch die ausge-wechselten Umschläge neuerlich selbst zu beschriften, was sowohl bei den 8 Triosonaten als auch bei den übrigen genannten 24 Werken fast ausschließlich der Fall ist und sogar noch später, bis in das Jahr seines Todes hinein (1729) durch Beispiele belegt werden kann.[39]

Im Folgenden die Aufstellung oben charakterisierter Abschriften der 8 Triosonaten Fux' aus der Hand von Abendt (mit – wie angeführt – fast ausschließlich von diesem selbst erneuerten Umschlägen), deren Ent-stehung aus genannten Gründen jeweils einige Jahre vor 1726 angesetzt werden könnte:[40]

K 368 = K 362	21. XI.	1726–42	42 (s. Abb. 4a und. 4b)
K 366 = K 363	6. XII.	1726–39	16
K 365	11. XII.	1726–39	25
K 367 = K 375	25. XI.	1726–44	36
K 370	18. XII.	1726–44	27
K 372	Jänner	1727–40	25 (Titelbl. nicht v. Abendt.)
K 395	26. XII.	1726–46	4
K 396	27. XII.	1726–49	6
[K 373	?	1727–47	30 (Titelbl. nicht v. Abendt)][41]

(Eine ähnlich auffällige Kummulierung der Aufführungsdaten innerhalb eines kleinen, allerdings späteren Zeitraums läßt sich auch noch bei den Abschriften einer weiteren Gruppe von 5 Triosonaten (K 389–93) beobachten. Sie stammen gleichfalls aus der HK, sind von ein und demselben Kopisten (?) geschrieben, und bei ihnen fallen die jeweils ersten Aufführungsvermerke in die Zeit zwischen 5. und 22. April des Jahres 1731, was in Hinblick auf naheliegende analoge Überlegungen zu der oben mit 1726/27 ins Auge gefaßten Archiv-Revision – mit gebotener Vorsicht – fragen läßt, ob nicht auch hier eine frühere Entstehungszeit anzunehmen ist.)

Verfährt man nunmehr analog zu den Triosonaten bei anderen Werkgattungen Fux', kann in einem ersten Schritt für folgende (Stimmen-) Abschriften, die von Abendt angefertigt wurden und mit ihren Aufführungsvermerken jeweils erst nach dem Tode dieses Kopisten einsetzen, wiederum mit 1729 ein sicherer *terminus ante quem* bestimmt werden. Naturgemäß sind auch hier wieder (mit wenigen, aber begründbaren Ausnahmen) die Titeleien der erneuerten Umschläge nicht mehr von Abendt selbst geschrieben:

Messen

K 6	*Missa Brevium ultima*	1731–43	24
K 8	*M. Confidentiae*	1740–51	2
K 16	*M. Fuge perversum mundum*	1730–32	3(auch Titelbl. von Abendt)[42]
K 17	*M. Humilitatis*	1733–40	20
K 33	*M. Sancti Caroli*	1732–40	5
K 35	*M. Sancti Josephi*	1733–41	16
K 42	*M. Una ex duodecim*	1733–39	12
K 52	*Dies irae*	1731–43	8
[K 53	*Domine Jesu Christe*	1731–43	7]

Vespern und Psalmen

K 60	Vesperae de Confessore	1755	1
K 61	*V. de Confessore*	1749–55	16
K 62	*V. de Confessore*	1740–64	11
K 65	*V. de B.M.V.*	1733–40	27
K 66	*V. de B.M.V.*	1755	4
K 72	*Dixit Dominus*	1732–38	3
K 75	*Dixit Dominus*	1732–50	23
K 76	*Dixit Dominus – Confitebor*	1740–55	10
K 80	*Beatus vir*	1736–42	5
K 82	*Beatus vir – Laudate pueri*	1740–46	8
K 85	*Laudate pueri*	1733–36	2
K 87	*Laudate pueri*	1736–40	5
K 89	*Laudate pueri*	1735–40	6
K 92	*Laudate Dominum*	1733–40	6
K 94	*Laudate Dominum. Magnificat*	1740–44	4
K 102	*Laetatus sum*	1735–39	5

Litaneien – Completorien

K 115	*Litaniae Lauretanae*	1744–54	2(s. Abb. 10)
K 116	*L. L.*	1744–53	13
K 117	*L. L.*	1740–57	7
K 118	*L. L.*	1743–75	74(nur z.T. v. Abendt)
K 121	*Litaniae. Sancta Maria*	1739–40	2
K 122	*Litaniae Lauretanae. Mater Divinae Gratiae*	1731–52	17

Motetten

K 165	*Mottetto de Resurrectione Domini*	1736–40	2
K 166	*M. de Resurrectione Domini. Ecce sacerdos magnus*	1735–37	3
K 170	*M. de Spiritu Sancto*	1737–49	15
K 179	*M. de Confessore. Justum deduxit Dominus*	1735–47	29
K 181	*M. de quovis Sancto. Celebremus cum gaudio*	1749	2

Hymnen

K 189	*Alma Redemptoris*	–	(auch Titelbl. von Abendt)[43]
K 193	*Alma Redemptoris*	1736–37	2(– " –)[44]
K 194	*A. R.*	1738–48	17
K 195	*A. R.*	1736–41	8
K 202	*A. R.*	1736–46	17
K 207	*Ave Regina*	1740	1
K 257	*Salve Regina*	–	(auch Titelbl. von Abendt)[45]
K 261	*Salve Regina*	1740	2(– " –)[46]

Ein zweiter Schritt betrifft die oben angesprochenen 24 Abschriften, sowohl aus der Hand von Abendt als auch von anderen Kopisten. Sie wurden ja (wie erwähnt) zusammen mit den genannten 8 Triosonaten gleichfalls 'Opfer' jener mit 1626/27 anzunehmenden Restaurierungskampagne in der HK und ließen sich demnach aus denselben Gründen wie letztere um einige Jahre früher datieren:

A: 14 Werke aus der Hand von Abendt mit ausgewechselten und fast ausschließlich von diesem selbst neuerlich beschrifteten Umschlägen bzw. Titelbl., den Zeitraum 22.XI.1726-6. VII. 1727 betreffend:

Messen

K 12	*Missa Dies mei sicut umbra*	29.XII.1726–54	32(Titelbl. nicht von Abendt)
K 21	*M. Ne intres in judicium*	2.II.1727–31	9
K 31	*M. Reconvalescentiae*	2.XII.1726–33	14
K 47	M. (Kyrie und Gloria)	26.XII.1726–31	8(Abb. 11)

Abb. 10. Aus den *Litaniae Lauretanae* K 115: Beginn der Sopranstimme

Plate 10. From the *Litaniae Lauretanae*, K.115. Beginning of the soprano part

Vespern

K 88	*Laudate pueri*	1.II.1727–40	12
K 91	*Laudate Dominum*	24.XII.1726–40	30
K 98	*Magnificat*	11.VI.1727–37	4
K 107	*Nisi Dominus aedificaverit.*		
	Beatus vir.	22.XI.1726–40	15
K 112	*Lauda Jerusalem*	22.XI.1726–37	6
K 113	*Lauda Jerusalem*	31.XII.1726–39	11

Motetten

K 171	*M. de B.M.V. Ave mundi*		
	spes Mariae	12.XII.1726–47	15
K 174	*M. de B.M.V. Benedicta*		
	quae lilium es.	6.VII.1727–29	3

Hymnen

K 191	*Alma Redemptoris*	1.XII.1726–35	8
K 196	*Alma Redemptoris*	21.XII.1726–48	41

B: 10 Werke – ausschließlich Hymnen – nicht aus der Hand von Abendt, den Zeitraum 8.II. – 5.IV. 1727 betreffend:

K 209	*Ave Regina*	5.IV.1727–34	4
K 212	*A. R.*	30.III.1727–34	5
K 215	*A. R.*	8.II.1727–42	23
K 216	*A. R.*	22.II.1727–41	34
K 217	*A. R.*	7.III.1727–49	46
K 218	*A. R.*	21.II.1727–39	12
K 221	*A. R.*	? III.1727–38	6
K 223	*A. R.*	? II.1727–57	18
K 225	*A. R.*	15.II.1727–41	15
K 226	*A. R.*	2.III.1727–64	12

Schließlich seien auch noch jene (überwiegend von Abendt angefertigten) Abschriften Fux'scher Werke genannt, bei denen die auf dem Titelblatt jeweils an erster Stelle stehenden Aufführungsvermerke in den Zeitraum von Mitte 1727 bis Ende 1729 fallen und die Köchel im Auge gehabt hat, als er von einer sogar bis in das Jahr 1729 zu beobachtenden 'unverhältnismässig grossen Anzahl von ersten Aufführungen sprach.' [47] Der auf diese Weise zurecht mit der genannten Revision von 1726/27 hergestellte Zusammenhang würde mit all den damit verbundenen Konsequenzen, inklusive vorliegender erneuerter (z.T. von Abendt neuerlich selbst beschriebener) Umschläge, auch hier wiederum mit gutem Gewissen eine jeweils um einige Jahre früher liegende Entstehungszeit anzunehmen erlauben:

Messen

K 3	*Missa Benjamin*	? IX.1728–39	8
K 30	*M. Quid transitoria*	21.IV.1729–59	42(s. Abb. 12)
K 34	*M. Sancti Joannis*	24. XII.1727–75	40
K 41	*M. Tempus volat*	17.VI.1729–52	37

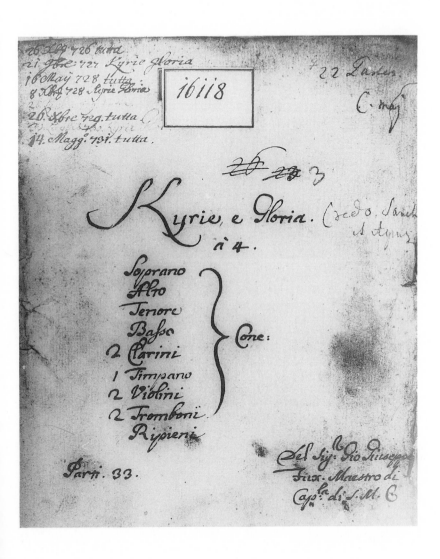

Abb. 11. Titelblatt der Messe K 47
Plate 11. Title-page of the Mass, K.47

Vespern

K 104	*Laetatus sum*	14.VIII.1727–40	8(auch Titelbl. von A.)
K 109	*Nisi Dominus*	22.IX.1728–40	13(– „ –)

Litaneien

| K 120 | *Litaniae. Sancta Dei genitrix* | 2.VII.1729–59 | 15 |
| K 123 | *Litaniae. Mater Salvatoris* | 7.IV.1729–54 | 23 |

Motetten

| K 175 | *M. de B.M.V. Christe fili summi patris* | 31.X.1728–52 | 22(auch· Titelbl. von A.) |
| K 182 | *M. Sanctorum Innocentium* | 28.XII.1729–59 | 7(– „ –, s. Abb. 13) |

Hymnen

K 190	*Alma Redemptoris*	26. XII.1729–38	5(auch Titelbl. von A.)
K 258	*Salve Regina*	2. VII.1727–31	5(– „ –)
K 260	*Salve Regina*	15.VII.1729–36	5(– „ –)
	(von anderen Kopisten)		
K 213	*Ave Regina*	18. III.1729	1
K 214	*Ave Regina*	23. II.1729–34	24
K 243	*In exitu Israel*	19. IV.1729–42	27
K 265	*Salve Regina*	18. X.1727–28	2

Gilt es abschließend ein Resümee aus vorliegendem Beitrag zu ziehen, wäre festzustellen, daß die aus der Identifizierung von Fux' Hauptkopist sowie aus den Folgen der mit den Jahren 1726ff. ins Auge gefaßten HK-Archiv-Revision resultierende Notwendigkeit bzw. Möglichkeit, sowohl einen Großteil der Triosonaten als auch zahlreiche andere Werke des Hofkapellmeisters teils mit Sicherheit vor 1729, teils um eine nicht näher bestimmbare Anzahl von Jahren früher als 1726/27 zu datieren, mehr und mehr zur Gewißheit werden läßt, was der bisherige Stand der Fux-Forschung vermuten ließ und worauf letztmals auch Gleißner[48] wiederum hingewiesen hat: daß nämlich Fuxens Schaffenskraft in der zweiten Hälfte des dritten Jahrzehnts des 18. Jahrhunderts tatsächlich rapide abgenommen hat und schließlich im vierten mehr oder weniger gänzlich versiegt ist. Einer endgültigen Klärung dieser Frage würde zweifellos die 'Konkretisierung' weiterer namentlich bekannter oder auch noch 'namenloser' Kopisten aus der Fux-Zeit näherbringen, was selbstverständlich in gleicher Weise auch für die (fraglos) noch in anderen Archiven als der ÖNB verstreuten und hier nicht erfaßten Abschriften Fux'scher Kompositionen durch Andreas Abendt gilt.

Abb. 12. Schriftprobe aus der *Missa quid transitoria* K 30

Plate 12. Handwriting sample from the *Missa quid transitoria*, K.30

Abb. 13. Schriftprobe aus der Motette *Sanctorum Innocentium* K 182

Plate 13. Handwriting sample from the motet *Sanctorum Innocentium*, K.182

Anmerkungen

[1] Walter Gleißner, *Die Vespern von Johann Joseph Fux. Ein Beitrag zur Geschichte der Vespernvertonung*, (Selbstverlag Glattbach, 1982), S. 63ff. u. 233ff.

[2] Gleißners Gleichsetzung der Schriftzüge des ebenda mit A bezeichneten Hauptkopisten der Vespern mit jenen Anton Salckis ist nicht haltbar und wurde vom Autor dieses Beitrags bereits zu einem früheren Zeitpunkt angezweifelt (s. *Johann Joseph Fux, Sämtliche Werke*, Serie VI, *Instrumentalmusik* 3, hrsg. von Josef-Horst Lederer (Graz 1990), Vorwort IX.).

[3] Reinhardt wird bei Gleißner nicht angeführt, muß aber (wie zu zeigen sein wird) dennoch in Betracht gezogen werden.

[4] Charakteristische Schriftproben von ihm finden sich im Verlauf des Textteils dieses Beitrags; vgl. diesbezügl. auch den Notenanhang bei Gleißner (S. 233ff.), den 'Kopist A' betreffend, wo bestimmte Spezifika dieses Notisten, wie Schlüsselung, Bezifferung, Pausen, etc. gesondert dargestellt werden.

[5] Das Titelblatt findet sich auch in: *The New Grove Dictionary of Music and Musicians*, hrsg. von Stanley Sadie (London, 1980), Bd. 5, S. 603.

[6] vgl. *Johann Joseph Fux, Sämtliche Werke* VI/3, Vorwort VIII.

[7] Die dennoch (sehr vereinzelt) zu beobachtende Existenz von Abschriften, bei denen Titelblatt und Notentext von X stammen und die mit ihren Aufführungsvermerken nach 1729 einsetzen, läßt sich relativ einfach und rasch erklären.

[8] s. L.R. v. Köchel, *Johann Josef Fux. Hofcompositor und Hofkapellmeister der Kaiser Leopold I., Josef I., und Karl VI. von 1698 bis 1740* (Wien, 1872), Beil. V, S. 360.

[9] s. Herwig Knaus, *Die Musiker im Archivbestand des kaiserlichen Obersthofmeisteramtes (1637-1705)* II, (Wien, 1967), S. 99.

[10] ibid., S. 139.

[11] ibid., S. 48.

[12] s. Gleißner, op. cit., S. 64.

[13] s. Köchel, op. cit., Beil. VI, S. 397.

[14] s. Köchel, *Die kaiserliche Hof-Musikkapelle in Wien von 1543 bis 1867* (Wien, 1869, S. 81.

[15] Köchel, *Johann Joseph Fux. Hofcompositor and Hofkapellmeister der Kaiser Leopold I., Josef I., und Karl VI. von 1698 bis 1740* (Wien, 1872). Beil, VI, S. 421.

[16] ibid., Beil. VI, S. 396.

[17] s. Gleißner, op. cit., S. 66.

[18] s. Adolf Koczirz, 'Exzerpte aus den Hofmusikakten des Wiener Hofkammerarchivs', *Studien zur Musikwissenschaft 1* (1913), S. 289.

[19] s. Fn. 15.

[20] s. Köchel, op. cit., Beil. V, 360.

[21] Den vollen Wortlaut der Eingabe s. bei Knaus, op. cit., S. 39.

[22] Köchel, op. cit. Beil. V, S. 360.

[23] Knaus, op. cit., S. 97.

[24] ibid. S. 160 (30.4.1692), III, S. 49 (28.8.1696). S. 65 (22.6.1699), S. 95 (10.10. 1701), S. 146 (11.4.1705).

[25] s. Koczirz, op. cit., S. 288; Abendt hat sowohl 1723 an der Reise der Hofkapelle nach Prag zur Kaiserkrönung als auch 1728 nach Graz zur Erbhuldigung Karls V, nicht mehr teilgenommen, was beides für ihn wohl bereits zu beschwerlich gewesen sein dürfte, zumal er damals doch schon 67 bzw. 72 Jahre alt war.

[26] Wann das Testament abgefaßt wurde, läßt sich nicht sagen, da bedauerlicherweise gerade jener Teil des Blattes, der das Datum trug, herausgeschnitten wurde.

[27] s. MGG 11/1963, 198ff. sowie Friedrich Wilhelm Riedel, *Kirchenmusik am Hofe Karls VI. (1711-1740). Untersuchungen zum Verhältnis von Zeremoniell und musikalischem Stil im Barockzeitalter (= Studien zur Landes- und Sozialgeschichte der Musik* 1) München/ Salzburg, 1977), S. 17ff.

[28] Knaus, op. cit., S. 105; s. auch ders., *Georg Matthias Techelmann. Sein Leben und seine Werke* (Phil Diss., Wien, 1959), VII.

[29] Köchel, op. cit., Beil. VI, S. 420; erwähnt wird von Fux allerdings nur die Abfassung der *Rubriche Generali,* nicht aber eine allfällige Kopistentätigkeit.

[30] Knaus, op. cit., II und III; s. Index.

[31] Daß Abendt im genannten 'Verzeichnuß' vom September 1729 als 'hohen Alters impotens' bezeichnet wird, muß nicht unbedingt (wie Gleißner < 65 > meint) bedeuten, daß er seine Tätigkeit 'nicht bis zum Lebensende' ausüben konnte – seine 'impotentia' kann ja auch bis zum Schluß eine zumindest eingeschränkte Tätigkeit erlaubt haben. Dafür spricht sogar, daß Abendt bei Köchel (Fux) nicht als 'pensioniert im Jahre 'angegeben wird, was bei vielen anderen Musikern aus der HK, die in den Ruhestand gingen, der Fall ist (z.B. bei Salcki!).

[32] Selbstverständlich kann dies nicht als ausschlaggebend, sondern nur als zusätzliche Unter-mauerung der für Abendt sprechenden Argumente gelten, da das Testament (wie gesagt) für einen Schriftvergleich nur eine sehr schmale Basis bietet.

[33] Sollte sich wider Erwarten-, und damit entgegen jeder realistischen Einschätzung der vorliegenden Fakten hinter X dennoch Kilian Reinhardt verbergen (seine Person wäre ja die einzige, die damit noch irgendwie in Einklang gebracht werden könnte), so hätte dies für die Datierung der Kompositionen von Fux aber ohnehin keine Bedeutung, da Reinhardt wie Abendt im Jahre 1729 verstarb.

[34] Selbstverständlich geht es hier in der Folge nicht darum, alle Werke aufzuzählen, die in Abschriften von Andreas Abend vorliegen, sondern es sollen vielmehr nur jene Kompositio-nen Fux' Erwähnung finden, bei denen der neue Erkenntnisstand eine andere (als die bisherige) Datierung erlaubt.

[35] Auf dem Umschlag einer Abschrift dieser Sonate aus dem Archiv der Ges. d. Musikfreunde Wien werden, beginnend mit 14. Okt. 1725, Aufführungen vermerkt (s. Köchel, op. cit., Beil. X, S. 154), was den *terminus ante quem* hier noch weitere 4 Jahre vorzuverlegen erlaubt.

[36] Köchel, op. cit., Beil X, S. 5.

[37] s. z.B. Antonio Caldaras *Ave Maris stella* (HK 165) oder Marc Antonio Zianis *Dixit, et Laudate Pueri à 4 voci* (HK 17427); bei letzterem z. B. setzen die Aufführungsdaten mit 28. Oktober 1726 ein, das Werk muß aber vor 1715 (Zianis Todesjahr) entstanden sein.

[38] z.B. Zianis *Confitebor* (HK 17410) und Fuxens *Alma Redemptoris* K 189, das *Salve Regina* K 257, die *Sonata pastorale* K 397 oder die Marienmotette *Pia mater, fons amoris* K 176. (Im übrigen alle aus der Hand Abendts und somit mit Sicherheit vor 1729 zu datieren.) Freilich ist nicht gänzlich auszuschließen, daß hier der Wechsel der Umschläge auch früher oder später als 1726/27 erfolgte.

[39] Daß es auch vereinzelt Abschriften mit (erneuerten) Titelblättern von der Hand Abendts gibt, bei denen die Aufführungsdaten erst nach 1729 einsetzen, wie z.B. die *Missa Fuge perversum mundum* K 16 (ab 1730), das *Alma Redemptoris* K 193 (ab 1736) oder das *Salve Regina* K 261 (ab 1740), bestätigt nur wieder, was oben in Hinblick auf die 'Rigorosität' der Revision gesagt wurde: im speziellen Fall dieser Werke hat Abendt eben noch zu Lebzeiten auch deren Umschläge selbst neu beschrieben, gespielt wurden dieselben aber erst wieder nach seinem Tode, also nach 1729.

[40] Um wieviele Jahre, muß (ausgenommen die erste hier angeführte Sonate [K 368 = K 362]; selbstverständlich offen bleiben und kann auch nicht annähernd gesagt werden, da der Zeitraum, der mit einem, mit Aufführungsdaten vollgeschriebenen Umschlagblatt abgedeckt wird, sehr stark variiert.

[41] Diese Sonate wird hier nur wegen ihrer Zugehörigkeit zur Werkgruppe der Triosonaten, also der Vollständigkeit halber, angeführt, denn streng genommen müßte sie in der letzten der in diesem Beitrag angeführten Gruppe von Werken stehen. Für sie hat demnach auch der dieselbe betreffende Kommentar Gültigkeit.

[42] vgl. Fn. 39; im übrigen zwischen 1711 und 1715 zu datieren, da Fux am Titelbl. als Vicekapellmeister bezeichnet wird.

[43] vgl. Fn. 38 u. 39.

[44] vgl. Fn. 39.

[45] vgl. Fn. 38 u. 39.

[46] vgl. Fn. 39.

[47] Köchel, op. cit., Beil. X, S. 5.

[48] Gleißner, op. cit., S. 82.

8 The secular-dramatic compositions of Fux: a general survey

Herbert Seifert

In 1961, John Henry van der Meer published a book in three volumes on Fux's stage works.[1] This study was based mainly on the manuscript scores in the Austrian national library; the only modern edition then available was that of the famous festival opera of 1723, *Costanza e Fortezza*.[2] Since that time, the situation has improved for scholars of Fux's secular dramatic works: the Johann Joseph Fux-Gesellschaft in Graz has issued the first two extant works of 1708,[3] and the score of *Elisa* (1719 and 1729) has been edited by the present writer. The serenata *Orfeo ed Euridice* (1715) is available in a facsimile edition.[4]

Fux's principal duty as a court composer and *Kapellmeister* was the production of sacred music, but he nevertheless composed the music for nineteen Italian secular-dramatic works, performed at the imperial court in Vienna. He was entrusted mainly with the composition of music for small-scale works, especially *serenate* (to 1720), whereas full-scale operas in three acts were usually set by Italian composers. Fux wrote only three works of the latter kind. As far as we can judge today, the style of these Italianate works by Fux does not differ fundamentally from that of his Italian contemporaries engaged at the imperial court. As a probable result of the musical taste of Charles VI, there is a notable increase of polyphonic texture in Fux's operas after 1716, although this trait is perceptible in the post-1716 works of his colleagues also.

Early dramatic works: 1698–1710

The first work Fux wrote for the stage after his appointment as court composer in 1698 was *Il Fato monarchico* (1700), a very unusual combination of spoken text, recitative and arias, with ballets by Johann Joseph Hoffer in addition to Fux's music. It is described on the title page of the libretto as 'Festa Teatrale rappresentata in accademia alla Sac. Ces., e Real maestà di Leopoldo I. Imperadore de' Romani, da Cavalieri suoi Paggi.' It was performed by boys of the court nobility as part of the carnival entertainments in February, 1700, in the court theatre, that is, the hall of the imperial palace, rebuilt after a fire in 1699.

The music of *Il Fato monarchico* does not survive;[5] neither does that of Fux's next dramatic work, written in 1701. On 18 July of that year the newly elected Benedictine Abbot of Melk monastery was welcomed on his return there by the students of the secondary school with the Latin musical play, *Neo-exoriens phosphorus*. Fux was at this time organist at the *Schotten-kirche*, the Benedictine church in Vienna, and probably knew the Abbot in this capacity. This may explain why it was Fux who provided the music for this allegorical act of homage to the new prelate.[6]

The music of Fux's most extensive opera is also lost: *L'Offendere per amare: overo La Telesilla* is the composer's only true *dramma per musica*; such large-scale theatrical entities were normally not part of Fux's duties at court, but were the responsibility of Fux's other colleagues, including Draghi (*Kapellmeister* until 1699), Marc' Antonio Ziani, Giovanni Bononcini and Carlo Agostino Badia.[7] In the exceptional case of *L'Offendere per amare*, Fux was commissioned to write an opera for the birthday of the wife of Crown Prince Joseph, Amalie Wilhelmine. This occasion fell on 21 April 1702, but the performance was delayed for some two months and took place on 25 June in the court theatre.[8] The libretto, by the court poet Donato Cupedo, is derived from Greek history, and its complex plot is ornamented with the well-established ingredients of Venetian opera: disguise, secret love, jealousy, lies, the conflict between love and duty, etc. There are, however, no comic elements. In musical terms, the complete lack of choruses is striking, as is the proportional disparity between the one duet and fifty-five arias.[9] Each of the three acts is concluded with a ballet, with music by Johann Joseph Hoffer.

Fux's next operatic commission concerned the Emperor's name-day, which fell on 15 November (St Leopold's day) 1702. A small-scale operatic work was generally performed on such occasions, and in this instance, Fux set the *poemetto drammatico per musica*, *La Clemenza d'Augusto* by Pietro Antonio Bernardoni, second court poet since 1701. This is an opera in one act, divided into thirteen scenes and concluded with a ballet. The plot is derived from Roman history: Ottavio forgives those who conspire against his life. The closing *licenza* draws the obligatory parallel between Ottavio's clemency and that of Leopold I, a virtue with which the Habsburg family was specially associated.[10] Two choruses and one duet are the only set numbers other than arias in this work, which was repeated for Crown Prince Joseph and his wife on 29 or 30 November 1702, on their return from the siege of Landau.[11]

In 1702, 1703 and 1706, Fux was commissioned to write overtures (*sinfonie*) for two *serenate* and an opera by Badia, Bononcini and Ziani respectively, all three of whom were at this time responsible for dramatic festivities (in addition to Attilio Ariosti). Fux himself was primarily occupied with church music in the early years of the eighteenth century, but in 1708 he set another *poemetto dramatico* by Bernardoni, the score of which is the first of Fux's secular-dramatic works to survive. *Julo Ascanio, Ré d'Alba* is in fact a *serenata*, a chamber piece performed on the name-day of Emperor Joseph I, 19 March 1708, in the imperial palace. The text is a very free adaptation of various legends from classical antiquity; most of the arias and the one ensemble before the final quintet are cast in octosyllabic verses, a form of syllabification which predominated in Italian texts for music in the late seventeenth century.

The *sinfonia* begins with two movements typical of French overture style, and continues with an adagio and a fugal presto, both of which derive from the Italian *sonata da chiesa*. Thus we find in this movement the mixed style favoured by Austrian musicians of the period, notably by Fux himself. The accompaniment of the set numbers differs widely, from simple continuo to strings and solo trumpet, according to the affection contained in the text. A pair of viols is used to special effect in the depiction of the pain of love; two chalumeaux and their bass are also featured in the aria scoring (Fux prescribed the chalumeau in eight of his operas and *serenate*).[12] One decidedly old-fashioned formal device in this work is the recurrence of a 3/2 arioso inserted during the course of a recitative and again at its conclusion, which thus forms a kind of refrain.[13]

The title role of *Julo Ascanio* was written for the alto castrato Gaetano Orsini, who sang important parts in all of Fux's operas except *Psiche* (see below, p. 146). Johann Joachim Quantz, who heard and accompanied him in 1723 in Fux's *Costanza e Fortezza*, praised him highly: 'the famous Gaetano Orsini . . . one of the greatest singers who ever lived, had a beautiful, equal and moving alto voice of great range, pure intonation, beautiful trill and extraordinarily fascinating [powers of] performance.'[14] Orsini sang two arias, whereas four each were assigned to the two female sopranos. In addition, two arias each were assigned to a tenor and bass.

Fux used exactly the same cast, Kunigunda Sutter, Anna Maria Lisi Badia, Orsini, Silvio Garghetti and Raniero Borrini, in another *serenata*, *Pulcheria*, which was performed two months after *Julo Ascanio*, near a grotto in the Favorita garden of the palace, on the occasion of the Empress's name-day (21 June). For this performance the audience was more public than for that of *Julo Ascanio*: in addition to the imperial family, it included an ambassador, ministers and ordinary members of the nobility.

Pulcheria is also a setting of a text by Bernardoni, which here concerns a rather conventionally amorous plot set in the Byzantine Empire. It compares technically with the text of *Julo Ascanio* (octosyllabic verse) and it contains the same number of set pieces (sixteen). In both cases, the title role is associated with the monarch. The libretto allows for one duet and final ensemble in addition to fourteen arias. Features which differ between both works include the style of introductory (instrumental) movement and the accompanimental texture of the arias. For *Pulcheria*, Fux composed an *intrada* for solo trumpet and strings, the trumpet playing only in the fast movements (first and fugal third), while the second movement comprises an *adagio* with string tremolo in quavers. The last movement is a chromatic *adagio* of six measures. Whereas in *Julo Ascanio* only three arias are accompanied by continuo alone, there are six such numbers in this work.

One aria is scored for chalumeau and flute *obbligato*[15] (in addition to the normal string parts), another juxtaposes oboes in unison and violins in pairs, and another, the text of which is martial, is scored for trumpet and orchestra. This last number is remarkable for its stylized dance rhythm (it is marked *Tempo di Minuette*) and for the *actual* accompaniment of the singer by two oboe parts (whereas such instruments normally play *between* the vocal phrases).[16]

In 1709, Fux was obliged to compose *serenate* for the same occasions, that is, the name-days of the imperial couple. The Emperor's name-day on 19 March was celebrated with *Il Mese di Marzo consacrato a Marte*, a setting of a libretto by the well-known Silvio Stampiglia, who in 1707 had been summoned to Vienna from Rome. Half of the small cast of four singers were sopranos, namely a woman described as 'Frühwirthin' and the castrato Domenico Tollini, also in a female role; Orsini sang the alto and Garghetti the tenor part. *Il Mese di Marzo* contains nine arias, a duet, two quartets and notably brief recitatives; it is the slightest of Fux's extant dramatic works, and the text he set is merely a fictional preparation for the closing *licenza*. The instrumental introduction is a three-movement, fast – slow – fast, Italianate *sinfonia*. For the first time in Fux's secular works we find an accompanied recitative of the kind already commonplace in the late seventeenth century, that is, sustained string chords to mark an important event in the libretto. In this case, Fux registers the consecration of the month March to the god Mars with this technique. Only two *obbligato* instruments are included in the scoring: a viol, to depict the pain of love, and a trumpet which conventionally ornaments an heroic aria.

The Summer afforded an opportunity for open-air performances of dramatic works. On the evening of July 15 1709 on the pond of the Favorita, the Empress Amalie Wilhelmine was honoured with the *serenata Gli Ossequi della Notte*. It is a work on a comparatively large scale, with strong orchestral forces to support a modest cast of four allegorical figures ('Night', 'Architecture', 'Sleep' and 'Silence') and two mythological personages (one of the muses and one of the three Graces). The dialogue comprises an act of homage to the Empress from the beginning of the text onwards. *Gli Ossequi* had in fact been written originally by the late court poet Cupeda in 1701 for the Empress Eleonore Magdalena Theresia's name-day (when it was set to music by Ziani); the text was revised somewhat for Fux's version. The singers were the sopranos Kunigunda Sutter and Tollini (in the principal roles of Notte and Urania), Orsini and another alto castrato Salvatore Mellini, the tenor Tomaso Bigelli and the bass Giovanni Battista Cativelli. Fux replaced three ensembles in this libretto with choruses; the closing chorus is markedly polyphonic in texture. A refrain is also sung by a quintet of soloists. There are two recitatives accompanied by string chords, that of 'Sleep' (*Sonno*) is marked *pianissimo*. Two pairs of trumpets participate in one aria and in the *sinfonia*, where for the first time in these works Fux demands two separate orchestral groups. This *sinfonia* consists of six movements in all: the first *allegro* is repeated at the close, and the third is a double fugue; the others comprise two *adagio* sections and a menuet. A 'love' aria is scored for viola d'amore and two viols. There are also unusual aria accompaniments which feature solo chalumeau with two violins and four viols, and another number includes three *concertino* ensembles, each of which comprises four violins. One aria is composed as a double fugue.

The next commission which Fux received for a dramatic composition was intended for the birthday of Joseph's younger brother, the Archduke Charles, who at that time was still resident in Barcelona as a pretender to the Spanish throne (as was his rival, Phillip of Anjou, in Madrid). On the evening of 1 October, 1710, the 'pastoral-heroic' composition *La Decima Fatica d'Ercole overo La Sconfitta di Gerione in Spagna* was performed in the Favorita. The text was by Giovanni Battista Ancioni, who had written a Lenten *sepolcro* oratorio for that year as his only other contribution to the Viennese court. *La Decima Fatica* belongs to that group of dramatizations of the myth of Hercules which frequently were employed in honour of various members of the Habsburg family, especially those who ruled in Spain. The same subject had been versified by Bernardoni some two years earlier in *Ercole Vincitore di Gerione*, with music by Badia, and Charles's birthday in 1710 was celebrated in Spain with the *serenata Ercole in Cielo* by Pietro Pariati and Andrea Stefano Fiorü.[17]

The cast of *La Decima Fatica* consisted of five singers, the title role being performed by the tenor Garghetti. Orsini also partook in an important role, and the three sopranos were Kunigunda Sutter, Tollini and, for the first time, Maria Conti-Landini, who thereafter took roles in all of Fux's operas until 1720. It is remarkable that the work contains as many as four choral numbers, but only one quartet. The heroic dimensions of the plot demand two trumpets and timpani, used in the warriors' chorus and in an aria sung by *Ercole*, whereas the opening chorus and one of the arias represent the pastoral qualities of the work. The choral episode is in typical 12/8 time and has the smoothly flowing rhythms, melodic shape and pedal points best known from Corelli's 'Pastorale' in the *concerto fatto per la notte di natale*, op. 6, no. 8. The scoring of this number for oboes, chalumeau, flute and strings also supports the pastoral impression. Only the first part and its reprise are sung by the whole choral ensemble in five parts; the middle section is given to two of the soloists.[18] This *serenata* is also introduced with a *sinfonia* in three movements (as is *Il Mese di Marzo*); it begins with a double fugue. One of the arias features a solo viol, another number is distinguished by the delicate texture of a chalumeau and theorbo.

The later dramatic works: 1711–1722

After the sudden death of Joseph I in April 1711, there was a break in the production of secular-dramatic works at court. Charles VI was crowned as Emperor in Frankfurt on his departure from Barcelona, and he reached Vienna in January 1712. Thereafter, the dismissed opera personnel were partly re-employed. It was not until the following year, however, that festive performances were gradually resumed. Fux, who had been deputy *Kapellmeister* since 1711, shared responsibility with the new court poet

Pariati for the chamber work commissioned for the birthday of Charles. This was *Dafne in Lauro*, which was first performed in the Favorita garden before dinner on 1 October, 1714. The two main roles, Apollo and Dafne, with four arias each, were sung by Orsini and Maria Conti-Landini; the soprano part, Diana, was assigned to a newly engaged singer, Regina Schoonjans, the sixteen-year-old soprano castrato Giovanni Vincenzi played Amore – often sung by boys – and the tenor Garghetti sang the role of Mercurio.

The subject of Apollo's unrequited love for Daphne has been repeatedly favoured in opera since its inception. Pariati, who had already contributed to the dramatic entertainments of Charles in Barcelona and had written plays and librettos for Italian courts and for Venice,[19] knew well how to provide musically suitable texts and thus inspired probably the finest operas by Fux. In his works for Spain, Pariati had compared Charles to Hercules; now he likened the Emperor to Jove, and the laurel which Daphne becomes could be used in the *licenza* as material for the new Emperor's laurel crown.

The libretto afforded Fux the opportunity to compose three choruses and two duets. The hunt which is an intrinsic part of the drama is prefigured in the *sinfonia* by an imitation of horn calls. One aria in the work is scored for Fux's preferred combination of chalumeau and flute, others are scored for solo theorbo and viol. Amore introduces himself with a *pianissimo* recitative with *portato* string chords repeated. In the *sinfonia* and in one aria Fux uses fugal technique; in a further number the structure comprises a freely varied chaconne.

The next occasion for a *serenata* by Fux and Pariati was the same celebration a year later. On 1 October, 1715, in one of the halls of the Favorita, *Orfeo ed Euridice* was performed. (Once again, Pariati had dramatized one of the oldest and most popular subjects of opera.) The singers of the title roles were Orsini and Conti-Landini,[20] Garghetti sang Plutone, Schoonjans his wife Proserpina, Amore was played by Tollini and the tenor Borrosini played Aristeo, also in love with Euridice.

The work contains four homophonic choruses, the first and last of these form scenes by recurring as refrains after arias. There are four duets, one of which also pairs with a choral number. The instrumental introduction begins with a pair of movements in French overture style and ends as an Italian *sinfonia* with a chromatic adagio and a minuet. One of Plutone's arias features conservatively picturesque scoring (two bassoons, cello and violone, generally *senza cembalo*) which conveys the gloom of the under-world. Other numbers are scored for solo violin and strings or for cello and continuo alone. Chalumeau and flute scoring (with figurative string writing in the middle section) characterizes an aria assigned to Orfeo. Orfeo's request to Plutone to recover his wife is conveyed in an *accompagnato* recitative with sustained string chords, and in the aria which follows it, scored for a melodic theorbo part and pizzicato strings (again without harpsichord support for the most part). Such instrumentation clearly suggests the lyre of Orpheus. The chorus of shades is introduced and probably reinforced by soprano-, alto- and tenor viols.[21] In Plutone's final aria, the string scoring articulates a triple fugal texture. The opera closes with a *licenza* which draws the expected parallel between the birthdays of the Emperor and Giove.

Fux's next secular-dramatic work was a genuine *festa teatrale*, a full-scale drama in three acts, and thus an exception in terms of Fux's operatic works as a whole. The occasion for this commission was the birth of a crown prince, the Archduke Leopold, on 13 April, 1716. *Angelica vincitrice di Alcina* was produced four times in September 1716, before several spectators, including several ambassadors and other foreign guests. Lady Mary Wortley Montagu was present at the second of these performances, and gave an enthusiastic report of it in a letter to Alexander Pope:

> Don't fancy, however, that I am infected by the air of these popish countries; I have, indeed, so far wandered from the discipline of the church of England, as to have been last Sunday at the opera, which was performed in the garden of the favorita, and I was so much pleased with it, I have not yet repented my seeing it. Nothing of that kind was ever more magnificent and I can easily believe what I was told, that the decorations and habits cost the emperor £30,000 sterling. The stage was built over a very large canal, and, at the beginning of the second act, divided into two parts, discovering the water, on which there immediately came from different parts 2 fleets of little gilded vessels that gave the representation of a Naval fight. It is not easy to imagine the beauty of this scene, which I took particular notice of: but all the rest were perfectly fine in their kind. The story of the opera was the enchantment of Alcina, which gives the opportunities for great variety of machines and changing of scenes, which are performed with surprising swiftness. The theatre is so large that 'tis hard to carry the eye to the end of it; and the habits, in the utmost magnificence, to the number of one hundred and eight. No house could hold such large decorations; but the ladies all sitting in the open air, exposes them to great inconveniences; for there is but one canopy for the imperial family; and the first night it was represented, a heavy shower of rain happening, the opera was broke off, and the company crowded away in such confusion, that I was almost squeezed to death.[22]

This opera was again the result of a collaboration between the *maestro di cappella* and the imperial poet Pariati, who had taken his plot from the Italian renaissance epic *Orlando furioso* (Ariosto). The love sequence of the Venetian drama, together with the jealousy which it provokes, provide the central momentum of this drama. Fux and Pariati were supported by the court architects and designers Ferdinando and Giuseppe Galli Bibiena, in their realization of this momentum and its surrounding circumstances. The elaborate stage machinery, which included the transformation of a sea monster into two ships, must have comprised a strikingly visual counterpart to the epic style of the text itself. The music was not all Fux's: one of the two ballet scores was provided by Nicola Matteis and the choreography was designed by the dancing masters Pietro Simon Levassori Della Motta and Alexandre Phillebois.

Angelica contains seven solo roles which were sung by the same singers as in *Orfeo* with the addition of the soprano Giovanni Vincenzi for the *licenza*. The work includes five ensembles – two quintets and three duets – together with four homophonic choruses, of which two are worked into scene-complexes, as in *Orfeo*. In this open-air opera, Fux calls for two orchestras with one to four trumpets per group. In the *intrada* and in the final chorus, all eight trumpets, with timpani, strings and winds are employed. A published illustration of one of the original performances allows us to see about sixty-eight instrumentalists in all between both orchestral groups. As in his other open-air compositions, Fux avoids soft-toned solo instruments.

The *intrada* to *Angelica* comprises three movements, a homophonic *allegro*, a *grave* in triple time and a double fugue with introduction. The sorceress Alcina sings her adjuration as an accompanied recitative. In this number, motivic figurations in the orchestral part are interpolated between the vocal phrases. These in turn are supported only by brief chords articulated in the (solo) violin parts. The orchestral motives in this recitative, and in the 'revenge' aria which follows it, are characterized by dotted rhythms, swift scales and tone repetitions.

The *pasticcio* opera *Teodosio ed Eudossa* was staged in Wolfenbüttel in this same year (1716) on the occasion of the birthday of a ducal relative of the Empress, and during the season 1718–19 it was also publicly performed in the opera house at Hamburg. The libretto of this three-act *dramma per musica* was written by Vicenzo Grimani, with music by Fux, Francesco Gasparini and Caldara. The music is lost, and we can only suppose that Fux contributed the setting of a single act.[23] We might deduce from this collaboration that Fux's operatic style was not considered to be especially different from that of his (two) colleagues, or from that of his Italian contemporaries in general. Another, more modest collaboration also supports this point of view. On 19 November 1716, Antonio Lotti's grand opera *Costantino* was given in celebration of the Empress's name-day.[24] Given Lotti's other commitments, only the main part of the music was his work. Fux had to write the French overture, and the *licenza* and *intermezzi* were both by Caldara.

For the same occasion in 1717 Fux was commissioned with a *festa teatrale* of the *serenata* type, *Diana placata*. The title does not disclose that Pariati had in fact versified the plot of Iphigenia in Tauris. The cast was the same as in *Angelica*, except that Domenico Tollini did not participate, due to the slightly smaller casting of six roles. The libretto of *Diana placata* provides for three choruses and two duets. The sacrifice of Iphigenia (redeemed by a happy outcome) does not take place on stage, but is described by Agamemnone in a recitative accompanied by string chords. The French overture includes a fugue with two countersubjects; an aria assigned to Agamemnone is also fugal in texture. One of the duets is scored for chalumeau and flute, an aria is scored for mandolin and strings.

A more demanding commission was the composition of the birthday opera for Empress Elizabeth in 1719. *Elisa*, performed on the evening of 28 August and on the afternoon of 14 September in the Favorita garden, was another re-working by Pariati of classical mythology. In this instance, the poet provided a treatment of the Dido legend (the spelling of the heroine's alternative name, Elissa, was adapted to that of the Empress). The stage design was by Giuseppe Galli Bibiena. The cast was similar to that of *Angelica*, except that one of the soprano roles was performed by the castrato Domenico Genovesi in place of Tollini, and in place of the second tenor Garghetti there was need of a second alto, Pietro Cassati. As eighth soloist, Christoph Praun sang the bass part. The opera also features a number of minor roles.

This production was deemed of such importance that the score was published by Jeanne Roger in Amsterdam (in addition to the normal publication of the libretto). Eight copies of the score are extant today in Austria, Germany, Paris, Stockholm, London and the United States. The scale of composition (twenty-six numbers in all) is not quite that of a full-length opera and as in *serenata* works there is no division into acts and/or scenes. There is only one stage setting and no ballets. Due to the open-air performance there are no solo instruments other than trumpets with timpani and four French horns (these latter as characteristic accompaniment for a chorus of hunters). An *introduzione* in two movements for two orchestral groups, each with four trumpets, serves as an opening to the work. The scene which follows this opening and the choral *licenza* which closes the work are both reminiscent of similar choral scenes in *Orfeo* and *Angelica*. The opening choral number of the opera features a refrain 'Viva Elisa, Elisa viva' assigned to a double chorus. Two other choruses incorporate soloistic *terzetti*. The opera also contains two *recitativi accompagnati* with motivic figurations for strings between the vocal phrases in a manner which recalls the use of this technique in *Angelica*.

Psiche is the title of the next *serenata* given by Fux on 19 November 1720, in celebration of the name-day of Elizabeth Christine. On this occasion, the text was by Apostolo Zeno, who also held the position of court poet in Vienna. Only the first fifteen of the twenty-three numbers are by Fux: he was prevented from completing the remainder most probably as a result of illness, and the last eight numbers were composed by his deputy, Caldara. When *Psiche* was repeated on 1 October 1722 for the Emperor's birthday, Fux set these remaining arias and choruses anew, so that a complete Fux setting of the text is in fact extant.

In the 1720 version, the cast was that of *Elisa*, except that Orsini was replaced by one 'Don Giulio', and Borrosini was not required because there was no tenor role. A cast of four sopranos, two of them castrati, and two male altos was completed by one lower voice, a bass. In the 1722 version the important role of Venere was no longer sung by a woman – Maria Conti-Landini had died in the meantime – but by the castrato Vincenzi. His former part, that of Psiche's sister Orgia, was taken by his colleague Giuseppe Monteriso. The plot, derived from ancient mythology, relates the history of Amor and Psiche. It seems probable that there was little or no stage design or scenic action, given that elaborate theatrical representation was not a feature of the small-scale *serenata*.

The overture to *Psiche* is once again a combination of French style in the first movement and Italianate design in the second (Larghetto) and third (Menuetto) movements. There are four five-part choruses, two of which include soloistic episodes, and one partly polyphonic duet. One aria which describes a monster features an accompanimental texture in which each of the string parts is organized in a distinctive rhythmic pattern. Another number includes Fux's preferred scoring for flute and chalumeau, with violins in unison. The most striking aria is assigned to Giove, and marked *su'l stile di Madrigale*, that is, it is written in *stile antico*, five-part counterpoint, with the vocal part and the four instrumental parts equally participating in *alla-breve* time. The formal design of this number, however, is the usual *da capo* structure. There are three *accompagnato* recitatives, one of which uses sustained string chords, while the other two feature rhythmic figurations in the instrumental parts, as described above.

During the wedding festivities of the Archduchess Maria Amalie and the Prince elector of Bavaria, Carl Albert, which took place on 6 October 1722, the *festa teatrale per musica, Le Nozze di Aurora,* was performed in the theatre of the Favorita. This was a scenically produced opera with prologue, one act and *licenza*, with stage decoration by Giuseppe Galli Bibiena. It contains twenty-nine vocal numbers and two ballets which were staged by Phillebois and Levassori Della Motta. Fux provided the music for the entire work, including the dance movements, which are distinguished by *ostinato* basses. Pariati's text provided for ten roles in his version of the Aurora myth: eight gods and goddesses, the man Titone and the allegorical Destino. The cast of this performance was largely that of the 1722 *Psiche*, with the addition of Borrosini and Orsini and two new female singers, Anna d'Ambreville (alto) and Maria Anna Schulz-Hilverding (soprano).

There are no less than eight choruses in *Le Nozze di Aurora*, some of which are used as refrains, but only three duets. An aria for Destino is written as a double fugue, Diana's song in praise of the hunt is scored for two horns and strings; in other arias the theorbo and violin feature as solo instruments. Amore's aria on the art of loving is 'pastorally' scored for two flutes, viola and 'cello, *senza cembalo*. The *sinfonia* is similar to that of *Pulcheria* in its scoring: four trumpets, timpani and strings. The second movement is a largo for strings alone, the third is a double fugue for the whole ensemble.

Costanza e Fortezza (1723)

The occasion for *Le Nozze di Aurora* was comparatively out of the ordinary. Fux's next operatic work was occasioned by the annual celebration of the Empress's name-day, but as this feast fell in 1723 during the festivities for the coronation of the imperial couple as King and Queen of Bohemia, a more elaborate entertainment than usual was commissioned. *Costanza e Fortezza*, which is a *festa teatrale* in three acts, was first performed in an open-air amphitheatre at Castle Hradschin in Prague on 28 August 1723, from 8 p.m. until 1 a.m. of the day following. A second performance took place at the same venue on 2 September.

The usual team for such festive operas (to which Fux, as a rule, did not belong) was assembled for this production: the text was by Pariati and the stage-designer was Galli Bibiena; the ballet composer Matteis and the choreographers Levassori Della Motta and Phillebois were likewise engaged for the presentation of this massive spectacle. It was an especially large-scale performance. Quantz, in his report on the first performance, writes of one hundred singers – choirs, four castrati, three (further) male and two female soloists – and some two hundred instrumentalists – including imperial musicians and other participants, such as Quantz himself, Carl Heinrich Graun and Silvius Leopold Weiss – an estimate which seems exaggerated.[25] One of the illustrations published with the libretto shows somewhat above a hundred musicians in the orchestra, which includes horns, although these are not prescribed in the score.[26] In a letter to his brother, Apostolo Zeno writes that the amphitheatre could hold four thousand people in all.

The cast of *Costanza e Fortezza* was made up of singers for the most part already familiar with Fux's operatic music. Only the soprano Rosa d'Ambreville (a sister of Anna's), the soprano castrato, Giovanni Carestini (a member of the imperial retinue of musicians at Vienna between 1723–25) and the tenor Giovanni Borghi were new to Fux's operas.

The plot of *Costanza e Fortezza* is taken from Roman history. Livy is the source of this free adaptation of the siege of Rome by the Etruscans at the end of the sixth century, BC. Tito Tarquinio (soprano) is trying to reconquer Rome with the help of the Etrurian king Porsenna (alto), who has fallen in love with Valeria (soprano), daughter of the consul Publio Valerio (bass). Tarquinio loves Clelia (alto); both Roman girls are captives of the Etruscans. Orazio, Clelia's fiancé, defends alone a bridge over the Tiber which is torn down behind him as he jumps into the river. To general astonishment, he is rescued. Muzio (alto), Valeria's lover, is captured when stabbing a man he believes to be Porsenna, but who is in fact the latter's treasurer. As expiation for this error, Muzio burns his hand. Because of this bravery he is released by the king. Tarquinio then tries to take Clelia by force, but is almost stabbed by her; only Erminio, Valeria's brother and in love with Clelia, prevents her from doing so. The consul Valerio offers peace, and Porsenna ceases to support Tarquinio. The *licenza* which follows is a hymn to Empress Elizabeth Christine.

Pariati chose Charles' device *constantia et fortitudine* as title and general theme of the opera. There are many symbolic allusions in the text, moreover, to contemporary history and politics. The musical setting of this text (conducted in performance by the deputy *Kapellmeister*, Caldara), comprises one of Fux's major works. With forty-two numbers it is by far the most extensive of his extant compositions. Sixteen of these numbers are choral episodes; the arias manifest polyphonically complex and expressly contrapuntal textures (which led Quantz to comment on the 'church style' of the work), and the rich scoring includes oboe, chalumeau and trumpet.[27] Despite its length, the opera contains only one *accompagnato* recitative, which includes orchestral figurations between the vocal phrases. The Italianate overture features two orchestral groupings with four trumpets and a pair of timpani in each.

Last works: 1725–1731

A small *festa teatrale* of the *serenata* type is *Giunone placata*, the dramatic composition written in celebration of the Empress's name-day in 1725. On this occasion, Pariati did not supply the text (for the first time since his court appointment), which was provided instead by the Ferrarese librettist Ippolito Zanelli. (*Giunone placata* would appear to be Zanelli's only text for Vienna.) Zanelli's dramatization of the jealousy of Hera comprises twenty-one vocal numbers with three choruses and one duet. The original singers of the four roles were Schoonjans, Orsini, Praun and the famous soprano Faustina Bordoni (afterwards the wife of Hasse). The Italian *sinfonia* is distinguished by its predominantly contrapuntal first movement. Harpsichord, cello and chalumeau are used to vary the orchestral texture throughout the course of the work. Unlike Fux's other dramatic works from 1709 onwards, *Giunone* does not contain an *accompagnato* recitative.

The Empress's birthday in August 1726 was also celebrated with a one-act *festa teatrale* by Fux and Pariati: this was to be the last collaboration between the composer and dramatist.[28] *La Corona d'Arianna* is a dramatization of another popular operatic subject, for which Galli Bibiena constructed an open-air theatre at the imperial court. The choreography for the two attached ballets was once again by Della Motta and Phillebois, with ballet music by Matteis. The seven roles were sung by the usual cast and a new soprano, Maria Conti-Lorenzoni. With a total of thirty-six numbers, this opera is second in length to *Costanza e Fortezza* in Fux's operatic output (*Angelica* has three fewer numbers). Eleven choruses constitute a considerable part of this music, but there is only a single duet. The *sinfonia*, scored for strings, four trumpets and timpani, is in three movements, the last being a reprise of the first. The middle movement is an imitative *larghetto*. Only one of the arias enjoys an instrumental scoring other than strings and/or continuo: Bacco sings 'Piö non empia mie trombe famose' in alternation with and paralleled by a virtuoso trumpet part.

By 1726 Fux was already in his sixty-sixth year and handicapped periodically by illness. Other, younger composers assumed the duties which he had fulfilled for almost three decades. When the imperial couple and a delegation from the court visited Graz in the autumn of 1728, Fux's *Orfeo ed Euridice* was performed there in celebration of the Emperor's birthday on 1 October. Exactly ten years after its first performance, *Elisa* was given in the Favorita on 28 August 1729. (Weather conditions prevented this repeat performance from being held in the garden, but a further performance on 8 September was held there.)

After an interval of five years in which Fux did not write a secular-dramatic work, the composer set *Enea negli Elisi, overo il Tempio dell'Eternità*, the first secular libretto for Vienna by the new court poet Pietro Metastasio. This *festa teatrale*, partly allegorical and partly mythological, is also in one act. It was performed on 28 August 1731 in the garden of the Favorita. Galli Bibiena provided the scenic decoration and stage machinery, and two ballets by Della Motta and Phillebois were included, the first of which had music by Matteis. The title role of Aeneas was sung by Orsini (who had sung the title role of *Julo Ascanio* in 1708). Other singers included Schoonjans, Genovesi, Praun and Borghi, all familiar from earlier Fux operas. Two new participants were the sopranos Theresia Reutter-Holzhauser and Anna Schnautz-Regenhofer.

The overture to *Enea* compares with that of *Elisa* and other festival operas in its scoring for two orchestral groups with four trumpets and timpani in each group (in addition to the usual body of strings and continuo). A *largo* for strings alone separates the fully scored outer movements. An invocation by Aeneas is set as *recitativo accompagnato*: this setting progresses from simple chordal support of the vocal line (in the strings) to the use of interjected string-figurations which intensify the mood of Aeneas's rhetoric after a storm breaks upon the scene. There are but twenty vocal numbers: of these four are choruses (in four vocal parts) and one is a duet. The instrumental texture of these numbers is also extremely limited: the only solo instrument to participate is the trumpet, in the main section of a single aria.

Conclusion

There are many general features which characterize the operas and *serenate* of Fux and those of his contemporaries at the Viennese court. These include the use of an orchestra which comprises two violin parts (frequently doubled by oboes), viola, cello and violone parts (the latter two *colla parte* as a rule), bassoon, harpsichord and occasionally the theorbo. The continuo embraces the keyboard instrument and the bass instruments identified here. The festive operas make frequent (prefatory) use of double groups of trumpets and timpani which function as a musical symbol of the imperial motto of Charles VI which we have seen embodied in the very title of Fux's opera *Costanza e Fortezza* (*constantia et fortitudine*).[29] Fux's orchestral resources also include the chalumeau, frequently combined with the flute, the horns (invariably in association with the hunt) and the violin, viola d'amore and other stringed instruments used soloistically or in *concertino* exchanges with the larger ensemble, as this discussion has shown.

Other features of these works betray a wholehearted adherence to conservative norms of formal design and content: the absolute majority of set pieces (especially arias) in *da capo* format (as against the dramatically contingent and formally inventive use of choral refrains and scene-complexes), the formalization of the recitative writing, especially with the formulaic cadences in which the voice leaps down a fourth from the tonic and the continuo part marks the cadence immediately afterwards, the use of *recitativo accompagnato* in its simpler form (with sustained string chords) and in its more elaborate guise (figurative orchestral motives between the vocal phrases) at moments of high drama, the preponderance of soprano and alto arias over tenor and bass numbers. As this general survey demonstrates, the secular-dramatic compositions of Fux can be regarded as an extremely well-defined application of the principles of serious (Italian) opera in the context of an imperial court which rigorously exploited them for the purposes of absolutist celebration and affirmation.

Notes

[1] John Henry van der Meer, *Johann Joseph Fux als Opernkomponist*, 3 vols (Bilthoven, 1961). The present essay is in great part indebted to this thorough study.

[2] *Costanza e Fortezza* was edited by Egon Wellesz as volume 35 of the series *Denkmäler der Tonkunst in Österreich* (Vienna, 1910).

[3] See *Julo Ascanio*, edited by Hellmut Federhofer, *Fux-Gesamtausgabe*, Series V, vol. 1 (Kassel–Graz, 1962) and *Pulcheria*, edited by Hellmut Federhofer and Wolfgang Suppan, *Fux-Gesamtausgabe*, Series V, vol. 2 (Kassel–Graz, 1969).

[4] See H.M. Brown, *Italian Opera, 1640-1770*, (Garland Press Facsimiles, New York, 1978).

[5] van der Meer, op. cit. pp. 45–6. See also Herbert Seifert, 'Die Aufführungen der Opern und Serenate mit Musik von Johann Joseph Fux', *Studien Zur Musikwissenschaft* 29 (1978), pp. 11, 14.

[6] See Friedrich W. Riedel, 'Neo-Exoriens Phosphorus. Ein unbekanntes musikdramatisches Werk von Johann Joseph Fux', *Die Musikforschung* 18 (1965), pp. 290–3.

[7] Cf. Herbert Seifert, *Die Oper am Wiener Kasierhof im 17. Jahrhundert* (Tutzing, 1985), pp. 556–82.

[8] Seifert, 'Die Aufführungen der Opern und Serenate mit Musik von Johann Joseph Fux', *Studien sur Musikwissenschaft* 29 (1978), p. 15.

[9] van der Meer, op. cit. pp. 47–57, elaborates on these observations.

[10] See Othmar Wessely, *Pietro Pariatis Libretto zu Johann Joseph Fuxens 'Costanza e fortezza'. Jahresgabe 1967 der Johann Joseph Fux-Gesellschaft* (Graz, 1969), p. 18.

[11] Seifert, *Die Oper am Wiener Kaiserhof im 17. Jahrhundert* (Tutzing, 1985), pp. 574–5 and 885–6.

[12] See Colin Lawson, Chapter 5 in this volume, also Gunther Joppig, 'Die hohen Holzblasinstrumente [Chalumeau und Oboe] im Schaffen von Johann Joseph Fux', *Johann Joseph Fux und die barocke Bläsertradition. Kongressbericht Graz 1985* (Tutzing, 1987), p. 71ff.

[13] See for example the recitative begun by Emilia (no. 8) on p. 47ff of *Fux-Gesamtausgabe*, Series V, vol. 1. For similar examples in seventeenth-century opera, see Seifert, op. cit. *Dic Oper*, pp. 296, 300, 302, 310, 327, 335ff., 346.

[14] Quoted by Wellesz, op. cit., p. IX.

[15] This combination was favoured also by other composers active in Vienna during Fux's tenure at the imperial court. See Ernst Kubitschek, 'Block- und Querflöte in Umkreis von Johann Joseph Fux – Versuch einer Übersicht', *Johann Joseph Fux und die Barock Bläsertradition. Kongressbericht Graz 1985* (Tutzing, 1987), pp. 109–17.

[16] See the introduction by Hellmut Federhofer to his edition of this opera, *Fux-Gesamtausgabe*, Series V, vol. 2 (Kassel–Graz 1969), p. VIff.

[17] Herbert Seifert, 'Pietro Pariati, poeta cesareo', *Pietro Pariati La carriera di un librettista* (Bologna, in press).

[18] van der Meer, op. cit., *Notenbeispiele*, pp. 33–5.

[19] See Gronda, op. cit., in press.

[20] It is worth noting that the vocal registers chosen by Fux for *Orfeo* and *Euridice* – alto and soprano – are those which Gluck used in his Viennese version of *Orfeo ed Euridice* some forty-seven years later.

[21] van der Meer, op. cit., p. 128, thinks it strange that the string parts are notated in c-clefs (soprano, alto and tenor), but there is enough evidence in Viennese scores from the seventeenth century to indicate that these clefs designate the use of viols. (Cf. Seifert, *Die Oper am Wiener Kaiserhof im 17. Johrhundert* (Tutzing, 1985), pp. 311ff., 316ff., etc.)

[22] *The Complete Letters of Lady Mary Wortley Montagu*, edited by Robert Halsband, (Oxford, 1965), vol. 1, pp. 262-3. Halsband notes on page 263 that 'the date of the premiere given in van der Meer [op. cit. vol. 1, pp. 135-6, 147] as 13 September (N.S.) . . . is incorrect. As stated in the Imperial Court records, the first performance of *Angelica* took place on Mon 14/3 September. It was next given on the following Sunday, 20/9 September – which must have been the uninterrupted performance attended by LM [Lady Mary Wortley Montagu].' Halsband refers to an entry in the *Hofzeremonialprotokoll* for 1716, fols. 210 and 214-15, as evidence for the date of these performances.

[23] See van der Meer, op. cit., vol. 1, p. 159.

[24] For a discussion of the authorship of the libretto of this work (Zeno and Pariati or Pariati alone), see Gronda, op. cit. (in press).

[25] See the edition of this work by Egon Wellesz op. cit. and also the present writer's forthcoming article on *Costanza e Fortezza* in *The New Grove Dictionary of Opera*.

[26] There is a parallel to be drawn between the use of horns here and their absence from the score and a similar disparity between score and performance on the last occasion on which *Messiah* was given under Handel's direction. In this performance also, horn players took part without being accounted for in the score. See Robert Donnington, *The Interpretation of Early Music*, 2nd edition (London, 1975), p. 586.

[27] See the present writer's forthcoming article on the opera (note 25).

[28] Herbert Seifert, 'Pietro Pariati, Poeta Cesareo', Pietro Pariati La carrierà di un librettista (Bologna: in press).

[29] A further degree of symbolism may attach to the use of double choirs of trumpets in this opera. A. Peter Brown in 'Caldara's trumpet music for the Imperial celebrations of Charles VI and Elizabeth Christine', *Antonio Caldara: Essays on his life and times* (Aldershot, 1987), pp. 43-5, argues that this arrangement of instruments also represents the 'Herculean Pillars' by which the Emperor was likened to the mythical hero in his claims to the throne of Spain.

9 The literary and dramaturgical aspects of the Viennese *Sepolcro* oratorio, with particular reference to Fux

Erika Kanduth

Any study concerned with the oratorios of Johann Joseph Fux must consider not only the wider context of artistic life at the Viennese court, but also the long tradition of the oratorio itself, since from the outset the genre tended to conform to fixed models.

The findings derived from research in musicology and theatre history are so extensive that only a few, relevant studies can be drawn upon here. Both earlier and later findings confirm the validity of the principles which underlie this present investigation: these principles are already implicit in baroque poetics (Crescimbeni, for example),[1] and they are reflected in successive phases of research into the history and development of the genre. In the case of Fux, Ludwig Ritter von Köchel has provided fundamental information on the oratorios in positivist terms, and on the range of musical activity in Vienna generally,[2] and subsequent research has determined the extent of Fux's contribution to sacred-dramatic music. Part of that contribution does not survive.[3]

This chapter is confined to a selective examination of the texts set by Fux, given the incomplete transmission of his works as a whole and the interchangeable structure of the oratorio text in this period. The study draws explicitly and implicitly on Gernot Gruber's investigation of the *sepolcro* oratorio in the seventeenth century as a background to similar works by Fux performed in Vienna between 1716 and 1740.[4] There are, of course, two approaches to works of this kind, namely through the texts alone and through the music. The treatment of the same subject in musical and poetic terms comprises a further point of reference.

The mutual efforts of poet, composer and performers in the production of oratorio at the Viennese court must be seen in terms of the function of sacred-dramatic works as a whole in the period. The oratorio was regarded as a product for immediate use, seldom given a second performance, and followed almost invariably with a newly commissioned work. The texts of such works, published largely as a matter of convenience and comprehension for the imperial audience, were rarely regarded as individual works of art to be taken separately from the music which they served, and their mobility and contingent nature exclude them from the immediate concerns of detailed literary analysis. It is not until the advent of such major figures as Zeno and Metastasio that the oratorio libretto becomes a matter of intensive literary communication and thus an object of critical commentary independent of musical considerations.[5]

The subject-matter of Fux's oratorios comprises biblical episodes (generally from the Old Testament), hagiographical dramas and settings of the Passion and Death of Christ. This last group falls within the devotional programme of the *sepolcro* tradition[6] and it includes six works, five of which are settings of texts by the court poet Pietro Pariati: *Il fonte della salute aperto dalla grazia nel Calvario* (1716), *Cristo nell'orto* (1718), *Gesù Cristo negato da Pietro* (1719), *La Cena del Signore* (1720), *Il testamento di nostro Signor Gesù Cristo sul Calvario* (1726). *La Deposizione dalla croce di Gesù Cristo, Salvator Nostro* (1728), is a setting of a text by Giovanni Claudio Pasquini. It is these Passion settings that are considered here.

Taken as a group, these texts trace the events of the Passion from the Last Supper (*La cena del Signore*) to the removal of Christ's body from the cross and His burial (*La deposizione*). It is useful, therefore, to consider them in an episodic (rather than strictly chronological) order. These poetic texts represent a vividly baroque stylization of the Passion which is comparable to pictorial and sculptural depictions of the Last Supper, the Agony in the Garden, the various other stations of the Cross, the crucifixion itself and the burial which follows. Just as the technical features of such depictions combine religious appeal with artistic endeavour, so likewise these texts complement the music in a combined synthesis of aesthetic and religious expression. In dramatic terms, the oratorios of which they form a part did not depend on the kind of sophisticated theatrical apparatus which was increasingly employed in secular-dramatic performances of the period, and so the inherently dramatic tension between text and music becomes all the more prominent. The setting for this musico-poetic synthesis was a representation of the sepulchre of Christ, erected in the court chapel.

Within the larger tradition of dramatic representations of the Passion which include references to the Holy Sepulchre and the Resurrection (and which dates from the late Middle Ages), the objective of baroque poetics was a stylized apotheosis of fixed schematic models that left little scope for individual commentary. Even in the case of Pariati, an author whose contribution to Fux's dramatic works is of special importance, we find that obligations of style and convention generally occlude the possibility of a personal sense of drama. Prescribed models of poetic and dramatic decorum (above all, the convention of the *sepolcro* itself) rule out an independent dramatic style. As a consequence, many of these libretti are, strictly speaking, routine in nature.[7] The individuality of the dramatist disappears in the face of conventional features which taken together comprise a typology of the *sepolcro* text.

It is clear from these performance conditions that there were no expectations on the part of the congregation which were not already anchored in the conventions of the *sepolcro* oratorio. Gernot Gruber's general observations on the genre in the later seventeenth century hold good for Fux's period also:

> (i) The unity in and between various works lies in their thematic focus upon the Holy Sepulchre as the object of veneration.
>
> (ii) Two semantic fields result from the different levels of textual content:
>   (a) the biblical narrative and its religious matter,
>   (b) the emotional moment of grief.
>
> (iii) Illustration and elaboration (of the central theme of the *sepolcro*) with the revelation of three cosmic levels, heaven, earth and hell.[8]

The sources of these texts were drawn largely from the Gospels. The poetic forms served particularly to emphasize the quotation of Christ's words and the psalms, both of which occur at key points in the respective texts. In some cases, as in Pasquini's *La deposizione*, Latin versions are added in the margins of the published libretti,[9] and the texts are generally enlivened and informed by the use of familiar biblical and other religious quotations.[10] In terms of baroque poetics, the principal interest of these texts lies in their differentiated use of literal translation as against a dramatic rendering of the sense of such quotations. Paraphrase, commentary and versification recast the Gospel and other texts as dramatic structures (dialogue, epic and lyric forms).

Both formal and thematic aspects of these texts are considered here in terms of the sequence which begins with the Last Supper, followed by Christ's agony in the garden of Gethsemane, the denial of Peter, Christ's promise of redemption (*Il testamento*) and His removal from the cross (*La deposizione*). In each of these episodes the plot is a fragmented composite of individual moments linked by recognizable Gospel texts. The pervasively elegiac mood in each libretto yields only at the close with the promise of salvation and the triumph of faith. Thus each episode undergoes a symbolic and allegorical transformation. Moral exegesis is the natural outgrowth of such transformation, and both plot and character are subordinated to this end. Thus the actual suffering of Christ in Gethsemane (in *Cristo nell'orto*) is seen from the perspective of the 'Contemplative Spirit', the 'Consoling Angel' and 'Divine Love'. The moral tenor of the text is determined by a further abstraction, 'Divine Justice'. Each of these characters contributes to the schematic propagation of religious ideas, which is presented in terms of redemption from Adam's original sin and the resolution of Christ's doubt. A vital aspect of this presentation of moral-religious ideas is the notion of Christ's ultimate victory, which 'Divine Justice' articulates in notably vengeful terms:

> Se Ingrato ed empio
> A sì gran Sagrificio il cor tu mostri,
> Io pur farò con egual rigore
> Le vendette di Cristo . . .

Thus in *Cristo nell'orto* the image of Christ suffering is transformed into that of Christ triumphant.

The title of *Il fonte della salute* implies the hope of salvation which is attained in dramatic conflict between a host of divine abstractions on one side and Ṣatan (personified as *Il Demonio*)* on the other. Both sides battle for the souls of a repentant and unrepentant sinner: ultimately both are saved although the former is pervasively contrite while the latter remains defiantly sceptical (until the resolution).

In *Il testamento di nostro Signor Gesù Cristo*, the Virgin Mary, John the Evangelist, the Angel Gabriel and the sinner receive Christ's assurance of salvation under the cross, which is contested by Lucifer. The dramatic tension is also provided here by the protagonists who represent the different spheres of Heaven, Earth and Hell. The battle of the *sepolcro* leads to redemption, where the mocking crowd of Hebrews, who demand of Christ that he effect His own salvation, and Satan, tempter of men, are defeated. The mood of divine admonition remains in case the repentant sinner would repay the mercy granted to him with ingratitude. As in *Il fonte della salute*, where the attitudes of the two sinners crucified with Christ are implied in the figures of the contrite and obstinate sinners, a sinner is also addressed in *Il testamento* in the person of *Il Peccatore*. The frame of associative reference, closely dependant on Gospel accounts, remains constant.

In contrast to the texts discussed thus far, the libretto of *La deposizione* penetrates deeply into the mourning of Good Friday. The contrast in dramatic terms is between the group of mourners (the Virgin Mary, Mary Magdalene, John the Evangelist, Joseph of Arimathea and Nicodemus) and the chorus of sinners. Much of the dialogue between these characters evokes the words of Christ on the cross which thereafter generate sentiments of remorse and moral commentary.

The various figures in these *sepolcro* texts embody qualities which bear out the pervasive theme of Good over Evil, the triumph of heavenly over demonic powers. The object of contention between these powers is, of course, sinful mankind, normally present as *Il Peccatore*. The sinner is led from the conflict to spiritual purification by the *persuasio* of the heavenly characters, but he remains vulnerable to the temptations of earthly pleasures. The synthesis of remorse and repentance which derives from the conflicting thesis and antithesis of good and evil becomes a dominant feature expressed in terms of a poetic concept which relies on linguistic variants of this essential theme of religious and moral redemption.

The leading roles, according to their respective functions, are imbued with sentiments of lamentation, reproach and admonition. This is particularly true of the allegorical personages: *L'Amor Divino* displays charity, *La Misericordia* shows merciful compassion, *La Giustizia Divina* commands the stern vocabulary of divine justice (and retribution). Mankind, therefore, faces these abstractions (and their opponents) with only free will as an

---

*In this chapter and in chapter 10, the names of characters from the Sepolcro texts are given in italics to distinguish them from biblica/personages and other sources.

independent agent of choice. That choice, of course, is eroded by the didactic function of the *sepolcro* text itself.

According to the conventions of baroque poetics, these abstract figures are dominated by their allegorical function. Through them, Christian doctrine becomes tangible. As victim of his own weakness and fate, Man is dependant upon divine authority which both comforts and judges him. To some extent, the allegorical matter in these texts accommodates a degree of psychological expression which embraces thought, feeling and volition (on the part of Mankind) and enhances the act of redemption. The profession of faith in such redemption is rendered differently in each of the various texts, but the basic import remains unchanged. The chorus in *Cristo nell'orto* summarizes this import as follows:

> Tu pur siegui amoroso
> Del Redentore i passi, Uomo redento.

In *Il fonte della salute*, the contrite and obstinate sinners finally confess together: 'Ci accolse Iddio'. Redemption is also the key factor in *Il testamento*, which concludes with the exhortation of the chorus:

> Peccatore, al suo Sangue, ed al suo pianto
> Grato ti vuol Gesù.

La deposizione, by contrast, expresses the importance of redemption in negative terms in its depiction of the mourners in helpless lamentation. The final chorus proclaims the guilt and sinfulness of Mankind as a whole:

> Nulla siam fuora, e dentro siam veleno
> E l'uomo nondimeno
> Il Sangue di Gesù sprezza e calpesta;

The thematic aspects of these *sepolcro* texts can be briefly summarized as follows: the episodes of traditional representation of the Passion story, derived from the Gospels, present Christ's sacrifice to the devout Christian who recreates this sacrifice in the devotions of Holy Week, and admonish him to renew his faith. The confrontation between his inclinations towards the profane, and spiritual contemplation, is conveyed through the metaphor of battle in which the heavenly powers (through the agency of divine abstractions) vanquish the forces of evil (personified by Lucifer or the demon).

These themes and motives are expressed through conventional formal structures. The two-part oratorio text (in the case of Fux's *sepolcro* works) contains an average of slightly more or less than five hundred verses. Within the prescriptions of this limit, the poet is also confined by the demands of a schematic alternation of recitative and aria, although this alternation embraces a pattern of thesis, antithesis and synthesis which accords with the principles of baroque poetics. The utterance of a sentiment, its elaboration and its abstraction in terms of religious doctrine is a familiar dramatic procedure in these texts which attests to the dominance of convention in the writing of *sepolcro* libretti. Howard Smither observes that 'The texts of Italian works called oratorios are either reflective or dramatic. The dramatic type usually employs the narrative element.[11] In its combination of poetic genres, such narrative contains epic qualities which also inform the descriptive writing; a lyrical element is expressed in the elegiac mood of the text and in various prayerful addresses which function as didactic sentiments.

The microstructures of the texts correspond with the macrostructures in a traditional alignment of theme and formal structure. The differentiation between linguistic units (verses) can be discerned in technical and rhetorical terms. Concerning metre, for example, Smither observes that

> Recitative texts in oratorios with Italian texts are poetic, and they usually employ a free mixture of seven- and eleven-syllable lines; aria and chorus texts generally use lines of one length throughout, with those of four, six and eight syllables being common.[12]

Beyond such formal correspondences, rhetorical *inventio* and *ornatus* distinguish the verses, to the extent that such rhetorical strategies are inevitably subordinate to religious dogma.

The prominence of the title of each *sepolcro* on the frontispiece of the extant libretti (in large block capitals) is sustained throughout the texts in question. The close of *Il fonte*, for example, reiterates the title (and thereby the central message of the work) in block capitals as follows:

Di SALUTE e Purità,
Questo è'l FONTE, o Peccatori;

In other works, this allusion to the title is more subtly made, although Fux's oratorio *Il trionfo della fede* (given in 1716, along with *Il fonte*) ends in precisely the same way.[13]

The opening chorus in these works either challenges the moral (and religious) status quo of the *sepolcro*, as in the *Coro di Giudei* in *Il testamento*, or it maintains the prevailing theme of guilt and (as yet unforthcoming) remorse, as in the *Coro di Peccatori* in *La deposizione*. In such verses the principle of thesis–antithesis–synthesis is also largely maintained. The challenge, the admonition and the promise which leads to the confession of faith are shown in the progress from sin to remorse, from offence to forgiveness, from suffering to redemption. The concepts of guilt and expiation are presented in a multiplicity of forms. This is especially true of the solo verses. In *Cristo nell'orto*, for example, *L'Amor Divino* presents the sinner with this formulation of guilt:

Osserva, o Peccator, qual sotto il peso
De le gravi tue colpe a terra inchina
La sua faccia Divina, e al Sommo Padre
Ora supplice il Verbo,

This in turn, effects the remorse of *L'Anima contemplativa*:

Qui dove sparger Sangue un Dio tu miri,
Spargi tu pur, cor mio, lagrime almeno.
E con i pianti miei, e i miei sospiri
Tutta la colpa ancor m'esca dal seno.

The metaphorical usage here of such imagery as 'blood' and 'tears' combines with the weeping and lamentation of the grieving lover, whose 'sighs and laments' signify the poet's reliance on secular imagery to a sacred purpose.

A fixed vocabulary is used to describe and characterise the evil which gives rise to such remorse. Man is *empio, superbo, ingrato*. Sin is relected in *viltà, miseria, delitto, pena,* and *dolore* and becomes *sacrilegio*. This semantic concentration of terminology creates a counterbalance to the faith, hope and divine charity which overcomes evil: the antithesis to such evil apostrophized in the *Gloria* and *Trionfo* of the divine principle.

The didactic principle of each text is most prominently expressed in a series of imperatives which occur in the apostrophe of guilt, the exhortation to repentance, the accusation of complicity and the consolations of hope which pervade the *sepolcro* libretti. In *Cristo nell' orto*, there is a particularly striking accumulation of such imperatives:

> *Respira, o Peccator . . . Vedi, o Mortale, . . . Taci, alma incauta . . . Osserva, o Peccator . . . Vieni, o Mortale . . . Piangi, Alma dolente . . . Tremane, o Peccator . . .*

Such directives clarify the ideas and evocations otherwise presented in the abstract.

Sublimation of the doctrinal message is also effected in prayer: prayerful address is particularly prominent in *La deposizione*, where the Virgin Mary begins by addressing God as *Padre* and continues with other intimate forms, including *Caro mio Redentore, Dolce mio Redentore, Adorato Gesù, Caro mio Dio* and *Forte e vivo mio Dio*. As well as such direct addresses, prayerful language is used metaphorically: the Virgin Mary employs the metaphor of Christ as spiritual food (*Il mio pane, il mio cibo*), while the recurring metaphor of Christ as light of the world appears in the apostrophe of St John as *figura etymologica* and synonym:

> O luce della mente,
> O verità lucente
> O verace splendor, che lume apporti
> A ogni Uom . .
> Tu sai ben ciò che brama
> Quest'acceso mio cor . . .

(The librettist Pasquini here quotes from the *Meditations* of St Augustine, a source used in several other passages throughout *La deposizione*).[14]

The synchronic presentation of events in the *sepolcro* texts is determined by foreknowledge of the events of the Passion as these are conveyed in the Holy Week liturgy. Christ's premonition of suffering in *Cristo nell'orto* typifies this synchronic presentation:

> Questo di dolor Calice amaro,
> De l'Onte, de'Flagelli, e de le Spine,
> De Chiodi, de la Piaghe, e de la Croce,
> Le amarezze vegg'io.

Analogous references to the blood of Christ are also made in the same text:

> Coronato di Spine,

Squarciato da' Flagelli,
E trafitto da Chiodi Ei verserallo ('He will shed His blood').

Both the Old and New Testaments are also drawn upon as analogous points of reference in the various moral addresses which occur throughout these *sepolcro* texts. Consider the following introductory address of *L'Amor Divino* to the sinner in *Cristo nell' orto*:

Respira, o Peccator. Te con la Colpa
Reo fece il primo Adamo, e trasse a morte;
Con la Grazia il Secondo
Te fa innocente, e te richiama in vita.

Il testamento di nostro Signor Gesù Cristo draws upon the words of Christ in direct quotation from the Gospels. His pronouncements run like a thread through this text, and their key importance is further emphasized (from a textual point of view) by the use of block capitals:

(Giovanni:) E appunto dal suo amor Cristo incomincia
il tenero Divin suo Testamento:
col dir: PERDONA, O PADRE,
AD ESSI, CHE NON SAN QUEL' CHE FANNO. [Luke 23: v. 34]

The consolation offered to *Il Peccatore* in the same text is expressed as follows:

. . . TEL DICO IN VERO:
OGGI TU SARAI MECO IN PARADISO. [Luke 23: v. 41]

The Angel Gabriel recalls the desperation of Christ with the exclamation:

MIO DIO, MIO DIO,
PERCHÈ M'HAI ABBANDONATO? [Matthew 27: v. 36, Mark 15: v. 33]

A phrase from the St John's Gospel (19: v.30), 'TUTTO È FINITO', is followed by the profession:

SIGNOR, NE LE TUE MANI
RACCOMANDO IL MIO SPIRTO. [Luke 23: v.46]

These word-for-word quotations function partly as a summons to the devout and are partly incorporated into the episodic presentation of the events of the Passion.

In this context, it should be emphasized that the texts of the scriptures remain the linguistic basis of the *sepolcro* texts, despite their constant variation, interpretation and assimilation.

The language of these texts is therefore a matter of symbolic and allegorical transformation. The listener (or reader of the libretti) is expected to comprehend the allusions and paraphrases of various source material (pre-eminently the scriptures, but also the writings of the Church Fathers) in a series of variations which belong ultimately to a tradition of quasi-liturgical practice and which afford him a wealth of metaphorical insight.

Once identified, the use of recurring metaphor in these texts appears to be a significant device. Thus in *Il fonte della salute*, the image of light is employed to characterize not Christ Himself, but the divine attribute of grace, as personified by *La Grazia Divina*:

> Ove più abbonda
> Infelice la colpa, ivi più splende
>
> . . . . .
>
> Or son fuoco, che strugge
> Le impure colpe: or sono ardor, che accende
> Di sacre fiamme un core: or raggio io sono . . .
> Ma sempre io d'acque vive e chiare, e belle
> Puro Fonte mi vanto . . .

This transition between metaphors of light and water is underpinned by the dominant theme of the fountain of salvation. The thirst for eternal life is quenched in its waters, the lips yearn for them. Nature provides a means of transfer from the physical to the spiritual. This is clearly borne out by the aria assigned to *La Grazia* in the wake of such usage:

> Corre a l'onda,
> Che l'alletta,
> Sitibonda
> La Cervetta;
> E la sete a l'or ristora.
> Tale ancora
> Il peccatore
> Cerca in me quel vivo umore,
> Che il risana, e l'innamora . . .

The analogy from the Old and New Testaments here combines the 'bitter waters' which Moses parted with the 'wood' which made the waters sweet. It is this *pars pro toto* which yields the climax of mystical connections, first in the cross itself and then in the Word (i.e., Christ Himself). The images employed for Christ are understood in the same (metaphorical) manner: *il pelicano pietoso, il mansueto Agnello*, and as the guardian *Pastore* (in *Il testamento*). Again and again such terms are invoked, following upon the basic gesture of *Ecce Homo*! with which *il testamento* begins.

In characteristically baroque fashion, the layers of linguistic and metaphorical allusion which distinguish these texts can ultimately be traced to scriptural sources. The ornamentation of these sources for moral and religious purposes should be regarded in terms of (quasi-liturgical) function rather than intrinsic value. The *texts* of the Viennese *sepolcro*, as they are represented in the oratorios of Fux, must be seen as part of a continuum which depended on tradition and convention. Not until the advent of Metastasio did the *sepolcro* text reach new and innovative poetic heights.

162   ERIKA KANDUTH

Notes

[1] In his study 'Giacomo Mazzoleni e l'oratorio a Rovigo sul finire del XVII secolo', *Tradizione e stile* (Como, 1989), pp. 187ff., Ivano Cavallini avails himself of the opportunity to remind the reader of Crescimbeni's poetological principles as he formulates them in his *Commentari intorno all'Istoria della volgar lingua* (Rome, 1702–11), vol. 1: 'Gli Oratori, Poesie già miste di drammatico, e di narrativo, ed ora tutte drammatiche, (. . .) si cantano con musica, e contengono, o morale o sacro argomento . . .'. This definition can serve as a basis for any consideration of the genre.

[2] Ludwig Ritter von Köchel, *Johann Joseph Fux* (Vienna, 1872, newly reprinted, Hildesheim, 1988). See chapter XII of this study, 'Die Oratorien von Fux', pp. 174ff.

[3] A revised list of Fux's sacred-dramatic music is contained in Rudolf Schnitzler's exhaustive source-study, *The Baroque Oratorio at the Imperial Court in Vienna* (in press). This confirms the loss of the *prima parte* of Fux's earliest (known) oratorio *Santa Dimpna* (1702) and of the entire music of his second-known oratorio *La Regina Saba* (1705). Schnitzler attributes two oratorios formerly attributed to Fux (*Santa Geltrude*, 1711 and *Ismaelle*, 1717) to Carlo Agostino Badia. The text of the first of these is by Giovanni Domenico Filippeschi and the second is by Bernardino Perfetti. The present note is derived from note 7 of Harry White's assessment of the *sepolcro* oratorios, Chapter 10 in the present volume.

[4] Gernot Gruber, *Das Wiener Sepolcro und Johann Joseph Fux. 1. Teil. Jahresgabe 1968 der Johann Joseph Fux-Gesellschaft* (Graz, 1972).

[5] For an extended critique of the period under discussion, however, see Robert Freeman's *Opera without Drama: Currents of Change in Italian Opera, 1675-1725* (Ann Arbor, 1981). See also the present writer's 'Metastasio viennese, I componimenti sacri', *Rivista di letteratura italiana* XIII (1984), nos 1–2, pp. 125ff.

[6] A tradition indigenous to Vienna and unquestionably independent of the dramaturgical and poetic principles advocated by Apostolo Zeno and his Italian contemporaries at court. Although Zeno and Pariati often collaborated, it is notable that Pariati was sympathetic to this tradition (and a vital contributor to the *sepolcro* genre) whereas Zeno was not.

[7] For a study of Pariati's secular works in particular and his career in general, see Naborre Campanini, *Un Precursore del Metastasio* (Florence, 1904). Cf. Othmar Wessely, *Pietro Pariatis Libretto zu Johann Joseph Fuxens 'Costanza e Fortezza'. Jahresgabe 1967 der Johann Joseph Fux-Gesellschaft* (Graz, 1969). See also G. Gronda, 'Per una ricognizione dei libretti di Pietro Pariati', *Civiltà teatrale e Settecento emiliano* (Bologna, 1986), pp. 115ff. The oratorio texts are not considered in this study.

[8] Gruber, op. cit., p. 13.

[9] See the print of this libretto, published by Johann Peter van Ghelen, located in the Austrian National Library music collection, A–Wn 25.236-B.M. See Schnitzler, op. cit., for a complete list of printed texts on which the present discussion is based. I am grateful to Dr H. Seifert for information on these libretti and to Dr H. White, who placed his copies of these texts at my disposal.

[10] Pasquini, for example, draws on the psalms and on the writings of St Augustine, among other sources.

[11] Howard Smither, *A History of the Oratorio* I *The Oratorio in the Baroque Era: Italy, Vienna, Paris* (Chapel Hill, 1977), p. 204.

[12] ibid., p. 205.

[13] Cf. the closing line of the final verse (*madrigal* chorus):
'E de la FEDE il bel TRIONFO adora.'

[14] It is interesting to observe that Pasquini uses these quotations as the source of meditative commentary (in the recitatives and even more frequently in the arias): this is especially true of his appropriation of the *Meditations* of St Augustine and of St Bernard's *Lamentations of the Blessed Virgin Mary*.

10 The *Sepolcro* Oratorios of Fux: An Assessment

Harry White

Within the past forty years, the regeneration of interest in music at the imperial court in Vienna from 1658 until 1740 has produced a significant corpus of scholarship which has profoundly enhanced our understanding of baroque style.[1] Documentary, archival, editorial and sociological studies brought to bear on the extent and function of music under the Habsburg Emperors Leopold I and his sons Joseph I and Charles VI have collectively demonstrated that the cultivation of music at the Viennese court comprises a complex and extremely fertile example of imperial patronage during the baroque period, which ranks in importance with other, similar examples of music under the duress of a conservative and powerful social structure. We might profitably suggest, as a result of this research, that the formulation and practice of certain musical genres in Vienna during the later seventeenth and early eighteenth centuries compares in stature with the cultivation of related genres in Leipzig, Rome and London, to cite three obvious centres of musical significance. The achievement of Bach in Leipzig, for example, can only be comprehensively grasped in terms of socio-religious conditions which determined the essentials of his work there; Handel's evolution of the English oratorio is likewise inconceivable without some sense of the fundamental social and aesthetic pressures on *opera seria* in London; the oratorios and chamber cantatas of Alessandro Scarlatti also reflect the vicissitudes of his operatic career and the social and religious circumstances which alternately inhibited and enhanced it. So it is with Fux: the range of Fux's assiduous contribution to several major genres of the baroque period was unquestionably determined by the context of an imperial court which sought to celebrate the 'two-fold triumph of counter-reformation and princely absolutism' in its extensive patronage of music.[2]

The comparative political stability of the Habsburg empire from 1660 to 1740, the personal predilection for music shared by Leopold I and his sons, and the cultural hegemony of Italian art (painting, poetry, architecture and music) are three vital factors in the social and cultural context which prevailed during Fux's tenure at Vienna, and the daunting corpus of music which he and his predecessors and contemporaries wrote in the service of the court was expressly informed by these factors. Given the fundamental research of Ludwig Ritter von Köchel and Alexander von Weilen towards the reconstruction of this context (especially in documentary and archival terms), the revival of research into the Austrian musical Baroque which occurred in the 1950s and which endures to the present day has greatly clarified our sense of the music and conditions of patronage which obtained at the Habsburg court.[3]

This is notably true of the various genres of secular- and sacred-dramatic music which the Habsburgs fostered in their emulation of Italian art. From the inauguration of a complete works edition of the music of Fux under the general editorship of Hellmut Federhofer in 1955 to the exhaustive catalogue of sources of the baroque oratorio at Vienna which Rudolf Schnitzler currently has in press, a host of genre studies, dissertations, historical surveys and source reports has focused upon the sacred- and secular-dramatic music of the Viennese court as a repertory imbued with the conservative ethos of its imperial context. The Viennese oratorio in general and the oratorios of Fux in particular have been comparatively prominent in this research. For the purposes of this assessment, it is useful to know that three of Fux's ten wholly extant oratorios have been published as volumes in the complete works edition;[4] the oratorios as a whole and one of them in particular have been discussed by Howard Smither,[5] and that these works have also been the subject of a doctoral dissertation by the present writer.[6]

Given this research, I should like to concentrate on the matter of style in the following discussion. The dynamic between poetry and music in these works which generates their inherent dramatic interest is one which Fux evolved as a direct result of external factors which by now are reasonably well known. The intrinsic means by which Fux discovered a musical style answerable to the demands of a notably doctrinaire concept of quasi-liturgical drama is of paramount interest. If it follows that such an element is contingent upon essential information as to the nature, content and performance practice of these oratorios, it is equally true that in the wake of such information (which is abundant, if necessarily incomplete in some respects), the enduring question provoked by these works concerns Fux's musical strategies in his response to the sacred-dramatic texts which he was assigned. In this respect, the present discussion may be regarded as a companion piece to Erika Kanduth's survey of sacred-dramatic texts which forms Chapter 9 of this volume.

Appendix I at the end of this chapter lists the twelve sacred dramatic works now ascribed to Fux,[7] of which ten are wholly extant. All ten postdate the composer's appointment as *Vize-Hofkapellmeister* by Charles VI in 1711: Fux became full *Kapellmeister* in 1715 and remained in this post until shortly before his death in 1741.[8] These ten works, written and first performed between 1714 and 1728, can be largely divided into Lenten oratorios (which comprise biblical drama and doctrinal allegory) and settings of the Passion designated for performance at a replica of the Holy Sepulchre of Christ erected in the court chapel in Vienna. Seven of the ten works are settings of texts by Pietro Pariati, court poet at Vienna from 1713 until his death in 1733. Prior to Apostolo Zeno's arrival in Vienna in 1718, Pariati was responsible for the large-scale secular libretti which dealt with historical and mythological subjects (these include texts set by Fux); during the same period, he contributed several texts for oratorios and shorter secular works. Robert Freeman has observed that Pariati's (secular) libretti for the court during these years are 'as modern as any of those . . . by Zeno after his arrival in Vienna',[9] and both Freeman and John Henry van der Meer maintain that Pariati's formal and technical achievements foreshadow many of the 'innovations' with which Zeno has been credited (a point of view maintained also by Howard Smither).[10] There is not much in Pariati's oratorio texts to suggest that he radically departed from the general structural principles advanced by his colleague Zeno, notwithstanding Pariati's cultivation of the *sepolcro* tradition of sacred drama which Zeno generally disdained.[11]

In critical and stylistic terms, it is the Lenten oratorios which to date have received most attention. The biblical dramas *La fede sacrilega nella morte del precursor S. Giovanni Battista* (1714) and *La donna forte nella madre de' sette Maccabei* (1715) have been published in modern editions, and *La fede sacrilega*, moreover, has been recently recorded in an outstanding performance by the Neuss ensemble Capella Piccola.[12] This oratorio is also selected by Howard Smither as a 'representative example' of the genre in Vienna during the later baroque, and the editors of *La fede sacrilega* and *La donna forte* provide extended critical appraisal of both works.[13] All of this being so, the greater part of this paper is devoted to a scrutiny of the six *sepolcro* oratorios which comprise Fux's most sustained contribution to sacred drama at the Viennese court. In the present context, we can perhaps clarify Fux's musico-dramatic achievement in respect of the *sepolcro* oratorio as an issue to be taken separately (in some respects only) from his earlier sacred-dramatic works. The biblical dramas, for example, represent a synthesis of biblical tragedy (in which the libretti show full-blown, operatic characterizations beyond the details of biblical narrative) which deserves to be distinguished from the admixture of literary and musical elements in the *sepolcro* works.

The *sepolcro* oratorios of Fux and Pariati (1716–1727)

The ensuing discussion divides into two sections. In the first of these, I survey the five *sepolcro* oratorios which Fux and Pariati wrote and which were performed between 1716 and 1727. This section thereby discloses the principal textual and musical strategies which taken together facilitate a scrutiny of Fux's musico-dramatic style in these works. In the second section, I seek to appraise Fux's last passion oratorio in some detail: his setting of Claudio Pasquini's *La deposizione dalla croce di Gesù Cristo Salvator Nostro*, first performed in 1728. This appraisal also refers in brief to a contemporary *sepolcro* oratorio by Fux's deputy, Antonio Caldara, for the sake of contextual comparison. The conclusions drawn at the end of this discussion widen the focus to include some commentary on Fux's oratorios as a whole.

The development of the Viennese *sepolcro* tradition at the imperial court has been extensively documented:[14] in brief, its essential characteristics comprise a form of sacred drama in the seventeenth century by which it is distinguished from other (Lenten) oratorios. Its formal structure (one, as against two parts), instrumentation, irregular arrangement of recitative and set number and manner of performance are factors which distinguish the *sepolcro* from the oratorio in the period 1660–1700. After the turn of the century, however, both types merge, and although important distinctions between the two still obtain, the intrinsic formal arrangement and musical structure yield to the more modern characteristics of an *oratorio al santissimo sepolcro.*[15]

In the case of Fux's *sepolcro* oratorios, the title-pages of the printed libretti largely refer to these works as 'componimento sacro' in order to distinguish them from the texts of ordinary Lenten oratorios. Furthermore, the wording on these title-pages gives clear information as to the manner and whereabouts of performance:

> CRISTO NELL'ORTO/ Componimento Sacro Per Musica/ Applicato al suo/ Santissimo Sepolcro,/ e cantato/Nell'Augustissima Capella/ Della /Sac. Ces. E. Cattolica Real/ Maestà / di/Carlo VI/ . . .Poesia del sig. Pariati Poeta di S. M. Ces. e Catt./ Musica del Sig. Gio. Gioseffo Fux Maestro di Capella di Sua Maestà Ces. e Catt.[16]

This information corroborates the reports to be found in contemporary journals and other sources (the *Rubriche generali* of Killian Reinhardt is one such source)[17] to the effect that Fux's *sepolcro* settings were performed 'in the manner of an oratorio' (i.e., in concert performance) at a replica of the holy sepulchre in the court chapel. The court copies of Fux's oratorios are notably scant in the provision of such information, and they merely confirm the tendency to regard these *componimenti sacri al sepolcro* as oratorios:

> Cristo nell'Orto./Oratorio/L'Anno 1718. . .etc. La Cena del Signore./ Oratorio/ L'Anno 1720. . . etc.[18]

Fux's *sepolcro* oratorios were performed as a rule on Good Friday or on the Tuesday of Holy Week (from 1718 onwards) in the afternoon: a sermon separated the first from the second part and the oratorio was usually followed with a short marian liturgy.[19]

Textual and musical changes in the new *oratorio al sepolcro* are paramount. Not only are libretti in the post-1700 period conspicuously lacking in the kind of elaborate directions and descriptions which characterise the seventeenth-century *sepolcro* text; they are also imbued – however gradually – with a different literary approach. Whereas the older *sepolcro* is typified by the exclusive participation of allegorical personages, and also by a corresponding neglect of biblical sources, the texts of the later *oratorio al sepolcro* are ultimately defined by the exclusive participation of actual personages and by an emphasis on biblical sources. Nevertheless, the process was slow to develop, and many of the meditative, speculative and doctrinal elements of the old *sepolcro* texts endure in the modern, eighteenth-century form.[20] In Fux's earliest text setting, all of the characters are allegorical: in his last setting, they are all actual and biblical.

Musical changes in the *sepolcro* after 1700 coincide with the widespread application of the techniques of contemporary opera to sacred drama by Carlo Agostino Badia, Marc' Antonio Ziani and other important predecessors of Fux's at the imperial court.[21] These changes are consolidated by Fux and Caldara, so that the music we are to survey here is in several vital respects of a piece with the musical content of Lenten oratorio and music drama generally in the period 1715-30. Many of the crucial distinctions between secular and sacred music in this period are textual rather than musical.

From 1716 until 1730 the greater number of *sepolcro* oratorios in Vienna were settings of texts by Pietro Pariati. His principal collaboration was with Fux, but he also provided texts for Caldara and other composers at the court. His five *sepolcro* libretti for Fux, together with Pasquini's *La deposizione*, represent a progression from the wholly allegorical to the wholly actual and all of them show some reliance on the Bible as a source of meditative verse. Table 1 shows the cast of characters in each of the *sepolcro* texts (with Fux's voice ranges for convenience of reference). The first of these works, *Il fonte della salute*, was performed on Good Friday, 1716 and repeated on the Tuesday of Holy Week, 1721. The extant published libretto dates from the latter year. Its inclusion of marginal references which indicate the sources on which the text is based is a feature it shares with one other libretto, *La deposizione dalla croce*. These sources are primarily biblical, and they include the Letters of St Paul, the Psalms, the Acts of the Apostles, the Book of Proverbs, the Lamentations of Jeremiah, the Apocryphal books and the Book of Ezekiel and some infrequent references to the Gospels. References to the church fathers, notably St Bernard and St Augustine, are also in evidence.

The wholly allegorical character of *Il fonte* is at odds with the predominantly biblical sources of the libretto. *Il fonte* is, however closely related in structure and theme to the didactic and doctrinal sentiments of Fux's other wholly allegorical oratorio, *Il trionfo della fede*, which was also given in 1716.[22] As in that libretto, the prevailing purpose of the text precludes the exposition of a chronological drama, and despite its biblical sources, *Il fonte* is far removed from the dramatic ideas proposed and adopted by Pariati's colleague Zeno and by Pariati himself in the biblical dramas which he also provided for Fux. The text of *Il fonte* divides between a contrite sinner who appeals to Christ for forgiveness and who is aided and counselled by 'Divine mercy', 'Grace' and 'Justice', as against an obstinate sinner who repudiates the warnings of these abstract characters and who is encouraged by a demon to do so. A lively exchange between the obstinate sinner, the demon and the divine abstractions in the second part of the work represents a struggle for the transgressor's soul: he is finally persuaded to approach the cross and seek mercy.

Abstract characterization and doctrinal meditation also predominate in the next of these libretti, *Cristo nell'orto* which was also given two performances, in 1718 and again in 1723. The one exception to the abstract

Table 1.   *The sepolcro oratorios*

(Note: S = Soprano; A = Alto; T = Tenor; B = Bass)

Il fonte della salute (1716)

La Grazia (S)
La Misericordia (S)
Il Peccatore Contrito (A)
Il Peccatore Ostinato (T)
Il Demonio (B)
Coro d'Angioli, Coro di Peccatori Penitenti; (SSSAT; SSSATB)

Cristo nell'orto (1718)

Cristo (B)
L'Amor Divino verso L'Uomo (T)
La Giustizia Divina (S)
Un Anima Contemplativa (S)
Un Angelo Confortatore di Cristo (A)
Coro di Angeli (SSAT; SSATB)

Gesù Cristo negato da Pietro (1719)

L'Amor Divino verso L'Uomo (A)
L'Umanità Peccatrice (S)
Pietro Apostolo (T)
Ballila, Ancilla di Caifa (S)
L'Odio di Giudei contro di Gesù (B)
Coro di Giudei Ostinati (SSATB)
Coro di Peccatori, che sperano la Redenzione (SSATB)

La cena del Signore (1720)

Gesù Cristo Salvator nostro (T)
Pietro Apostolo (T)
Giovanni Apostolo (S)
Un Anima Contemplativa (S)
Lo Spirito Profetico (A)
Giuda il Traditore (B)
Coro degli Apostoli (SSATB)

Il testamento di nostro Signor Gesù Cristo sul Calvario (1726)

La Santissima Vergine (S)
L'Angelo Gabriele (A)
Giovanni l'evangelista (A)
Il Peccatore (T)
Lucifero (B)
Coro di Giudei; di Scribe e Farisei; di Peccatori (SATB)

La deposizione dalla croce di Gesù Cristo Salvator Nostro (1728)

Maria Vergine (S)
Maria Maddalena (S)
Giovanni Apostolo (A)
Gioseppe d'Arimatea (Discepolo) (T)
Nicodemo (Discepolo) (B)
Coro di Peccatori (SATB)

personages is Christ himself. As against *Il fonte, Cristo nell'orto* addresses a particular episode from the Gospels not obliquely but directly: the suffering of Christ in the Garden of Gethsemane. Although the extant libretto does not include the marginal references featured in the text of *Il fonte*, it is clear that the dramatic passages in this libretto are drawn from the fourteenth and fifteenth chapters of St Mark's Gospel. The explicitly dramatic events of this account are omitted by Pariati (notably the betrayal of Christ by Judas and His subsequent arrest), and literal action is generally usurped by abstract meditation, in keeping with the *sepolcro* tradition. The moral commentary furthered by the divine graces combines with the consolations of a 'comforting angel' and a 'contemplative soul', in order to amplify the central concern of the text, which is Christ's obedience to the point of death. Actual quotations from the biblical account, including a twice repeated statement of 'Not my will, but thine be done', are pressed into service of this commentary rather than to advance the drama.

The title of *Gesù Cristo negato da Pietro* (1719) promises a more explicit dramatic treatment than the earlier Pariati texts but in fact the poet continues to favour a blend of biblical and abstract material. Only two characters are actual (Peter and the daughter of Caiaphas), and the chief dramatic interest lies in the limited characterization of Peter. His denial is included in the second part of the oratorio, and this in turn leads to expressions of shame and remorse in the closing recitative and aria verses of the work. This slender dramatic material is amplified by the commentary of 'sinful mankind' and 'divine love'. The latter is directly involved in what drama there is at the point of Peter's denial:

> Pietro: Io quell'uom non conosco. Il dico e'l giuro.
> L'Amor Divino: Ah Pietro! Che dicesti? Che giurasti?!

Halfway between direct participation of this kind and the moral commentary represented by the choral texts is the position of the 'hatred of the Jews directed against Jesus': this personage conveys the mockery elicited by Christ's claims to divinity.

With *La cena del Signore* (1720), Pariati achieves a more satisfactory integration than before of the *sepolcro* tradition of abstract commentary and the Arcadian ideal of biblical drama. In this respect *La cena* is something of a watershed among the six passion oratorios of Fux. Pariati reduces the number of abstract characters to two and increases the actual persons to four. Within the framework of the Lord's Supper, Pariati includes several dramatic elements from the various Gospel accounts, including Christ's washing of His disciples' feet, His announcement that 'one of you will betray me', the protestations of Judas and the other disciples, the institution of the Eucharist and the dialogue between Christ and His disciples which follows in the Gospel. Christ, Peter, John and Judas partake in the drama which the abstract characters (the 'prophetic spirit' and a 'contemplative soul') comment upon. The length of these deliberations dissipates the impact of the story itself.

Six years separates *La cena* from the final Fux–Pariati *sepolcro* oratorio, *Il testamento di nostro Signor Gesù Cristo sul Calvario* (1726). It was given on the Tuesday of Holy Week, and on the same occasion on the year following. The text is drawn directly from the Gospel of St John and it relates the last words of Christ on the cross to His mother and to St John the Evangelist. Pariati adds the Angel Gabriel, Lucifer and a sinner. A chorus of Jews, Scribes and Pharisees is introduced to reinforce the mockery of Christ in the text, but Pariati notably excludes Christ Himself from the drama. Perhaps in the light of Zeno's recommendations it is significant that Christ's words are reported but not directly uttered.[23] Thus St John narrates Christ's invocation to His father ('forgive them, for they know not what they do') and thereafter proceeds to speculate on this statement. The Angel Gabriel is likewise introduced with his narration of Christ's promise to the repentant sinner crucified beside Him ('I tell you truly, today you will be with me in Paradise'). Thus the cardinal points of the drama are related but inevitably diminished by this narrative–speculative pattern which weakens the impact of the biblical account. The prominence of this account in *Il testamento* is nevertheless a vital advance over the exclusively meditative verse of Pariati's first *sepolcro* text for Fux. The five texts taken together demonstrate the currency of the older *sepolcro* tradition which Pariati modified in order to accommodate some degree of scriptural drama within the framework of moral speculation which remains essential to the later development of the *sepolcro* oratorio in the eighteenth century.[24] Pariati's use of actual personages and his greater dependence on Gospel-based narratives are both features which reflect the influence of the Arcadian academy and in particular the influence of Zeno.

The musical organization of these texts is also governed by convention: the provision for recitative and set number in fairly strict alternation which the libretti expressly recognize is reflected also in Fux's adherence to a well-tried and durable mode of musical articulation. Thus there are two principal considerations which inform the development of musical style in these oratorios. One is the essentially unchanged structural dependence which extends even to expressive norms (instrumentation and the range of affective feeling); the other is Fux's imaginative manipulation and dramatic response within the constraints imposed by adherence to conventional expectations. The *sinfonie*, recitatives, choruses, smaller vocal ensembles and *da capo* arias which comprise these sacred dramas can be classified in purely formal terms, therefore, as a generally unremarkable application of the principles of serious opera to the doctrinaire poetics of the *sepolcro* tradition.

Beyond this kind of classification, other generalizations also apply. The Passion oratorios of Fux manifest little stylistic development in formal terms, but they do afford evidence of an intense exploration of counterpoint as a primary mode of dramatic articulation. If the recitatives for the most part are conventionally alert to the rhetorical dynamics of Pariati's verse, the arias (and occasionally the smaller vocal ensembles) probe the relationship between schematic poetry, formalized affection and musical technique well beyond the banal requirements of a formal *da capo* structure. The choral writing, moreover, evinces a command of vocal and instrumental textures which transcends the ritual sentiments of the texts in question.

Fux prefers the simple binary structure of a French overture in his
Passion oratorios: four of the five Pariati settings are headed by *sinfonie*
which adhere to this structure. The prominence of counterpoint as a means
of dramatic expression and objectification is signalled in the repeated use of
double-fugal expositions which comprise the fast movement of such
numbers. The opening of *Il fonte* features a *Largo-Andante* design which
embraces a textural contrast between chordal homophony and a chromatic
fugue subject which typifies the expressive norm employed in the other
introductory movements (see Example 1). It is useful to note that the
sequential intervallic structure and comparative length of the fugue subject
in this example are features which are common to Fux's instrumental
fugues as a whole. The conception of fugal technique in the arias, however,
differs considerably.[25]

Example 1

Each of the remaining three French overtures affords some degree of variation of this conservative pattern. In *Gesù Cristo negato*, for example, Fux scores the *sinfonia* in five real parts rather than four, in order to accommodate a *concertante* exchange between a solo violin and the larger ensemble. In *La cena del Signore*, this *concertante* texture is applied in the fugal movement which consequently alternates formal counterpoint with five passages for solo violin and continuo. In the concluding section of this movement, fugal material is abandoned in favour of a *tutti* version of the solo material.

Only in *Cristo nell' orto* does Fux depart from the binary pattern of a French overture: the opening movement here reverts to the older scheme of a church sonata in its alternation of fast and slow movements, although Fux employs an added bass part to develop an ambitious fugal texture in the third of the four sections. An expanded version of this older structure is also used in Fux's final *sepolcro* oratorio, *La deposizione dalla croce*.[26]

In his comprehensive study of Fux's secular dramatic works, J.H. van der Meer argues that the doctrine of affections, propounded in the eighteenth century by Mattheson, Marpurg, Quantz and other near-contemporaries of Fux, is of extreme importance to Fux's musical style. Van der Meer maintains that in his choice of tonality, tempo, vocal style, melodic contour and harmonic pattern, etc., Fux is governed by considerations of this doctrine, and that consequently his operas should be regarded as the outgrowth (in part) of a conscious deployment of musical rhetoric.[27] It is difficult, nevertheless, to ascertain the extent to which the complex terminology and systematic codifications of German music theory actually impinged on the compositional process of Fux's dramatic works in general. van der Meer puts the case as follows:

> The question as to whether Fux was aware of musical rhetoric, given that it was mainly developed in protestant Germany by such authors as Burmeister, Nucius, Thuringius . . . can be answered in this sense very probably in the affirmative: the doctrine of musical rhetoric was also expounded by the Jesuit Kircher, and Fux was a student of the Jesuit Ferdinandeum.[28]

The closing chapter of the *Gradus ad Parnassum* (1725) does contain a number of rhetorical points of instruction which modestly support this argument. In this chapter, *De Stylo Recitativo*, Fux confines himself, however, to fairly general comments on the question of *Affektenlehre*, and he is explicit only in terms of those musical figures required for elementary (grammatical) punctuation, including the comma, semi-colon, period, question mark and exclamation mark.[29] His musical illustrations, moreover, are restricted to accompanied recitative and there is scarcely more than a superficial acknowledgment of grammatically-derived rhetoric as a force in musical thought:

> Recitative style is none other than musical speech with changing expression or oratorical delivery. Therefore, just as an orator attends to the different branches of oratory, modulating his voice in an inciteful manner, or in a gentle or uplifting way, or in a depressed manner, he takes pains to improve his style of expression: the composer must do likewise with regard to the variety of the text.[30]

When we return to Fux's music, it is not especially taxing to discover an abundance of systematic figures which bear out this general advice. The use of sequences, figurative imitation of the sense of the text, unusual or sudden extension of the vocal range as a gestural device and literal 'word-painting' is plainly evident. In the context of the oratorios – and in particular these Passion oratorios – it is reasonable to advance the use of such figures by simple illustration and to avoid the complex and often ambiguous terminology which these devices receive in theoretical abstraction. Nevertheless, I should emphasize that the correspondence between such theoretical description and the music itself is an issue of material relevance to our understanding of Fux's contribution to baroque style.[31]

Three kinds of recitative are apparent in the *sepolcro* oratorios. First, there is a pervasive continuo recitative which sets the free verse in generally syllabic declamation with the addition of vocal decoration of affective words; such recitative is grammatically organized according to the prescriptions of the *Gradus* (and the example of contemporary Italian practice, for that matter). The second kind is a matter of orchestral accompaniment rather than melodic alteration: held chords are used to emphasize cardinal points of dramatic interest in the text. Fux conservatively employs such *accompagnato* emphasis towards the close of either (or both) parts of the oratorio. The third kind is also a matter of orchestral commentary which intensifies the rhetorical expression of the text by means of rapid (*agitato*) string figuration inserted between the vocal phrases. A harmonic feature of Fux's recitative accompaniments generally (especially the latter two) is the tendency to use the chord of the flattened supertonic as a cadential approach to the conclusion of texts which convey distress or sorrow.[32]

Two *accompagnato* recitatives are conventionally located near the close of both parts of *Il fonte*. These do not increase the range of *vocal* expression otherwise available in the continuo recitatives, as in the tenth number of the oratorio which dramatizes the rebuke of *La Misericordia* against the obstinate sinner.[33] The continuo recitative assigned to Christ in *Cristo nell' orto* (no. 21, 'Ah! qual patire agonizzante un Dio') exemplifies the use of rhetorical figures which are not materially intensified in the one *accompagnato* number (13) which articulates Christ's invocation that 'this bitter cup be taken from me'.

The occurrence of four orchestral recitatives in the second part of *Gesù Cristo negato*, however, signifies the greater prominence of dramatic material in this work in comparison with the preceding two. These recitatives concern the denial of Christ by Peter and the events which surround it. Thus in no. 32, *L'Umanità Peccatrice* laments the vulnerability of Christ and asks of the whereabouts of angels to defend Him. Fux uses the third kind of technique described here to register the despair of the text (see Example 2a). A more modest orchestral gesture (*accompagnato* chords) is used to underline the tragic exclamations of *L'Amor Divino* upon Peter's actual denial: the latter, together with this *accompagnato* response, are quoted in Example 2b. These three excerpts illustrate the operatic thrust of Fux's recitative technique. The first of them combines a vigorous vocal line characterized by broad strokes and a sudden extension of the range to underline the word *fulmini* with a frankly dramatic contrast of *piano* and *forte* instrumental figurations; Peter's denial in the second extract is nakedly set as a continuo recitative of shameless simplicity while the third extract in response to this allows the descending vocal line to move in affective, sequential reproaches which are steadily supported by the string chords.

Example 2a

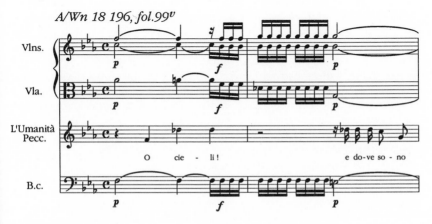

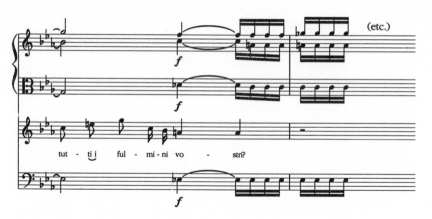

Example 2b

There are three orchestral recitatives in *La cena del Signore*, of which two are used to highlight the words of Christ by means of simple chords.[34] The most striking recitative, however, is reserved for the *Spirito Profetico*, who condemns outright the scepticism and disbelief of Judas. The semiquaver string figure which instrumentally registers the high indignation of the character is comparable to the figure quoted in Example 2a above.[35] Chordal realization of the continuo part is also employed in both accompanied recitatives in *Il Testamento*, assigned here to *La Santissima Vergine*, but in neither case does the range of melodic (vocal) expression extend beyond the reach of the continuo numbers in the work.

Johann Mattheson explicitly recommends Fux's choral writing as an outstanding example of oratorio style in *Der vollkommene Capellmeister* and he also quotes 'a beautiful duet by Fux' to illustrate the felicities of vocal chamber music.[36] Both types of number are prominent in the oratorios generally, although as a rule only one small ensemble is included in the *sepolcro* works.

The text of *Il fonte* provides for three choral numbers, a chorus of angels which opens the work, a chorus of penitent sinners which is located in the libretto at the close of the first part and a combined chorus of sinners and angels in six parts with which the oratorio ends. The 1716 score of *Il fonte* includes only the first and last of these numbers, which suggests that the chorus at the end of the first part was added for the 1721 performance.[37]

Fux's oratorio choruses, which frequently adhere to the disposition of the solo vocal parts,[38] are designated by the term 'Madrigale' on the court copies of the scores. Such large-scale numbers are conventionally used to close the two parts of the oratorio, but smaller numbers are introduced according to the demands of the text. In the *sepolcro* oratorios, however, Fux uses a large-scale chorus to begin each work: these numbers rarely are scored for the full vocal resource and they frequently signify some degree of involvement in the drama (as a 'chorus of sinners' etc.). The closing choruses, by contrast, summarize the moral lesson drawn at the end of the drama and exploit an elaborate structural design, as in the number which ends *Il fonte*, 'Di salute e purità'. The instrumental introduction to this number comprises a fugal exposition and the vocal writing is scored in six parts. The antiphonal grouping which this range facilitates is explored by Fux in a movement which alternates massive vocal homophony with passages of imitative counterpoint.

Of the three choral numbers in *Cristo nell'orto*, the first calls for special comment here. Those which close the first and second parts respectively are cast in the multi-thematic design which characterizes most such numbers, but the opening *coro di Angeli* (SSAT) is structured instead in seven

Example 3

A/Wn 18 194 fol.7ᵛ

sections which group as AABB'ACD formally and which adhere to a ternary harmonic scheme also (f–c–f). The internal sections are set for sopranos (B) and altos (B') only, with continuo accompaniment. The 'A' sections, dispensing with counterpoint and elaborate orchestral support, are characterized by the homorhythmic, declamatory style which distinguishes much of the choral writing throughout these Passion settings. Example 3 cites the opening phrase of this chorus to illustrate that style here.

None of the three choruses in *Gesù Cristo negato* departs from the stylistic norms established in the two previous works, whereas the three choral numbers in *La cena del Signore* include some features peculiar to this oratorio. The work conservatively opens with a chorus which is then half repeated as the sixth number in the first part. The omission of a chorus from the end of this part is a possible consequence of this repeat. A remarkable integration of textual and musical considerations of formal structure is attempted by Fux in the closing chorus, which is organized according to a recurring 'rondo' principle. The chorus divides into ten sections of which the first, fourth, sixth and eighth are identical and instrumental. These sections unite the piece (in the absence of textual repetition) and the overall design emerges thus, AbcAdAb'A BC, if 'A' is allowed to stand for the recurring instrumental episode. 'B' and 'C' indicate the closing sections, which uniquely are scored for continuo accompaniment only. The homogeneity of the vocal writing throughout compensates somewhat for this textural imbalance and for the sudden disappearance of the recurring instrumental section. In this movement also, Fux's choral homophony is the most imposing and memorable aspect of the vocal writing and it attains particular dramatic importance as an articulation of sorrow. The immediate impact of such choral movements is in striking contrast to the more usual refinement and abstraction of such emotions by means of counterpoint (and other techniques) in the arias.

Il Testamento increases the choral numbers to four, but apart from one curious textural feature, these numbers manifest exactly similar techniques to those discussed thus far.[39]

Fux's smaller ensembles are generally confined to a single number per work (in the *sepolcro* settings); the exception is *Il fonte*, which contains a trio in addition to the conventional duet. Both ensembles are scored for continuo accompaniment only, and both are derived from the Italianate chamber style of thematic imitation and affective decoration over a supporting bass. Fux's modification of this style includes the participation of the continuo in thematic counterpoint and the vital addition of *obbligato* wind scoring (although not in the case of these two numbers). The trio in *Il fonte* unites the three divine abstractions (*La Misericordia, La Grazia, La Giustizia*) for the only occasion throughout the work. It is cast in *da capo* format. The text conveys a concerted moral attack on the obstinate sinner which is rhetorically organized into three anaphoric statements and a final dismissal, all of which is repeated in a second verse. The first verse is as follows:

> Dio ti vuole, e non intendi
> Dio ti chiama, e non rispondi

> Dio ti parla, e tu non senti
> Va superbo: ingrato va.

This textual strategy is paralleled in Fux's setting: the three voices consecutively introduce the sequence phrase by phrase (with skilful overlaps) and combine for the dismissal. Example 4a quotes the opening of the number and the intensified idiom which registers the last line (Example 4b). The formal organization of the music sustains the structural clarity of the text. Two statements of the first verse comprise the 'A' section of the piece in F, with a musical subdivision between the sequence and dismissal; the 'B' section is in the relative minor (d) with a further subdivision between the second sequence marked *adagio* and the dismissal, marked *allegro*. Thus the balance between cumulative reasoning and outright condemnation in the text is exactly mirrored in the music. Example 4b indicates how the intensification of the vocal counterpoint, which combines with the elaboration of *'ingrato'*, is used by Fux to dramatize the rhetorical force of the text.[40]

Example 4a, b

A/Wn 18 190 foll. 76-77^{r-v}

As with *Cristo nell'orto* and *Gesù Cristo negato, La cena del Signore* contains a single small ensemble placed towards the conclusion of the work and shared between *L'Anima Contemplativa* and *Lo Spirito Profetico*. 'O beate l'alme umane' (no. 38) differs considerably from the other duets in these oratorios because of its elaborate scoring: chalumeau, two violin parts, viola, trombone and continuo, that is, six instrumental parts in all. The instrumental sections sustain a *concertante* texture which refers to the texture of the opening *sinfonia*, and a clear distinction is made between the *tutti* and *concertino* groupings: it is the latter which comprise the wind ensemble.[41] The vocal sections receive elaborately different scorings drawn from this range of colour so as to mark the descriptive and contemplative progressions in the text. Verse I is scored for chalumeau, trombone and continuo; its repeat is accompanied by the whole ensemble; the second verse is set for strings and continuo only; the repeat of Verse II, that is, the end of the middle section, is set for continuo only. This kind of textural progression, in combination with the close, Italianate vocal counterpoint, greatly heightens the dramatic pitch of Fux's dramatic resource. Although not as elaborately wrought, the duet in *Il testamento* between *La Vergine* and *L'Angelo Gabriele* ('Venite Angioli tutti', no. 32) bears comparison with this number in its scoring for chalumeau, trombone and continuo. A degree of *concertante* participation marks the repeat of both verses of the text, which are initially set with continuo accompaniment only.[42]

Notwithstanding the expressive range and suppleness of Fux's recitatives, choral numbers and vocal ensembles, it is the remarkably imaginative exploitation of the *da capo* aria which comprises Fux's most enduring contribution to sacred-dramatic music. While the sheer scale and impact of his choral movements in particular distinguish his treatment of the Roman Catholic oratorio from its cultivation elsewhere,[43] it is Fux's immensely resourceful manipulation of contrapuntal, *concertante, obbligato* and treble-dominated textures which represents the essence of his dramatic style. This style is less overtly reliant upon fugal counterpoint in the arias of his later oratorios than is the case in earlier works, but counterpoint nevertheless endures as the singlemost distinctive resource in Fux's range of expressive techniques.

The arias of *Il fonte* employ a wide range of instrumentation and technical means which illustrate Fux's usage in the other oratorios surveyed here. In many instances, formal counterpoint is replaced by a closely established motivic relationship between the vocal and instrumental parts. The first aria assigned to *La Misericordia*, for example, is built on two contrasting ideas first presented in the principal ritornello and subsequently used to generate the melodic structure of the first and second verses respectively. Example 5a quotes these ideas and Example 5b part of the first verse: the elaboration of 'sciolto' in this latter example is derived from the second ritornello idea.

Example 5a, b

The principal ritornello of the aria which introduces *La Grazia* exemplifies another device employed by Fux as a viable alternative to formal counterpoint: a treble-dominated texture which draws upon the rhythm of a stylized dance movement. The opening is cited in Example 6. The vocal sections of such arias, including the present instance, combine this texture with the habitual omission of the continuo, a reduction which clearly affects the balance of sound throughout.

Example 6

A/Wn 18 190 fol. 27ʳ

Elaborate vocal decoration characterizes the five arias in *Il fonte* which are set for continuo accompaniment only (notwithstanding the occasional addition of a closing ritornello scored in four string parts). Such decoration is rhetorically alert to the sense of the text, as in the circular figure which decorates the word 'disarma' in the first aria assigned to the *Peccatore Ostinato* (Example 7). This usage closely compares to the decoration of 'sciolto' shown in Example 5b.

Example 7

A/Wn 18 190 foll.31ᵛ-32ʳ

Three of the seventeen arias in *Il fonte* are scored for instrumental combinations that provide some relief from the dual norm of continuo and string scoring (in four parts) which prevails in Fux's oratorios as a whole. Virtuoso *concertante* exchanges between bassoons, strings and continuo dominate the texture of the demon's aria in the first part of the oratorio, and the recurrence of a bassoon figure in particular is used to articulate the progression of the aria text which urges the obstinate sinner to transgress as he pleases. In the following aria, the *Peccatore Contrito* is set against a baryton *obbligato* and two bass parts (cello and continuo) which create a distinctive texture enhanced in turn by the reversal to conventional four-part string scoring in the closing ritornello. Example 8 cites the beginning of the 'B' section of this aria (second verse of the text) to illustrate the interaction between the *obbligato* part, the vocal writing and the supporting bass parts which typifies the texture in the body of the aria itself.

Example 8

A/Wn 18 190 foll.55ᵛ-56ʳ

The final aria assigned to *La Grazia* towards the conclusion of the oratorio incorporates texture and instrumentation which Fux uses repeatedly (with some variation) to encode moral commentary: chalumeau and trombone in imitative figurations over a steady continuo.[44]

Only one aria in *Il fonte* is fugal: the contrite sinner's reproach of his obstinate counterpart (no. 26, 'Sai perché, vil peccator') employs a double-fugal exposition in its principal ritornello which subsequently generates the pervasively contrapuntal texture in the remainder of the aria. Example 9 quotes the opening of the number to illustrate the characteristically terse subject and countersubject which between them provide the thematic substance of the piece.

Example 9

A/Wn 18 190 fol.71^v

Example 10

A/Wn 18 190 foll. 98^v-99^r

One other technique used in *Il fonte* also contributes to Fux's expressive resources elsewhere in these oratorios. The final aria assigned to *Il Demonio* makes use of a dramatic instrumental figuration which registers the turmoil and distressed defeat of the character in a manner that relates closely to the third kind of recitative discussed above. Example 10 quotes the opening vocal motto and this ensuing figure which Fux integrates into the formal structure as a systematic reinforcement of the sentiments of the text.[45]

The remaining arias in *Il fonte* correspond to the types outlined here. Fux maintains a stringent relationship between the vocal and bass lines of his continuo arias (in which the vocal decorations are dramatically figural intensifications of the text nevertheless controlled by firm bass support). His homophonic, treble-dominated ritornelli establish a desirable contrast to this tense relationship, so that the broad assimilation of stylized dance movements becomes a matter of deliberate simplification of utterance by comparison with the explicitly complex textures of contrapuntal or *concertante* techniques on one side and with the embellished continuo numbers on the other.

A similar range of textures is available in the seventeen arias of *Cristo nell'orto*. Ostinato figures, the omission of the continuo in vocal sections and the participation of *concertante* string and wind writing in the advancement of the motivic argument are abundantly in evidence. In each instance, the interdependence between vocal and instrumental music is heightened by the use of ritornello material which defines the main terms of dramatic articulation before the singer begins.[46]

If a systematic range of techniques is clearly discernible throughout the oratorios in their entirety, a constant feature of individual works within this corpus is the refinement and variation of these techniques in response to the local, dramatic requirements of a particular text. Two arias in *Cristo nell'orto* are fugally wrought, and the first of them opens the *parte seconda* of the work. 'Tanto fece e non contento' (no. 23), assigned to *L'Amor Divino*, compares closely with the mood, placement, textual content and musico-dramatic treatment of the aria 'Sai perché' from *Il fonte* discussed above. Both numbers are concerned with moral remonstration (although the precise affections naturally differ), both occur in the first half of the *parte seconda* and both are fugal textures in g, with instrumental scoring in four string parts (including continuo). Example 11 quotes the first repeat of the opening verse of 'Tanto fece' which illustrates the crucial difference between this fugal treatment and that of 'Sai perché'. In this example, the subject and countersubject combine against a free vocal part which is unrelated to either of these ideas. However involved the contrapuntal texture overall (and the vocal writing clearly relates contrapuntally to the fugal ideas), the expressive ardour of the vocal part achieves a compelling independence which subtly alters the musical perspective and balance.[47]

Example 11

A/Wn 18 194 fol.68ᵛ

The systematic derivation of vocal decoration from instrumental thematic material is nevertheless a procedure which Fux persistently adopts in support of a highly affective text. The impassioned rebuke of sinful mankind made by *La Giustizia* (no. 29, 'Sul tuo capo, scellerato') exemplifies the use of this procedure in *Cristo nell'orto*. The principal ritornello projects three elements which are rigorously deployed throughout the aria: a forthright, rhythmically square melodic gesture and two complementary motives, one scalic the other chromatic, which between them disclose the expressive scope of the remainder. Such motivic economy and the rhythmic counterpoint which it produces are both vital elements in Fux's aria technique.

Other strategies in *Cristo nell'orto* enhance this technique: the use of trombone in place of viola in the scoring of the aria assigned to *Un Angelo Confortatore* in the *parte seconda* (no. 31) results in a texture which exploits the trombone both in terms of its distinctive sonority and its contrapuntal contribution to the musical development. As Wolfgang Suppan observes, the trombone functions as an *obbligato* indication of certain expressive factors, principally sorrowful contemplation.[48]

Gesù Cristo negato sustains the techniques examined thus far in this discussion, and the arias manifest the range of fugal, motivic, treble-dominated and *obbligato* textures employed in the two preceding Passion works. There are, nevertheless, important modifications and additions to this technical range which enlarge our understanding of Fux's contribution to the *da capo* structure.

Concerted arias are in the majority in *Gesù Cristo* (ten out of a total of sixteen arias) and the first of them is distinguished by a thickly textured accompaniment which is uncharacteristic of the other concerted numbers. These latter juxtapose elaborate ritornelli with vocal sections that are largely confined to simple continuo accompaniment only. Thus the first aria assigned to *Pietro Apostolo* (no. 7) in which he boasts of his love for Christ and his readiness to face death on His behalf encodes the affection of exhibitionism in a ritornello figure which, with one exception, is *absent* from the vocal sections. This expressive contrast, between a stylized, courtly dance in dotted rhythm and a largely unornamented, forthright vocal line, does not occlude thematic coherence: the continuo line maintains the dotted rhythm of the ritornello sections throughout the vocal sections; in one exceptional instance, moreover, the voice and upper parts exchange material derived from the principal ritornello.

The fugal arias in this work are also characterized by a dependence on continuo accompaniment in most of the vocal sections; in both cases, Fux restricts his counterpoint to the exposition of a *single* fugue subject as against his normal practice of double-fugal expositions.[49] The first of these arias is also unusual in its choice of mode and text. The threatening sentiments of the character in question, *L'Odio di Giudei* (no. 9, 'L'innocenza non vive sicura'), are encoded in an angular fugue subject in a major key which is generally confined to the instrumental ritornelli, although one extended passage combines the independently conceived vocal melody against the fugal (thematic) material.[50]

This modification of fugal technique, which disappears thereafter from the arias of Fux's remaining two *sepolcro* oratorios, is accompanied by the introduction of paired imitation as a contrapuntal technique of equal significance. It first appears in the second aria assigned to *L'Amor Divino* in the *parte prima* (no. 13, 'Chi ha vergogna divantar'). Examples 12a and b show how two motivic ideas are simultaneously introduced in the principal ritornello and subsequently deployed in the first vocal section to provide the vocal and melodic interest. The variety of accompanimental textures maintains this contrapuntal device: paired imitation between voice and ensemble, continuo and vocal part, upper strings and vocal part, etc.[51]

Example 12

A/Wn 18 196 foll. 42ᵛ-43ʳ

Fux also maintains the placement of an *obbligato* aria towards the end of the *parte seconda* as a conventional feature in *Gesù Cristo*, and it is assigned here to *L'Umanità Peccatrice* (no. 33, 'Da Christo si pio'). The aria is scored for trombone and continuo. The virtuosity of the solo instrument in the ritornelli is juxtaposed here with simple continuo writing in the vocal sections, a trait which bears out this general tendency in the other arias of *Gesù Cristo* also.

The relaxation of formal contrapuntal techniques in this oratorio adumbrates the absence of fugal counterpoint in particular from the arias of its successor, *La cena del Signore*. With one exception, the arias in this work do not feature any kind of formal contrapuntal texture and homophonic and *obbligato* textures consequently predominate. Moreover, the use of vocal

and instrumental figures in combination necessarily results in a wide
manifestation of *informal*, motivic counterpoint in the arias of *La cena*, as in
the first aria of the work, which is assigned to *Lo Spirito Profetico* (no. 3,
'Alme sante sì sperate'). The treble-dominated ritornello and a sequentially-
developed vocal figure which between them convey the joyful import of the
text are tacitly combined in a texture of contrapuntal organization. The
main feature of this organization is a lively rhythmic structure.

A different kind of rhythmic structure pervades the first aria assigned to
Giuda (no. 14, 'Di quest' opra'), which relies on an *ostinato* figure in the
continuo as against a leading violin idea with the subordinate strings in
support. The *ostinato* is used in the continuo part throughout the
statements of the first verse ('A') in order to encode the sinful repudiations
of Judas; Examples 13a and b quote from the close of this 'A' section and
from the ensuing ritornello respectively, to illustrate the thematic function
of the *ostinato* figure and the simplified, informal contrapuntal texture
which it supports throughout the number.

Example 13a

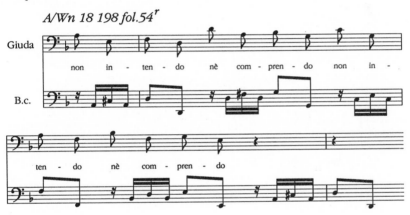

Example 13b

Example 14 illustrates the treble-dominated, 'pre-classic' texture which commonly usurps the function of strict counterpoint in the arias of Fux's later oratorios: the latter is used once only here, in the second aria assigned to Judas (no. 34, 'L'impossibil del mistero'), which is briefly illustrated in Example 15. Once again, Fux prefers the paired imitation of ideas (with a third idea articulated in the viola and subsequently absorbed into the fabric) to fugal texture, and the use of this imitation results in a perceptibly brisk, vivacious mode of expression which emphasizes motivic development at the expense of pervasive (formal) counterpoint.[52]

Example 14

It is noteworthy that the arias in *La cena* are confined to string scoring (the one *obbligato* aria features a solo violin) but the elaborate scoring of the duet in this work (see above) compensates somewhat for this restriction.

Example 15a

The arias in *Il testamento* are also distinguished in the main by a high degree of treble-dominated textures and by a corresponding absence of formal counterpoint. But Fux also consolidates his tendency to replace such formal techniques with rhythmic figurations and *concertante* textures which provide a satisfactory context for the dramatization of the verse. Examples 16 and 17 respectively illustrate the broad division of style which informs these arias: a sweeping homophony which relies on a simplified concept of melodic structure and a continued reliance on intricate, if informal, rhythmic and melodic counterpoint.

Example 15b

A/Wn 18 198 fol.115ᵛ

In addition, the cultivation of *concertante* and *obbligato* textures in this oratorio demonstrates Fux's continued sensitivity to the inherently dramatic content of the *sepolcro* text. The aria assigned to *Lucifero* in the *parte seconda* (no. 34, 'Son de l'uomo'), is scored in three actual parts for unison violins, four unison bassoons and continuo. The extreme simplicity of the vocal writing in this number allows the development of the figurative instrumental material to determine the mood and projection of the text. In a similar way, the *obbligato* violin part in the closing aria of the oratorio, assigned to *La Vergine* (no. 38, 'Si tempra il mio martir'), largely defines the rhetorical expression of sorrow which the text conveys. The contrast of

vocal sections with and without the *obbligato* counterpoint is itself a
dramatic strategy used to specific effect. The pervasively sorrowful mood of
the *sepolcro* narrows to an intimate consideration of grief which is
registered by this combination of instrumental commentary and vocal
statement.

Example 16

Example 17

La deposizione dalla croce: Fux and Pasquini

La deposizione dalla croce di Gesù Cristo Salvator Nostro, a 'componimento sacro per musica', was first given on the Tuesday of Holy Week, 23 March 1728. As with the other works surveyed here, it was performed before a replica of the Holy Sepulchre erected in the court chapel.[53] This performance was recorded in the *Wienerisches Diarium* on the day following in these terms:

> Dienstag/den 23sten dito. . ./nach Mittag. . .in der kaiserl. grossen Hof-Capelle der Italiänischen Predig/als auch dem lebten Italiänisch gesungen *oratorio* bey/ welches *La Deposizione dalla Croce di Gesù Cristo Salvator nostro*: die Herabnehmung Jesu Christi/ unsers Erlösers/von dem Creuz/ benamset ware/ von dem Herrn Gio. Claudio Pasquini, so in würtl. kaiserl. Diensten ist/ in Poesie verfasset/ und von dem Herrn Johann Joseph Fux/ kaiserl. CappellMeister in die Music gebracht worden.[54]

Pasquini wrote at least seven sacred-dramatic texts in all for the imperial court chapel, in whose service he was from 1725, when he came under the protection and influence of Apostolo Zeno.[55] His libretto *La deposizione dalla croce* represents a definitive example of the *sepolcro* oratorio text under the influence of Italian dramaturgical practice in the second and third decades of the eighteenth century.[56] It bears close comparison with Pariati's later *sepolcro* libretti in its elimination of allegorical personages and its concentration upon the Bible and the writings of the church fathers. Its simple structure reduces the *sepolcro* to a doctrinal meditation which closely paraphrases these sources, and its inclusion of reported events, the removal of Christ from the cross and the preparation for His burial, frames the series of contemplations which comprise the bulk of the verse.

Pasquini casts *La deposizione* for five typical personages, all of them taken from various biblical accounts of the Passion: *Maria Vergine* (S), *Maria Maddalena* (S), *Giovanni Apostolo* (A), *Giuseppe d'Arimatea* (T) and *Nicodemo* (B). To these he adds a *Coro di Peccatori* (SATB). The latter opens the text with a verse imbued with pathetic fallacy: 'The earth shook, the sun hid its rays, the mountains gaped and we?, We yet have hearts of stone':

Tremò la terra, e il sole
Nascose i raggi suoi,
S'apriro i monti, e noi?
E noi di scoglio abbiamo ancora il core.

Thereafter each of the characters is introduced in turn. A central consideration in *La deposizione* is the grief of the Virgin, and Pasquini combines
hyperbolic invocation and close, biblical paraphrase in order to convey it.
Thus her first appearance culminates in an aria text drawn from the Book of
Lamentations: 'Oh all ye who pass this way attend and see if there is any
sorrow like unto my sorrow':

O voi tutti, che passate
Per la via qui dove Amore
A morir condusse un Dio;
Soffermativi, e guardate
Se può darsi ugual dolore
All'intenso dolor mio.

This plea provokes a response from *Giovanni* (whom the Virgin addresses
as 'caro mio Figlio'), and in his first aria it is the Virgin's suffering, rather
than the death of Christ, which he meditates upon. Other concerns are
raised with the subsequent introduction of *Gioseppe, Maddalena* and
Nicodemo. The familiar pattern of free verse and aria text accommodates
dialogue between these three on the removal of Christ from the cross, with
moral explications of the significance of this addressed to *Maddalena* by
Gioseppe. These culminate in the latter's first aria, a paraphrase from
Isaiah: 'All we like sheep have gone astray . . .':

Quasi Agnelle tutti noi
Traviammo dal sentiero . . .

The remorse of Mary Magdalene (which Pasquini projects as a counterpart
to the sorrow of the Virgin) finds expression in a more personal idiom
which is characterized by metaphorical intensity. Her eyes 'shall become
two founts, two streams of bitter tears' until her 'guilt is washed away':

Di lagrime amare
Saran questi lumi
Due fonti, due fiumi,
Finché la mia colpa
Lavata sarà.

To this point the text offers pathetic fallacy and self-rebuke in the chorus
of sinners, intense grief (the Virgin), consolation (*Giovanni*), moral
commentary (*Gioseppe*) and personal remorse (*Maddalena*). Each of these
concerns is directly or indirectly stimulated by the immediate circumstances
of Christ's death on the cross. The final aria in the *prima parte* widens this
focus to predict the fall of Jerusalem. The text of *Nicodemo*'s aria, drawn
from Hosea (3:4), abruptly alters the mood from sorrowful contemplation
to vengeful clairvoyance. 'You (Jerusalem) shall pay the just price of your
fierce cruelty on the crumbling towers and abandoned walls (of the city)':

> Sulle Torri diroccate,
> Sulle mura desolate,
> Pagherai la giusta pena
> Di tua fiera crudeltà;

The action of the *prima parte* ends with *Gioseppe*'s decision to shroud the body of Christ. This in turn leads to a choral paraphrase of psalm twenty-one, verse 25: 'They have pierced my hands and my feet, they have numbered all my bones.'

The *parte seconda* sustains the admixture of biblical paraphrase, orderly exposition of character and moral deliberation which comprises the content of the *prima parte. Giovanni* consoles, the Virgin laments, *Gioseppe* and *Nicodemo* moralise and *Maddalena* yearns for forgiveness. *Nicodemo*'s characteristic declaration that 'none is without guilt' in his final aria is repeated at the opening of the closing chorus which meditates on divine sacrifice as against human culpability.

Fux's musical treatment of this text is summarized in Appendix II below. His musical articulation of Pasquini's text profits from individual scrutiny in that the technical resources surveyed in this discussion can thereby be seen in the context of an oratorio in its entirety. Preceded by a nine-section *introduzione* scored for five real parts, *La deposizione* begins with a chorus which is governed by a pictorial approach to the hyperbole and pathetic fallacies of the text. The opening phrase, 'Tremò la terra', for example, is articulated in a monotonal rhythmic gesture which echoes the sense of the verbal image (see Example 18). This gesture is introduced without

Example 18

preamble and without accompaniment. The stark beginning, with its rhetorically suggestive (vocal) range of an octave and a half, yields to an independent string figure and successive vocal entries which culminate in a shift to the dominant minor of the principal tonality. The following phrases ('e il sole nascose i raggi suoi/ s'apriro i monti/ e noi?') are met by a series of antiphonal exchanges in the vocal parts which are also demarcated by a semiquaver figure in the upper strings. The leading role of the soprano (which the other voices follow) lends interrogative urgency to 'e noi?'; this question in turn is relieved by the broad, chromatic and rhythmic pull of the response 'di scoglia abbiamo ancora il core'. These pictorialisms are sustained in the second verse of the chorus. Although Fux naturally inclines towards a ternary harmonic organization, the impulse which determines the shape of the number as a whole is finally gestural rather than formal.

A different kind of gestural impulse is used to organize the first aria of the oratorio, in which *Maria Vergine* contemplates the extent of her sorrow. Whereas the choral writing is immediate in its figurative response to the text, the ritornello material in this aria (part of which is quoted in Example 19) matches the comparatively restrained tone of Pasquini's re-working of the text from Lamentations. Fux employs a circular instrumental motive which throws the simple declamation of the text into relief. If there is an inherent formal and expressive problem in the continued application of this motive for the lengthy duration of this aria (which runs to 121 measures before the *da capo*), there is also a sensitive relationship established between Pasquini's biblical paraphrase and Fux's obligations to baroque style. In precise terms, the ritornello material objectifies the affections of the text which are then more freely expressed in the vocal writing:

Exanple 19

A/Wn 18 204 fol.14ᵛ ff.

Gioseppe's aria in the *prima parte* (no. 7, 'Quasi agnelle tutti noi') is also a biblical paraphrase, as we have seen. It is the culmination of a recitative exchanged between *Giovanni, Nicodemo* and *Maddalena,* in which these characters are introduced into the work. Example 20a quotes part of this recitative and an excerpt from the aria (beginning with the vocal motto and first ritornello). The recitative conveys the dramatic content of the text fairly rapidly. Fux does not extend the range of expression to include elaborate rhetorical figures, but confines himself here to a plain rendition in which monotones are commonplace. (Affective words, however, such as *Maddalena*'s 'incrudelir', are modestly highlighted.)

Example 20a

The aria itself, by contrast, discloses a highly systematic use of rhythmic figuration, chromatic sequence and invertible counterpoint in order to register the spiritual turmoil and disarray of *Gioseppe*'s text. Three elements are specifically discernible in the instrumental parts and these work in counterpoint against the vocal theme, which is independently derived from the opening motto. These three elements are (i) a long-note, descending motive in the first violin part, (ii) a semiquaver/quaver motive in the second violin part and (iii) a tied chromatic descent in the continuo. Furthermore, the vocal decorations which Fux uses to dramatize affective words are taken over directly from the instrumental material, as the elaboration of *traviammo* in the present example clearly demonstrates. Example 20b cites the opening of the middle 'B' section of the aria in which the second element identified here is transferred to the continuo; the half verse and its repetition are conventionally separated by short references to the principal ritornello and Fux sets the text in this section syllabically (notwithstanding one brief decoration). Such a reduction of texture is a conservative feature of the middle sections of Fux's arias generally, but the reduction in this case actually clarifies one important feature of the motivic structure of the aria as a whole, namely, its reliance on invertible counterpoint.[57]

The formal and harmonic organization of this material is perhaps its least impressive feature. 'Quasi agnelle' adheres to a full-blown *da capo* structure with motto, opening, internal and closing ritornelli and a middle section of substance. The repetition of so much cogently derived material, however, which this structure involves, weakens the dramatic impact of the aria. There is an undesirable tension between the apposite nature of Fux's vocal and instrumental motives and their continued reiteration.[58] The harmonic path is also limited. The following scheme shows how it is applied throughout the aria.

Vocal motto and principal ritornello: a
Verse I : a to e

Internal ritornello: e
Verse I repeat: a to d to a
Closing ritornello: a
Verse II (first half): F to g to F
Internal ritornello: F
Verse II (second half): F to C
Internal ritornello: C to a

This kind of formal design and harmonic scheme are both representative of Fux's procedures generally.

Example 20b

The continuo aria is a vital resource in these oratorios, and its spare texture frequently affords a clear indication of Fux's dramatic reconciliation of prescribed form and affective depiction.[59] Somewhat over a third of these arias have a closing ritornello orchestrated for strings in four parts attached as a substitute for the *da capo* reprise. In the case of *La deposizione*, *Maddalena's* first aria is thus designed, and Example 21 quotes three excerpts which comprise Fux's response to the metaphorical conceit of the text (discussed above). The continuo ritornello, the repeat of the first verse and part of the orchestral ritornello at the close are shown in this example. The first of these offers a rhythmically alert continuo line, the contour of which is defined by the flattened supertonic in measures 2 and 7, the octave leaps and the rhythmic pattern of the opening measures. This material establishes the musical context for the verse itself. The second excerpt shows material from the continuo ritornello (particularly the octave leaps and tied crotchets) in support of a plain, vocal articulation of the first line of text followed by a melodic sequence to match the verbal sequence ('due fonte, due fiumi'). The elaboration of 'sarà' is an independent decoration. The third excerpt shows how Fux adapts the original ritornello as a contrapuntal summary of the musico-dramatic content of this setting. Three elements, therefore, define the emotional impact of the text within the constraints of a predictable formal scheme and a limited instrumental resource. The expressive qualities of the number as a whole can be reduced to this identification of stylistic and technical features which also include one further, vital component. This is the *constant* nature of the contrapuntal dynamic which exists between the vocal and continuo parts. If the latter moves unobtrusively during points of vocal decoration (with subtle allusions to the opening ritornello), the exchange of rhythmic movement elsewhere is an unmistakable feature of the vocal–continuo relationship. It is this relationship which supports the musical interest under the exacting conditions of lengthy repetition and formal expectations.

The final aria in the *prima parte* is assigned to *Nicodemo*. As with 'Quasi agnelle', 'Sulle torri diroccate' depends on a systematic manipulation of

Example 21

instrumental motives which are contrapuntally combined in the ritornelli
and adapted in the vocal sections. The elaboration of these techniques in
this aria to convey the destruction of Jerusalem testifies to Fux's preference
for such heavily scored motivic textures in his later sacred-dramatic music
over the claims of abstract, formal counterpoint. The rhythmic vigour and
motivic sequences of the string writing in 'Sulle torri diroccate' are
inevitably contrapuntal to a degree, but it is the variation of basic motivic
cells which is the paramount technical strategy. In terms of dramatic music,
this technique provides for a complex of (instrumental) motives which
determines the affective range of the aria as a whole. The vocal writing is by
comparison notably plain (notwithstanding instrumentally derived elaborations of the verb 'pagherai'), and it is subordinate to the expressive
gestures of the ritornello sections.

Three arias in the *parte seconda* add significantly to the expressive range
of techniques analysed here. The *concertante* texture employed by Fux in
the aria 'O beate l'alme umane' is also evident in the first of these arias
which comprises the definitive expression of the Virgin's grief in *La
deposizione*. 'Aveva ancor bambino' is an intensely worded contrast
between the infant born to the Virgin and the wounded ('piagato'), bleeding
('svenato'), torn ('lacero'), battered ('pesto') and crushed ('infranto') body
she now beholds.[60] For this potent accumulation of adjectives, Fux combines
rhetorical-vocal syntax with ritornelli of considerably complex scoring and

texture. These ritornelli are scored for chalumeau and strings in five real parts. The principal ritornello is elaborately divided into three sections, the first of which (mm 1–12) rehearses the Virgin's vocal melody at the opening of the first verse; the second section (mm 13–16) features a descending sequence for strings alone and the last (mm 16–24) assimilates both previous sections. The ritornello material accommodates a *concertino* grouping between chalumeau and first violin against the *tutti* ensemble, and both verses (and their repetition) receive a distinct scoring based on this or a similar contrast of groupings. Example 22a indicates the level of this contrapuntal texture in the repeat of the first verse and 22b shows the two principal ideas employed in the opening ritornello. It is these ideas which modify and inform Fux's subsequent vocal articulation of the series of adjectives which compound feeling in the text, and the overall result is one of controlled expression which is instrumentally defined and objectified.

Fux's interest in *obbligato* textures is paramount in the *parte seconda* of this work. A duet between *Maria Vergine* and *Giovanni* (no. 28) scored for two trombones and continuo recalls the trio-sonata texture and chamber style so skilfully combined in *Il testamento*; the use of violin and bassoon as *obbligato* instruments in two arias is equally notable. The violin *obbligato* is juxtaposed with paired imitation in the only aria which makes use of formal counterpoint in *La deposizione*.[61] Fux brilliantly resorts to two contrasted ritornelli in *Maddalena*'s aria (no. 24 'Caro mio Dio'), which are separated by a vocal motto. These ritornelli are used to register the two levels of moral ardour and personal intensity which characterize the text. *Maddalena* yearns for the divine fear which 'little by little' would suffuse the natural

Example 22a

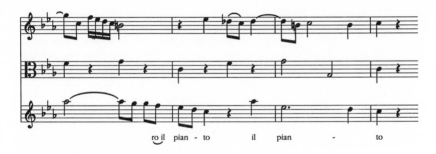

ro il pian - to   il   pian   -   to

Example 22b

A/Wn 18 204 fol. 78ʳ-79ᵛ

mm 1-4

mm 13-16

coldness of her heart. Both ritornelli are partly quoted in Example 23. The first is a passage of paired imitation in which the chain of suspensions objectifies the moral purpose and yearning conveyed in the text. The second is a soloistic episode for violin which graphically prefigures the personal longing as a separate issue. Fux allows this solo material to combine with the vocal writing (after a simple statement of the text with continuo only), and he frames the vocal sections with the first ritornello which constantly recurs in part as a point of stability and moral reference between the vocal sections. Here, as in 'Aveva ancor bambino', two kinds of counterpoint, one formal, the other incidental, dramatize the textual sentiment by means of an exhaustive exploration of the formal constraints of the *da capo* structure.[62] The final aria in the work is the third such in the *parte seconda* which augments the technical and textural resources of the arias in the *parte prima*. It is assigned to *Nicodemo* (no. 30, 'Se pura più nel core') and its combination of *obbligato* bassoon figurations and virtuoso vocal writing conveys the extravagant terms of moral culpability with which *Nicodemo*'s text is imbued.

Example 23a

A/Wn 18 204 fol.113ᵛ

Example 23b

A/Wn 18 204 fol.114ʳ⁻ᵛ

Example 23c

In sum, what I would wish to argue here is that the systematic richness of scoring, colour, technique and expressive usage which distinguishes Fux's approach to the text of *La deposizione* is informed by two factors. One is an adherence to established formal conventions which pose an inherently dramatic problem of design *versus* expressive impact. The other is an immensely resourceful use of textural and technical strategies (most of them intrinsically if informally contrapuntal) in order to circumvent this problem. Given the predetermined conventions, both textual and musical, which obtain in the *oratorio al santissimo sepolcro*, Fux's *La deposizione* may be advanced as a definitive and imaginative example of this tradition of sacred-dramatic music.

La passione di Gesù Cristo: Caldara and Metastasio

Antonio Caldara's setting of Metastasio's *La passione di Gesù Cristo* was performed in the court chapel in Vienna on 3 April 1730. Its design and content permit a useful comparison between the oratorios of Fux and those of one of his ablest contemporaries in Vienna. Appendix III below summarizes the musical disposition of *La passione* for the purposes of comparing the general layout of this work and that of Fux's *La deposizione*, performed some two years previously.

At almost every level *La deposizione* invites comparison with *La passione*. Fux's oratorio is the most 'modern' text set by the composer in that it reflects the norms of biblical drama prescribed by the Viennese colony of the Arcadian *accademia* in general, and those of Zeno in particular.[63] Metastasio was Zeno's successor as imperial court poet, and his sacred-dramatic libretti for Vienna share much in common with those of the older writer. Of these seven texts, one is hagiographical, five are based on the Old Testament and one – *La passione* – is based on the Gospels. As with Zeno, Metastasio draws frequently upon the church fathers and his text emphasizes reflection and narration at the expense of action. It is not difficult to recognize *La deposizione* and *La passione* as two of a kind, written under the same stylistic and dramaturgical principles established by Zeno, absorbed by Pasquini and essentially upheld (if undoubtedly modified) by Metastasio.

Three factors especially are shared by these texts: (i) they were intended for the same audience, place of performance and period (the imperial household, the *sepolcro* erected in the court chapel and Holy Week, 1728 and 1730, respectively); (ii) the libretti have three characters in common: *Giovanni, Maddalena* and *Gioseppe/Giuseppe* (*La passione* has *Pietro* in addition; *La deposizione*, as we have seen, adds *Maria Vergine* and *Nicodemo*); (iii) both texts were widely admired as 'definitive' versions of the Passion, to judge by the number of subsequent settings both within and beyond Vienna.

The principal distinction between *La passione* and *La deposizione* lies in the characterization of the central personage in each text. We have seen that this is *Maria Vergine* in the latter. *La Passione* is organized around the character of *Pietro*.[64] Metastasio imbues his characterization of *Pietro* with tragic status in that *Pietro* dominates the drama as the greatest figure of guilt and anguish throughout the text. The vivid hyperbole of his opening recitative absorbs much of the pathetic fallacy expressed by the *coro* in *La deposizione* within the confines of an individual character. *Pietro* describes his state of mind having denied Christ in terms which are very similar to those of Pasquini's *Tremò la terra.*[65] *Pietro* also introduces each of the remaining characters into the text. His questions provoke an account of Christ's suffering on the cross, the crowning with thorns and other elements of the Gospel account, which are here provided by *Giovanni* and *Giuseppe; Maddalena* meanwhile contemplates the extent of her sorrow (as in *La deposizione*) and *Giuseppe* condemns Jerusalem in an extravagant simile which sustains the hyperbole of *Pietro*'s diction and the poetic conceits employed by *Maddalena.*[66]

Thus *Pietro* is the dramatic agent of sorrow whose interrogations further the progress of the drama which the others recount and contemplate. Much of the *parte seconda* continues with this pattern of instigation (*Pietro*) and consequent narration, but the dramatic mood is shifted from sorrow to righteous anger directed, as in *La deposizione*, against Jerusalem. The language gradually becomes remote from the direct circumstances of the Passion although *Maddalena*'s aria recovers the thread of personal sorrow. The final aria, assigned to *Pietro*, is an extraordinary avowal of hope, in which Christ is compared to an experienced swimmer who rescues the struggling infant from the waves: the sea (and by extension, the swimmer) is used as a metaphor for life itself.[67]

In brief, this libretto divides between a *parte prima* largely given over to narration, and a *parte seconda* which contemplates the implications of the Passion as a point of departure for moral scrutiny. In both parts, the advantage of *Pietro*'s dominance is that our sense of perspective on these events is enhanced.

The characterization and structure of *La deposizione* are somewhat weaker and more complex. *Maddalena* rivals *Maria Vergine* in Pasquini's text, although the latter does attain a primary position at the outset and at the culminating point of her expression of grief ('Aveva ancor bambino'). Nevertheless, the range of literary expression, the general pattern of Gospel narration and contemplation and the alternation of sorrow with righteous anger which both texts share, support the view that they stem from a commonly understood approach to the *sepolcro* tradition in its later manifestation.[68]

Just as Pasquini's text compares in structural and linguistic terms to that of Metastasio, so also Caldara's musical response compares with that of Fux. From the orchestral *introduzione*, with its double-fugal second movement, to the alternation of massive, declamatory textures and more lightly scored soloistic imitation in the three choruses of *La passione*, Caldara's setting shows the same formal constraints and many of the same strategies which distinguish Fux's oratorio. If the recitative in Caldara's case appears sometimes rushed (and there are no *accompagnato* recitatives in *La passione*)[69] the set numbers are characterized by many of the contrapuntal, *obbligato, concertante* and treble-dominated techniques used by Fux in *La deposizione*. A deficiency in Caldara's oratorio is the limited instrumentation: all but one of the set numbers is scored for strings and continuo, the exception being an aria for *Giovanni* (no. 26) which is scored for trombone and continuo.

Nevertheless, the arias in *La passione* are technically comparable to those in *La deposizione*. Caldara's pervasive manipulation of ritornello material in motivic counterpoint against vocal elaborations which are themselves largely derived from the principal ritornello is a feature of the work's opening aria (assigned to *Pietro*). This feature is exactly similar to Fux's procedure in 'Sulle torri diroccate' from *La deposizione*. This reliance on instrumentally-conceived motives in an essentially contrapuntal context for the purposes of dramatizing the text is a vital characteristic of Fux's later style and it is prominent also in *La passione*.

The *obbligato* arias in *La passione* are likewise comparable to Fux's soloistic writing in *La deposizione*. The Caldara work employs solo violin to dramatize the poignant contrast urged by *Pietro* between his desolate guilt and *Giovanni*'s 'happy sorrow' in the former's second aria (no. 15, 'Tu nel duol felice sei') in a manner which closely compares with the soloistic commentaries of the violin writing in *Maddalena*'s aria 'Caro mio Dio' in *La deposizione*. Caldara's treatment of the prediction of the fall of Jerusalem in *La passione* is also strongly suggestive of the influence of Fux. The catalogue of disasters recounted in the recitative yields to a more stable, abstract prediction in the aria text; the music likewise proceeds from free, rapid declamation to an orderly, fugal aria.[70]

Caldara's complex organization of counterpoint in this number, assigned to *Giuseppe* (no. 22, 'All'idea de' tuoi perigli'), compares with Fux's fugal procedures in his arias. The vocal insistence upon and dramatization of a single word juxtaposed with an internal ritornello of unremitting abstract counterpoint is a feature of this aria which is repeatedly found in Fux's fugal arias.[71]

Formal counterpoint is in fact more prominent in the arias of *La passione* than it is in those of *La deposizione*. One ritornello is organized in canon (no. 20, 'Ritornerà fra voi', assigned to *Giovanni*) and the strict counterpoint thereby articulates the objective prediction of Christ's return to avenge His death, while the freely derived vocal elaborations (partly combined *against* the canonic writing) dramatize the affective implications of the text.

In the arias which use simpler techniques a comparison between Fux and Caldara is also pertinent. The characterization of *Maddalena* in Caldara's oratorio is not as effectively achieved as Fux's depiction of the same character in *La deposizione*, but the musical means compare. This is especially true of the first appearance of the character in both oratorios. Metastasio's text, 'Vorrei dirti il mio dolore' shares with Pasquini's 'Di lagrime amare' a reliance on hyperbole which Caldara sets by means of three elements: (i) a vigorously imitative ritornello; (ii) a circular, chromatic vocal motto which is doubled in thirds in the strings (the continuo is silent during the vocal sections); (iii) a comparatively restrained use of vocal decoration. Fux's treatment of Pasquini's text depends similarly on four elements that produce a texture which in its rhythmic and motivic astringency is preferable to the instrumental doubling, absence of continuo support and limited harmonic movement which deprive the Caldara version of much dramatic power.[72]

The overall design of both oratorios, the musical characterization of *Pietro* and *Maria Vergine* respectively, the portrayal of the fall of Jerusalem and the treatment of *Maddalena* are points of contact between these oratorios which reinforce the view that Fux and Caldara worked from a thoroughly well-tried concept of sacred-dramatic music which significantly affected the contribution of each composer. Until a more complete study of Caldara's oratorios is available, it is difficult to determine the extent to which Fux led and Caldara followed in this commonly understood approach to sacred drama. In the meantime, this brief comparison underlines the fact that Fux's blend of *sepolcro* traditions and the expressive resources of serious opera (and, of course, *oratorio volgare*) was not unique to the composer and that on the contrary it also served as a durable formula for other composers.

Conclusion

David Poultney has observed that 'the lifetime of Alessandro Scarlatti (1660–1725) coincides with the golden age of oratorio in both its Italian and Latin forms'.[73] The oratorios of Scarlatti's exact contemporary, Fux, belong in part to this 'golden age' and deserve evaluation in terms of the best of *oratorio volgare* in the later baroque. The scope of these sacred-dramatic works permits us to suggest that Fux was to Vienna as Scarlatti was to Rome in the development of oratorio. If Fux did not possess the latter's outstanding gift for vocal melody, or the stylistic versatility of his colleague Caldara, he nevertheless brought to perfection a local and well-defined version of Italian oratorio. He infused the genre with a coherent and highly effective sense of musical drama and in so doing, he created a form recognizably independent of similar achievements in Rome, if also manifestly indebted to those achievements and to those of his immediate predecessors and contemporaries in Vienna.

All forms of Italian oratorio in the later Baroque bear a close, stylistic relationship to contemporary opera. It has not been part of this assessment to consider Fux's oratorios in relation to his secular-dramatic works,[74] but it is useful in this conclusion to point out that Fux's secular dramas manifest the same dependence on Italian models (and to a lesser extent, German and French precedents also) which informs his oratorios. The same concept of musical articulation and dramatic method, moreover, is evident in both secular- and sacred-dramatic works, and Fux's technical and textural strategies and resources in both closely compare.[75]

The texts of Fux's oratorios reflect the conventional, poetic and dramatic changes which took place in the Viennese oratorio in the eighteenth century. The earliest of them, *Santa Dimpna, Infanta d'Irlanda* (1702), is a hagiographical drama which clearly belongs to the Roman tradition of oratorio as a sacred counterpart to opera which developed *c*.1700, and to which Scarlatti and Caldara both made important contributions.[76] The biblical libretti, *La fede sacrilega, La donna forte* and *Il disfacimento di Sisara*, likewise invite comparison with the texts of Italian oratorios in the first decades of the eighteenth century. Several of Scarlatti's oratorios in particular are settings of biblical texts (on Ishmael, Judith, Samson, the Assumption of the Blessed Virgin, etc.), and the subjects of Fux's biblical oratorios are also those of his contemporaries in Vienna, versified by Apostolo Zeno and other court poets, and set by Caldara, Badia and other composers attached to the imperial chapel.

Although regional differences naturally obtain between the biblical libretti set by Fux and those set by his Roman and Venetian contemporaries, the general structure, length and dramatic disposition of these libretti are similar.Although Pariati's texts reflect the influence of Zeno, it is not surprising to find that the inherent dramatic qualities and moral stance of his libretti also characterize the style of oratorio texts cultivated under the patronage of the Arcadian academy in Rome.[77] As a Lenten substitute for operatic texts, such libretti had to satisfy the demand for fully accomplished characterization, even as they sought to dramatize the moral or spiritual meaning of the biblical event in question. In Pariati's biblical libretti *La fede sacrilega nella morte del Precursor S. Giovanni Battista* (1714) and *La donna forte nella madre de' sette Macabei* (1715), as in *Il disfacimento di Sisara* (1717), the development of characterization extends far beyond the requirements of moral explication. These texts are explicitly dramatic in their exploration of conflict, anguish and tragic circumstance.[78]

Vienna's most distinctive achievement in the oratorio libretto is the virtually unbroken series of Passion texts used for performances at the Holy Sepulchre erected in the court chapel from 1700–40. Pariati, as imperial poet, figured prominently in this series from *c.*1715 onwards, and the texts he wrote comprise a sustained and vital contribution to the Italian oratorio which is notably independent of the achievement of his contemporaries in Italy. Whereas settings of the Passion were 'relatively few' in Italy,[79] they were frequent and of long standing in Vienna. The quasi-liturgical performances of *sepolcro* oratorios in the court chapel are as central to Vienna as are the extravagant entertainments to the oratories and palaces of Rome in the early eighteenth century.

Fux was responsible for many of these performances. The Passion texts which he set typify a more general trend in the Italian oratorio text, towards an emphasis on 'the varied emotional states of the characters rather than the events of a religious story' in the later Baroque.[80] We have seen how these libretti gradually discard abstract personages in favour of actual characters, whose 'behaviour' is governed by the prescriptive guidelines of Zeno and Pariati. In formal terms, these texts compare with Roman models in their 'relatively inflexible alternation of poetic units intended for recitatives and arias'.[81] This alternation of recitative and aria is essential to the construction of all texts set by Fux. Thus there is no notable structural difference in this respect between a later Scarlatti oratorio libretto (*La Giuditta*, 1700, for example), and a late Fux libretto. In terms of length, poetic form, metrics, syllabification, rhyme and number of characters, there is little fundamental change in thirty years. Notwithstanding the exceptional length of some of Zeno's texts, the externals and technical characteristics of a Viennese libretto are those of a Roman one. Although the subject matter can vary widely, David Poultney's division of Scarlatti's libretti into biblical, hagiographical and allegorical categories is one which could usefully serve Fux's oratorios also, with the important addition of a separate category for the Passion texts. The musical externals of a Roman oratorio in the early eighteenth century and a Viennese work of the same period are also very similar, notwithstanding the virtual absence of choral texts in Scarlatti's oratorios. Just as Arcangelo Spagna, speaking for Roman librettists in 1708, dispensed with the need for a chorus,[82] Pariati apparently assumed the inevitability of one, given the permanent choral resources available in the court chapel. In Rome and Vienna, as in Venice or Bologna, practical circumstances determined whatever variation might be brought to bear on the external structure of sacred musical drama.

The inevitability of such a structure obtained with equal force, however, in Rome and Vienna, and in other centres where the oratorio developed as a sacred counterpart to serious opera. David Poultney, in his assessment of Scarlatti's oratorios, adverts to a formal limitation which bears on the recurrence of formal schemes in Fux's oratorios:

> It is clear that Scarlatti's later oratorios [i.e., after 1695] become ever more schematicized in design and content. Seldom, or never, is there a higher level of organization than a recitative and the da capo aria that follows it.[83]

In the same way, the oratorios of Fux uniformly adhere to the general scheme of *sinfonia, prima parte* (*coro*) and *parte seconda* (*madrigale*), within which recitatives and *da capo* set numbers are systematically alternated. The added feature of an opening *coro* is also a formal trait of the six *sepolcro* oratorios. The composer's musico-dramatic response, therefore, is determined by these invariables, no matter what the dramatic situation. The torture and persecution of the Maccabees, the despair of Sisara, the anguished indecision of Herod, the crucifixion of Christ, the effrontery of Judas, the remorse of Mary Magdalene: all such events and feelings are articulated within the boundaries of such comparatively inflexible structures. Given the concept of musical drama which underlies these structures, it must be acknowledged that Fux's primary dramatic problem concerns the excessive repetition of musical ideas (and textual material) in his adherence to the formal demands of such structures, above all the full-blown *da capo* aria. Fux's dramatic articulation of these libretti is, however, greatly strengthened by the techniques which we have surveyed in this assessment. Massive choral homophony to project the concerted grief of the Passion, intricate choral counterpoint to throw sections of the text into high relief, rhetorical figures which are alert to the dramatic import and structure of the recitative texts or which intensify the affection of an aria text, an extremely sophisticated range of contrapuntal techniques and textures (motivic, paired, fugal, *concertante, obbligato*) which objectify and dramatize the poetry, and colourful scoring for wind, strings and continuo which enhance it: all of these elements contribute to Fux's definitive approach to the Italian oratorio as it developed in Vienna.

In his treatment of the *da capo* aria, we find the point of closest contact between Fux and his Roman contemporaries, for in his choral writing he is isolated from the prevailing style of the Italian oratorio in Rome and elsewhere in Italy.[84] The kind of dramatic role afforded to the chorus in Fux's work is quite foreign (for the most part) to the oratorios of Scarlatti and his Italian colleagues. Beyond Vienna, one has to look to the choral movements in Bach's passions or the later dramatic oratorios of Handel, to find large-scale sacred-dramatic works in which the chorus is as prominent or more so.

The solo numbers in these works, however, share a great deal in common with the style and content of the *da capo* aria as it has been perceived in the sacred-dramatic music of Scarlatti and Caldara.[85] David Poultney, for example, finds four main elements in the arias of Scarlatti's mature oratorios, three of which can clearly be discerned also in Fux's arias: (i) a greater interest in portraying the general affection in the music than in literal fidelity to every nuance of the text; (ii) a freely developed vocal line characterized by elaborate melismas (*Fortspinnung*); (iii) a schematicized harmonic procedure that depends on formulaic contrast of tonal centres; (iv) a varied use of scoring and instruments, sometimes in *obbligato* and *concertante* textures and occasionally in one part which is contrapuntally combined with the continuo line. Only the second element here is generally untypical of Fux's *da capo* arias, wherein the vocal line is normally determined by the opening ritornello, and where the vocal decorations are frequently elaborations of a motive announced in this (opening) section. (Free elaboration is of course a feature of some of the continuo arias especially, as I have shown in this discussion.)

The aria which David Poultney chooses to illustrate these elements in Scarlatti, a lament of the Virgin Mary for the dead Christ in *La vergine addolorata* (1717),[86] confirms the similarity of approach to dramatic articulation which informs the arias of Scarlatti and Fux. The Scarlatti number ('Figlio, à morte') invites comparison with the Virgin's lament in *La deposizione* ('Aveva ancor bambino') because of its subject matter and general context. In both areas, the sophisticated ritornello material 'defines the emotional state of a character before (s)he himself (herself) expresses it'.[87] The *concertante* texture of the Scarlatti number, scored for solo and *tutti* strings and continuo, is not nearly as varied or complex as the Fux aria, but the principle of instrumental objectification and subsequent vocal elaboration is essentially the same in both cases. If there are significant differences between them, these lie perhaps in the sharply profiled and expressive vocal contour of the Scarlatti aria by comparison with Fux's greater dependence on an interaction between vocal and instrumental material.

The 'highly contrapuntal relationship between the vocal and instrumental lines' which characterizes many of Scarlatti's sacred-dramatic arias[88] is strongly maintained throughout the oratorios of Fux. The densely motivic texture of several numbers in the Passion settings, along with several expressly fugal arias in these works and elsewhere, establish beyond doubt that the composer's use of counterpoint is far more prominent and dramatically purposeful than in the solo numbers of the Italian oratorio generally. Fux's arias represent an integrated synthesis of counterpoint, orchestration and dramatic articulation not easily available elsewhere in the sphere of Italian oratorio. Quite apart from the special case of the fugal arias, they exemplify Fux's interest in counterpoint as a primary means of stylized dramatic expression. This interest extends beyond the arias to every component of the oratorios (with the obvious exception of the recitatives) and it helps to defeat the stylistic difficulty presented by so much repetition (largely confined to the arias). Fugal technique is an obvious resource in the introductory movements and many of the choral numbers feature imitative textures. In his use of textures which are informally or incidentally contrapuntal (such as the actively contrapuntal relationship between vocal and continuo parts in continuo arias and the use of rhythmic motives in a treble-dominated texture), Fux absorbs his preference for such techniques into a compelling engagement with the special qualities of the text in question.

Counterpoint is not the only significant feature of Fux's dramatic resource, although its prominence represents Fux's most distinctive trait. In other arias, the use of stylized dance rhythms and prototypes (minuet, gavotte, sarabande) reflects a general movement towards 'pre-classic' textures in the Viennese oratorio which Howard Smither and Ursula Kirkendale have both identified as a characteristic of Caldara's sacred-dramatic music also.

We can conclude that the oratorios of Fux are distinguished by their choral writing, their sheer variety of instrumental colour and variety of texture and by their remarkably versatile use of counterpoint to formal and dramatic ends. While Fux clearly absorbed modern Italian techniques, he forged a synthesis of these and his own innate resources to produce a body of work which definitively represents the enormous contribution made in Vienna to the Roman Catholic oratorio in the early eighteenth century. These works greatly enrich our understanding of that contribution and our sense of the composer's achievement as a whole.

Notes

[1] For a survey of this scholarship as it applies to Fux, see Hellmut Federhofer, '25 Jahre Johann Joseph Fux-Forschung', *Acta musiocologica* 52 (1980), Fasc. II, pp. 155–94, and the bibliography of Fux studies and editions by Ingrid Schubert which forms Chapter 12 of the present volume.

[2] Robert Kann, *A History of the Habsburg Empire 1526-1918* (California, 1974), p. 151.

[3] See Hellmut Federhofer, art. cit., *passim* and the same writer's 'Johann Joseph Fux und die Gegenwart', Chapter 1 of the present volume.

[4] These are, respectively, *La Fede Sacrilega nella Morte del Precursor S. Giovanni Battista* (1714), K 291, edited by Hugo Zelzer, *Fux-Gesamtausgabe*, Series IV, vol. 1 (Graz, 1959); *La Donna Forte nella Madre de' Sette Maccabei* (1715), K 292, edited by Othmar Wessely, *Fux-Gesamtausgabe*, Series IV, vol. 2, (Graz, 1976); *Il Trionfo della Fede* (1716), K 294, edited by Harry White, *Fux-Gesamtausgabe*, Series IV, vol. 3, (in press).

[5] Howard Smither, *A History of the Oratorio I The Oratorio in the Baroque Era: Italy, Vienna, Paris* (Chapel Hill, 1977), pp. 365–415, including a discussion of *La fede sacrilega*.

[6] Harry White, 'The Oratorios of Johann Joseph Fux' (Diss., The University of Dublin, 1986).

[7] Two oratorios previously attributed to Fux by Hellmut Federhofer in 1959 and subsequently listed in the present author's survey of oratorio sources published in 1985, have now been established as the work of Carlo Agostino Badia by Rudolf Schnitzler in his forthcoming study, *The Baroque Oratorio at the Imperial Court in Vienna* (Vienna, in press). Professor Schnitzler is currently preparing a detailed study of these misattributions, which concern the oratorios *S(anta) Geltrude* and *Ismaelle* which data from 1711 and 1717 respectively. See also Hellmut Federhofer, 'Unbekannte Kirchenmusik von Johann Joseph Fux', *Kirchenmusikalisches Jahrbuch* 43 (1959), pp. 113–54 and Harry White, 'Erhaltene Quellen der Oratorien von Johann Joseph Fux: Ein Bericht', *Kirchenmusikalisches Jahrbuch* 67 (1983/5), pp. 123–31.

[8] Fux's initial court appointment as composer dates from 1698. For a brief account of his career see the article 'Fux, Johann Joseph' by Hellmut Federhofer in *The New Grove Dictionary of Music and Musicians*, edited by Stanley Sadie (London, 1980), vol. 6, pp. 43–6. The standard work on this subject is Ludwig Ritter von Köchel's study *Johann Joseph Fux* (Vienna, 1872, newly reprinted, Hildesheim, 1988). Hereafter: Köchel/Fux.

[9] Robert Freeman, *Opera without Drama: Currents of Change in Italian Opera, 1675-1725* (Ann Arbor, 1981), p. 138.

[10] ibid., p. 138 and also John Henry van der Meer, *Johann Joseph Fux als Opernkomponist* (Bilthoven, 1961), vol. II, p. 25ff.

[11] Although Zeno held his biblical dramas in high esteem, he did not concern himself with the special form of Passion text required for the performance of oratorical works at the Holy Sepulchre erected in the court chapel during Holy Week. For further discussion of this matter, based on an examination of Zeno's *Poesie sacre drammatiche* published in 1735 and research by Robert Freeman and Howard Smither, see the present author's dissertation (as note 6), pp. 31–7.

[12] Released in 1989 on the Thorofon label as *Johann Joseph Fux. Oratorium Johannes der Taüfer*.

[13] See the editions cited in note 4 above.

[14] See especially Gernot Gruber, *Das Wiener Sepolcro und Johann Joseph Fux 1. Teil. Jahresgabe 1968 der Johann Joseph Fux-Gesellschaft* (Graz, 1972); Rudolf Schnitzler, 'The

Sacred-Dramatic Music of Antonio Draghi' (Diss., University of North Carolina at Chapel Hill, 1971); Howard Smither, op. cit., p. 365ff., Friedrich W. Riedel, *Kirchenmusik am Hof Karls VI (1711-1740)* (Munich–Salzburg, 1977), p. 33ff.; Howard Smither, 'Oratorio and Sacred Opera 1700-1825: Terminology and Genre Distinction', *Proceedings of the Royal Musical Association*, 105, (1979–80), p. 97ff.; Harry White, op. cit., pp. 257–69.

[15] Gernot Gruber summarizes this merge of *sepolcro* and oratorio as follows: 'Das *sepolcro* stand in der zweiten Hälfte des 17. Jahrhunderts an Bedeutung und Umfang der Pflege zumindest gleichrangig neben den *oratorio volgare* und verschmolz mit diesem nach 1700 zum *Oratorio per il santo sepolcro*.' See Gernot Gruber, 'Die Musik der ausserliturgischen kirchlichen Feier', *Geschichte der Katolischen Kirchenmusik*, edited by K.G. Fellerer (Kassel, 1976), p. 143.

[16] From the libretto issued by the court publisher at Vienna, Johann van Ghelen.

[17] Of the seven references to the performance of oratorio and related genres contained in the *Rubriche generali per le Funzioni Ecclesiastiche Musicali di tutto l'Anno* by Killian Reinhardt, 'Maestro de Concerti Musicali di dett'Aug: (ustissima) Capella,' which dates in manuscript from 1727, the following excerpt most directly bears on passion music: 'Ma invece *si canta il sepolcro in forma d'Oratorio* con le litanie della B.M.V. e "sub tuum praesidium" in fine.' (Vienna, Austrian National Library, siglum 2503, fol. 27). Present author's emphasis.

[18] Wording on the court copies held in the Austrian National Library, *sigla* A–Wn Mus. Hs. 18 194 and 18 198 respectively.

[19] See the extract from Reinhardt's *Rubriche generali* cited in note 17 above. Some of the reports of Fux's *sepolcro* oratorios in the court circular *Wienerisches Diarium* also include references to the recitation of 'the litany'. See White, op. cit., p. 562.

[20] For further on this point, see White, op. cit., p. 267ff. The term *componimento sacro* appears to have been reserved for oratorios intended for performance at a replica of the Holy Sepulchre in the court chapel.

[21] For a summary of stylistic features in the sacred-dramatic music written by Fux's immediate predecessors and contemporaries at the Viennese court see White, op. cit., pp. 16–28. This summary is based on research by Egon Wellesz, Naborre Campanino Robert Freeman, Rudolf Schnitzler, Hermine Williams, Theophil Antonicek and Lawrence E. Bennett, Cf. Smither, op. cit., p. 393ff. See also Ludwig Ritter von Köchel, *Die kaiserliche Hof-Musikkapelle in Wien von 1543 bis 1867* (Vienna, 1869) and *Beilage* VIII (*Verzeichniss der Opern, Serenaden, Feste teatrali und Oratorien, welche am kaiserlichen Hofe in Wien von 1631 bis 1740 gegeben wurden*) of Köchel/Fux, pp. 485–572; Alexander von Weilen, *Zur wiener Theatergeschichte* (Vienna, 1901) and Franz Hadamowsky, 'Barocktheater am wiener Kaiserhof: mit einem Spielplan (1625–1740)', *Jahrbuch der Gesellschaft für wiener Theaterforschung* (1951–2), pp. 7–115.

[22] See Appendix I below.

[23] Zeno advised against the inclusion of divine persons in sacred drama.

[24] See Erika Kanduth's discussion of this (moralizing) aspect in her essay on the literary and dramaturgical features of the *sepolcro* oratorio, Chapter 9 of the present volume.

[25] See the discussion of various fugal arias below.

[26] Fux also adds a second bass part (for keyboard and *violone*) in the *introduzione* of this work (discussed below).

[27] van der Meer identifies several rhetorical devices in Fux's operas which he describes by means of the musico-rhetorical terminology developed by Burmeister, Kircher and Bernhard. See van der Meer, op. cit., vol. 3, p. 252ff.

[28] ibid., p. 209.

[29] Johann Joseph Fux, *Gradus ad Parnassum* (Vienna, 1725), facsimile edition introduced by Alfred Mann, *Fux-Gesamtausgabe*, Series VII, vol. 1 (Graz, 1967), p. 274ff.

[30] Fux, op. cit., p. 274. The original Latin reads as follows:

> Stylus recitativus aliud non est, quam sermo musicae modulis expressus, sive oratoria elocutio. Quemadmodum enim Declamator pro vario Orationis genere, varie quoque vocem flectit, modo incitando, modo remittendo, modo extollendo, modo deprimendo, ejus habitum affectus induere studet, quem animo exprimere concepit: idem compositori musices, pro textus varietate faciendum est.

The English translation used here is by the present author.

[31] A readily available instance of rhetorical organization in Fux's oratorios can be found in the opening recitative of La fede Sacrilega, edited by Hugo Zelzer, Fux-Gesamtausgabe, Series IV, vol. 1, (Graz, 1959), p. 6, wherein Aronte's appeal to King Herod is shaped by melodic sequence (which matches the anaphoric sequences of the text) and decorative vocal extension (hyperbole or pleonasmus) respectively.

[32] An especially clear instance of this harmonic usage can be seen at the close of Deborah's first recitative in the prima parte of Il Disfacimento di Sisara, where the words 'nostra duol acerbo' are underlined by this chordal device. See A–Wn Ms. 18 192, fol. 28ʳ.

[33] For the vocal ranges of the characters in question, see Table 1 above.

[34] This 'highlighting' compares with Bach's similar usage in the setting of Christ's words in the passions.

[35] Such comparable usage in the case of two texts which are utterly different in meaning demonstrates Fux's systematic dependence on 'stock' figures to register high emotion, whatever the verbal content in question.

[36] See Ernest Harris, Johann Mattheson's Der vollkommene Capellmeister, A Revised Translation with Critical Commentary (Ann Arbor, 1981), pp. 665–6, where this duet is reproduced in facsimile.

[37] Rudolf Schnitzler, The Baroque Oratorio at the Imperial Court in Vienna, (Vienna in press) lists two sources for the score of the 1721 performance under the sigla A–Wn Mus. Hs. 17 308 and D–MEIr Ed 126ⁿ respectively.

[38] For example Il fonte della salute includes a six-part vocal disposition for its closing madrigal (SSSATB) which corresponds to the number and disposition of the six soloists.

[39] This is a short section for altos alone (with every other part, including the continuo, silent) in the opening Coro di Scribei e Farisei of the work. (See A–Wn Mus. Hs. 18 200, foll. 7ᵛ–8ʳ.)

[40] For a similar intensification of vocal counterpoint and decoration see the treatment of the same word ingrato in the duet between L'Umanità Peccatrice and L'Amor Divino in the parte seconda of Gesù Cristo negato (A–Wn Mus. Hs. 18 196, fol. 96ʳ.)

[41] See also Colin Lawson's discussion of this number in Chapter 5 of the present volume.

[42] ibid. and also Wolfgang Suppan's account of Fux's wind scoring, Chapter 6 of the present volume.

[43] See the conclusion of this paper.

[44] See the discussion of such numbers in Lawson, op. cit. and Suppan op. cit.

[45] A similar technique pervades the first aria assigned to Christ, 'Mira o cieco peccator' in Cristo nell'orto.

[46] See, for example, the aria 'Fu d'amore, opra superna' assigned to La Giustizia Divina in this work, discussed and quoted in White, op. cit., pp. 299, 351 respectively.

[47] The second fugal aria in Cristo nell' orto, also assigned to Christ (no. 39, 'Tu vedrai'), reverts to the practice of deriving the vocal material from the principal fugue subject exposed in the opening ritornello.

[48] See Suppan op. cit.: 'The sound of the instrument [trombone] would appear to be closely

identified with the concept of 'suffering and death' in the [*sepolcro*] oratorios, and it is employed as an *obbligato* instrument generally towards the close of the work in question.'

[49] Quoted in White, op. cit., pp. 357–8.

[50] For further discussion of these fugal numbers see ibid., p. 308–9, 311.

[51] ibid., p. 309ff.

[52] The distinction drawn here between 'paired imitation' and fugue is a useful one, in that it helps to clarify the nature of Fux's contrapuntal resourcefulness. As a matter of technical exactitude, the opening ritornello of the aria illustrated in Example 34 here does not pursue the thematic (and counter-thematic) rigour formally associated with fugal texture. Instead, Fux's contrapuntal pairing of ideas is contingent upon motivic structures which taken together generate the aria. Nevertheless, it is clear that the vocal line is an unambiguous reworking of the motive first outlined in the upper violin part in measure one of the piece. The present writer has a survey of fugal and related textures in Fux's sacred-dramatic music in preparation.

[53] See the title page of the libretto published by Johann Peter van Ghelen, a copy of which is in the Austrian National Library (A–Wn 25.236-B.M.).

[54] *Wienerisches Diarium* no. 24, 24 March 1728. (Tuesday the 23rd inst . . . in the afternoon . . . (were given) in the great imperial court chapel the Italian sermon and also the fine oratorio sung in Italian entitled *La Deposizione dalla Croce di Gesù Cristo Salvator nostro*: The removal of Jesus Christ our Saviour from the Cross, versified by Giovanni Claudio Pasquini, [presently] in the imperial service and set to music by Johann Joseph Fux, imperial *Kapellmeister*).

[55] For details of Pasquini's career see the entries on the librettist in *Enciclopedia dello Spettacolo* (Rome, 1960), VII, pp. 1727–30, and in *Dizionario Enciclopedico della Letteratura Italiana* (Unedi: Laterza, 1967), IV, pp. 282–4.

[56] The text of *La deposizione* was subsequently set by composers in Dresden, Venice and Mannheim. See White, op. cit., p. 272. Cf. the discussion of Metastasio's text *La passione di Gesù Cristo* below.

[57] In this example, the counterpoint between the continuo and the vocal part underlines the thematic coherence of Fux's initial ritornello material, from which this middle section is strictly derived.

[58] One contemporary copy of the score, held in the Austrian National Library (Sig. A–Wn S.A. 68. B.21), is distinguished by several diagonal and other markings which clearly indicate cuts in the performance of certain arias. In the case of 'Quasi agnelle', these markings imply the loss of the vocal motto and first ritornello, in addition to measures 21–36, with a consequent loss of some twenty-six measures in all before the *da capo*. Such pruning may have resolved the undesirable conflict between thematic coherence and lengthy repetition identified in the present discussion.

[59] I mean to suggest here that Fux's use of the continuo aria permits us to examine his exploitation of the *da capo* structure and its associated range of expressive techniques (systematic vocal elaboration and a pervasively contrapuntal relationship between vocal and supporting (bass) parts) in its clearest manifestation.

[60] Cf. the discussion of 'O beate l'alme umane' and 'Aveva ancor bambino' in Colin Lawson's essay, Chapter 5 of the present volume.

[61] Howard Smither in *A History of the Oratorio* I (Chapel Hill, 1977), p. 409, classifies this number as one which begins with a 'double-fugal' exposition. But 'paired imitation' would seem to be a more accurate designation, given the absence of a clearly delineated and exactly stated fugal 'subject' here. Cf. note 52 above.

[62] For a more detailed discussion of this number, see White, op. cit., p. 422ff.

[63] See the discussion of the texts of Fux's *sepolcro* oratorios above and Robert Freeman, *Opera Without Drama* (Ann Arbor, 1981) *passim*.

[64] Although a comparison between the role of *Pietro* in Metastasio's text and that of the same character in Pariati's *Gesù Cristo negato da Pietro* might appear instructive, Pariati's inclusion of allegorical personages and his general adherence to the meditative (indigenous) traditions of the Viennese *sepolcro* in *Gesù Cristo negato* are considerations which suggest that the coincidence of the same character in both libretti is a less useful basis for comparison than the very similar treatment and depiction of *Maria Vergine* and *Pietro* in *La deposizione* and *La passione* respectively.

[65] Nature trembles at *Pietro*'s crime. Every bird he hears accuses him of his inconstancy, the sun is hidden in shame, the earth trembles, he is frightened and confused: *Ogni augello che ascolto/ Accusator dell'incostanza mia/. . .Perchè langue e si oscura/ Fra le tenebre il sole?/. . . A che la terra. . .trema. Nulla so, bramo assai, tutto pavento.*

[66] *Giuseppe* asserts that the turbulent sea (*torbido mar*) takes greater account of its fearful travellers than does Jerusalem of Christ's suffering. His preceding recitative speaks of *le mure distrutte, à terra sparsi gli archi, le torri: incenerite il tempio, Dispersi i sacerdoti . . .* These apocalyptic terms invite immediate comparison with *Gioseppe*'s aria text *Sulle torri diroccate* in *La Deposizione*.

[67] The text of this aria is as follows:

> Se a librarsi in mezzo all'onde
> Incomincia il fanciuletto,
> Con la man gli regge il petto,
> Il canuto nuotator.

[68] It is useful to observe that whereas Zeno did not directly contribute to this tradition, his prescriptive influence on the dramaturgical approach to the setting of the Passion in Vienna comprises the link between the later Passion texts of Pariati and Pasquini and Metastasio's *La Passione*.

[69] The court copy of this work is located in the Austrian National Library, Music collection (A–Wn Mus. Hs. 17 131). A facsimile reproduction is available in *The Italian Oratorio*, edited by Joyce L. Johnson and Howard Smither, vol. 11 (New York, 1985).

[70] Compare Fux's treatment of the same textual matter, discussed above. Fugal counterpoint (as against paired imitation) is frequently used to objectify comparatively restrained expressions of sorrow or of tragic import.

[71] Compare Caldara's vocal elaboration of the word *detestar* in this aria (A–Wn 17 131, fol. 62ʳ. ff., quoted in White, op. cit., p. 441) and Fux's treatment of similar words (*vanto, pianto*) in the fugal aria from *Il Disfacimento di Sisara*, ibid., pp. 504–10.

[72] There may, however, be a simple clash of styles in evidence here. Caldara's musical portrayal of *Maddalena*, especially in this final aria, 'Ai passi erranti', relies on a greatly simplified textural resource which is at odds with Fux's baroque stylizations. In such terms, Caldara's music manifests a drastic reduction of expressive techniques (for an example of which see the passages from this aria quoted in White, op. cit., p. 447), which is diametrically opposed to the contrapuntal and *obbligato* complexities of 'Caro mio Dio' in *La deposizione*.

[73] David Poultney, 'Alessandro Scarlatti and the Transformation of Oratorio', *The Musical Quarterly* lix (1973), pp. 584–601; p. 584.

[74] This relationship is considered in White, op. cit., pp. 69–74.

[75] See note 74 above and also van der Meer, op. cit., *passim*.

[76] Scarlatti's *Il martirio di Santa Susanna* (Florence, 1706) and Caldara's *Il martirio di Santa Caterina* (Rome, 1708) are relevant examples of the larger tradition to which *Santa Dimpna* belongs.

[77] See Smither, op. cit. p. 258ff., for an account of the style of hagiographical and biblical libretti cultivated by important members of the Roman academy, including the Cardinals Pamphili and Ottoboni and Prince Francesco Maria Ruspoli.

[78] See the discussion of these libretti in White, op. cit., pp. 103–20.

[79] Scarlatti is known to have set only two versions of the Passion and only one version was set by Caldara before he settled in Vienna. (See the work-lists attached to Malcolm Boyd and Donald Grout, 'Scarlatti (i) Alessandro', *The New Grove Dictionary of Music and Musicians*, edited by Stanley Sadie (London, 1980), vol. 16, pp. 549–67 and Robert Freeman, 'Caldara, Antonio', ibid., vol. 3, pp. 612–16.)

[80] David Poultney ascribes this change of emphasis to Scarlatti (see Poultney, art. cit. p. 584).

[81] Smither, op. cit., p. 305.

[82] ibid., p. 298, where Spagna's observations on the question of the chorus in oratorio are paraphrased. The expectations of early eighteenth-century audiences, the influence of opera and the uneven ability of composers to write well for choral resources are advanced by Spagna as justifications for the omission of choral numbers.

[83] Poultney, art. cit., p. 595.

[84] The inclusion of choral episodes for an ensemble of soloists, as in Handel's *La Resurrezione* (1708) is a feature of the Italian oratorio which must be distinguished from the pre-eminent role of the chorus in Fux's oratorios, above all in the *sepolcro* works.

[85] For a discussion of Caldara's Roman oratorios, see Smither, op. cit., pp. 355–61, which follows Ursula Kirkendale, *Antonio Caldara: Sein Leben und Seine Venezianisch-römischen Oratorien* (Graz and Cologne, 1966), pp. 257–317.

[86] See Poultney, art. cit., pp. 599–601.

[87] ibid., p. 598.

[88] Smither, op. cit., p. 341.

Appendix I The sacred-dramatic compositions of Johann Joseph Fux (year, and where known, date of first performance given)

1 *Santa Dimpna, Infanta d'Irlanda* (text by ? Giovanni Andrea Lorenzani). Lent, 1702.

2 *La regina saba* (text by Piermaria Ruggieri). Lent, 1705.

3 *La fede sacrilega nella morte del Precursor S. Giovanni Battista* (text by Pietro Pariati). Lent, 1714.

4 *La donna forte nella Madre de' sette Maccabei* (text by Pietro Pariati). Lent, 1715.

5 *Il trionfo della fede* (text by Bernardino Maddali). 5 March 1716.

6 *Il fonte della salute aperto dalla grazia nel Calvario* (text by Pietro Pariati). 10 April 1716 (Good Friday).

7 *Il disfacimento di Sisara* (author unknown). 18 February 1717.

8 *Cristo nell'orto* (text by Pietro Pariati). 12 April 1718 (Tuesday of Holy Week).

9 *Gesù Cristo negato da Pietro* (text by Pietro Pariati). 7 April 1719 (Good Friday).

10 *La cena del Signore* (text by Pietro Pariati). 26 March 1720 (Tuesday of Holy Week).

11 *(Il) testamento di nostro Signor Gesù Cristo al (sul) Calvario* (text by Pietro Pariati). 16 April 1726 (Tuesday of Holy Week).

12 *La deposizione dalla croce di Gesù Cristo Salvator Nostro* (text by Giovanni Claudio Pasquini). 23 March 1728. (Tuesday of Holy Week).

Appendix II La deposizione dalla croce di Gesù Cristo Salvator Nostro (1728)

Overall disposition and contents. Abbreviations: 'a 4' = Violins 1, 2, Viola, Basso (including Cello, Violone, Cembalo/Organ Bassoon). B.c. = Basso continuo (Cembalo/organ and Cello/Violone). D.C. = *Da capo*. S = Soprano, A = Alto, T = Tenor, B = Bass.

Number	*Character*	*Principal Key*	*Scoring and technique*
Introduzione.	———	a	Five real parts, including two bass lines scored for cellos and bassoons (i) and violoni and keyboard (ii). The design is multisectional; nine sections in all, beginning with A (*Largo*) B (*Allegro*), both of which are repeated. The central movement is a double fugue.
1.	Coro di Peccatori	a	SATB and 'a 4'. Basso line specifies 'Violoni, violoncelli, fagotti, organo'. Gestural, broadly homophonic and antiphonal texture.
2. Recit.	Maria Vergine(S)	–	B.c.
3. Aria	"	g	'a 4'. *Tempo giusto*. 3/4 Circular, treble-dominated motive and texture. Chromatic colouring. D.C.
4. Recit.	Giovanni (A)	–	B.c.
5. Aria	"	E-flat	'a 4'. Common time. Single motive exploited in rhythmic counterpoint between outer string parts and vocal part. Basso part marked *senza organo e tiorba* on vocal entry. D.C.
6. Recit.	Nicodemo(B)	–	B.c.
7. Aria	Gioseppe(T)	a	'a 4'. *Andante* 3/4. Begins with vocal motto. Invertible and motivic counter-point. D.C.

225

8. Recit. accomp.	Nicodemo	–	'a 4'. *coll'arco continuato; senza organo.* Held string chords. The number continues thereafter as a continuo recitative.
9. Aria	Maria Maddalena(S)	b	B.c., with closing ritornello scored 'a 4'. 3/4. Rhythmic organization of continuo line and verbal-vocal sequences. D.C.
10. Recit.	Nicodemo	–	B.c.
11. Aria	"	C	'a 4'. *Allegro.* Common time. Rhythmic counterpoint. D.C.
12. Recit.	Giuseppe	–	B.c.
13. Coro.	Coro di Peccatori	e	'a 4'. *Largo.* Common time. Instrumental introduction in paired imitation adapted in ensuing vocal setting.

PARTE SECONDA

14. Recit.	Gioseppe	–	B.c.
15. Aria.	Giovanni	d	'a 4'. 6/8. Begins with vocal motto. Treble-dominated texture, but principal ritornello closes with semiquaver motive used in counterpoint against the vocal melody (above and below). D.C.
16. Recit.	Maria Vergine	–	B.c.
17. Aria	"	c	Chalumeau and strings 'a 4'. *Tempo giusto.* Common time. *Obbligato* exchanges between chalumeau and vocal part, also various concertino groupings, especially between chalumeau and first violin part. Textural contrast systematically employed in ritornello sections. D.C.
18. Recit.	Maria Maddalena	–	B.c.

19. Aria	Gioseppe Giovanni	f	'a 4'. *Larghetto*. 3/4. Treble-dominated, chromatic texture. D.C.
20. Recit.		–	B.c.
20a. Recit. accomp.	Maddalena Maria	–	'a 4'. Sustained string chords.
21. Aria	Maddalena	A	'a 4', including *violino solo*. *Andante*. Common time. Two distinct ritornelli, separated by a vocal motto, which feature paired imitation and *obbligato* scoring respectively. The vocal sections characterized by interplay between the violin solo and the vocal part and separated one from the other by the recurrence of the first ritornello. D.C.
22. Recit.	Maria Vergine	–	B.c.
22a. Recit. accomp.		–	'a 4'. Sustained string chords.
23. Duet	Giovanni Maria Vergine, Giovanni	B-flat	Two trombones (separate parts) and Basso. 3/4. Imitative texture throughout, although the trombones are silent during the vocal sections. D.C.
24. Recit.	Gioseppe Nicodemo	–	B.c., but preceded by string chords.
25. Aria		F	Bassoon and basso continuo. *Affetuoso*. Common time. *Obbligato* exchanges between bassoon and vocal part. D.C.
26. Madrigal	Coro di Peccatori	c	SATB, 'a 4'. Fugal instrumental introduction, vocal entries in paired imitation, declamatory, homophonic texture ensues.

Appendix III *La passione di Gesù Cristo* (1730) (Caldara)

Abbreviations as in Appendix II

Number	Character	Principal key	Scoring and technique
Introduzione.	–	a	'a 4'. Common time. French overture: chordal movement, *grave*; double-fugal *andante*.
1. Recit.	Pietro(A)	–	B.c.
2. Aria	"	f	'a 4'. *Largo.* Common time. Treble-dominated texture and vocal decoration. D.C.
3. Recit.	Pietro	–	B.c.
4. Coro.	Coro di Seguaci Gesù	g	SATB and 'a 4'. *Andante.* Common time. Main (A) section homophonic and declamatory. Middle (B) section for soloists, imitative and without orchestral support. D.C.
5. Recit.	Pietro. . .	–	B.c.
6. Aria	Maddalena (S)	d	'a 4'. 3/4. Vocal motto. *Concertante* texture with instrumentally-derived vocal decoration. *Dal Segno.* (Motto omitted on reprise.)
7. Recit.	Giovanni (T). . .	–	B.c.
8. Aria	Giuseppe (B)	B-flat	Violins and viola in unison and basso. *Allegro.* Common time. Vigorous, *obbligato* style and vocal decoration. D.C.
9. Recit.	Pietro	–	B.c.
10. Aria	Giovanni	c	'a 4'. Common time. Imitative and sequential instrumental texture. D.C.
11. Recit.	Pietro. . .	–	B.c.
12. Aria	Maddalena	g	'a 4'. *Andante.* 3/4. Treble-dominated ritornello material. Some vocal elaboration. D.C.

13. Recit.	Pietro...	–	B.c.
14. Aria	"	e	Violins (in one part), viola, basso. (3 parts). *Andante*. Common time. Sequential, treble-dominated instrumental writing. Some *concertante* exchanges between ensemble and vocal part. D.C.
15. Recit.	Giovanni... Maddalena,	–	B.c.
16. Duet	Pietro	E-flat	'a 4'. *Largo*. 3/2. Chordal string texture. Middle (B) section scored for continuo accompaniment only. Voices frequently consecutive and discrete rather than in close imitation. D.C.
17. Coro.	–	c	SATB with instruments *colla parte* and an additional basso part. *Andante*. Common time. Imitative vocal entries at beginning, thereafter largely homophonic.

PARTE SECONDA

18. Recit.	Pietro...	–	B.c.
19. Aria	Giovanni	a	'a 4'. Common time. Canonic counterpoint between upper strings. D.C.
20. Recit.	Giuseppe	–	B.c.
21. Aria	"	D	'a 4'. Cut common time. Double-fugal texture in which vocal part is fully involved and from which vocal melismas are derived. D.C.
22. Recit.	Pietro	–	B.c.
23. Aria	"	g	Violins in unison and basso continuo (i.e., 2 parts). *Andante*. 3/4. Vocal part strictly derived from *obbligato* curve of continuous quaver movement in violin part. D.C.
24. Recit.	Maddalena...	–	B.c.
25. Aria	Giovanni	E-flat	Trombone and basso continuo. *Andante*. Common time. *Obbligato* instrumental writing replicated in vocal part. D.C.

26. Recit.	Maddalena	–	B.c.
27. Aria	"	B-flat	'a 4'. *Moderato.* 2/4. Homophonic elaboration of syncopated figure, subsequently subjected to imitative treatment. Continuo omitted during vocal sections. Vocal part tends to double upper strings. D.C.
28. Recit.	Pietro	–	B.c.
29. Aria	"	d	'a 4'. *Andante.* Common time. Elaborate homophonic semiquaver figure in principal (and subsequent) ritornello sections is replicated in vocal part. D.C.
30. Recit.	Maddalena...	–	B.c.
31. Coro.	–	a	SATB with instruments *colla parte* and an additional basso part. Common time. Alternating *Grave* (homophonic, declamatory) and *Andante* (successive imitation) sections.

11 Bemerkungen zu den Kompositionen von Johann Joseph Fux zum *Offertorium**

Rudolf Walter

Seit den Offertorienkompositionen von Giovanni Pierluigi da Palestrina, Orlando di Lasso und William Byrd im ausgehenden 16. und beginnenden 17. Jahrhundert wurde dieser Satz des *Proprium Missae* ohne cantus firmus komponiert, während bei *Introitus*- und *Graduale*-Vertonungen bis in die Zeit von Johann Joseph Fux, und darüber hinaus, *cantus firmus*-Verwendung prakti ziert wurde.[1] Im 17 Jahrhundert bervorzugten die Komponisten neben solistischen Offertorien-Kompositionen in der 1. Hälfte doppelchörige Anlagen, das Konzertieren von 2 Chören (Mikołaj Zieleński, Steffano Bernardi, Andreas Hofer [ungedruckte Sätze] u.a.); in der 2. Hälfte entwickelten sie kantatenähnliche Gebilde für Soli, Ripieni und Instrumentalbegleitung (Abraham Mergerle, Andreas Hofer [Druck Salzburg 1677], Johann Georg Reichwein u.a.). Das *Offertorium* bildete in der 1. Hälfte des 18. Jahrhunderts in Kathedral-, Stifts- und Klosterkirchen mit figuraler Kirchenmusik den einzigen Teil des *Proprium Missae*, der während des ganzen Kirchenjahres vokal ausgeführt zu werden pflegte (in der Kaiserlichen Hofkapelle in Wien erklang zudem der *Introitus* in traditionellen *a-cappella*-Kompositionen).[2] Durch die bei Meßkompositionen mehr und mehr üblich gewordene Auffassung des *Kyrie* als feierlicher Eröffnung, des *Dona* als festlichem Finale und die dadurch bedingten längeren Vertonungen blieb für *Introitus* und *Communio* keine Zeit verfügbar. Sie wurden darum weggelassen. Die Gesänge zwischen den Lesungen *Epistel* und *Evangelium* – *Graduale* und *Alleluja* mit Vers, bzw. *Tractus* – wurden lediglich an den Sonntagen der Advents- und Fastenzeit vorgetragen, im übrigen Kirchenjahr wurde seit dem 17. Jahrhundert an ihrer Stelle Instrumentalmusik üblich, die nach Festrang in Besetzung und Ausdehnung differieren konnte.

In den konzertanten Offertoriumkompositionen, die seit der 1. Hälfte des 17. Jahrhunderts entstanden, bezog man betont den Sologesang ein.

---

*See list of abbreviations on pages 252–3.

Wahrscheinlich ohne dies zu wissen, knüpfte man damit an die ursprüngliche Gestalt dieses Propriumsatzes an, denn bis ins 11. Jahrhundert waren beim *Offertorium* melodisch sehr reiche Soloverse üblich gewesen.[3] Solisten wurden beschäftigt in Solo- und Ensemblemotetten und in Kompositionen für Solo (Soli) und Chor.

Ein neues Element bildete seit dem späteren 17. Jahrhundert die freiere Textwahl für Offertorien. Während in Advents- und Fastenzeit an den liturgischen Texten festgehalten wurde, stellte man für Hochfeste, Heiligenfeste und nicht in Bußzeiten fallende Sonntage längere und kontrastreichere Texte zusammen, über deren Quellen wir später handeln werden. Durch Gliederung der Vertonungen in Sinfonien (Sonaten, Sonatinen), *Secco-* und *Accompagnato*-Rezitative, Arien, Ensembles und Chorsätze wurden kleine Kirchenkantaten entwickelt. Dieser Prozeß lief im deutschsprachigen Raum in der katholischen und evangelischen Kirchenmusik im Prinzip parallel. Die Unterschiede lagen in der Sprache der Texte (in der katholischen Kirche lateinisch, in der evangelischen landessprachlich) und in der Ausdehnung (die Offertorien-Kantaten waren knapper, weil Hauptmusik die *Ordinarium*vertonung, die Messe, blieb; in der ev. Kirche bildete dagegen die Kantate das musikalische Zentrum). Selbst zur Kirchenlied-Einbeziehung in die ev. Kantate läßt sich bei kath. *Offertorium*-Kompositionen eine gewisse Parallele aufzeigen in den Zitaten gregorianischer Melodien (sie wurden allerdings nur gelegentlich, nicht regelmäßig verwirklicht).

Einen gedruckten Hinweis auf die neuen, nicht-liturgischen Texte finden wir im Titel des 1694 in Augsburg gedruckten Offertorienbandes von Thomas Eisenhuet. Dort heißt es: *Offertoria de Festis, Tempore et Communi novis textibus, Ariis, Fugis et Stylo recitativo.* In den musikalischen Begriffen Arie, Fuge und *Stylus recitativus* wird gleichzeitig die kantatenartige Vertonung bezeichnet. Zeitlich war dies nicht die früheste Publikation dieser Art, u.a. enthielten Bd. 2 und 3 des *Cultus harmonicus* von dem Heiligenkreuzer Zisterzienserpater Alberik Mazak, Wien 1650 und 1653, Offertorienkompositionen auf nicht-liturgische Texte.[4]

Auf italienische Offertorien-Drucke des späten 17. und frühen 18. Jahrhunderts hat Friedrich Wilhelm Riedel hingewiesen.[5] Deshalb seien hier einige Belege aus Süddeutschland und der Habsburger-Monarchie erwähnt (wobei zu betonen ist, daß der wohl größere Teil figuraler Kirchenmusik, also auch der Offertorien, aus diesem Raum ungedruckt blieb). Nach Zeitbrauch waren dies Stimmendrucke (ohne Partitur). In Neudruck ist bisher nur eine Auswahl aus der Publikation von R.I. Mayr vorgelegt worden.[6]

Abraham Megerle, *Ara musica*, Salzburg, 1647
Alberik Mazak, *Cultus harmonicus*, Bd. 2, Wien, 1650, und Bd. 3, Wien, 1653
Andreas Hofer, *Ver sacrum seu flores musices*, Salzburg, 1677
Johann Melchior Cäsar (Kaiser), *Trisagion musicum*, Würzburg, 1683
Johann Georg Reichwein, *Sacra thyamata, id est Offertoria per festa majora*, Regensburg, 1688
Thomas Eisenhuet, *Offertoria de Festis, Tempore et Communi...*, Augsburg, 1694

Caspar Prentz, *Grana Thuris*, Regensburg, 1695

Johann Caspar Ferdinand Fischer, mindestens 6 *Offertoria* aus den Jahren um 1700 (in Kopien überliefert)[7]

Rupert Ignaz Mayr, *Gazophylacium musico-sacrum*, Augsburg, 1702

Cajetan Kolberer, *Partus IV, continens 30 Offertoria festiva...*, Augsburg, 1710

Idem, *Partus V, proferens alia 20 Offertoria*, Augsburg, 1719

Johann Joseph Ignaz Brentner, *Offertoria solenniora 4 vocibus et instrumentis*, Prag, 1717

Benedikt Anton Aufschnaiter, *Aquila clangens exaltata ... sive Duodena Offertoria*, Passau, 1719

Meinrad Spieß, *Laus Dei in sanctis ejus, 20 Offertoria...*, Mindelheim, 1723

Johann Valentin Rathgeber, *Sacra Anaphonesis per 24 Offertoria*, Augsburg, 1726

Idem, *Holocaustum Ecclesiasticum Coelo et Mundo oblatum, continens Offertoria Festivalia* [LX], Augsburg, 1734/35

Česlav Vaňura, *Cultus Latriae seu duodecim Offertoria solemnia*, Prag, 1736

Vom Kaiserlichen Hofkapellmeister Johann Joseph Fux blieb kein Offertorien-Jahrgang erhalten wie vom gleichzeitigen Vicekappellmeister Antonio Caldara, doch nach bisherigem Wissen um 56 vollständige Kompositionen in Abschriften und mehrere Titel von verschollenen.[8] Caldara hatte um 1718/19 34 Sätze für die Sonntage des Kirchenjahres mit Ausnahme der auf einen Sonntag fallenden Hochfeste und mit Ausnahme der Advents- und Fastensonntage geschaffen. Caldaras Vertonungen sind auf die liturgischen Texte komponiert und im *stile ordinario* gesetzt, d.h. für 4 Vokalstimmen (*Soli e Ripieni*), 2 Violinen und Generalbaß + colla parte-Bläsern für die *Ripieni*.[9] Das Zugrundelegen der liturgischen Texte bezeugt, daß Kaiser Karl VI. die liturgische Tradition möglichst beachtet sehen wollte.

Als Gründe für das Bevorzugen nicht-liturgischer Texte für die Offertorien an Hochfesten, Heiligenfesten und Sonntagen außerhalb der Advents- und Fastenzeit durch Fux und seine Zeitgenossen waren wohl mehrere Gesichtspunkte bedeutsam. Grundsätzlich war für die gültige Zelebration der Messe seit dem Trienter Konzil allein der vom Priester am Altar gesprochene Text maßgeblich. Zum zweiten erschienen die liturgischen Texte für festliche Hochämter mit Inzens zu knapp.[10] Selbst die *Cappella Pontificia* in Rom sang nachweislich seit der 2. Hälfte des 16. Jahrhunderts nach dem choraliter vorgetragenen *Offertorium* häufig eine textlich passende Motette als Einlage, wie die *Diari* belegen.[11] Weiter boten die wenig dramatischen liturgischen Offertorientexte dem Komponisten keinen Anlaß zur Darstellung der Affekte, d.h. zu kontrastierenden Anlagen. Schließlich strebte man nach Texten, die sich mehrfach im Kirchenjahr verwenden ließen. Bei Fux offenbaren Titel wie: *pro omni tempore, de quolibet Sancto, de Confessore, de Martyribus* u.a. diese Tendenz.

Die Kompositionen zum *Offertorium* sind bei Fux *Offertorium* oder *Motetto* betitelt. Bei Zeitgenossen kommt auch die Bezeichnung *Concertus* vor (J.C.F. Fischer). Gabriele Krombach schreibt in 'Die Vertonungen liturgischer Sonntagsoffertorien am Wiener Hof', daß in der 1. Hälfte des 18. Jahrhunderts *Offertorium* in der Hauptsache für Vertonungen des liturgischen Textes, *Motetto* für Vertonungen frei zusammengestellter oder neu gedichteter Texte verwendet wurde.[12] Zum Teil trifft dies für Fux zu.

Doch begegnen wir der Bezeichnung *Offertorium* für den frei gewählten Text *Jubilate*, der aus einem Vers der Apocalypse und aus der *Introitus-Antiphon* des 3. Sonntags nach Ostern besteht. Das Material stammt allerdings nicht aus der Kaiserlichen Hofkapelle, sondern aus Stift Schlierbach. Andrerseits ist die Vertonung des liturgischen Textes *Reges Tharsis* für Epiphanie auf Material der Wiener Hofkapelle *Motetto* bezeichnet. Eine nicht geringe Zahl einschlägiger Kompositionen ist nicht in Materialien der Hofkapelle überliefert,[13] sodaß bei der gegebenen Quellenlage eine einwandfreie Klärung dieser Frage nicht möglich scheint. Jeder Chorregent dürfte die Offertorienkompositionen von Fux nach seinem Brauch eingeordnet und beschriftet haben. Zudem scheint Zeitbrauch gewesen zu sein, die Bezeichnungen *Offertorium* und *Motetto* mehr oder weniger synonym zu gebrauchen. Bei Fux' Zeitgenossen Fischer läßt sich eine Namensänderung durch den *Regens chori* nachweisen. Das im Notenmaterial des Kreuzherrenklosters Prag *Concertus de S. Cruce* benannte *Jubilate* ist im Musikalieninventar des gleichen Klosters als *Offertorium* verzeichnet.[14]

Nach bisherigem Wissenstand vertonte Fux an liturgischen Texten die Offertorien der 4 Adventssonntage, der Vigil von Weihnachten, des Festes Epiphanie, des Aschermittwoch, von 3 Ferialtagen der Fastenzeit, des 4. Fastensonntags, des 17. und 23. Sonntags nach Pfingsten und des *Commune de Confessore non Pontifice (Missa I)* sowie der Totenmesse.[15]

Bei den drei Offertorien für Ferialtage der Fastenzeit (K 154–156) erscheint ungewöhnlich, daß Fux den Text zweimal von Anfang bis Ende singen läßt. Im gregorianischen Choral (und im Meßtext) wird beim *Offertorium* vom Freitag nach dem 2. Fastensonntag K 154 der erste Satz wiederholt: *Domine, in auxilium meum respice.* Bei den Offertorien vom Mittwoch und Freitag nach dem 3. Fastensonntag K 155 und 156 wird kein Wort wiederholt. Vermutlich wegen der Knappheit der Texte entschloß sich der Komponist zu dieser vollständigen Wiederholung. Das Verfahren wiederholte er im *stilus mixtus* beim *Offertorium Reges Tharsis* für Epiphanie K 168. Den ersten Vortrag übergab er hier den Solisten, den zweiten dem Chor. Die Komposition leitete er durch eine *Sinfonia* ein und gliederte er durch eine thematisch verwandte zweite *Sinfonia* vor dem abschließenden *Alleluja*, das als eigener Abschnitt ausgebaut ist. Das 70 Takte lange *Reges Tharsis* mag ein Musterbeispiel bilden, wie ein Komponist des Hochbarock zu einem knappen liturgischen Text eine Kontraste bietende Vertonung entwickelte. Vom liturgischen Standpunkt sind die vollständigen Wiederholungen des Offertoriumtextes in den beschriebenen vier Fällen Willkürlichkeiten.

Riedel konnte nachweisen, daß die in *Denkmäler der Tonkunst in Österreich* (DTÖ), Bd. 3, abgedruckte Vertonung *Veritas mea* eine Komposition von Giovanni Pierluigi da Palestrina ist. Sie wurde wohl von Fux im Unterricht als Beispiel verwendet, sodaß es zu dieser Fehlzuschreibung kam. Der Fux-Schüler Jan Dismas Zelenka, Kirchenkapellmeister am Hof zu Dresden, versah sie nämlich mit colla parte-Begleitung und mit dem Autornamen Fux.[16]

Der Verfasser stellte fest, daß das bei Andreas Liess genannte *Offerto-*

rium de Quadragesima, L 31, ebenfalls vom römischen Meister des 16. Jahrhunderts stammt. Dieses ist *Pars I* des *Responsorium I pro Feria 5. post Dominicam I. Quadragesimae,* eine Komposition mit *soggetto ostinato.*[17] An dem Stimmenmaterial, das aus dem Kreuzherrenkloster Prag stammt, erscheint irreführend, daß der Titel auf dem Umschlag *Cum tribularer si nescirem* lautet. In den Stimmen beginnt der Text zutreffend *Tribularer si nescirem.* Im Kurzkommentar hat Liess diesen Punkt nicht erwähnt.[18]

Bei den frei zusammengestellten Texten für Kompositionen im *stilus mixtus* lassen sich sechs Arten von Quellen nachweisen. Trotz vieler Recherchen läßt sich in manchen Fällen nicht alles belegen.[19] Vor allem können die barocken Neudichtungen nur als Vermutungen bezeichnet werden, die Texte scheinen nicht als geistliche Dichtungen eines bestimmten Autors selbständig publiziert worden zu sein.

Die Quellen lassen sich folgendermaßen charakterisieren:

1 Texte aus anderen Meßgesängen und/oder aus dem Offizium des Tages (das bedeutet aus dem Brevier).
2 Übernahmen aus anderen liturgischen Formularen (das heißt Formularen, die nicht zu dem betreffenden Tag gehören).
3 Verbindungen von liturgischen Texten des Tages (Festes) mit einem Zitat (auch mit mehreren) aus dem Alten oder Neuen Testament.
4 Hymnenartige Dichtungen des frühen oder hohen Mittelalters.
5 Verbindung von liturgischen Texten des Tages mit barocken Zusätzen oder Neudichtungen.
6 Barocke Neudichtungen.

Lassen wir für jede Gruppe einige Belege folgen:

1 E 46 *Offertorium de Dominica*
Jubilate, alleluja. Vicit leo de tribu
Juda, radix David. Alleluja. [Fine]
Jubilate Deo omnis terra, alleluja.
Psalmum dicite nomini ejus,
alleluja.
Date gloriam laudi ejus, alleluja.
[da capo al fine]

3. Sonntag nach Ostern: 1. u. letztes Wort der Introitus-Antiphon. Apoc 5, 5:

3. Sonntag nach Ostern: vollständige Introitus-Antiphon.

2 K 164 *Mottetto de Venerabili*
Caro mea vere est cibus, et sanguis
meus vere est potus.
Qui manducat meum carnem, et
bibit meum sanguinem, in me
manet et ego in illo.

Fronleichnam: Beginn des Evangelium (Joh 6, 56 und 57).

3 K 170 *Motetto de Spiritu Sancto*

O ignis coelestis,/ o gratiae testis,/   Eine Sequenz des 13. Jh. enthält
o mentium pax.   einen gedanklich verwandten
     Beginn:[20]

Frigentes accende,/a noxis   O ignis spiritus paracliti,
defende,/o caelica fax.   vita vitae omnis creaturae,
     sanctus es, vivificando formas.

Factus est repente de coelo sonus,   Pfingstsonntag: aus der Epistel
tamquam advenientis spiritus vehe-   (Act Ap 2, 2).
mentis, et replevit totam domum,
ubi erant sedentes.

Linguis loquuntur omnium;   Pfingsten: Laudes-Hymnus, 3.
Turbae pavent gentilium, o nova res,   Strophe, mit Zusätzen (o nova res
Musto madere deputant,   bzw. o magna res).
Quos Spiritus repleverat, o magna
res.

Beata nobis gaudia   Gleicher Laudes-Hymnus, 1. Stro-
Anni reduxit orbita,   phe, mit Zusatz von alleluja.
Cum Spiritus Paraclitus,
Illapsus est Apostolis.
Alleluja.

4 L 43 *Motetto per la Madonna Santissima*

Paries quidem Filium, et virgi-   Annuntiatio B.M.V.: Aus der Matu-
nitatis non patieris detrimentum: tin, Versus von Responsorium 3.
efficieris gravida, et eris semper   Aus dem Evangelium des Festes
intacta, ut benedicta dicaris inter   (nach Luc 1, 28).
mulieres.

Huc terrae gigantes
pro coelo pugnantes
Maria vos amat,
ad arma conclamat,
conferte vos.   Wohl barocke Neudichtung

Pugnate strenue
Mariae nomine,
haec lauros parabit,
certantes juvabit,
et proteget vos.
Alleluja.   Alleluja erscheint als häufiger
     Zusatz in den Kompositionen zum
     Offertorium. Meist wird es in
     einem eigenen Abschnitt
     durchgeführt.

5 K 162 *Offertorium pro festo Assumptionis B.V.*[21]

Hodie Maria virgo caelos ascendit: gaudete, quia cum Christo regnat in aeternum.	Assumptio B.M.V.: Magnificat-Antiphon der 2. Vesper.
Gratulemur in hac die, in qua sanctae fit Mariae celebris assumptio:	Sequenz 'Gratulemur in hac die', Strophen 1, 2, 9, 10 (von 26) (AH, Bd. 54, S.325).
Dies ista, dies grata, qua de terra* est translata in caelum cum gaudio.	*in AH: terris
Virgo sancta, virgo munda, tibi nostra sit jucunda vocis jubilatio;	
Nobis opem fer desursum et post hujus vitae cursum tuo junge filio.	

6 K 178 *Motetto de Confessore*

Iste sanctus pro lege Dei sui certavit usque ad mortem, et a verbis impiorum non timuit, fundatus enim erat super firmam petram.	Commune unius Martyris extra tempus paschale: Magnificat-Antiphon der 1. Vesper.
Gloria et honore coronasti eum, Domine, et constituisti eum super opera manuum tuarum.	Aus der gleichen Vesper: Versiculum et Responsum.

7 K 179 *Motetto de Confessore*

Justum deduxit Dominus per vias rectas, et ostendit illi regnum caelorum.*	Commune Confessoris non Pontificis: Versikel in der Laudes. *im Brevier: Dei.
Amavit eum Dominus et ornavit eum, stolam gloriae induit eum.	Gleiches Formular: Versikel in der Matutin.
Alleluja.	Alleluja wurde hinzugefügt.

8 K 177 *Motetto de S. Michaele Archangelo*

Concussum est mare et contremuit terra, ubi Archangelus Michael descendebat de caelo.	In Dedicatione S. Michaelis Archangeli: 1. Antiphon in der Matutin.
Princeps gloriosissime, Michaele Archangele, esto memor nostri, hic et ubique semper precare pro nobis Filium Dei.	Gleiches Formular: Magnificat-Antiphon der 2. Vesper (ohne Alleluja).

Laudemus Dominum, quem laudant angeli, quem Cherubim et Seraphim,Sanctus, Sanctus, Sanctus proclamant.

Ebenda: 2. Antiphon in der Matutin.

Alleluja.

Alleluja wurde hinzugefügt.

9 K 159 *Offertorium de Apostolis*
Estote fortes in bello, et pugnate cum antiquo serpente:

Commune Apostolorum et Evangelistarum: Magnificat-Antiphon der 2. Vesper (1. Satz).

Tradent enim vos in conciliis, et ante reges et principes* ducemini propter me, in testimonium illis et gentibus.

Ebenda: Magn.–Ant. der 1. Vesper. *Im Antiphonale Romanum: praesides.

Quis separabit nos a caritate Christi?An tribulatio, an angustia, an fames, an nuditas, an periculum, an persecutio, an gladius?

Paulus ad Romanos 8, 35.

Non nos separabit a caritate Christi.

Ebenda: nach 8, 39.

10 K 160 *Offertorium de Venerabili*
Sacris solemniis juncta sint gaudia, et ex praecordiis sonent praeconia; Recedant vetera, nova sint omnia, corda, voces et opera.

Ad Processionem Corporis Christi: Hymnus I, Strophe 1.

Lauda Sion Salvatorem, Lauda ducem et pastorem, In hymnis et canticis.

In Festo Corporis Christi: Sequentia, Strophe 1 et 2.

Quantum potes, tantum aude: Quia major omni laude, Nec laudare sufficis.

Angelorum esca nutrivit* Dominus populum suum, et panem de caelo praestitit† eis.

Gleiches Formular: 2. Antiphon in den Laudes (ohne alleluja). *im Brevier: nutrivisti;† ebenda: praestitisti.

Quem qui manducat in *Deo* manet et *Deus* in eo.

Nach dem Evangelium des Festes (Joh. 6,57). Die originalen Worte me und ego sind durch *Deus* ersetzt.

Nobis datus, nobis natus Deus noster cibus fit. Se videndum dat edendum, apud nos ut semper sit.	Wohl Neudichtung nach Zitat der ersten 4 Worte aus der 2. Strophe des Vesperhymnus vom Fest.
Alleluja.	Alleluja ist hinzugefügt.

11 L 33 *De Nativitate Christi*

O admirabile commercium; creator generis humani, animatum corpus sumens, de Virgine nasci dignatus est: et procedens homo sine semine, largitus est nobis suam Deitatem.	In Circumcisione Domini: 1. Antiphon in den Laudes.
Venite, gentes, et adorate regem* vestrum, Deum nostrum.	In Nativitate Domini: In der Matutin Ende des Versus von Responsorium 7 (erweitert). *Im Antiphonale Romanum: Dominum.
Quid agis, Bethlehem, si hospitem gratiosum tam turpiter beneventas?	Wohl Neuformulierung
In stabulo nasci vult, pabulo pasci humano vult, pastores dant ei honores.	Wohl Neudichtung

12 K 169 *Motetto de Ascensione Domini*

Ponis nubem ascensum tuum, Domine, qui ambulas super pennas ventorum.Confessionem et decorem induisti, amictus lumine sicut vestimento.*	In Ascensione Domini: Responso- rium 8 in der Matutin (ohne alleluja). *im Brevier: vestimentum.
Pandite portas, principes, vestras, ecce adventat gloriae rex. Pavet infernus, tremit infestus Daemonum grex.	Nach Ps. 23, 7 Sequenzstrophe oder Neudichtung
Dominus in Sion magnus et excelsus, nimis exaltatus est super omnes deos, in caelo paravit sedem suam.	In Ascensione Domini: Antiphonen 8,7,9 der Matutin (leicht gekürzt).

Gaudent chori angelorum
civiumque beatorum
concinunt victoriam,
de peccato triumphato
gratulantur Domino.

1. Zeile nach AH, Bd. 1, S.174.

Cumque intuerentur in caelum
euntem*, dixerunt: Alleluja.

Gleiches Formular: 2. Antiphon
von Vesper I, II und Laudes.
*nach euntem fehlt das Wort
illum.

13 K 182 *Motetto Sanctorum Innocentium*

Isti, qui amicti sunt stolis albis,
qui sunt et unde venerunt?

Apoc 7, 13.

et dixit mihi: Hi sunt, qui venerunt
de tribulatione magna, et
dealbaverunt stolas suas in
sanguine agni.

SS. Innocentium Martyrum:
7. Antiphon der Matutin (mit
leichten Wortänderungen).

Innocui agnelli, infantuli tenelli,
quae sola gentis spes.
Atrociter necantur, hae rosae
suffocantur, o dira foeda res.

Wohl Neudichtung

Hi empti sunt ex hominibus
primitiae Deo et agno, et in ore
ipsorum non est inventum
mendacium.

Apoc 14, 4 und 5.

Salvete, flores martyrum
novaeque turbae caelitum,
quos Christus habet rex,
o candidae animulae,
o amate, purpurate grex.

Wohl Neudichtung, an die 1.
Zeile des Laudes-Hymnus vom
gleichen Formular (28.XII.)
anknüpfend. (Mit AH Bd. 50,S.27,
stimmt ebenfalls nur die 1. Zeile
überein.)

14 K 175 *Motetto de B.M.V.*

Christe Fili summi Patris,
per amorem tuae matris
cujus venter te portavit
et te dulci lacte pavit.

Ad Christum oratio, Strophen
1–3 (von 9). In der letzten
Zeile der 3. Strophe leicht
geändert (AH Bd. 31, S.48).

15 K 161 *Offertorium de B.M.V.*

Lingua mea dic tropaea
virginis puerperae,
quae inflictum maledictum
miro transfert genere.

Mariale, Rhythmus II,
Strophen 5–8 von Bernhardus
Morlanensis, Monachus Clu-
niacensis (um 1140) (AH Bd. 50,
S.428).

16 K 172 *Motetto de B.M.V.*
Ave, o puerpera, fons jucunditatis
o dulcis* Christifera, flos virgi-
nitatis in succursum propera nobis
tribulatis pacis adfer munera nobis
tuis natis.

Ave, o puerpera, Strophen
1–3 (von 12) (AH Bd. 3, S.177)
*in AH praedulcis.

17 K 171 *Motetto de B.V.*
Ave, mundi spes, Maria,
ave mitis, ave pia,
ave plena gratia,
omnis boni copiosa.*

Ave, mundi spes, Maria,
Strophe 1–6 (von 22).
(Philipp Wackernagel, Das
deutsche Kirchenlied, Bd. 1,
Leipzig 1864, S.142 f.)
*bei Wackernagel: copia.

18 E 99 *Motetto*
Deus, in adjutorium meum intende,
quoniam mala me undique
premunt, et non est, qui eruat.

Eröffnungsversikel der Horae
diurnae (Fux zitiert die zugehörige
gregorianische Melodie).

Peccavi quidem et malum coram te
feci, sed, eheu, quam poenitet me.

Nach Ps. 50, 6.

O Deus, peccavi,
te sero amavi,
ex corde suspiro ad te.

Me magis dilexi,
te Deum despexi,
hoc paene exanimat me.

Wohl Neudichtung

Ast numquid laus tua in fines
terrae, quoniam misericors et mi-
serator Dominus. Anne abbreviata
est manus tua? Non, non.

Nach Ps. 47, 11;
nach Ps. 110, 4;
Zitat aus Isaias 59, 1.

Tu, o Deus, es peccantis una spes:
latronem exaudisti,
et mihi spem dedisti.

Zitat aus der Sequenz, *Dies
irae*, Strophe 13.

In te ergo sperabo, et non con-
fundar in aeternum.

Nach dem letzten Versikel
des *Te Deum*.

19 K 183 *Motetto*
Omnis terra adoret te, Deus, et
psallat tibi: psalmum dicat nomini
tuo, Domine.*

2. Sonntag nach Epiphanie:
Introitus-Antiphon.
*im Graduale Romanum: Altissime

O nomen dulce, o nomen suave,
O Jesu nomen delectabile,
O mel in ore, melos in aure
et pio jubilus in pectore.

Benedic, anima mea, Domino,
et omnia quae intra me sunt,
nomini sancto ejus.

In Officio feriali in Precibus
ad Primam: Vers. et Resp.

Marcescite flores, arescite rores,
cessate odores, praeeminet nomen
Jesu super omnia.

Wohl Neudichtung

Abeste sapores, perite liquores,
migrate colores, transcendit nomen
Jesu mundi gaudia.

Sit nomen Domini benedictum,
in saeculorum saecula.

In der Liturgie häufig verwendeter
Vers. et Resp. u.a. beim Pontifi-
kalsegen. In Festo SSmi Nominis
Jesu in mehreren Horen
verwendet. Das Responsum heißt
dort: ex hoc nunc, et usque in
saeculum.

Omnes inde delectamur,
dum in Jesu consolamur
laeto modulamine.
In adversis adjuvamur,
ad amorem inflammamur
cordis hoc solamine.

Alleluja.

20 K 174 *Motetto de B.M.V.*
Benedicta, quae lilium es castitatis,
veni in auxilium nobis, tuis natis,
Flecte tuum filium prece pietatis,
ut post hoc exilium simus cum
beatis.

Wohl Neudichtung in der Vaganten-
strophe. In Vers 1 scheint Fux die
Worte 2 und 3 vertauscht zu
haben Nach dem rhythmischen
Schema muß die Wortfolge lauten:
Benedicta lilium, quae es castitatis.

Tu in mulieribus sola causa pacis,
clarior sideribus stella solem paris,
quaeque sanctis omnibus plus
auxiliaris,
junge coeli civibus nos,
o stella maris.

Benedictus filius tuus, o sacrata,
per te sit propitius, dimittat peccata,
conculcetur fortius passio innata,
dentur nobis ocius gaudia beata.

Fructus tuus, regia virgo et decora,
veniat de regia poli absque mora,
dona det cum venia nobis gratiora
tua per suffragia, rutilans aurora.

Aus dem Gesamtformular des betreffenden Tages oder Festes stammen die Texte von E 46, K 164, K 170, K 162, K 169. Übernahmen aus anderen liturgischen Formularen stellen dar K 178 (*Motetto de Confessore aus Commune unius Martyris*), K 183 (Zum Fest *Jesu Namen*, das am 2. Sonntag nach Epiphanie begangen wurde, wird ein Vers. et Resp. des ferialen Offizium genommen) und L 33 (eine Komposition zu Weihnachten eröffnet eine Antiphon von Beschneidung des Herrn). Kombinationen von Tagestexten und Bibelzitaten finden wir in K 159 und 182, an Bibelstellen knüpft an und ein Sequenzzitat enthält E 99. Verbindungen von Tagestexten mit Neudichtungen begegnen in K 160, 169, 182. Die vermutlichen Neudichtungen knüpfen manchmal an liturgische Hymnen oder hymnenartige Dichtungen des Mittelalters an: K 160 und 182 an liturgische, K 169 an einen mittelalterlichen. (Zu K 169 steht ein Parallelfall in AH, Bd. 50, S.27: dort ist ebenfalls die 1. Zeile vom 28. XII. zitiert.). Eine barocke Neudichtung dürfte K 174 sein, in diesem Text ist die sogenannte Vagantenstrophe benützt, deren Verse aus 7 + 6 Silben bestehen. In der Vertonung der 1.Zeile stellte Fux das Relativpronomen an zweite Stelle, er läßt singen: *Benedicta, benedicta, quae lilium es castitatis.*[22] Das mag wegen der vom Komponisten gewählten Wiederholung des ersten Wortes und zu besserer Verständlichkeit des Textes beim Hören geschehen sein. Dadurch wurde die erste Zeile unregelmäßig und zwar als einzige in den 4 Strophen des Gedichts. Sie entspricht nicht mehr den 7 + 6 Silben, die Teilungsstelle des ersten Verses fällt in das Wort 'lilium'.

Neben Strophen liturgischer Hymnen in K 160 und 170 beobachten wir in den Texten mehrere Übernahmen aus Sequenzen. Diese Beispiele sind:

1 K 160: Strophe 1 und 2 der Fronleichnams-Sequenz *Lauda Sion Salvatorem.*
2 K 170: vermutlich 2 Innenstrophen einer Hl. Geist-Sequenz.
3 K 162: die in der Liturgie nicht mehr verwendete Sequenz *Gratulemur in hac die*, 1., 2., 9., 10. Strophe (AH Bd. 54, S.325).
4 E 99: Zitat aus der Requiem-Sequenz *Dies irae*, Strophe 13.

Für die *Vertonung* lassen sich folgende Grundsätze beobachten: Für Rezitative wird in der Regel Prosatext, für Arien gereimter Text zugrunde gelegt. Besteht die Textvorlage ausschließlich aus gereimten Strophen, wie in K 161, 171, 172, 175, wird auf Rezitative verzichtet. Die knappste Form mit ausschließlichem Prosatext stellt dar E 46 *Jubilate*, das aus Chorsatz, Altarie und Wiederholung des Chorsatzes besteht.

Auf die Worte *Amen* oder *Alleluja* wird nicht selten ein eigener Schlußabschnitt gesetzt. Dies war Zeitbrauch und findet sich auch bei R.I. Mayr, J.C.F. Fischer, A. Caldara und anderen. Enthält der Text keines dieser Worte am Ende, kann der Schlußabschnitt auf den letzten Satz des gewählten Textes geformt sein: K 161, E 99, E 101 u.a.

Bei den Solo-Motetten entspricht die Form von E 80 nahezu der von Johann Joachim Quantz 1752 charakterisierten Anlage 'welche aus zweyen Arien und zweyen Recitativen besteht, und sich mit einem Halleluja schließt'. Hier fehlt lediglich das Rezitativ am Anfang.[23] K 165 repräsentiert dagegen diesen Typ übervollständig. In dieser Solo-Motette reihte Fux eine Einleitung (20 Takte), ein *Recitativo accompagnato* (in der 2. Hälfte R. secco), eine erste *da capo*-Arie, ein weiteres *Recitativo accompagnato*, eine zweite *da capo*-Arie (die nur vom Generalbaß begleitet wird) und ein abschließendes Alleluja als dritte *da capo*-Arie. K 162, *Gratulemur in hac die* belegt, daß die *da capo*-Arie auch für Texte angewandt wird, die der liturgischen Tradition entstammen (und nicht nur für barocke Neudichtungen). Solo-Motetten sind wiederholt mit 4-st. Chor einfacherer Setzart abgeschlossen, wofür K 162, 167, 173 u.a. Beispiele sind.

In den mir zugänglich gewesenen rund 30 Offertorienkompositionen von Fux im *stilus mixtus* eröffnen wiederholt Vorspiele die Vertonung, deren formale Funktion wir später erwähnen: K 168, 170, L 33 und 44, E 100 und 101. Hier sei mitgeteilt, daß sie stets knapp und ohne Taktwechsel, meist imitatorisch gearbeitet sind. Nachspiele von Arien kommen wiederholt vor, Nachspiele des kantatenartigen Zyklus lassen sich nur vereinzelt beobachten, in der Regel schließen die Kompositionen mit dem begleiteten Vokalsatz. Ausnahmen bilden K 165, die österliche Solomotette mit Trompetensolo,[24] die mit dem 11-taktigen Ritornell endet, und E 45, das Alt/Tenor-Ensemblestück *Odorosae charae rosae*, in dessen *Alleluja*-Finale die beiden Violinen einen Takt überhängenden Schluß (in der zweigestrichenen Oktave) hören lassen.

Für die Entstehungszeit der Sätze gibt es keine präzisen Daten, doch einige ungefähre Anhaltspunkte. Das sind:

1 Datierungen im Notenmaterial.
2 Aufführungsdaten auf den Umschlägen.
3 Notenschreiber, deren Tätigkeit zeitlich bekannt ist.

Eine ungefähre Datierung enthalten die Advents-Offertorien, auf deren Partituren Fux Vice-Kapellmeister tituliert ist.[25] Dieses Amt hatte er 1713-15 inne. 6 *Motetti con Istromenti* blieben in Meiningen in einem Konvolut erhalten, auf dem als Besitzervermerk eingetragen steht (Kürzel aufgelöst): Anton Ulrich Dux Saxoniae 1727.[26] Das sind Kopien von E 57, 80, 97, 98, 99, 100, die sich der damals in Wien lebende Herzog anfertigen liess. Diese Kompositionen sind demzufolge spätestens 1727, wahrscheinlich früher entstanden. Die Kopie von E 45 in Stift Göttweig ist 1725 datiert.

Bei den in Köchels Verzeichnis der Kompositionen von Fux mitgeteilten

Aufführungsdaten scheiden jene für die Datierung aus, die nach Fux' Tode liegen (K 159, 160, 163), auch wohl jene, die um 1730 beginnen (K 165, 166, 167, 168, 170), weil bei beiden Gruppen die Umschläge erneuert worden sein dürften. Anhaltspunkte können wohl lediglich jene geben, die in den ersten Jahren des Meisters als Hofkapellmeister beginnen. Das sind K 172, das ab 1717 und K 173, das ab 1718 aufgeführt wurde.

Für K 165, die österliche Solomotette für Tenor, beginnen die Aufführungsdaten 1736. Daß Fux diese Komposition als rund 75-Jähriger verfaßte, scheint ausgeschlossen. Riedel wies nach, daß die Stimmen ein Kopist schrieb, der zwischen 1707 und 1723 belegbar ist.[27]

Die Frage nach dem Compilator bzw. Dichter der frei gewählten Texte ist nun zu stellen. Da ein Name nirgends erwähnt ist, sind wir auf Vermutungen angewiesen. Die gleiche Situation ist bei Zeitgenossen gegeben, etwa bei J.C.F. Fischer. Selbst in einem sorgfältig geführten Musikalieninventar wie dem der Prager Kreuzherren wird kein Autor bei frei gewählten kirchenmusikalischen Texten genannt.

Die offensichtlich genaue Kenntnis der Meß- und Offiziumstexte, des Alten und Neuen Testaments und von Dichtungen der kirchlichen Tradition legt die Vermutung nahe, daß ein Priester die Texte redigierte. Dabei wäre naheliegend an den jeweiligen Hofprediger zu denken, da Abstimmung von Predigt-und Gesangstexten ein bekannter und berechtigter Wunsch vieler Seelsorger ist. In den Jahren von Fux' Tätigkeit als Hofkomponist und Hofkapellmeister waren als Hofprediger stets Jesuitenpatres eingesetzt, die aus Österreich oder Süddeutschland stammten.[28] Den in klassischem Latein gründlich geschulten Angehörigen der *Societas Jesu* scheint der Stil der Neudichtungen zu widersprechen (u.a. die Verwendung der Vagantenstrophe). Als weitere Möglichkeit ist der jeweilige Hofpoet zu erwägen. Das waren gewöhnlich italienische Literaten, mitunter Priester, weil hauptsächlich italienische Texte für Oratorien, *Sepolcri* und Opern zu verfassen waren. Einige Italianismen in den freieren Offertorientexten weisen in diese Richtung. Das sind etwa das Gerundium in der Zeile *nullos formidando dolores* in K 181, die Umschreibung *Me habeto excusatum/apud Christum, tuum natum* in K 171 und das Verbum 'beneventare' im Rezitativ von L 33 *Quid agis, Bethlehem, si hospitem gratiosum tam turpiter beneventas?*[29] In den Kapellmeister-Jahren arbeitete Fux hauptsächlich mit den Hofpoeten Pietro Pariati und Claudio Pasquini als Verfassern von *Sepolcri* und Oratorien zusammen.[30] So scheint nicht auszuschließen, daß Hofpoeten die Texte der Offertorien bereitgestellt haben können.

Von Pasquinis Sepolcrotext *La Deposizione dalla croce* blieb außer der Partitur der zeitgenössische Textdruck erhalten.[31] In unserem Zusammenhang sind darin die am Rande beigedruckten Quellenangaben aufschlußreich. Sie zitieren ausschließlich Quellen, die in lateinischer Sprache verfaßt sind und belegen ausgebreitete Kenntnis der einschlägigen theologischen Literatur, von der wir oben sprachen. Ähnlich wie manche freieren Offertorientexte stellt dieser Sepolcrotext eine Neudichtung, mindestens eine Neuformulierung dar.

Die vorstehenden Erwägungen sind alle bloße Vermutungen. Bearbeiter bzw. Dichter kann ein unbekannter Priester oder Ordensangehöriger in Wien gewesen sein. 1696 bis 1702 hatte Fux als Organist der Schottenkirche geamtet und sicher manche dieser gebildeten Benediktinerpatres näher kennen gelernt. So könnte unter ihnen (auch unter Angehörigen anderer Orden in Wien) sich jener wichtige Helfer befunden haben. Fux selbst könnte den einen oder anderen knappen Text redigiert haben (etwa E 46), kaum alle. Seine theologischen Kenntnisse waren wohl nicht so gründlich und seine beruflichen Pflichten ließen wohl kaum die entsprechende Muße. Anregungen und Wünsche dürfte er diesem Helfer schon mitgeteilt haben. Das könnte etwa gewesen sein, daß er kontrastreiche Aussagen, Vorlagen für Rezitative, Arien und Chöre sowie nicht zu knappe Satzfolgen wünschte.

Die Offertorien für Advents- und Fastenzeit setzte Fux im *stylus a capella*, dem *stile antico*. Wie er in den *Gradus ad Parnassum* 1725[32] ausführte, war dieser in der Kaiserlichen Hofkapelle in zwei Varianten üblich a) als unbegleiteter Chorgesang, b) als von Melodieinstrumenten und Generalbaß mitgespielter Chorgesang. Bei der zweiten Art ließen sich höhere Ansprüche an die Singstimmen stellen: schwierigere Intervalle, kompliziertere Rhythmen, längere Phrasen u.ä.

Betrachtet man die Offertorien für die 4 Adventssonntage, von denen Fux jene für den 1. und 4. in den *Gradus* vollständig abdrucken ließ,[33] bemerkt man bald, daß sie keineswegs nach gleichem Formmuster gearbeitet sind. Der deutlichste Unterschied besteht zwischen dem ersten und vierten, von denen das erste in Motettenart auf selbst erfundene *soggetti* (außer dem Kopfmotiv, das den Beginn des gregorianischen *Offertorium* nachzeichnet), das vierte als *cantus firmus*-Komposition gestaltet ist. Im Kommentar von Fux fehlt ein Hinweis auf das nach Kadenz und nach zusätzlicher Pause ansetzende *non confundentur*. Diesen ungewöhnlichen Ansatz wiederholt er sogar variiert, da er den letzten Textsatz *etenim universi . . .* zur formalen Abrundung wiederholt (Takt 66 und 85). Beim *Ave Maria*, in dem die neuen *Soggetti* wiederholt nach Klauselschluß einsetzen (Takt 13, 19, 27, 47, 57), läßt er den Schüler Joseph diesen Punkt ansprechen. Der Lehrer erwidert, daß die Struktur des gregorianischen Themas die Ursache dafür sei. Dennoch sei in dieser Komposition der beständige Fluß der Stimmen gewahrt, was die Hauptsache bilde.[34]

Im Revisionsbericht zu *DTÖ* Bd. 3 stellt Johann Evangelist Habert zum *cantus firmus* fest: Von wo er [Fux] den Choral genommen hat, läßt sich nicht nachweisen.[35] Dieser *cantus firmus* enthält in der Mitte die Wiederholung der Worte *in mulieribus*, ein Verfahren, das in vergleichbaren Choralgesängen nicht vorkommt (die 5. und 6. cantus firmus-Zeile sind gleich textiert). Das bestärkt die Vermutung, daß Fux der Autor dieses *cantus firmus* sein dürfte. Trotz mixolydischem Beginn und Schluß des *cantus firmus* schließt Fux die Komposition mit einer jonischen Kadenz. Damit weicht er von der Tradition ab. Auch dieser Punkt ist im Kommentar des Lehrbuches nicht angesprochen.

Das *Offertorium* für den 2. Adventssonntag ist 2-teilig, jenes für den 3. Adventssonntag 3-teilig gegliedert. Mag diese Anlage beim ersten von Palestrinas Komposition des gleichen Textes angeregt sein,[36] so ist das

Ergebnis recht verschieden. Palestrina gliederte in 60 + 23 *tempora* in gleichem Zeitmaß, Fux hingegen in 34 *Alla breve-* und 30 *Tempo ordinario-tempora*. Bei Palestrina ist die Vertonung der Worte *Ostende nobis, Domine* wesentlich kürzer, bei Fux wesentlich länger als der Offertorien-Beginn. Der zweite Teil erhält bei ihm stärkeres Gewicht. Beim *Offertorium* des 3. Adventssonntags hat möglicherweise der liturgische Charakter des Sonntags *Gaudete* die Vertonung mitgeprägt. In den Introiten vom 3. Advents- und 4. Fastensonntag läßt die katholische Kirche bereits im ersten Wort (*gaudete* bzw. *laetare*) die Vorfreude auf Weihnachten bzw. Ostern anklingen. Sie dokumentiert diese auch in der rosaroten Farbe des Messgewands (statt der violetten). Der liturgische Text vom 3. Adventssonntag stammt aus Ps. 84, 2 und erste Hälfte von 3. Fux nahm die 2. Hälfte des 3. Verses hinzu und bildete eine dreiteilige Formanlage. In der Vertonung bediente er sich einer Reprise: für den zusätzlichen Halbvers griff er auf das 3. *soggetto* des Einleitungsteils zurück. Dieses imitierte er nun 37 Takte lang, also deutlich gesteigert, während er es beim ersten Auftreten 14 Takte durchgeführt hatte. Musikalisch entstand so eine dreiteilige Anlage, die dem *Responsorium* mit Vers und (variierter) Wiederholung der zweiten Hälfte des *Responsorium* ähnelt. Hier äußert sich – wenn auch in bescheidenem Maß – das Streben nach Kontrast in einer Offertorienkomposition auf liturgischen Text im *stylus a capella*.

Zu den Fastensonntagen konnte bisher nur eine Offertoriumkomposition von Fux gefunden werden, *Laudate Dominum* für den 4. Fastensonntag. In den Musikalienbeständen der schlesischen Zisterzienserklöster Grüssau und Leubus ist sie überliefert.[37] Die Kopie in Grüssau ist 1748, jene in Leubus 1755 datiert, möglicherweise erhielt der *Regens chori* in Leubus diese von seinem Grüssauer *Confrater*. Bezüglich Kompositionen von Fux gibt es in den schlesischen Klostermusikalien eine einzige Parallele. Das ist eine *Missa solemnis ex C* à 4 v, 2 Vl, 2 Cl, Timp, Org, con Violone aus der 1. Hälfte des 18. Jahrhunderts ohne Herkunftsbezeichnung.[38] Wie die Offertoriumkomposition 1748 nach Grüssau gelangt ist, als Schlesien bereits zu Preussen gehörte, konnte bisher nicht geklärt werden. Denkbar ist, daß ein in Wien Theologie studierender Mönch sie zu erhalten wußte und in das Heimatkloster mitbrachte.

Im Minoritenkonvent Wien befindet sich ein *Offertorium, Justitiae Domini*, für den 3. Fastensonntag, das den Komponistennamen Fux trägt. Riedel erkannte, daß eine Bearbeitung des *Tractus* zum 1. Fastensonntag K 143 vorliegt.[39] Diese Parodie dürfte der Hofkapellmeister kaum selbst eingerichtet haben.

Laudate Dominum stellt einen Beleg für den *stylus a capella* mit *colla parte*-Instrumenten und Generalbaß dar. Die erwähnte liturgische Sonderstellung des Sonntags *Laetare* dürfte Fux zu dieser Stilwahl veranlaßt haben. Der stützende Instrumentalsatz ist in beiden Kopien 2 Vl, Vla und Organo übertragen, im Original dürften beide Violinen den Sopran, Alt-Trombone den Alt, Tenor-Trombone den Tenor, Fagott und Generalbaß den Baß dupliert haben. Die Führung der Vokalstimmen ist intervallmäßig, rhythmisch und in manchen Phrasenausdehnungen anspruchsvoller behandelt als in Sätzen des *stilus antiquus*. Das belegt sogleich der erste Abschnitt *Laudate Dominum*. Diesem liegen 2 Themen zugrunde, das in Halben und Vierteln abwärts ausgefüllte Quartintervall und eine weithin in Achteln kontrapunktierende Gegenstimme, in der Sexten abwärts und in der Weiterführung auch der Tritonus abwärts eingesetzt sind. Mehrfach kommen madrigalische Abschnitte vor: *psallite nomini ejus* und *omnia quaecumque voluit*. Der letzte Abschnitt *omnia, quaecumque voluit, fecit...* ist imitatorisch ähnlich breit ausgeführt wie der Anfang. Die 76 Takte umfassende Komposition erläutert die Erklärung von Fux in den *Gradus*: [*stylus a capella, Organo, aliisque instrumentis instructus*] *qui majori, & modulandi, & canendi, vagandique gaudet libertate.*[40]

Der *stilus mixtus* wurde am Wiener Hof in der Amtszeit von Fux ebenfalls in zwei Varianten gepflegt: als *stile mediocre* und *stile solenne*. Diese Unterscheidung ist in den *Gradus* nicht mehr behandelt, sie war für einen 2. Band aufgespart, der nie erschienen ist. Doch wird diese Einteilung in den *Rubriche Generali* von Kilian Reinhardt eingehalten.[41] Der *stile mediocre* wurde für Vokalstimmen (*Soli e Ripieni*) mit bescheidener Instrumentalbesetzung, dem sogenannten *Kirchentrio* gepflegt, beim *stile solenne* traten Clarini (gelegentlich Clarini e Trombe) mit oder ohne Timpani hinzu.

Dem hervorragenden Ensemble von Vokalisten und Instrumentalisten entsprechend, das ihm in der Kaiserlichen Hofkapelle anvertraut war, hat Fux beide Stilarten in mehreren Varianten gepflegt. Im stile mediocre schrieb er:

a) für 1 Solisten,
b) für mehrere Solisten,
c) für 1 Solisten und Chor,
d) für mehrere Solisten und Chor.

In ähnlicher Weise sind die Kompositionen im stile solenne besetzungsmäßig unterschiedlich angelegt. Von der Trompetenverwendung her läßt sich gliedern in:

a) mit 1 Clarino,
b) mit 2 Clarini,
c) mit 2 Clarini e Timpani,
d) mit 2 Clarini, 2 Trombe e Timpani.

Tromboni in solistischer Funktion enthät *Christe, Fili summi Patris*, K 175. Doch sind die Ansprüche nicht mit jenen im *Alma redemptoris*, K 186[42] zu vergleichen, wo in *Sonatina* und *Aria* virtuose Ansprüche gestellt sind. In K 175 spielt im einleitenden Solo-Terzett für Sopran/Alt/Tenor die Alt-Trombone die Violoncello-Stimme bis auf kleine Varianten mit. Im Terzett *Te per ipsum rogo supplex* für Alt/Tenor/Baß alternieren schlichter Vokalsatz und Instrumentalsatz miteinander. Trotz der bescheidenen technischen Ansprüche steigert der Posaunenklang den Ausdrucksgehalt.

Der Chor ist 4-stimmig, in verhältnismäßig wenigen Fällen 5-stimmig besetzt, verdoppelt ist dabei der Sopran. Belege bilden K 183, K 44, E 101, K 53, E 17. Auffallend ist die häufig 5-stimmige Besetzung in Requiemkompositionen, auf die Riedel bereits aufmerksam machte. Diese scheint auf einer Tradition am Kaiserhof zu beruhen.[43]

Ein beträchtlicher Teil der Kompositionen von Fux zum *Offertorium* sind für Hochfeste bestimmt. In der Reihenfolge des Kirchenjahres sind dies: Weihnachten 3. Messe, K 167, Epiphanie K 168, Ostersonntag K 165, Christi Himmelfahrt K 169, Pfingstsonntag K 170. Dazu kommen die Marienfeiertage Purificatio K 172, Assumptio K 162, Nativitas K 175. Weiter gehören dazu wohl das Fest des Erzengels Michael K 177 und Offertorienvertonungen zum Requiem (für Allerseelen bzw. Beerdigungsgottesdienste) K 53, K 55, K 56, L 27, E 16.

Für die fehlenden Feste *Annuntiatio B.M.V.,* Peter und Paul, Allerheiligen konnte Riedel in den Beständen der Hofkapelle keine anderen zeitgenössischen Vertonungen finden. Im Kalendarium setzte er deshalb ein: Motetto proprio. Für Fronleichnam wies er für 1721 und 1733 Aufführungen von zwei Kompositionen Caldaras nach. Da Fux in K 160 und 164 geeignete Kompositionen verfaßte, kann in dem einen oder anderen Jahr an diesem Fest eine Fux-Komposition erklungen sein. K 160 wurde nur in St. Peter, Wien, überliefert, K 164 in der Hofkapelle, doch mit offensichtlich erneuertem Umschlag (Aufführungstermine nach dem Tod von Fux, vom 9.2.1742 bis 12.3.1744). In aller Vorsicht läßt sich deshalb die Vermutung äußern, daß Fux für *Annuntiatio B.M.V.,* Peter und Paul, Allerheiligen – oder mindestens für das eine oder andere dieser Feste – Kompositionen zum *Offertorium* verfaßt haben kann, die verloren gingen.[44]

Vergleicht man bei den genannten Kompositionen zu hohen Festen Festrang und gewählte Besetzung, läßt sich eine gewisse künstlerische Freiheit in der Besetzungsart beobachten. Die Komposition für Ostern K 165 ist eine Solo-Motette. Ein chorisches *Alleluja* statt des solistischen hätte die Wirkung zweifellos gesteigert. Die 5-st. Chorbesetzung ist bei K 183 und bei den Offertorien des Requiem für einen herausgehobenen Anlaß verwirklicht. *Omnis terra,* nur *Motetto* beschriftet, dürfte dem Text nach für das Fest *Namen Jesu* bestimmt sein. Da es nicht im Bestand der Hofkapelle überkam, wissen wir nicht, ob es an diesem Fest verwendet wurde. K 53 gehört zu dem Requiem, das für Angehörige des Kaiserhauses, für Prinz Eugen und für Kaiser Karl VI. als Beerdigungsrequiem erklang.[45] Doch die ebenfalls 5-st. Chorsätze K 44 sind *per ogni santo* und E 101 *de quocumque Sancto* bezeichnet, also für keinen ungewöhnlichen Anlaß bestimmt. Abweichungen von der Norm beobachten wir auch bei der Orchesterbesetzung. Die Offertorien für Weihnachten, Epiphanie, Christi Himmelfahrt und Pfingsten – um nur diese Hochfeste zu nennen – verwenden keine Clarini. Sie sind also im stile mediocre verfaßt, wenn auch textlich und musikalisch reich gegliedert. Ähnliche Abweichungen liegen bei der Paukenverwendung vor. Bei den mir zugänglich gewesenen Offertorienkompositionen sind nur in drei Timpani besetz. Das sind K 162, E 98 und E 100. K 162, *Hodie Maria virgo caelos ascendit* ist für *Assumptio*

B.M.V.; E 98, *Gloria tua est Domine*, enthält keine Zuschreibung (Titel *Motetto*) und E 100 *O sancte n.* [*nominande*] ist für ein beliebiges Heiligenfest gedacht. Die festliche Komposition für Sonntage nach Ostern E 46 *Jubilate* weist hingegen keine Paukenstimme auf. Möglicherweise darf man für dieses nicht in der Hofkapelle überkommene Stück Verlust der Paukenstimme annehmen.

Der geschilderte Befund läßt erkennen, daß bei den Offertorien nicht jede Einzelheit reglementiert gewesen scheint. In der vokalen und instrumentalen Besetzung blieb dem Komponisten eine gewisse Wahlfreiheit. Bei den Messen wurden die Kriterien des *stile mediocre* und *solenne* genau befolgt, sodaß bei den Offertorien Ausnahmen zugestanden wurden.

Eine eigene Species scheinen die Offertorienkompositionen für 4 Solisten und Generalbaß zu bilden. Sie verwenden keine Violinen, etwa für *Sinfonia*, gliedernde Zwischenspiele oder zur Bereicherung von Solo- oder Ensembleabschnitten. Die Faktur entspricht dem *stile antico* mit Instrumentalbegleitung, die Instrumentalbegleitung ist jedoch auf den Generalbaß reduziert, weil ausschließlich Solisten singen. Solistenstimmen wurden in der Wiener Kirchenmusik der 1. Hälfte des 18. Jahrhunderts nicht von Instrumenten dupliert.[46]

Zwei Belege sind nach bisheriger Kenntnis erhalten: K 163 und 179. Beide Materialien entstammen der Kaiserlichen Hofkapelle, die Umschläge tragen zahlreiche Aufführungsvermerke. Bei K 163 reichen sie vom 12. Oktober 1741 bis 17. Dezember 1749 (der Umschlag wurde offensichtlich erneuert), bei K 179 vom 4. Oktober 1735 bis 27. Februar 1747, das sind 20 bzw. 29 Aufführungen.[47] K 163, *Ave salus mundi* ist *Motetto de Venerabili*, K 179, *Justum deduxit Dominus* ist *Motetto de Confessore* betitelt. Das erste dürfte für die Votivämter zum Altarssakrament am Donnerstag, das zweite für Bekennerfeste eingesetzt worden sein.

Der Tonsatz dieser Stücke ist durch deutlich aufgelockerte Vierstimmigkeit gekennzeichnet. Immer wieder wird Chorspaltung verwendet, werden Phrasen von Sopran + Alt durch Tenor + Baß wiederholt oder fortgesetzt und umgekehrt. In den technischen Ansprüchen für die Stimmen überschreitet Fux nicht den Maßstab, der etwa in *Alleluja*-Schlüssen für Ripieni eingehalten ist, selbst nicht bei *amavit eum Dominus* in K 179 (Takt 25 ff.). Die Anforderungen sind jedoch gesteigert gegenüber dem *stile antico* mit *colla parte-* Instrumenten, sodaß man wohl von einer eigenen Species sprechen darf, wenn auch nur wenige Belege vorliegen. In den *Gradus* hat Fux diesen Typ nicht behandelt. Forscht man nach dem Sinn dieser Gestaltungsart, lassen sich wohl drei Gesichtspunkte der Kapellpraxis als Gründe nennen. Zum ersten sparten diese Sätze Probenarbeit. Die Solisten hatten ihre Parte allein zu studieren. Besetzte man Sopran und Alt nicht mit Sängerinnen oder Kastraten, sondern mit Knabensolisten, wurden nur die im Blattsingen gewandteren Stimmführer benötigt. Zum anderen boten diese motettischen Sätze eine Gelegenheit, die Solisten als Ensemble in einem längeren Satz vorzustellen. Zum dritten war dies eine Möglichkeit, zu künstlerischer Ensembledisziplin zu erziehen, arien-, duett-, oder terzettartige Abschnitte sind darin nämlich nicht enthalten. Jeder Solist hatte sich ständig einzuordnen.

In der Formanlage enthält K 179 eine Reprise. Der Aufbau lautet nach soggetto-Abschnitten: a,b,c,d,a¹,e. Das erste soggetto wird vor dem Alleluja-Abschnitt erneut durchgeführt, doch in abgewandelter und verkürzter Weise. Diese Form bildet eine gewisse Parallele zu K 150, dem im stile antico komponierten Offertorium zum 3. Adventssonntag. Dort lautet das oben beschriebene Formschema: a,b,c,d,c¹. Wiederholt wird der 3. Abschnitt. Fux wählte die Formanlage nicht nach Schemata, sondern jeweils dem Text entsprechend individuell.

Einige *Hinweise zur Formgestaltung* und zur Verwendung der Instrumentalabschnitte dabei sollen unsere Bemerkungen beschließen. Bei einem Meister wie Johann Joseph Fux braucht nicht im einzelnen belegt zu werden, daß die formale Gestaltung keine Schematik aufweist. In großer Mannigfaltigkeit ist sie verwirklicht.

Als Grundtyp läßt sich wohl auch bei den Offertoriumkompositionen im *stilus mixtus* die reihende Anlage wie bei den Belegen des *stilus antiquus* bezeichnen. Je nach Textstruktur kann Wechsel von Rezitativ, Arie (Ensemble) und Chor oder Chor, Solo (Ensemble), Chor vorliegen (bei den 6 Strophen von K 171, *Ave mundi spes, Maria*: S-Solo / Chor / A-Solo / Chor /T-Solo/ Chor, wobei die 3 Chorabschnitte – obwohl unterschiedlich gesetzt – eine Art Ritornell der Besetzung bilden). Dazu kann eine einleitende Sinfonia als abgeschlossener Abschnitt oder als Einleitung des ersten Vokalsatzes kommen.

Ein solcher auf den ersten Blick gereiht scheinender Zyklus kann durch motivische Bezüge eine gewisse Abrundung aufweisen. In E 100 liegt die Quarte des 1-st. Vokalbeginns dem *Alleluja*-Thema des Schlußabschnitts als konstitutives Intervall zugrunde. Ebenso ist in E 98 der ebenfalls 1-st. Quartanfang im Thema des Schlußsatzes in Umkehrung und diatonisch ausgefüllt verwendet. In E 105 bewegt sich der zweite, nur vom Generalbaß gestützte Ansatz des Solotenors im Raum der kleinen Sexte g es¹, wobei die Randtöne auf betonter Zeit liegen. Den gleichen Ambitus weist das Thema der Schlußfuge auf.

Formal vereinheitlichende Wiederaufnahmen von Abschnitten liegen in folgenden Zyklen vor:

1. In E 46, wo der Anfangschor wiederholt wird.[48]
2. In L 33, wo der Chor *Venite, gentes* als 3. und 6. Abschnitt zu singen ist.
3. In K 166 (einem 10-teiligen Gebilde), wo die Aria *Plaudite* an 5. und 7. Stelle zu erklingen hat.
4. In K 159, wo der Anfangschor *Estote fortes in bello* in ritornellartiger Weise dreimal eingesetzt ist. Das Soloquartett singt dazwischen zwei kontrastierende Abschnitte mit Generalbaß. Dadurch entsteht eine rondeauartige Form.

Nicht alle Offertorienkompositionen von Fux im *stilus mixtus* beginnen mit einer *Sinfonia (Sonata, Sonatina)*. K 161 eröffnet mit Rezitativ, E 99 hebt mit einem *Adagio* an, auch E 105 setzt zum *passus duriusculus* des Instrumentalbasses adagio ein (Gesangstext: *Oravi*). Die *Sinfonia* ist ferner nicht immer als eigener Abschnitt durch Kadenz abgeschlossen. In L 44 (10

Takte), E 46 (9 Takte), E 100 (7 Takte), E 101 (12 Takte) u.a. geht sie unmittelbar in den Vokaleinsatz über. Vereinzelt ist das Instrumentalvorspiel zur formalen Gliederung wiederholt. Das liegt vor:

1. In K 170, wo die *Sinfonia* an 1. und 3. Stelle des 7-sätzigen Zyklus steht. Der Instrumentalsatz ist beidemal 17 Takte lang, doch divergieren die Takte 10–15. Die Echowiederholung der Takte 10–13 der Erstfassung wird dadurch bei der Wiederholung eliminiert.
2. In K 177, wo die den eröffnenden Chorsatz rahmende Einleitung (4 Takte) am Anfang in den Chorsatz unmittelbar hineinführt.
3. In K 168, wo eine Sonatina an 1. Stelle, eine (scheinbar) andere an 3. Stelle des 4-sätzigen Zyklus erscheint. Die erste steht im 4/4-Takt und weist 11 Takte auf, die zweite benützt 3/4-Takt und mißt gleichfalls 11 Takte. Die Themen sind motivisch verwandt: das Kopfmotiv der zweiten Sonatina ist eine freie Umkehrung der Führung in der 1. Violine (2. Takt) in der ersten Sonatina.

Anmerkungen

*In der Studie sind folgende Abkürzungen verwendet:
K = Numerierungen der Kompositionen von Fux durch L. Ritter v. Köchel
L = Numerierungen weiterer Funde von Andreas Liess
E = Ergänzungen; Numerierungen zusätzlicher Funde durch Hellmut Federhofer

Apoc	=	Apocalypse
AH	=	Analecta Hymnica
GA	=	*Gesamtausgabe*
DTÖ	=	*Denkmäler der Tonkunst in Österreich*
KmJb	=	*Kirchenmusikalisches Jahrbuch*
ÖNB	=	Österreichische Nationalbibliothek, Musikabteilung, Wien

K und K Hofburgkapelle = Kaiserliche und Königliche Hofburgkapelle

S	=	Sopran
A	=	Alt
T	=	Tenor
B	=	Baß
Rip	=	Ripieni
Vl	=	Violino
Vla	=	Viola
Vle	=	Viole
Vlta	=	Violetta
Vc	=	Violoncello

Viol	=	Violone
Cb	=	Contrabasso
Corn	=	Cornetto
Tromb	=	Trombone
Fag	=	Fagotto
Cl	=	Clarino
Tr	=	Tromba
Timp	=	Timpani
Org	=	Organo
Bc	=	Basso continuo

[1] Cf. *Denkmäler der Tonkunst in Österreich (DTÖ)*, Bd. 3, wo Kompositionen mit Choralintonationen und auch *cantus firmus*-Kompositionen von Fux publiziert sind.

[2] Friedrich W. Riedel, *Kirchenmusik am Hofe Karls VI. (1711-1740)* (München–Salzburg, 1977), S.117f.

[3] Josef Jungmann, *Missarum solemnia*, Bd. 2, (Wien,[5] 1962), S.34ff. – C. Ott, *Offertoriale sive versus off. cantus greg.* (Tournai, 1935).

[4] Vgl. das Inhaltsverzeichnis von Bd. 2 in: Alois Niemetz, *800 Jahre Musikpflege in Heiligenkreuz* (Heiligenkreuz, 1977), S.33 (von Bd. 3 wurde bisher kein vollständiges Exemplar gefunden).

[5] Riedel op.cit., *S.155*.

[6] *Erbe deutscher Musik, Landesdenkmale Bayern*, Bd. 1, hrsg. von Karl Gustav Fellerer (Braunschweig, 1936).

[7] Rudolf Walter, 'Zu J.C.F. Fischers geistlicher Vokalmusik. Neue Funde', *Archiv für Musikwissenschaft* XXXII, (1975), S.69f.

[8] Ein dem derzeitigen Forschungsstand entsprechendes Werkverzeichnis von J.J. Fux fehlt. Neben Ludwig Ritter von Köchel, Johann Josef Fux (Wien, 1872; Hildesheim, 1988), Beilage X, sind hauptsächlich folgende Ergänzungen zu nennen: Andreas Liess, *J.J. Fux*, (Wien, 1948), S.57ff.; Hellmut Federhofer, 'Unbekannte Kirchenmusik von J.J. Fux,' *KmJb* 43 (1959), S.122ff.; H. Federhofer und F.W. Riedel, 'Quellenkundliche Beiträge zur J.J. Fux-Forschung', *Archiv für Musikwissenschaft* 21 (1964), S.118ff.

[9] Gabriele Krombach, 'Modelle der Offertoriumskompositionen bei A. Caldara, J.G. Albrechtsberger und J. Preindl', *KmJb* 72 (1988), S.130f.

[10] Ähnliche Textwahl aus dem Tagesformular und gleichzeitige Belege dafür, daß dem Komponisten die liturgischen Texte zu knapp erschienen, beobachten wir in R.I. Mayrs *Gazophylacium musico-sacrum. Dominus regnavit* (Nr. 5) ist Versus all. + Off. der Missa in Aurora in Nativitate Domini; *Passer invenit* (Nr. 14) ist die (textreiche) Communio des 3. Fastensonntags; Ascendit Deus (Nr. 23) ist Off. + Communio in Ascensione Domini.

[11] Die Diari werden aufbewahrt in der Biblioteca Vaticana, Rom, Fondo Cappella Sistina.

[12] Gabriele Krombach, *Die Vertonungen liturgischer Sonntagsoffertorien am Wiener Hof* (München–Salzburg, 1986), S.18.

[13] Belege bilden die solennen Kompositionen K 162 (Stift Kremsmünster), E 43 (Kreuzherren Prag), E 46 (Schlierbach), E 98 und E 100 (M. Reger-Archiv Meiningen), E 101 (Mährisches Museum Brünn).

[14] Rudolf Walter, 'Der Kirchenkomponist J.C.F. Fischer', *Musica sacra* 97, (1977), S.344f.

[15] Das Offertorium *Exaltabo te à 4* ist im Musikalien-Inventar der Prager Kreuzherren als Off. des 11. Sonntags nach Pfingsten verzeichnet, mit dem es übereinstimmt. Dieses Inventar befindet sich in der Univ.- Bibl. Brünn. Ob die Komposition erhalten blieb, läßt sich erst überprüfen, wenn der in der Musikabteilung des Nationalmuseums Prag archivierte Notenbestand aus dem Kreuzherrenkloster der Forschung vollständig zugänglich ist.

[16] *Riedel* op. cit., S.122. *Palestrina-Gesamtausgabe*, hrsg. von Franz Xaver Haberl, (Leipzig, 1862–1903) Bd. 9, S.190ff. Wolfgang Horn, *Die Dresdner Hofkirchenmusik 1720–1745* (Kassel u.a., 1987), S.100. *Zelenka-Dokumentation. Quellen und Materialien*, hrsg. von O. Landmann, W. Reich, W. Horn, Th. Kohlhase, Bd. 1, (Wiesbaden, 1989), S.34.

[17] *Giovanni Pierluigi da Palestrina-Gesamtausgabe* Bd. 2 (Leipzig, 1881), S.81ff. Zum soggetto ostinato in dieser Komposition vgl. Paul Patrick Macey, 'Josquins "Miserere mei Deus"; Context, Structure and Influence' (Diss. University of California, Berkeley 1987), S.158ff.

[18] Liess, op. cit., S.68.

[19] Für wiederholte liebenswürdige Unterstützung bei der Herkunftsbestimmung der nicht-liturgischen Offertorientexte dankt der Verfasser herzlich Herrn Dr. Ludwig Schuba, Univ.-Bibl. Heidelberg. – Zu den Textquellen der liturgischen Offertorien vgl. Helmut Hücke, Die Texte der Offertorien, in: *Festschrift für H. Husmann*, München 1970, S. 193 ff.

[20] Diese ist in einer Handschrift in Wiesbaden überliefert. vgl. Joseph Kehrein, *Sequenzen des Mittelalters aus Handschriften und Drucken* (Mainz, 1873), S.109 f.

[21] Der Text von K 162 ist als Dichtung der Barockzeit bezeichnet in: *Fux-Gesamtausgabe* Reihe III, Bd.1 (Graz 1961), Vorwort S.VII.

[22] Freundlicher Hinweis von Herrn Prof. Dr. R. Düchting, Seminar für Mittellatein der Univ. Heidelberg.

[23] Johann Joachim Quantz, *Versuch einer Anweisung, die Flöte traversière zu spielen* (Berlin, 1752), S.288.

[24] Gedruckt in *DTÖ*, Bd. 101/102, (Graz/Wien, 1962), S.127ff.

[25] *DTÖ*, Bd. 3, Revisionsbericht S.97.

[26] Christian Mühlfeld, 'Die Meininger Musikbibliothek', *Neue Zeitschrift für Musik* 79 (Leipzig 1912), S.219.

[27] Riedel op. cit., S.191.

[28] Cölestin Wolfsgruber, *Die K. und K. Hofburgkapelle und die K. und K. Geistliche Hofkapelle* (Wien, 1904), S.607f.

[29] Freundliche Hinweise von Herrn Prof. Dr. W. Berschin, Seminar für Mittellatein der Univ. Heidelberg.

[30] Köchel, op. cit., Kompositoinsverzeichnis S.132 ff. und Gustav Renker, *Das Wiener Sepolcro* (Phil. Diss. Wien, 1913), S.97.

[31] Wien, 1728. Eine Ablichtung vermittelte liebenswürdiger Weise Herr Prof. Dr. H. Federhofer, Mainz.

[32] Der Titel des Lehrbuchs ist als Plural zu verstehen, wie der Titelkupfer (Treppe mit mehreren Stufen) erläutert (*Fux-Gesamtausgabe*, Reihe VII, Bd. 1 (Kassel u.a., 1967).

[33] *Gradus*, S.247–54 und 256–61.

[34] *Gradus*, S.262.

[35] *DTÖ*, Bd. 3, S.99.

[36] *Palestrina-Gesamtausgabe*, hrsg. von Franz Xaver Haberl, (Leipzig, 1862–1903) Bd. 9, S.6ff.

[37] Die Kopie von 1748 entdeckte der Verfasser bei der Aufnahme des Musikalienbestandes in der Marienkirche Grüssau 1978, die Kopie von 1755 befindet sich in den schlesischen Klostermusikalien, die seit 1945 in der Musikabteilung der Univ. -Bibl. Warschau aufbewahrt werden. Im Grüssauer Exemplar lautet der Komponistenname Fux, im Leubuser Exemplar Gioseppe Fux.

[38] Signatur Mf 306.

[39] Riedel, op. cit., S.128. Vgl. auch: F.W. Riedel, *Das Musikarchiv im Minoritenkonvent zu Wien, Catalogus musicus I* (Kassel, 1963), S.16.

[40] *Gradus*, S.262.

[41] Kilian Reinhardt, *Rubriche generali per le Funzione Ecclesiastiche Musicali di tutto l'Anno . . . In Vienna d'Austria l'Anno MDCCXXVII* (Österr. Nat. -Bibl. Wien, Signatur S.m. 2503). Der Leitung der Musikabteilung der ÖNB Wien dankt der Verfasser für Vermittlung eines Mikrofilms.

[42] Gedruckt in *Fux-Gesamtausgabe*, Reihe III, Bd. 1, S.99ff.

[43] Friedrich W. Riedel, *Kirchenmusik am Hofe Karls VI. (1711-1740)* (München–Salzburg, 1977) S.183.

[44] vgl. 'Verlorene Quellen' in Federhofer/Riedel, 'Quellenkundliche Beiträge zur J.J. Fux-Forschung', *Archiv für Musikwissenschaft* 21 (1964) S.135 und 137.

[45] Köchel, op. cit., Kompositionsverzeichnis S.33.

[46] Johann Sebastian Bach ließ gelegentlich Solistenparte durch Instrumente mitspielen. Beispiele sind: Arie Nr. 8 in der Matthäus-Passion BWV 244, wo die Sopranstimme von Flauto traverso I unisono dupliert wird; Weihnachtsoratorium BWV 248, Arie Nr. 4, wo die Altstimme nicht ständig, doch zweimal je 8 Takte von Violine I und Oboe I unisono mitgespielt wird (T.17–24 und 45–52); ebenda Arie Nr. 19, wo die Altstimme von Flauto traverso I in der Oberoktave verdoppelt ist.

[47] Köchel, op. cit., Kompositionsverzeichnis S.73 und 78.

[48] Einzelausgabe (mit Aufführungsmaterial), Altötting 1991.

Anhang

Verzeichnis der bisher bekannten Kompositionen von Johann Joseph Fux
zum Offertorium
A. Liturgische Texte

I. In reinem a cappella-Stil[1]

1 Ad te, Domine, levavi a 4 v.	Dom. I. Adventus	K 153
2 Deus, tu convertens a 4 v.	Dom. II. Adventus	K 149
3 Benedixisti, Domine a 4 v.	Dom. III. Adventus	K 150
4 Ave Maria a 4 v.	Dom. IV. Adventus	K 151
5 Tollite portas a 4 v.	Vigilia Nativitatis	K 152
6 Exaltabo te, Domine a 4 v. (m.B.c?)	Feria IV. Cinerum Inv. der Kreuzherren in Prag[2]	
7 Domine, in auxilium meum a 4 v.	Feria VI. p. Dom. II. Quadrages.	K 154
8 Domine, fac mecum a 4 v.	Feria IV. p. Dom. III. Quadrages.	K 155
9 Intende voci or. meae a 4 v.	Feria VI. p. Dom. III. Quadrages.	K 156
10 De profundis clamavi a 4 v. (m.B.c?)	Dom. XXIII. p. Pentecosten	L 39

II. In begleitetem a cappella-Stil

11 Laudate Dominum, quia benignus a 4 v. Offertorium de Tempore	2 Vl, A-Vla con Org Dom. IV. Quadrages.	E 158

III. In mediocrer Besetzung

12 Reges Tharsis et insulae Motetto	a 4 v. 2 Vl, Corn, 2 Tromb, Fag, Vc, Viol, Org Epiphania Domini	K168
13 Oravi Deum meum Offertorium de Tempore	a 4 v. 2 Vl, 3 Tromb, Org Dom. XVII. p. Pentecosten	E 105
14 Veritas mea	a 4 v. 2 Vl, Vla, Org Commune Conf. non Pont.	L 32
15 Domine Jesu Christe	a 5 v. 2 Vl, Vla, 2 Corn, 2 Tromb, Fag, Vc, Viol, Org Missa pro Defunctis	K 53

16	Domine Jesu Christe	a 4 v. 2 Vlta, Org Missa pro Defunctis	K 55
17	Domine Jesu Christe	a 5 v. 4 Vle, 2 Tromb, Fag, Org Missa pro Defunctis	K 56
18	Domine Jesu Christe	a 4 v. 4 Vle, 3 Tromb, Org Missa pro Defunctis	L 27

IV In solenner Besetzung

| 19 | Domine Jesu Christe | a 5 v. Vla, 2 Cl, 2 Corn, 2 Tromb, Org Missa pro Defunctis | E 16 |

B. Nicht-liturgische Texte[4]

I. In mediocrer Besetzung für Solo bzw. Soli

20	Motetto de B.M.V. *Pia mater, fons amoris*	a S, 2 Vl, Fag, Vc, Viol, Org	K 176
21	Motetto Sanctorum Innocentium *Isti, qui amicti sunt*	a T, 2 Vl, Fag, Vc, Viol, Org	K 182
22	Motetto *Laetare, turba caelitum*	a S, 2 Vl, Fag, Vc, Viol, Org	E 80
23	Motetto *Ad arma decantate*	a B, 2 Vl, Vla, Vc, Cb, [Org]	E 97
24	Motetto *Confitebor*	a B, 2 Vl, Bc	E 56
25	Motetto *Voces laetae, voces canorae*	a B, 2 Vl, Vla, Org	E 58
26	Motetto de B.M.V. *Benedicta, quae lilium es*	a 2S, 2 Vl, Fag, Vc, Viol, Org	K 174
27	Motetto de Venerabili *Caro mea*	a 2S, Vc, Viol, Org	K 164
28	Motetto *Ecce clara fulget dies*	a S/B, 2 Vl, Cb, [Org]	E 57
29	Offertorium de B.M.V. *Odorosae charae rosae*	a A/T, 2 Vl, Org	E 45
30	Motetto de Resurrectione Domini *Ecce sacerdos*	a T/B, 2 Vl, Fag, Vc, Viol, Org	K 166
31	Motetto de B.M.V. *Ave, o puerpera*	a S/A/T, 2 Vl, Vc, Viol, Org	K 172

32 Motetto de Martyre *Iste est sanctus, qui contempsit*	a S/A/T, Vc, Viol, Org	K 180
33 Motetto de Confessore *Iste sanctus pro lege Dei*	a A/T/B, Vc, Viol, Org	K 178
34 Motetto de Venerabili *Ave salus mundi*	a 4 Soli, Vc, Viol, Org	K 163
35 Motetto de Confessore *Justum deduxit Dominus*	a 4 Soli, Vc, Viol, Org	K 179

II. In mediocrer Besetzung für Solo (Soli) und Ripieni

36 Motetto de Nativitate Domini *Plaudite Deo nostro*	a S, 4 Rip, 2 Vl, Vla, 2 Tromb, Fag, Vc, Viol, Org	K 167
37 Motetto della Madonna SS. *Ave pia stella maris*	a S, 4 Rip, 2 Vl, Corn, 2 Tromb, Fag, Vc, Viol, Org	K 173
38 De Nativitate Christi *O admirabile commercium*	a S/A, 4 Rip, 2 Vl, 3 Tromb, Org	L 33
39 Motetto de Ascensione Domini *Ponis nubem ascensum tuum*	a S/T, 4 Rip, 2 Vl, Corn, 2 Tromb, Fag, Vc, Viol, Org	K 169
40 Motetto de quovis Sancto *Celebremus cum gaudio*	a S/T, 4 Rip, 2 Vl, Corn, 2 Tromb, Fag, Vc, Viol, Org	K 181
41 Offertorium de B.V.M. *Lingua mea dic tropaea*[5]	a T/B, 4 Rip, 2 Vl, 2 Tromb, Vc, Viol, Org	K 161
42 Motetto de B.V.M. *Ave mundi spes Maria*	a S/A/T, 4 Rip, 2 Vl, Corn, 2 Tromb, Fag, Vc, Viol, Org	K 171
43 Motetto *Deus in adjutorium*	a S/T/B, 4 Rip, 2 Vl, Org	E 99
44 Offertorium de Apostolis *Estote fortes*	a 4 Soli e Rip, 3 Vle, Corn, 2 Tromb, Fag, Vc, Viol, Org	K 159
45 Offertorium de Venerabili *Sacris solemniis*	a 4 Soli e Ripieni, 2 Vl, Corn, 2 Tromb, Fag, Vc, Viol, Org	K 160
46 Motetto de Spiritu Sancto *O ignis coelestis*	a 4 Soli e Rip, 2 Vl, Corn, 2 Tromb, Fag, Vc, Viol, Org	K 170
47 Motetto de B.V.M. *Christe, fili summi patris*	a 4 Soli e Rip, 2 Vl, Corn, 2 Tromb, Fag, Vc, Viol, Org	K 175
48 Motetto de S. Michaele Arch, *Concussum est mare*	a 4 Soli e Rip, 2 Vl, Corn, 2 Tromb, Fag, Vc, Viol, Org	K 177

49	Motetto *Omnis terra adoret*	a 5 Soli e Rip, 2 Vl, Corn, 2 Tromb, Fag, Vc, Viol, Org	K 183
50	Motetto per ogni Santo *Coelum plaude*	a 5 Soli e Rip, 2 Vl, Vla con Fondamento	K 44

III. In solenner Besetzung für Solo

51	Motetto de Ressurectione Domini	a T, 2 Vl, Vla, Cl, Fag, *Plaudite, sonat tuba* Vc, Viol, Org	K 165

IV. In solenner Besetzung für Solo (Soli) und Ripieni

52	Offertorium pro Festo Assumptionis B.V.M. *Hodie Maria virgo*	a S, 4 Rip, 2 Vl, 2 Cl, Timp, Viol, Org	K 162
53	Offertorium de Dominica *Jubilate alleluja*	a A, 4 Rip, 2 Vl, 2 Cl con Org	E 46
54	Motetto per la Madonna SS. *Paries quidem filium*	a B, 4 Rip, 2 Vl, Vla, 2 Cl con Org	L 43
55	Motetto *Gloria tua est Domine*	a S/T/B, 4 Rip, 2 Vl, 2 Cl, Timp, Cb, [Org]	E 98
56	Motetto *O sancte N:, lumen ecclesiae*	a 4 Soli e Rip, 2 Vl, 2 Cl, 2 Tr Timp, Cb, [Org]	E 100
57	Motetto de quolibet Sancto *Accurrite, fideles*	a 5 Soli e Rip, 2 Vl, 2 Vle, 2 Cl, Viol et Org	E 101

C. Verlorene Kompositionen[6]

I. In mediocrer Besetzung für Solo (Soli)

58	Motetta (!) de Nomine Jesu	a B, 2 Vl, Viol, Org	E 76
59	Offertorium *Flammis Cor.*		E 132

II. In mediocrer Besetzung für Solo (Soli) und Ripieni

60	Offertoria(!) de Venerabili	a 4 v., 2 Vl, 2 Tromb ad lib, Fag, Vc, Viol, Org	E 75
61	Motetto de Apostolis	a 4 v., 2 Vl, Vc, Org	E 78
62	Motetto de B.M.V.	a 4 v., 2 Vl, 2 Tromb, Viol, Org	E 79

63	Motetta(!) de omni Sancto	a 4 v., 2 Vl, Viol, Org	E 81
64	Offertorium de Communi Confessoris	a 4 v., 2 Vl, 2 Tromb, Fag, Vc, Viol, Org	E 83
65	Offertorium de SS. Trinitate *Eja gentes*	a 4 v., 2 Vl, Org	E 143
66	Offertorium *Ave maris stella*		E 131

III. In solenner Besetzung für Soli

| 67 | Offertorium de Dedicatione | a S/B, 2 Vl, 2Cl, 2 Tr, Timp, 2 Tromb, Fag, Vc, Viol, Org | E 82 |

IV. In solenner Besetzung für (Soli und) Ripieni

| 68 | Motetta(!) de Resurrectione | a 4 v., 2 Vl, 2 Cl, Org | E 77 |
| 69 | Offertorium *Quod capis* | (Unter *Offertoria cum Tubis* eingetragen) | E 130 |

Anmerkungen

[1] Die in Prager Archiven nachgewiesenen Nr. 6 und 10 waren nicht erreichbar. Möglicherweise sind sie mit Basso continuo (und duplierenden Instrumenten) versehen, sodaß sie Gruppe AII zuzuordnen wären.

[2] Im 1738–59 angefertigten Musikalieninventar der Kreuzherren, Prag, steht *Exaltabo te, Domine* für Dom. XI. p. Pent. eingetragen, mit dem es übereinstimmt. Mehrfache Verwendung im Kirchenjahr gilt auch für Nr. 1 (Feria IV. p. Dom. II. Quadrages.; Dom. X. p. Pent.) und für Nr. 7 (Dom. XVI. p. Pent.).

[3] Zum Off. *Justitae Domini*, E 44. vgl. F.W. Riedel, *Kirchenmusik an Hofe Karls VI. (1711-1740)* (München–Salzburg, 1977), S.128, Anm. 94.

[4] Die Reihenfolge richtet sich nach der Besetzung, nicht nach dem Kirchenjahr.

[5] Bei L. Ritter v. Köchel, *J.J. Fux, Werkverzeichnis* irrtümlich: trophaea.

[6] Nur Titel erhalten (cf. H. Federhofer in: *KmJb* 43 (Köln, 1959), S.137 und 143).

Nachtrag

Persönliche Studien in den Musikarchiven von Prag brachten folgende Korrekturen und Ergänzungen (wiederholte schriftliche Anfragen waren unbeantwortet geblieben):

1 L 39 'De Profundis' ist kein Offertorium, sondern eine vollständige Vertonung von Psalm 129 mit Doxologie (266 Takte). Das Offertorium 'De profundis' ist zu streichen.

2 L 29 ist vollständig betitelt: 'Motetto Lux perpetua de pluribus Sanctis'. Darum gehört es zu den Kompositionen für das Offertorium Die Streicher duplieren lediglich die Singstimmen, somit ist es beim begleiteten a cappella-Stil einzureihen.

3 L 32 ist vollständig betitelt: 'Offertorium Veritas mea de Uno Sancto'. Der Text ist 'Offertorium' im Commune Confessorum non Pontificum. Die Streicher duplieren lediglich die Singstimmen, es ist ebenfalls beim begleiteten a cappella-Stil einzuordnen.

4 L 27, Das Inzipit des Offertorium zum Requiem 'Domine Jesu Christe' ist unvollständig mitgeteilt. Die Komposition beginnt mit Alt-Solo.

5 Im 'Verzeichnis der bisher bekannten Kompositionen von J.J. Fux zum Offertorium' bleibt die Zahl der Kompositionen gleich. Die Gruppe II 'in begleitetem a capella-Stil' erhöht sich auf 3 Titel:
   10. Laudate Dominum, quia benignus . . .
   11. Veritas mea . . .
   12. Lux perpetua lucebit sanctis (dieser Text ist kein liturgisches Offertorium, sondern 'Antiphona ad Magnificat' im Commune Apostolorum et Martyrum tempore paschali – und zwar: erste Satzhälfte).
   In Gruppe III. In mediocrer Besetzung sind die Nummern zu ändern:
   13. Reges Tharsis et insulae . . .
   14. Oravi Deum meum . . .

12 Bibliographie des Fux-Schrifttums/A Fux bibliography

Ingrid Schubert

Einleitung

Der 250. Todestag von Johann Joseph Fux bietet willkommenen Anlaß, den vorliegenden Versuch zu wagen. Ausgangspunkt dafür war das 1980 von Hellmut Federhofer – der auch die vorliegende Arbeit unermüdlich mit wertvollen Ratschlägen gefördert hat, wofür ihm mein aufrichtiger Dank gilt – publizierte Werk '25 Jahre Johann Joseph Fux-Forschung' mit einem Verzeichnis von Schriften über Fux dieses Zeitraumes.

Die von Federhofer aufgestellte Systematik wurde im wesentlichen übernommen, wodurch sich ein umfangreiches Sachregister, das den Rahmen eines Aufsatzes sprengen würde, erübrigt. Lediglich zwei weitere Kapitel *VIII Ikonographie* und *IX Discographie* wurden angefügt. Jeder Titel ist prinzipiell nur einmal angeführt. Bei Überschneidungen der Thematik wurde bei der Zuordnung primär vom Titel ausgegangen, weshalb bei der Suche nach bestimmten Themengruppen auch verwandte Kapitel heranzuziehen sein werden. Innerhalb der einzelnen Abschnitte wurde eine alphabetische, bei mehreren Titeln ein und desselben Autors eine chronologische Ordnung vorgenommen. Das Schrifttum wurde dabei einerseits bis zu Fuxens Lebenszeit erweitert, andererseits bis an das Jahr 1990 herangeführt.

Problematisch war die Auswahl der Titel. So wurden wichtige Publikationen der Fux'schen Umwelt ebenso mit einbezogen, wie Titel der Grenzbereiche. Arbeiten, deren Inhalt nicht primär Fux gilt, wurden nur dann aufgenommen, wenn jener substanziell berührt wird. Dabei wurden des öfteren die Seiten, auf denen Fux Erwähnung findet – in einigen speziellen Fällen mit raisonnierenden Anmerkungen – angegeben. Bei Aufsätzen dieser Art wurden zuerst der Gesamtumfang, dann die betreffenden Seiten in Klammer angeführt. Lexikonartikel, die nach Köchels Fux-Biographie erschienen, fanden keine Berücksichtigung, ältere nur dann, wenn sie Quellenwert besitzen. Kritiken von Aufführungen und Rezensionen von Büchern blieben im allgemeinen unberücksichtigt; nur wenn sie neue wissenschaftliche Erkenntnisse enthielten, schien ihre Aufnahme wünschenswert. Infolge der umfangreichen Quellenforschungen durch Federhofer und Riedel blieb die Erwähnung von Bibliothekskatalogen mit Verzeichnissen von Fux-Werken auf die Zeit ab 1964 beschränkt. Nicht eingearbeitet hingegen wurden diverse Musikgeschichten und Bibliographien. Um einen annähernd objektiven Stand zu geben, wurden Titel im Zweifelsfalle eher aufgenommen als weggelassen. Bei Büchern wurde der Verlag bewußt nicht angegeben, da eine Zuordnung auch anhand des Ortes möglich sein muß. Bei sämtlichen Titeln wurde versucht, diese im Original einzusehen; bei einigen gelang es trotz mehrmaliger Anstrengungen nicht. Sie sind mit einem Asteriskus* versehen.

Das bereits von Federhofer eingefügte Kapitel der wissenschaftlichen Ausgaben wurde um praktische Ausgaben und Bearbeitungen erweitert, einerseits um auch den Bedürfnissen der ausübenden Musiker gerecht zu werden, andererseits weil sie auch wertvolle Ergänzungen enthalten. Da die Ausgaben des öfteren neu aufgelegt wurden, ist hier der Verlag zur besseren Unterscheidung beigegeben. Nicht näher eingegangen wurde auf die verschiedenen Stimmausgaben (Grundlage bildet meistens die Partitur) – sie sind in den betreffenden Fällen bei den Verlagen zu erfragen. In der Anordnung sind die Einzelausgaben nach K-Nummern, gefolgt von den Werken mit E-Nummern und jenen ohne Nummer, gereiht. Auch die nicht eingesehenen Noten wurden mit einem Asteriskus versehen und diejenigen, welche zum Zeitpunkt der Fertigstellung des Manuskriptes (Frühjahr 1990) noch käuflich erwerbbar waren, mit einem Kreuz†.

Im Kapitel der Ikonographien wurde von einer Auflistung diverser Szenenbilder von Fux-Aufführungen Abstand genommen; dies bleibt der Theaterwissenschaft vorbehalten.

Die Angaben zur Discographie sind ausschließlich dem *Bielefelder Katalog Klassik 1953-1990* entnommen. Sie verzeichnen den jeweiligen Jahreszuwachs der Schallplatten, um so eine gewisse Übersicht über die Wertschätzung des Komponisten zu geben. (Abkürzungen für Plattenfirmen mögen dem jeweiligen Band des Kataloges entnommen werden.)

Da eine solche Arbeit nicht ohne die Hilfe von Kollegen, Bibliotheken, Verlagen und Instituten möglich wäre, sei diesen zwar pauschal, aber nicht minder herzlich gedankt.

Die Autorin ist sich bewußt, daß vorliegende Bibliographie, die einer zukünftigen Fux-Forschung den Zugriff erleichtern soll, nicht vollständig sein kann und ist für Ergänzungen dankbar.

* * * * *

Introduction

The 250th anniversary of the death of Johann Joseph Fux offers a welcome opportunity to attempt the following work. Its starting point was '25 Jahre Johann Joseph Fux-Forschung' published in 1980 by Hellmut Federhofer with an index of writings on Fux in this period. Professor Federhofer also tirelessly encouraged the present work with valuable suggestions and my sincerest thanks are owed to him.

The classification established by Federhofer has been adopted in its essentials and has thus made superfluous an extensive list of categories which would exceed the limits of an essay. Just two further sections, *VIII Ikonographie* and *IX Discographie*, have been added. As a rule each item is cited only once. Where subjects overlap, classification has been based primarily on the title, so that related sections will have to be considered when referring to specific subject areas. Within the individual sections an alphabetical sequence has been adopted; a chronological sequence has been adopted for multiple items by the same author. The bibliography accordingly extends to cover the period from Fux's life up to the present.

The choice of entries was a difficult one. Important publications from Fux's period have been included, along with more peripheral studies. Works whose content did not primarily relate to Fux have been included only when he is substantially treated. In such cases the pages which contain references to Fux are specifically cited – in some cases with an explanatory annotation. In such articles the total number of pages has been given, followed by the relevant pages in brackets. Dictionary articles published after Köchel's biography of Fux have not been taken into account; older ones appear only if they have value as sources. Reviews of performances and of books have been generally excluded; their inclusion seemed desirable only if they contained new scholarly findings. As a result of the extensive source studies by Federhofer and Riedel, the inclusion of library catalogues with indices of Fux works has been restricted to the period from 1964. Similarly, various musical histories and bibliographies have not been included. In order to provide a more or less objective picture, in cases of doubt titles have been included rather than excluded. In the case of books, the publisher has not been cited as it seemed feasible to include the *place* of publication as an alternative. There has been an attempt to give all titles in the original; in some cases, despite repeated efforts, this was not possible. Such titles are indicated by an asterisk.

The section on scholarly editions previously provided by Federhofer has been extended to include performance editions and arrangements, on the one hand to meet the needs of practising musicians, on the other because they also include worthwhile additional material. Since the editions have frequently been newly revised the publisher is also given for the sake of precision. No distinction was made between the various editions of the parts (the musical score is usually the authority) – these can be requested from the publishers in the relevant instances. The individual editions have been classified in the order of K numbers, followed by E numbers, and those without numbers. The unclassified works are indicated by an asterisk and those which were still in print at the time of completion of the manuscript (spring 1990) are indicated by a cross†.

In the chapter on iconography it has been decided to dispense with a list of various stage-sets of Fux performances; this is a matter for theatre studies.

The items in the discography have been taken exclusively from the *Bielefelder Katalog Klassik 1953-1990*. In each case the year of recording is indicated in order to afford some sense of the composer's reputation. (Abbreviations for record companies may be found in the relevant volume of the catalogue.)

I wish to express general and yet heartfelt thanks for the assistance of colleagues, libraries, publishers and institutes without which such an undertaking would not be possible.

I am aware that the following bibliography, designed to facilitate Fux research in the future, cannot pretend to be complete and I should be grateful for additional submissions.

Abkürzungen

ADEVA	Akademische Druck und Verlagsanstalt
AfMw	*Archiv für Musikwissenschaf*
Bd., Bde.	Band, Bände
bearb.	bearbeitet
Ders., Dies.	Derselbe, Dieselbe
DTÖ	*Denkmäler der Tonkunst in Österreich*
Faks.	Faksimile
Fotomechan.	Fotomechanisch
GA	*Gesamtausgabe*
hrsg.	Herausgeber, herausgegeben
i. d. R.	in der Reihe
JAMS	*Journal of the American Musicological Society*
KmJb	*Kirchenmusikalisches Jahrbuch*
Mf	*Die Musikforschung*
MQ	*The Musical Quarterly*
ND	Nachdruck, Neudruck
NZfM	*Neue Zeitschrift für Musik*
o. J.	ohne Jahr
o. O.	ohne Ort
ÖMZ	*Österreichische Zeitschrift für Musikwissenschaft*
ÖNB	Österreichische Nationalbibliothek
Pl. Nr.	Platten Nummer
s. a.	siehe auch
s. d.	siehe dort
StMw	*Studien zur Musikwissenschaft*
u. d. T.	unter dem Titel
UE	Universal Edition
v.	von
VfMw	*Vierteljahresschrift fur Musikwissenschaft*
vgl.	vergleiche

I Biographie

Anonym: 'Über den Zustand der Musik in Böhmen', *Allgemeine musikalische Zeitung* 2 (Leipzig, 1799–1800) Sp. 488–94 [494: 'Fux dirigierte das 200 Personen starke Orchester' bei der Krönung Karls VI.].

Anonym: 'Die kaiserliche Hofcapelle unter Kaiser Carl VI.', *Allgemeine musikalische Zeitung, mit besonderer Rücksicht auf den Österreichischen Kaiserstaat* 3 (Wien, 1819) Nr. 48, Sp. 385–87 [die 1730 bei Karl VI. angestellten Musiker werden aufgezählt, u.a. 'Fuchs' als Hofkapellmeister].

Anonym: 'Uebersicht der Geschichte der kaiserlich königlichen Hoftheater in Wien, bis zum Jahre 1818; besonders in Hinsicht auf die Oper', *Allgemeine musikalische Zeitung* 24 (Leipzig, 1822) Nr. 15, Sp. 233–42 [238, 240: Fux wird als Leiter eines vollendeten Orchesterspiels und Kapellmeister Karls VI. erwähnt].

Antonicek, Theophil: 'Der Hofkapellmeister', *ÖMZ* 42 (1987) S.217–21.

Batz, Karl: 'Zwei Meister des musikalischen Barock im Umfeld der Universität zu Ingolstadt. Johann Josepf Fux und Georg Muffat', *Ingolstädter Heimat Blätter. Beilage zum Donau Kurier* 43 (1980) S.21–2.

Biba, Otto: 'Kaiserin Wilhelmina Amalia und die Musik', *ÖMZ* 45 (1990) S. 66–73 [71: Fux als Kapellmeister bei der Kaiserin-Witwe; Foto des Ölbildes von Buck].

Erbach, L.: 'Kaiser Karl VI. und sein Kapellmeister', *Musikalische Jugendpost* Jg. 4, Nr. 19 (Stuttgart, [1889]) S. 289–90.

Federhofer, Hellmut: 'Joh. Jos. Fux zum Gedenken', *Österreichisches Liederblatt* 1 (1955/56) S. 1–5 [mit Bildnis].

Ders.: 'Biographische Beiträge zu Georg Muffat und Johann Joseph Fux', *Mf* 13 (1960) S. 130–42.

Ders.: 'Musikleben in der Steiermark', in *Die Steiermark. Land – Leute – Leistung* (Graz, 2/1971) S. 614–60 [632–4].

Ders. – Rudolf Flotzinger: 'Musik in der Steiermark. Historischer Überblick', in *Musik in der Steiermark. Katalog der Landesausstellung 1980*, hrsg. v. Rudolf Flotzinger (Graz, 1980) S. 15–83 [40–3].

Federhofer-Königs, Renate: 'Studien zu Johann Joseph Fux', *Musica* 13 (1959) S. 146 [Besprechung von Liess' Fuxiana].

Flotzinger, Rudolf: 'Fux und Graz', in *58. Bachfest der Neuen Bachgesellschaft. 24.–29. Mai 1983 Graz. Johann Sebastian Bach und der österreichische Raum* (Graz, 1983) S. 77–80.

Ders.: *Johann Joseph Fux. Stationen und Gefährten auf dem Weg von Hirtenfeld nach Wien = Jahresgabe der Johann-Joseph-Fux-Gesellschaft* 14 (Graz, 1984). – auch in *Fux-Studien* (s. d. sub III).

Ders.: 'Musik im Spannungsfeld zwischen Universität und Stadt. Der

Universität Graz zum 400-Jahr-Jubiläum gewidmet', *Blätter für Heimatkunde* 59 (1985) S. 33–45 [34].

Ders.: 'Johann Joseph Fuxens Weg von Hirtenfeld nach Wien', in *Johann Sebastian Bach und Johann Joseph Fux. Bericht über das Symposion anläßlich des 58. Bachfestes der Neuen Bachgesellschaft 24.–29. Mai 1983 in Graz*, hrsg. v. Johann Trummer und Rudolf Flotzinger (Kassel etc. 1985) S. 38–48.

Ders.: Abhandlung über die 'Sonderpostmarke "Europa-Cept 1985 (325. Geburtstag von Johann Joseph Fux – Europäisches Musikjahr 1985)".' Ausgabetag: 3. Mai 1985.

Grosheim, G. C[hristoph]: *Chronologisches Verzeichniß vorzüglicher Beförderer und Meister der Tonkunst nebst einer kurzen Uebersicht ihrer Leistungen* (Mainz, 1831) [S. 48: Das Todesjahr von Fux wird fälschlich mit 1733 angegeben].

Haas, Robert: 'Bach und Wien', in *Kongress-Bericht. Gesellschaft für Musikforschung. Lüneburg 1950*, hrsg. v. Hans Albrecht u.a. (Kassel etc., 1950) S. 129–31.

Hamann, Heinz Wolfgang: 'Neue Quellen zur Johann Joseph Fux-Forschung', in *Bericht über den Internationalen Musikwissenschaftlichen Kongreß Kassel 1962*, hrsg. v. Georg Reichert u. Martin Just (Kassel, 1963) S. 158–61.

[Hanslick, Eduard]: 'Feuilleton. Musikalische Neuigkeiten. III. "Beethoven's Leben", von Thayer. "Johann Joseph Fux" von Köchel', *Neue Freie Presse. Morgenblatt* (Wien, 1871, 31. Oktober), Nr. 2581, S. 1–3 [2–3: Hanslick betrachtet Köchels Buch als zu umfangreich. Fux sei nur als Theoretiker über die Grenzen bekannt. Ihm fehle die Genialität].

Hofmann, Siegfried: 'Die Ingolstädter Jahre des späteren Wiener Hofkapellmeisters Johann Joseph Fux', *Ingolstädter Heimatblätter* (Beilage zum Donau Kurier) 39 (1976) S. 1–2.

Jontes, Günther: 'Johann Josef Fux in Leoben', *Blätter für Heimatkunde* 49 (Graz, 1975) S. 91–3 [es handelt sich nicht um den Komponisten, sondern um einen gleichnamigen Namensträger].

Kern, Anton: 'Ein Rätsel um einen großen Steirer gelöst', *Kleine Zeitung* (Graz, 29. Juni 1949), 46./2. Jg., Nr. 148, S. 7.

Ders.: 'Johann Josef Fux. Neue biographische Forschungen', *Musica orans* 3/1 (Graz – Wien, 1950) S. 8.

Klug, Peter: 'Persönlichkeiten aus dem steirischen Bauernstand', in: *Katalog der Ausstellung der steirische Bauer. Leistung und Schicksal von der Steinzeit bis zur Gegenwart. Eine Dokumentation*, hrsg. v. Fritz Posch = *Veröffentlichungen des Steiermärkischen Landesarchives* 4 (Graz, 1966) S. 596–8.

Knaus, Herwig: *Die Musiker im Archivbestand des kaiserlichen Obersthof-*

meisteramtes (1637-1705) Bd. 3 = *Österr. Akademie der Wissenschaften, phil.-hist. Klasse, Sitzungsberichte* Bd. 246/1. *Veröffentlichungen der Kommission für Musikforschung* 10 (Wien, 1969) [S. 80-2, 98, 112-13].

Köchel, Ludwig Ritter von: *Die Kaiserliche Hof-Musikkapelle in Wien von 1543 bis 1867* (Wien, 1869) [S. 66, 72, 108].

Kundigraber, Hermann: 'Das Geburtshaus von Johann Joseph Fux', *Tagespost* Nr. 46 vom 15. Febr. (Graz, 1941), S. 6 [die Zuschreibung stellte sich jedoch als Irrtum heraus; vgl. unten F. Posch].

Liess, Andreas: 'Neues aus der biographischen Johann Joseph Fux-Forschung', *Mf* 5 (1952) S. 194-200.

Ders.: 'Johann Joseph Fux', *Das Musikleben* 5 (1952) S. 254-5.

Morel, Fritz: 'Organisten und Kapellmeister am Wiener Hof um 1700', *Musik und Gottesdienst* 21 (1967) S. 81-90 [86-7].

Neukomm, Edmond: 'Curiosités Musicales. Biographiques et autres', *L'art Musicale. Journal de Musique* 8 (1868, 23. Janvière) S. 58-9 [59: berichtet über die Anekdote von Kaiser Karl VI. und Fux anläßlich der Aufführung einer Fux-Oper, sowie über Fuxens Reise nach Prag in einer Sänfte].

Nyáry, Albert: *A Bécsi udvar a XVII. szazad végén* (Budapest, 1912) [S. 62-3: erste wirklich nachweisbare Aufführung eines Instrumentalwerkes von Fux am Kaiserhof im ersten Jahr seiner Anstellung].

Posch, Fritz: 'Das Geburtshaus von Johann Josef Fux', *Neue Chronik zur Geschichte und Volkskunde der innerösterreichischen Alpenländer*, Nr. 24 (Graz, 19. Dez. 1954) = Beilage zu Nr. 293 der *Südost-Tagespost*, S. 2.

Ders.: 'Heimat und Herkunft des Johann Josef Fux', *Mitteilungen des Instituts für Österreichische Geschichtsforschung* 63 (1955) S. 396-402.

Riedel, Friedrich Wilhelm: 'Johann Joseph Fux und die römische Palestrina-Tradition', *Mf* 14 (1961) S. 14-22 = *Jahresgabe 1961 der Johann-Joseph-Fux-Gesellschaft* [3].

Ders.: 'Zur "Missa SSmae Trinitatis" von Johann Joseph Fux', in *Symbolae historiae musicae. Hellmut Federhofer zum 60. Geburtstag*, hrsg. v. Friedrich Wilhelm Riedel u. Hubert Unverricht (Mainz, 1971) S. 117-21.

Schelle, Eduard: 'Feuilleton. Ein Musiker aus der guten alten Zeit Wiens', *Die Presse (Wiener Politisches Blatt)* Jg.25, Nr. 12 (1872) s.1-3.

Schenk, Erich: 'Ein wichtiger Fund zur Biographie von Johann Joseph Fux', *Anzeiger der phil.-hist. Klasse der Österreichischen Akademie der Wissenschaften* Jg. 1949, Nr. 20 (Wien, 1950) S. 480-3.

Schmid, Anton: *Christoph Willibald Ritter von Gluck. Dessen Leben und tonkünstlerisches Wirken* (Leipzig, 1854) [S. 23 wird das Todesdatum genannt].

Schneider, Constantin: 'Die Kirchenmusik im St.-Stephans-Dom zu Wien.

Ein geschichtlicher Überblick', *Musica Divina. Monatsschrift für Kirchenmusik und Liturgie* 21 (1933) S. 67–77 [74–5].

Schubart [Ludwig]: 'Proben einer Geschichte der Tonkunst, 2: Aus der Geschichte der deutschen Musik, von Luther bis auf Kaiser Karl den sechsten', *Allgemeine musikalische Zeitung* 6 (Leipzig, 1803–4) Sp. 253–60 [259–60].

Schubert, Ingrid: 'Steirische Musiker in der Welt', in *Musik in der Steiermark, Katalog der Landesausstellung 1980*, hrsg. v. Rudolf Flotzinger (Graz, 1980) S. 205–34 [207–10, mit Bildnis].

Suppan, Wolfgang: 'Johann Joseph Fux. Zur 300. Wiederkehr seines Geburtstages', *Musica 14* (1960) S. 808.

Ders. – Bogner, Harald: 'Johann Joseph Fux. Ein Steirer als "Kaisserlicher Hofkompositor"', *Sonate. Steirisches Musikjournal* 0 (1990) S.11–12 [mit Bildnis].

W. H.: 'Alte und neue Zeit', *Allgemeine musikalische Zeitung* 27 (Leipzig, 1825) Nr. 11, Sp. 173–83 [177: Fuxens *missa canonica*, hrsg. v. Gottfredo Schicht, wird gerühmt und daß er zu denen gehöre, die die Gattung der Kirchenmusik in Deutschland berühmt gemacht haben].

Wolfsgruber, P. Cölestin: *Die k. u. k. Hofburgkapelle und die k. u. k. geistliche Hofkapelle* (Wien, 1905) S.197.

II Quellen

Bárdos, Kornél: *Sopron zenéje a 16–18. században. A müvek tematikus jegyzékét összeállitotta Vavrinecz Veronika* (Budapest 1984) [S.420: K 26 und eine Messe in C, die weder bei Köchel noch Liess genannt ist].

Baselt, Bernd: 'Die Musikaliensammlung der Schwarzburg-Rudolstädtischen Hofkapelle unter Philipp Heinrich Erlebach (1657–1714)', in *Traditionen u. Aufgaben der Hallischen Musikwissenschaft = Wissenschaftliche Zeitschrift der Martin-Luther-Universität*, Halle–Wittenberg, Sonderbd. (Halle–Wittenberg 1963) S.105–34 [bes. S.108: verschollene Werke von Fux werden angeführt].

Bužga, Jaroslav: 'Skladatelský odkaz Jana Dismase Zelenky' [The compositional legacy of Jan Dismas Zelenka], *Hudební Věda* 16 (1979) S.305–15 [307–10].

Ders.: 'Zelenkas Musikinventar aus der katholischen Schloßkapelle in Dresden', *Fontes artis musicae* 31 (1984) S.198–206. [199–201, 205].

Chrysander, Friedrich: 'Geschichte der Braunschweig-Wolfenbüttelschen Capelle und Oper vom sechzehnten bis zum achtzehnten Jahrhundert', *Jahrbücher für musikalische Wissenschaft* 1 (1863), S.145–286 [266: Aufführung von *Teodosio ed Eudossa* in Hamburg 1718].

Deutsch, Otto Erich: '*Franz Schubert. Theamtisches Verzeichnis seiner Werke in chronologischer Folge*, Neuausgabe in deutscher Sprache, hrsg. v. Werner Aderhold = *Neue Ausgabe sämtlicher Werke* VIII, 4 (Kassel etc., 1978) S.335 [sub D 577: Bearbeitungen Schuberts von Teilen des *Singfundaments*].

Dokoupil, Zpracovali V. a Telec, Vladimir: *Hudebni staré tisky ve fondech Universituí Knihovny v Brne* (Brno, 1975) S.151-2 [Nr. 584 *Cristo nell' orto* u. 586 *Die Stärke und Beständigkeit*].

Elliott, Robert – White, Harry M.: 'A Collection of Oratorio Libretti, 1700–1800 in the Thomas Fisher Rarebook Library, University of Toronto', *Fontes artis musicae* 32 (1985) S.102–14 [107].

Federhofer, Hellmut: 'Unbekannte Kirchenmusik von Johann Joseph Fux', *KmJb* 43 (1959) S.113-54 = *Jahresgabe 1959 der Johann-Joseph-Fux-Gesellschaft* [1].

Ders.: 'Zur Musikpflege im Benediktinerstift Michaelbeuern (Salzburg)', in *Festschrift Karl Gustav Fellerer zum sechzigsten Geburtstag am 7. Juli 1962*, hrsg. v. Heinrich Hüschen (Regensburg 1962) S.106–27 [Verschollene Werke von Fux].

Ders. – Riedel, Friedrich Wilhelm: 'Quellenkundliche Beiträge zur Johann Joseph Fux-Forschung', *AfMw* 21 (1964) S.111–40, Nachtrag, S.253–4.

Federhofer-Königs, Renate: 'Zur Musikpflege in der Wallfahrtskirche von Mariazell Steiermark', *KmJb* 41 (1957) S.117–35 [132–3].

Fellerer, Karl Gustav: 'Verzeichnis der kirchenmusikalischen Werke der Santinischen Sammlung' (Forts.), *KmJb* 29, Jg. 1934 (Köln, 1935) S.125–41 [132].

Freeman, Robert N.: *The Practice of Music at Melk Abbey. Based upon the Documents, 1681-1826* = *Österr. Akademie der Wissenschaften, phil.-hist. Klasse, Sitzungsberichte* Bd. 548. *Veröffentlichungen der Kommission für Musikforschung* 23 (Wien, 1989) [u. a. Erwähnung der Abschrift zweier Triosonaten und *Die Fuchsische Solmisation*, sowie Archivmaterial über *Neo-Exoriens Phosphorus* und Besoldung an Fux].

Gericke, Hannelore: *Der Wiener Musikalienhandel von 1700 bis 1778* = *Wiener musikwissenschaftliche Beiträge* 5 (Graz–Köln, 1960).

Gmeinwieser, Siegfried: *Die Musikhandschriften in der Theatinerkirche St. Kajetan in München. Thematischer Katalog* = *Kataloge Bayerischer Musiksammlungen* 4 (München, 1979) [S.XI, XVI; Nr. 454-6, 858, 1046, Nr. 4, 1048].

Grasberger, Franz: *Die Musiksammlung der österr* [eichischen] *Nationalbibliothek* (Wien, 1978) S.40-2.

Haberkamp, Gertaur: *Die Musikhandschriften der Benediktiner Abtei Ottobeuren. Thematischer Katalog* = *Kataloge Bayerischer Musiksammlungen* 12 (München, 1986) [Nr. 379-86; S.15, 261-2].

Herrmann-Schneider, Hildegard: *Die Musikhandschriften des Dominika-nerinnenklosters Lienz im Tiroler Landesmuseum Ferdinandeum.* *Thematischer Katalog* = *Beiträge zur Musikforschung in Tirol* 1 (Innsbruck, 1984) [S.176].
Dies.: *Die Musikhandschriften der St. Michaelskirche in München.* *Thematischer Katalog* = *Kataloge Bayerischer Musiksammlungen* 7 (München, 1985) [S.XXI–XXII; Nr. 49, 380-3, 754].

Hochstein, Wolfgang: 'Liturgische Kirchenkompositionen in Hand-schriften der Staats- und Universitätsbibliothek Hamburg', *KmJb* 70 (1986) S.51–110 [S.65, 66: *Messa Canonica* K 7].

Kecskeméti, István: 'Johann Joseph Fux ismeretlen zenei kézirata' [Eine unbekannte Musikhandschrift von J.J. Fux], [= E 37], in *Az Országos Széchényi Könyvtár Evkönyve* 1958 (Budapest 1959) [Jahrbuch 1958 der Nationalbibliothek Széchényi] S. 238–46 [mit deutscher Zusam-menfassung].

Kellner, Altman: *Musikgeschichte des Stiftes Kremsmünster* (Kassel-Basel, 1956) [u. a. S.317: Beziehungen zu L. Christian, 350: die in Kremsmünster aufbewahrten Werke werden aufgezählt; 438–529: Beziehungen zu G. Pasterwitz].

Lang, Gerda: 'Zur Geschichte und Pflege der Musik in der Benediktiner-Abtei zu Lambach. Mit einem Katalog zu den Beständen des Musikarchives'. 3 Bde. Mschr. Diss. (Salzburg, 1978), Bd. 2 [S.174-5].

Marx, Hans Joachim: 'Some Corelli attributions assessed', *MQ* 56 (1970) S.88–98 [91: Quellenlage zu K 322].

Mattheson, Johann: *Der Musicalische Patriot* (Hamburg, 1728) [S.189 Aufführung von *Theodosio* 1718].

Mitterschiffthaler, Karl: *Das Notenarchiv der Musiksammlung im Zisterzienserstift Wilhering (Drucke und Handschriften)* = *Tabulae musicae Austriacae* 9 (Wien, 1979) [S.109].

Moser, Hans Joachim: 'Eine Pariser Quelle zur Wiener Triosonate des ausgehenden 17. Jahrhunderts: Der Codex Rost', *Festschrift Wilhelm Fischer zum 70. Geburtstag überreicht im Mozartjahr 1956* = *Innsbrucker Beiträge zur Kulturwissenschaft*, Sonderheft 3 (Innsbruck, 1956) S.75–81 [fälschliche Zuschreibung einer Triosonate an J.J. Fux].

Mühlfeld, Christian: 'Die Meininger Musikbibliothek', *NZfM* 79 (1912) S.217–21 [219, 221].

Nemeth, Carl: 'Eine unbekannte Sinfonia von J. J. Fux' [= E 63], *ÖMZ* 16 (1961) S.525–8.

Nettl, Paul: 'Weltliche Musik des Stiftes Ossegg (Böhmen) im 17. Jahrhundert', *Zeitschrift für Musikwissenschaft* 4 (1921/22) S.351–7 [Erwähnung verschollener Werke von Fux].

Ders.: 'Das Prager Quartierbuch des Personals der Krönungsoper 1723',

Anzeiger der phil.-hist. Klasse der Österr. Akademie der Wissenschaften Nr. 1, Jg. 1957, *Mitteilungen der Kommission für Musikforschung* 8 (Wien, 1957) S.1–7.

Pazdírek, François: *Manuel Universel de la Littérature Musicale.* Bd. 9 (Wien, o. J.) S.616.

Die Matrikel der Ludwig-Maximilians-Universität. Ingolstadt-Landshut-München I, *Ingolstadt* II, 2, hrsg. v. Götz Frh. von Pölnitz (München, 1940) [S.1139].

Quoika, Rudolf: 'Barocke Kirchenmusik in Ingolstadt', *KmJb* 49 (1965) S.125–43 [130–1, 139–40].

Riedel, Friedrich Wilhelm: *Quellenkundliche Beiträge zur Geschichte der Musik für Tasteninstrumente in der zweiten Hälfte des 17. Jahrhunderts (vornehmlich in Deutschland)* = *Schriften des Landesinstituts für Musikforschung Kiel* 10 (Kassel–Basel: 1960).

Ders.: *Das Musikarchiv im Minoritenkonvent zu Wien (Katalog des älteren Bestandes vor 1784)* = *Catalogus Musicus* 1 (Kassel, 1963).

Ders.: 'Neo-Exoriens Phosphorus'. Ein unbekanntes musikdramatisches Werk von Johann Joseph Fux', *Mf* 18 (1965) S.290–3.

Ders.: 'Die Kirchenmusik im Benediktinerstift Göttweig', *Singende Kirche* 13 (1965/66) S.196–202 [198].

Der Göttweiger Thematische Katalog von 1830, hrsg., kommentiert und mit Registern versehen v. Friedrich Wilhelm Riedel, 2 Bde. = *Studien zur Landes- und Sozialgeschichte der Musik* 2,3 (München–Salzburg, 1979).

Schaal, Richard: 'Quellen zur Musiksammlung Aloys Fuchs', *Mf* 16 (1963) S.71.

Ders.: 'Handschriften-Kopien aus der Wiener Musiksammlung von Aloys Fuchs', in *The Haydn Yearbook* 7 (1970) S.255–80 [267].

Schütz, Karl: *Musikpflege an St. Michael in Wien.* = *Österr. Akademie der Wissenschaften. Phil.- hist. Klasse, Sitzungsberichte* Bd. 369. *Veröffentlichungen der Kommission für Musikforschung* 20 (Wien, 1980) S.120–1.

Sehnal, Jiří: 'Das Musikinventar des Olmützer Bischofs Leopold Egk aus dem Jahre 1760 als Quelle vorklassischer Instrumentalmusik', *AfMw* 29 (1972) S.285–317 [300, 304, 317].

Sonnleithner, Leopold von: 'Musikalische Skizzen aus Alt-Wien', *ÖMZ* 16 (1961) S.50–62 [58].

Stadlmayr, Johann: *Hymnen,* hrsg. v. Johannes Ev. Habert = *DTÖ* III/1 (Wien, 1896) RB [S.37–8].

Průvodce. Po archivních fondech. Ústavu dějin hudby Moravského musea v Brně 4, red. Theodora Straková (Brno, 1971).

Ecclesia metropolitana Pragensis. Catalogus collectionis operum artis musicae. Composuit Jiri Stefan. Bd 1 = *Catalogus artis musicae in Bohemia et Moravia cultae. Artis musicae antiquioris catalogorum* 4, 1 (Prag, 1983) [S.303–313].

Trolda, Emil: 'Tote Musik. (Ein Beitrag zur Musikgeschichte Böhmens.)', *Musica divina* 7 (1919) S.71–2, 111–12, 139–44 [140].

Vander Straeten, Edmond: *La musique aux Pays-Bas avant le XIXe siècle Tome I* (Bruxelles, 1867) [S.86–9].

Weinmann, Alexander: *Handschriftliche thematische Kataloge aus dem Benediktinerstift Melk* = *Tabulae musicae Austriacae* 10 (Wien, 1984).

White, Harry M.: 'Erhaltene Quellen der Oratorien von Johann Joseph Fux. Ein Bericht', *KmJb* 67 (1983) S.123–31.

Ders.: 'Zwei Oratorientextbücher in der Thomas Fisher Library, University of Toronto', *Musik und Kirche* 57 (1987) S.191–5 [K 300, *La deposizione dalla Croce*].

Die Musikalien der Grafen von Schönborn-Wiesentheid. Thematisch bibliographischer Katalog. bearb. v. Fritz Zobeley, T. I: *Das Repertoire des Grafen Rudolf Franz Erwein von Schönborn (1677–1754)*, Bd. 1, 2 (Tutzing, 1967, 1982).

III Gesamtdarstellungen – Kleinere Beiträge Allgemeinen Inhalts – Lexikonartikel

Anonym: 'Wiens musikalische Kunst-Schätze' (Fortsetzung) [In Briefen eines Reisenden. Fünfter Brief], *Allgemeine musikalische Zeitung* 30 (Leipzig, 1828) Nr. 3, Sp. 35–41 [die Angaben entsprechen jenen von Kandler (s.d.) in der *Allgemeinen musikalische Zeitung, mit besonderer Rücksicht auf den Österreichischen Kaiserstaat*].

Anonym: 'Johann Josef Fux-Gedenkfeier', *Zeitschrift der internationalen Musikgesellschaft* 5 (1903–1904) S.461.

Beck, P. Michael: 'Johann Joseph Fux. Biographische Skizze', *Gregorianische Rundschau* 9 (1910) S.52–6.

Neues Universal-Lexikon der Tonkunst, hrsg. v. Eduard Bernsdorf. Bd. 2 (Dresden, 1857) S.74–5.

Day, Thomas: 'Palestrina in history: a preliminary study of Palestrina's reputation and influence since his death'. Phil. diss. (Columbia Univ., 1970).*

Dlabacž, Gottfried Johann: *Allgemeines Historisches Künstler-Lexikon für Böhmen und zum Theil auch für Mähren und Schlesien*. Bd. 1 (Prag, 1815) Sp. 436–8.

Dommer, Arrey von: *Musikalisches Lexikon* (Heidelberg, 1865) S.131–2.

Dworczak, Karl Heinz: 'Der steirische Palestrina. Zum 200. Todestag von Johann Joseph Fux', *Tagespost* Nr. 44 vom 13. Februar (Graz, 1941) S.3 [mit Abbildung des Ölgemäldes von Buck].

Elvert, Christian Ritter de: *Geschichte der Musik in Mähren und Oesterr.- Schlesien mit Rücksicht auf die allgemeine, böhmische und österreichische Musik-Geschichte* = *Schriften der historisch statistischen Sektion* 21 (Brünn, 1873) [S.174-8, 190].

Federhofer, Hellmut: '25 Jahre Johann Joseph Fux-Forschung', *Acta musicologica* 52 (1980) S.155-94, auch erschienen als *Jahresgabe der Johann-Joseph-Fux-Gesellschaft* [11] (Graz, 1981).

Federhofer-Königs, Renate: 'Aufgaben und Ziele der Johann-Joseph-Fux-Gesellschaft', *Mf* 12 (1959) S.213.

Flotzinger, Rudolf: *Die Anfänge der Johann Joseph Fux-Forschung* = *Jahresgabe der Johann-Joseph-Fux-Gesellschaft* 12 (Graz, 1982). – auch in *Fux-Studien* (s. d.).

Ders.: *Vinzenz Fux. Ein erster Bericht* = *Jahresgabe der Johann-Joseph-Fux-Gesellschaft* 13 (Graz, 1983). – auch in *Fux-Studien* (s. d.).

Ders.: *Fux-Studien* = *Grazer Musikwissenschaftliche Arbeiten* 6 (Graz, 1985). Die gesammelten Beiträge finden sich jeweils als *Jahresgabe der Johann-Joseph-Fux-Gesellschaft* H. 12, 13, 14.

Gerber, Ernst Ludwig: *Historisch-biographisches Lexikon der Tonkünstler* (1790-1792) und *Neues Historisch-biographisches Lexikon der Tonkünstler* (1812-1814). Mit den in den Jahren 1792 bis 1834 veröffentlichten Ergänzungen sowie der Erstveröffentlichung handschriftlicher Berichtigungen und Nachträge, hrsg. v. Othmar Wessely, Bd. 2: *Neues Historisch-biographisches Lexikon* Sp. 225-230, Bd. 4: Ergänzungen-Berichtigungen-Nachträge (Graz, 1969) S.147-53, 340.

Ders.: 'Biographische Beyträge. Fux', *Allgemeine musikalische Zeitung* 8 (Leipzig, 1805-06), Sp. 369-75.

Heinse, Wilhelm: 'Hildegard von Hohenthal'. Erster und zweiter Theil. *Sämmtliche Werke*, hrsg. v. Carl Schüddekopf, Bd. 5 (Leipzig, 1903) [S.107, 180, 214].

[Kandler, Franz Sales]: 'Beyträge zu Biographien. Johann Joseph Fuchs, k.k. Hof-Capellmeister', *Allgemeine musikalische Zeitung, mit besonderer Rücksicht auf den Österreichischen Kaiserstaat* 4 (Wien, 1820) Nr. 25, Sp. 199-200; Nr. 43, Sp. 343-4; Nr. 53, Sp. 422-4; Nr. 54, Sp. 428-30 [u.a. 1660 in Ober-Steyer geboren, 1695-1735 Kaiserl. Ober-Capellmeister. Sterbedatum nicht bekannt.].

Karpf, Roswitha Vera: 'Die ganze Welt ist Bühne'. Musik und Repräsentation bei der Erbhuldigung von 1728', *Theater in Graz* = *Historisches Jahrbuch der Stadt Graz* 15 (1984) S. 53-77. [64-5, 69, 75-7; u.a. Aufführung von *Orfeo ed Euridice*].

Köchel, Ludwig Ritter von: *Johann Josef Fux, Hofcompositor und Hofkapellmeister der Kaiser Leopold I., Josef I. und Karl VI. von 1698-1740* (Wien, 1872, ND Hildesheim–New York, 1974).

Liess, Andreas: 'Johann Joseph Fux', *Musik im Ostalpenraum = Das Joanneum* 3 (Graz, 1940) S.85–104.

Ders.: *Wiener Barockmusik = Wiener Musik-Bücherei* 3 (Wien, 1946).

Ders.: *Johann Joseph Fux. Ein steirischer Meister des Barock. Nebst einem Verzeichnis neuer Werkfunde* (Wien, 1948) [mit Bildnis].

Ders.: 'Bach, Fux und die Wiener Klassik', *Musica* 4 (1950) S.261–5.

Ders.: 'Johann Joseph Fux', *NZfM* 118 (1957) S.285–6 [mit Photo des Ölgemäldes von Buck].

Ders.: *Fuxiana = Österreich-Reihe* 53 (Wien, 1958).

Ders.: 'Johann Joseph Fux', in *Tausend Jahre Österreich. Eine biographische Chronik*, hrsg. v. Walter Pollak. Bd. 1: *Von den Babenbergern bis zum Wiener Kongreß* (Wien–München, 1973) S.264–72.

Oesterreichische National-Encyklopädie oder alphabetische Darlegung der wissenswürdigsten Eigenthümlichkeiten des österreichischen Kaiserthums, (von Gräffer und Czikann), Bd. 2 (Wien, 1835) S.256 [ohne Angabe von Geburts- und Sterbedatum].

Oehler, Joseph: *Geschichte des gesamten Theaterwesens zu Wien* (Wien, 1803) [S.71–8].

Antonio Caldara: Essays on his life and times, hrsg. v. Brian W. Pritchard (Aldershot, 1987).

Riedel, Friedrich Wilhelm: 'Der "Reichsstil" in der deutschen Musikgeschichte des 18. Jahrhunderts', *Bericht über den internationalen Musikwissenschaftlichen Kongress Kassel 1962*, hrsg. v. Georg Reichert und Martin Just (Kassel etc., 1963) S.34–6 [Parallelen zwischen Fux und J. B. Fischer von Erlach].

Ders.: 'Abt Berthold Dietmayr von Melk und der kaiserliche Hofkapellmeister Johann Joseph Fux. Zur Musikkultur Niederösterreichs im Barockzeitalter', *Unsere Heimat* 36 (Wien, 1965) S.58–64.

Ders.: *Kirchenmusik am Hofe Karls VI. <1711–1740>. Untersuchungen zum Verhältnis von Zeremoniell und musikalischem Stil im Barockzeitalter = Studien zur Landes- und Sozialgeschichte der Musik 1* (München–Salzburg, 1977).

Ders.: 'Die Musik bei der Erbhuldigungsreise Kaiser Karls VI. nach Innerösterreich 1728', *Florilegicum Musicologicum. - Hellmut Federhofer zum 75. Geburtstag*, hrsg. v. Christoph Hellmut Mahling (Tutzing, 1988) S.275–86 [276, 278–9, 281, 283–5: verschiedene Fux-Werke gelangten zur Afführung].

Romé, Helmut: 'Johann Joseph Fux, ein Meister des deutschen Barocks. Zur Wiederkehr seines 300. Geburtstages', *Deutsche Sängerschaft* 65 (1960) S.45–50 [47: Photo des Ölbildes von N. Buck].

Encyclopädie der gesammten musikalischen Wissenschaften, oder Universal-Lexicon der Tonkunst. Bearbeitet von M. Fink u.a. unter dem Redacteur Dr. Gustav Schilling, Bd. 3 (Stuttgart, 1836) S.104–7.

Schnabl, Carl: 'Johann Joseph Fux, der österreichische Palestrina. Eine biographische Skizze' [mit Bildnis], *Jahrbuch der Leo-Gesellschaft* (Wien, 1895) S.153–162.

Schubart, Christian Friedrich D.: *Schubart's Leben und Gesinnungen. Von ihm selbst, im Kerker aufgesetzt.* Theil 1 (Stuttgart, 1791) [S.179–80: er bedauert, daß Caldara, Fux etc. nicht mehr gelesen werden und deren 'köstliche Partituren mit Staub bedeckt sind'.]

Schubert, Ingrid: 'Johann-Joseph-Fux-Gesellschaft', *ÖMZ* 37 (1982) S.346.

Seifert, Herbert: 'Zur neuesten Fux-Forschung. Kritik und Beiträge', *Studien zur Musikwissenschaft* 38 (1987) S.35–52.

Suppan, Wolfgang: 'Tonkünstler des Barocks. Johann Josef Fux', in *Steirische Ehrengalerie*, hrsg. v. Kulturreferat der Steiermärkischen Landesregierung (Graz, 1960) S.16–19 [auf S.17 Photografie der Büste von Otmar Clemencic].

Ders.: 'Höhepunkte abendländischer Musikgeschichte (I). Im Dienste dreier Kaiser: Der Barockmeister Johann Josef Fux', *Die Blasmusik* 22 (1972) S.29–30.

Sutter, Berthold: 'Johann Josef Fux. Lebensgang und Werk', *Weststeirische Volkszeitung*, 22.4.1950 [mit Bildnis].

Ders. – Mezler-Andelberg, Helmuth: 'Johann-Joseph-Fux-Gesellschaft', in *58. Bachfest der Neuen Bachgesellschaft. 24.–29. Mai 1983 in Graz. Johann Sebastian Bach und der österreichische Raum* (Graz, 1983) S.102–3.

Tank, Ulrich: *Studien zur Esterházyschen Hofmusik von etwa 1620 bis 1790 = Kölner Beiträge zur Musikforschung* 101 (Regensburg, 1981) [S.59, 64, 79, 86, 91, 171–2, 179, 207, 297].

Walther, Johann Gottfried: *Musicalisches Lexicon oder Musicalische Bibliothec* (Leipzig, 1732) S.269.

Wellesz, Egon: *Fux = Oxford Studies of Composers* 1 (London, 1965).

Wisoko, Karl: 'Fux und die Hofmusikkapelle', *ÖMZ* 15 (1960) S.132–4.

Wurzbach, Constant von: *Biographisches Lexikon des Kaiserthums Oesterreich* Bd. 5 (Wien, 1859) S.41–2; Bd. 28 (Wien, 1874) S.339 [hier wird das Todesdatum ergänzt].

IV Beziehungen zu Zeitgenossen

Albert, Herzog zu Sachsen: 'Im Zeichen des "Weißen Goldes". Die Häuser Wittelsbach und Wettin als Förderer des Meißner Porzellans', *Deutsche Tagespost* No. 47 (Würzburg, 1980, 16. April) S.9 [über die von Johann Joachim Kaendler (1706–1775) modellierte Porzellangruppe des 'Fuchses am Cembalo', die auf die künstlerische Beziehung zwischen Fux und Faustina Hasse-Bordoni spöttisch Bezug zu nehmen scheint].

Blumauer, Manfred: 'Eine Ellipse, gezogen um Bach und Fux', *Parnass. Die österreichische Kunst- und Kulturzeitschrift* 3, 5 (1983) S.70–1.

Brixel, Eugen: 'Die Bläsertradition des Grazer "Ferdinandeums" vor und um 1700', *Alta Musica* 9 (Tutzing, 1987) S.25–37.

Burney, Charles: *Carl Burney's der Musik Doktors Tagebuch seiner musikalischen Reisen*. Bd. 2: *Durch Flandern, die Niederlande und am Rhein bis Wien* [S.177: er hörte in der Vesper 'eine vortreffliche alte Musik von Fuxens Komposition']; Bd. 3: *Durch Böhmen, Sachsen, Brandenburg, Hamburg und Holland* [S.130–1: Die bekannte Charakteristik der Oper *Costanza e Fortezza* als 'mehr kirchenmässig als theatralisch, aber sehr prächtig. . . . Fux selbst aber hatte das Podagra']. Aus dem Englischen übersetzt von C.D. Ebeling (Hamburg, 1773; Faks. ND, hrsg. v. Richard Schaal. = *Documenta musicologica*, R. 1, 19 (Kassel etc., 1959).

Federhofer, Hellmut: 'Johann Joseph Fux und Joseph Haydn', *Musica* 14 (1960) S.269–73 = *Jahresgabe 1960 der Johann-Joseph-Fux-Gesellschaft* [2].

Ders.: 'Johann Joseph Fux und Johann Mattheson im Urteil Lorenz Christoph Mizlers', in *Speculum musicae artis. Festgabe für Heinrich Husmann zum 60. Geburtstag am 16. Dezember 1968*, hrsg. v. Heinz Becker und Reinhard Gerlach (München, 1970) S.111–23.

Ders.: 'Das Vermächtnis von Johann Joseph Fux an Johann Sebastian Bach,' in *Johann Sebastian Bach und Johann Joseph Fux. Bericht über das Symposion anläßlich des 58. Bachfestes der Neuen Bachgesellschaft 24. - 29. Mai 1983 in Graz*, hrsg. v. Johann Trummer u. Rudolf Flotzinger (Kassel – Basel 1985) S.16–21.

Forkel, Johann Nikolaus: *Ueber Johann Sebastian Bachs Leben, Kunst und Kunstwerke* (Leipzig, 1802; hrsg. mit Einleitung und ausführlichem Nachwort v. Joseph M. Müller-Blattau, Augsburg, 1925) [S.47, 62 u. Nachwort des Hrsg. S.106–7].

Fürstenau, Moritz: *Zur Geschichte der Musik und des Theaters am Hofe zu Dresden*. T.2: *Musik und Theater am Hofe der Kurfürsten von Sachsen und Könige von Polen* (Dresden, 1862) [S.72–5: J.D. Zelenka u. Fux].

Gmeyner, Alice: 'Die Opern M.A. Caldaras. Ein Beitrag zur Geschichte der italienischen Oper in Wien'. Mschr. diss. (Wien, 1927) [S.15, 23–5, 75–6, 199–200 u. ö.].

Hawkins, Sir John: *A General History of the Science and Practice of Music*.

2 Bde. (London, 2/1875; NA v. Othmar Wessely, i. d. R. *Die großen Darstellungen der Musikgeschichte in Barock und Aufklärung* 5, Graz, 1969) Bd. 2 [S.773–5: *Gradus* wird behandelt].

Heyde, Herbert: 'Blasinstrumente und Bläser der Dresdner Hofkapelle in der Zeit des Fux-Schülers Johann Dismas Zelenka (1710–1745)', *Alta Musica* 9 (Tutzing, 1987) S.39–65.

Zelenka-Dokumentation, Quellen und Materialien. In Verbindung mit Ortrun Landmann u. Wolfgang Reich vorgelegt v. Wolfgang Horn u. Thomas Kohlhase. 2 Bde. (Wiesbaden, 1989).

Küchelbecker, Johann Basilius: *Johann Basilii Küchelbeckers Allerneueste Nachricht vom Römisch-Kayserl. Hofe* (Hannover, 2/1732) [S.172].

Lester, Joel: 'The Fux-Mattheson correspondence: an annotated translation', *Current Musicology* 24 (1977) S.37–62.

Mann, Alfred: 'Haydn as student and critic of Fux', in *Studies in eighteenth-century music. A tribute to Karl Geiringer on his seventieth birthday*, hrsg. v. Howard Chandeller Robbins Landon (London, 1970) S.323–32.

Ders.: 'Padre Martini and Fux', in *Festschrift für Ernst Hermann Meyer zum sechzigsten Geburtstag*, hrsg. v. Georg Knepler (Leipzig, 1973) S.253–5.

Marpurg, Friedrich Wilhelm: *Historisch-Kritische Beyträge zur Aufnahme der Musik.* 5 Bde. (Berlin, 1754–78; repr. ND Hildesheim, 1970) I (1754–55): S.210, bes. 216–20, Bericht über die Uraufführung der Oper *Costanza e fortezza* in Prag sub *Herrn Johann Joachim Quantzens Lebenslauf, von ihm selbst entworfen* [S.197–250]; S.437 u. ö. II (1756) S.322; 327–8, 347, 351 sub *Gedanken über Herrn Daubens Generalbaß in drey Accorden* von D. Gemmel [S.325–66, 464–74]. III (1757–58) S.468, 472–6, 479 sub *Unpartheyische Gedanken, über die richtige Denkungsart des Herrn Daube in Seinem Vorbericht . . .* v. Friedr. Wilhelm Sonnenkalb [S. 465–86]. IV (1758–59) S.229 sub *Herrn Sonnenkalbs Fortsetzung der unpartheyischen Gedanken . . .* [S.196–244].

Mattheson, Johann: *Critica Musica*, Bd. 2 (Hamburg, 1725; Faks. ND Amsterdam, 1964) [S.185–206].

Ders.: *Der Vollkommene Capellmeister* (Hamburg, 1739; Faks. ND hrsg. v. Margarete Reimann i. d. R. *Documenta Musicologica* 1, V Kassel etc., 1954) [S.256, 345, 349–50, 362, 393].

Ders.: *Grundlage einer Ehrenpforte* (Hamburg, 1740; ND hrsg. v. Max Schneider, Berlin, 1910) [S.42, 79, 172, 232, 378, 401].

Mizler, Lorenz: *Musikalische Bibliothek oder Gründliche Nachricht nebst unpartheyischem Urtheil von alten und neuen musikalischen Schriften und Büchern.* 4 Bde. (Leipzig, 1739–1754; ND Hilversum, 1966) Bd. 2 (1743) [T. IV S.118–22], Bd. 3 (1752) [S.281, 500, 564].

Montague, Lady Mary Wortley: Brief v. 14. Sept. 1716 an Alexander Pope [über *Alcina*-Aufführung] in *The Complete Letters*, hrsg. v. Robert Halsband, Bd. 1: *1708–1720* (Oxford, 1965; Litogr. ND, 1967) S.262–4.

Nicolai, Friedrich: *Beschreibung einer Reise durch Deutschland und die Schweiz im Jahre 1781*, Bd. 4 (Berlin–Stettin, 1784) [S.524–5, 560 sub *Von der Musik in Wien*: S.524–5 wird Fux u.a. von Quantz gelobt].

Oschmann, Susanne: 'Die Oratorien Jan Dismas Zelenkas (1679–1745)'. Diss. (Köln, 1984). [Fux wird mehrmals in Zusammenhang mit den Affekten erwähnt].

Pečman, Rudolf: 'F.X. Richter und seine Schrift "Harmonische Belehrungen oder gründliche Anweisung zu der musicalischen Tonkunst und regulairen Composition" ', in *Die Wechselwirkung von Instrumentenbau und Kompositionsweise sowie Editionsfragen der Frühklassik: Konferenzbericht der 8. wissenschaftlichen Arbeitstagung Blankenburg/Harz 1980 = Blankenburger Studien zur Aufführungspraxis und Interpretation von Instrumentalmusik des 18. Jahrhunderts* 14 (Blankenburg, 1981) S.53–7 [geht von Fuxens *Gradus* aus].

Pohl, Carl Ferdinand: *Joseph Haydn*. 2 Bde. (Berlin, 1875 u. Leipzig, 1882) Bd. 1 [bes. S.56–8, 68, 176–8, 205–6].

Riedel, Friedrich Wilhelm: 'Musikgeschichtliche Beziehungen zwischen Johann Joseph Fux und Johann Sebastian Bach', in *Festschrift Friedrich Blume zum 70. Geburtstag*, hrsg. v. Anna Amalie Abert und Wilhelm Pfannkuch (Kassel, 1963) S.290–304 = *Jahresgabe 1963 der Johann-Joseph-Fux-Gesellschaft* [5].

Ders: 'Johann Sebastian Bach und die österreichische Barockmusik', in *58. Bachfest der Neuen Bachgesellschaft. 24.–29. Mai 1983 in Graz. Johann Sebastian Bach und der österreichische Raum* (Graz, 1983) S.73–6.

Scheibe, Johann Adolph: *Critischer Musikus* (Leipzig, 2/1745; reprogr. ND Hildesheim, 1970) [S.304, 341, 468, 549, 652, 762].

Schenk, Erich: 'Kuhnau und Fux', in *Anzeiger der phil.-hist. Klasse der Österr. Akademie der Wissenschaften* Jg. 1965, Nr. 23 (Wien, 1966) S.359–66.

Schenkman, Walter, 'Theory und Practice: Mattheson's Differing Key Arrangements, Part I', *Bach. The Quarterly Journal of the Riemenschneider Bach Institute* 12, 3 (1981) S.2–10.

Seifert, Herbert: 'Die Bläser der kaiserlichen Hofkapelle zur Zeit von J. J. Fux', *Alta Musica* 9 (Tutzing, 1987) S.9–23.

Spitta, Phillipp: *Johann Sebastian Bach*. 2 Bde. (Leipzig, 4/1930) Bd. 2 [S.603–6].

Stegemann, Michael: 'Antonio Vivaldi und Johann Joseph Fux. Anmerkungen zu einer hypothetischen Feindschaft', *NZfM* 145, H. 6 (1984) S.12–15.

Stollbrock, L[udwig]: 'Leben und Wirken des k.k. Hofkapellmeisters und Hofkompositors Johann Georg Reutter jun.', *VfMw* 8 (1892), S.161–203, 289–306 [bes. S.162–74 u. 195–7, 200].

Tebaldini, Giovanni: *L'archivio musicale della Capella Antoniana in Padova* (Padova, 1895) [u. a. S.155–8 Briefe Vallottis an Fux].

Johann Sebastian Bach und Johann Joseph Fux. Bericht über das Symposion anläßlich des 58. Bachfestes der Neuen Bachgesellschaft 24.–29. Mai 1983 in Graz, hrsg. v. Johann Trummer und Rudolf Flotzinger (Kassel–Basel, 1985).

Wessely, Othmar: *Johann Joseph Fux und Johann Mattheson = Jahresgabe 1964 der Johann-Joseph-Fux-Gesellschaft* [6] (Graz, 1965).

Ders.: *Johann Joseph Fux und Francesco Antonio Vallotti = Jahresgabe 1966 der Johann-Joseph-Fux-Gesellschaft* 7 (Graz, 1967).

Ders.: 'Johann Joseph Fux im Urteil der Umwelt und Nachwelt', *ÖMZ* 25 (Wien, 1970). S.579–85.

Ders.: *Johann Joseph Fux. Persönlichkeit. Umwelt. Nachwelt = Jahresgabe 1979 der Johann-Joseph-Fux-Gesellschaft* [10] (Graz, 1979).

Ders.: 'Bach und Fux – zwei Stil-Welten?', in *Johann Sebastian Bach und Johann Joseph Fux. Bericht über das Symposion anläßlich des 58. Bachfestes der Neuen Bachgesellschaft 24.–29. Mai 1983 in Graz*, hrsg. v. Johann Trummer und Rudolf Flotzinger (Kassel, 1985) S.75–81.

Wolff, Christoph: *Der Stile antico in der Musik Johann Sebastian Bachs. Studien zu Bachs Spätwerk = Beihefte zum Archiv für Musikwissenschaft* 6 (Wiesbaden, 1968) [S.3, 7, 9f. u. ö.].

Wollenberg, Susan: 'The Keyboard Suites of Gottlieb Muffat (1690–1770)', *Proceedings of the Royal Musical Association* 102 (London, 1975/76) S.83–91.

V Kompositorisches Schaffen

Adler, Guido: 'Ferdinand III, Leopold I, Joseph I. u. Karl VI. als Förderer der Musik', *VfMw* 8 (1892) S.252–74 [271–2: Aufführung der Oper *Elisa*].

Ders.: 'Zur Geschichte der Wiener Messenkomposition in der zweiten Hälfte des XVII. Jahrhunderts', *StMw* 4 (1916) S.5–45.

Allacci, Lione: *Drammaturgia accresciuta e continuata fino all'anno 1755* (Venezia, 1755; Fotomechan. ND Torino, 1961) [Sp. 88, 197, 242, 283, 289, 570, 588].

Altenburg, Detlef: *Untersuchungen zur Geschichte der Trompete im Zeitalter der Clarinblaskunst (1500–1800)* 3 Bde. = *Kölner Beiträge zur Musikforschung* 75 (Regensburg, 1973) Bd. 1 [S.399].

Ders.: 'Instrumentation im Zeichen des Hofzeremoniells. Bemerkungen zur Verwendung der Trompete im Schaffen von Johann Joseph Fux', *Alta Musica* 9 (Tutzing, 1987) S.157–68.

Anonym: Besprechung der *Messa canonica* [Leipzig, Peters], in *Allgemeine musikalische Zeitung* 17 (Leipzig, 1815) Sp. 263–4 [vgl. auch Ausgabe K 7].

Anonym: '*Pulcheria*' [Rezension der Aufführung Innsbruck 7. 8. 1986], *Oper + Konzert* 24, 10 (1986) S.8–9 [der Autor geht geringfügig auf das Werk ein].

Bauer, Anton: *Opern und Operetten in Wien. Verzeichnis ihrer Erstaufführungen in der Zeit von 1629 bis zur Gegenwart* = *Wiener Musikwissenschaftliche Beiträge* 2 (Graz–Köln, 1955).

Becker, Heinz: 'Das Chalumeau im 18. Jahrhundert', in *Speculum musicae artis. Festgabe für Heinrich Husmann zum 60. Geburtstag am 16. Dezember 1968*, hrsg. v. Heinz Becker und Reinhard Gerlach (München, 1970) S.23–46 [32, 34, 45f.].

Benedetto, Renato di: 'The Sonate a quattro of Angelo Ragazzi (1736)', in *International Musicological Society. Report of the 11th Congress Copenhagen 1972* (Copenhagen, 1974) S.356–65.

Bletschacher, Richard: *Rappresentazione sacra. Geistliches Musikdrama am Wiener Kaiserhof* = *dramma per musica* 1 (Wien, 1985) [S.29f., 184–211 = Text von *La fede sacrileg* in Übersetzung].

Botstiber, Hugo: *Geschichte der Ouvertüre und der freien Orchestersuite* = *Kleine Handbücher der Musikgeschichte nach Gattungen* (Leipzig, 1913) [bes. S.77–81].

Brenn, Franz: 'Die Meßkomposition des Johann Joseph Fux. Eine stilistische Untersuchung'. Mschr. diss. (Wien, 1931).

Chew, Geoffrey Alexander: 'The Christmas pastorella in Austria, Bohemia and Moravia'. Diss. (Manchester, 1968) [bes. S.105–9: über *Pastorella* und *Sonate pastorali* und Anhang S.26–54: Übertragung der *Pastorella*, bisher ohne E-Nummer].

Day, Thomas: 'Echoes of Palestrina's *Missa ad fugam* in the eighteenth century', *JAMS* 24 (1971) S.462–9 [Vergleich mit Fuxens *Missa di San Carlo*].

Deutsch, Otto Erich+: 'Das Repertoire der höfischen Oper, der Hof- und der Staatsoper. Chronologischer Teil', *ÖMZ* 24 (1969) S.369–421 [384–7, 389, 393].

Eckstein, Pavel: '[Pulcheria] Brno', *Opera* 25 (1974) S.1090–2 [1091: Kurze Inhaltsangabe der Oper].

Federhofer-Königs, Renate: 'Ziele und Stand der Fux-Ausgabe', *Musica* 13 (1959) S.340–1.

Fellerer, Karl Gustav: *Der Palestrinastil und seine Bedeutung in der vokalen Kirchenmusik des achtzehnten Jahrhunderts. Ein Beitrag zur Geschichte der Kirchenmusik in Italien und Deutschland* (Augsburg, 1929) [bes. S.292–6].

Flotzinger, Rudolf: 'SOL–DO–MI–RE–DO. Ein subiectum und seine (Be) Deutung', *Studien zur Musikwissenschaft* 33 (1982) S.13–20.

Ders. – Klebel, Bernhard – Schubert, Ingrid: 'Einführung zu Werken von Johann Joseph Fux', in *58. Bachfest der Neuen Bachgesellschaft. 24.–29. Mai 1983 in Graz. Johann Sebastian Bach und der österreichische Raum* (Graz, 1983) S.96–101 [S.96–7: K 322, 326, 342; S.97–8: K 270; S.98–9: K 354; S.99: K 291; S.100: K 165; S.100–1: E 113].

Fitzpatrick, Horace: *The Horn and Horn-playing and the Austro-Bohemian Tradition from 1680 to 1830* (London etc., 1970) [S.60 u.ö.].

Gleißner, Walter: 'Die Vespern von Johann Joseph Fux. Ein Beitrag zur Geschichte der Vespernvertonung'. Diss. (Mainz, 1981) (Glattbach, 1982).

Gregor, Joseph: *Kulturgeschicte des Balletts. Seine Gestaltung und Wirksamkeit in der Geschichte und unter den Künsten* (Wien, 1944) [S.232–3: Aufführung von *Angelica vincitrice di Alcina* 1716].

Gruber, Gernot: *Das Wiener Sepolcro und Johann Joseph Fux. 1. Teil = Jahresgabe 1968 der Johann-Joseph-Fux-Gesellschaft* [9] (Graz, 1972).

Haas, Robert: *Die Musik des Barocks = Handbuch der Musikwissenschaft* (Wildpark–Potsdam, 1929) [S.159 u.ö.].

Johann Joseph Fux und die barocke Bläsertradition. Kongreßbericht Graz 1985, hrsg. v. Bernhard Habla = *Alta Musica* 9 (Tutzing, 1987) [die Aufsätze Fux betreffend finden sich auf S.1–212].

Hadamowsky, Franz: 'Barocktheater am Wiener Kaiserhof. Mit einem Spielplan (1625–1740)', in *Jahrbuch der Gesellschaft für Wiener Theaterforschung 1951/52* (Wien, 1955) S.7–117.

Halpern, Vita: 'Die Suiten von Johann Joseph Fux'. Mschr. diss. (Wien, 1917).

H[euß], A[lfred]: '*Costanza e Fortezza*. Besprechung der Ausgabe in *Denkmäler der Tonkunst in Österreich*', *Zeitschrift der Internationalen Musikgesellschaft* 12 (1910–1911) S.89–91.

Hilmera, Jiří: ' "Costanza e Fortezza". Několik poznatků k scénografií barokního divadla' ['*Costanza e Fortezza*'. *Einzelne Erkenntnisse zur Szenographie des Barocktheaters], Divadlo* 4 (1958) S.258–66.*

Ders.: 'Costanza e fortezza'. Giuseppe Galli-Bibiena und das Barocktheater in Böhmen', *Maske und Kothurn* 10 (1964) S.396–407.

Ders.: 'Mise en scène de l'opéra solennel "Costanza e fortezza" au chateau de Prague en 1723', *Baroque* 5 (1972) S.129–32.

Hilscher, Elisabeth: 'Joseph I. (1678–1711) und Karl VI. (1685–1740) als

Widmungsträger musikalischer Werke. Zum historischen und geistesgeschichtlichen Umfeld der Widmungskomposition'. Mschr. dipl. Arb. (Wien, 1989).

Hofmann, Ulrike: 'Die Serenata am Hofe Kaiser Leopold I. (1658–1705)'. Mschr. diss. (Wien, 1975) [S.21, 51].

Horiguchi, Hisako: 'Karudara to fukkusu no opera jokyoku' [A study of the opera overtures by A. Caldara and J. J. Fux], in *Daigoro Arima – Festschrift*, S.213–46 [in Japanisch].*

Joppig, Gunther: 'Die hohen Holzblasinstrumente (Chalumeau und Oboe) im Schaffen von Johann Joseph Fux', *Alta Musica* 9 (Tutzing, 1987) S.67–87.

Kamper, Otakar: *Hudební Praha v XVIII. věků* (Praha, 1935) [über *Costanza e Fortezza*].

Kaufmann, Harald: *Eine bürgerliche Musikgesellschaft. 150 Jahre Musikverein für Steiermark* (Graz, 1965) [S.98, 107 u. ö.: mehrere Fux-Aufführungen seit 1890].

Khittl, Klaus: 'Herodias heißt das Ereignis. "La Fede Sacrilega" von Johann Joseph Fux in der Universitätskirche', *Die Presse. Unabhängige Zeitung für Österreich* (Wien, 11. Juli 1980) S.5.

Kier, Herfrid, 'Kiesewetters historische Hauskonzerte. Zur Geschichte der kirchenmusikalischen Restauration in Wien', *KmJb* 52 (1968) S.95–119 [97, 109, 118: Aufführung der *Messa canonica* und *La Depositione della Croce di Giesù Cristo*].

Kindermann, Heinz: *Theatergeschichte Europas.* Bd. 3: *Das Theater der Barockzeit* (Salzburg, 1959).

Körner, Friedrich: 'Aufführungspraktische Hinweise zur Renaissance barocker Clarin- und Trompetenspieltechniken', *Alta Musica* 9 (Tutzing, 1987) S.169–76.

Koller, Walter: *Aus der Werkstatt der Wiener Klassiker. Bearbeitungen Haydns, Mozarts und Beethovens = Münchner Veröffentlichungen zur Musikgeschichte* 23 (Tutzing, 1975) [S.130–3: Oktavfigur bei Fux, Monn, Beethoven].

Kovac, Roland: 'Studien zur Harmonik in der Klaviermusik des Spätbarock'. Mschr. Diss. (Wien, 1951) [bes. S.174–210; alle behandelten Werke sind dem Bd. 85 der *DTÖ*, hrsg. v. Erich Schenk, entnommen].

Kubitschek, Ernst: 'Block- und Querflöte im Umkreis von Johann Joseph Fux. Versuch einer Übersicht', *Alta Musica* 9 (Tutzing, 1987) S.99–119.

Larsen, Jens Peter: 'Die Triosonate von Johann Joseph Fux im Wiener Musikleben um 1740', in *Musicae Scientiae Collectanea. Festschrift Karl Gustav Fellerer zum siebzigsten Geburtstag am 7. Juli 1972,* hrsg. v. H. Hüschen (Köln, 1973) S.356–62.

Lawson, Colin: *The Chalumeau in Eighteenth-Century Music. Studies in British Musicology* 6 (Ann Arbor, 1981) [bes. S.39–46, 178].

Leslie, Murray: 'Innsbruck. Fux revival', *Opera* 29 (1978) S.58 [Besprechung von *Psyche*].

Lewinski, Wolf-Eberhard von: 'Idealfall einer Ausgrabung. P.A. Cestis "Orontea" bei der "Festwoche der Alten Musik" in Innsbruck / J. J. Fux "Pulcheria" ', *Opernwelt. Die internationale Opernzeitschrift* 27 (1986) S.38–9 [39].

Liess, Andreas: *Die Trio-Sonaten von J.J. Fux. An Hand der Manuskripte der Wiener Nationalbibliothek. Eine Studie zum dynamischen Geschichtsbild im süddeutschen Spätbarock = Neue deutsche Forschungen. Abt. Musikwissenschaft* 9 (Berlin, 1940).

Loewenberg, Alfred: *Annals of Opera (1597–1940)* Bd. 1: Text (Genf. 2/ 1955) [Sp. 141 Aufführung von *Elisa*, Sp. 148 Aufführung von *Costanza e Fortezza* u.a. 1938 in engl. Sprache in Northampton, Mass.].

Lossmann, Hans: 'Graz: Barocke Fest- und Fleißaufgabe', *Die Bühne. Das Österreichische Theatermagazin*. Nr. 317 (1985) S.32–33 [er bringt eine kurze Werkkritik].

Lotschak, Peter: 'Angelica', *Postille* 4 (Graz: Jänner, 1985) S.[8–9; Beschreibung der Charaktere].

Mark, Michael L.: 'The Introduction of the Clarinet into the Orchestra', *Woodwind World Brass & Percussion* 15, 3 (1976) S.14–17, 42, 57 [S.14, 16: *Concentus Musico-instrumentalis* u. *Constanza e Fortezza*].

Van der Meer, John Henry: *Johann Josef Fux als Opernkomponist*, 3 Bde. = *Utrechtse bijdragen tot de Muziekwetenschap* 2 (Bilthoven, 1961) [beschränkt sich nicht nur auf das Opernschaffen].

Ders., Rezension über D. Altenburg, *Untersuchungen zur Geschichte der Trompete im Zeitalter der Clarinblaskunst (1500–1800)* (s. d.), *Mf* 30 (1977) S.120–3 [122: führt ein weiteres Werk von Fux zu diesem Thema an].

Melkus, Eduard: 'Die Oper "Psiche" von Johann Josef Fux', *ÖMZ* 33 (1978) S.368–75.

Merbach, Paul Anton: 'Das Repertoire der Hamburger Oper von 1718 bis 1750', *AfMw* 6 (1924) S.354–72 [Aufführungsdaten der Oper *Teodosio*].

Moser, Andreas: 'Zur Genesis der Folies d'Espagne', *AfMw* 1 (1918/19) S.358–71 [367–8: *Follia* aus *Concentus musico-instrumentalis*].

Ders.: 'Der Violino piccolo', *Zeitschrift für Musikwissenschaft* 1 (1919) S.377–80 [379].

Nagy, Michael: 'Holzblasinstrumente der tiefen Lage im Schaffen von Johann Joseph Fux', *Alta Musica* 9 (Tutzing, 1987) S.89–98.

Nef, Karl: *Geschichte der Sinfonie und Suite* (Leipzig, 1921) [bes. S.88–90].

Nemeth, Carl: 'Eine unbekannte Sinfonia von J. J. Fux', *ÖMZ* 16 (1961) S.525–8.

[Programmheft] *Angelica vincitrice di Alcina* anläßlich der Uraufführung 1985 in Graz, Redaktion Carl Nemeth [u. a. S.8–61 Faksimile des deutschen Textes].

Nettl, Paul: '*Besprechung von DTOe*, Bd. 85' [s. Ausgaben], *JAMS* 2 (1949) S.110–12.

Ders.: 'Das Prager Quartierbuch des Personals der Krönungsoper 1723', in *Anzeiger der phil.-hist. Klasse der Österreichischen Akademie der Wissenschaften* Jg. 1957, Nr. 1 = *Kommission für Musikforschung* 8 (Wien, 1957) S.1–7.

Newmann, William S.: *The sonata in the Baroque era* (Chapel Hill, 1959) [bes. S.255–8].

Planyavsky, Alfred: *Geschichte des Kontrabasses* (Tutzing, 2/1984) [bes. S.215–27].

Reichert, Georg: 'Zur Geschichte der Wiener Messenkomposition in der ersten Hälfte des 18. Jahrhunderts'. Mschr. diss. (Wien, 1935).

Reimann, Margarete: 'Materialien zu einer Definition der Intrada', *Mf* 10 (1957) S.337–64 [344–5: Hinweis auf die Beziehung improvisierter Trompeterfanfaren zu Intraden mit konzertierenden Trompeten, speziell zur Fuxschen Intrada aus der *Serenade* bezeichneten ersten *Partita* des *Concentus musico-instrumentalis*].

Renker, Gustav: 'Das Wiener Sepolcro'. Mschr. diss. (Wien, 1913).

Riedel, Friedrich Wilhelm: 'Der Einfluß der italienischen Klaviermusik des 17. Jahrhunderts auf die Entwicklung der Musik für Tasteninstrumente in Deutschland während der ersten Hälfte des 18. Jahrhunderts'. *Studien zur italienisch-deutschen Musikgeschichte* 5 = *Analecta Musicologica* 5 (1968) S.18–33.

Riemann, Hugo: 'Die französische Ouverture (Orchestersuite) in der ersten Hälfte des 18. Jahrhunderts (Fortsetzung)', *Musikalisches Wochenblatt* 30 (1899) Sp. 65–7.

Rietsch, Heinrich: 'Der "Concentus" von J.J. Fux', *StMw* 4 (1916) S.46–57.

Rohde, Gerhard: 'Huldigungsoper fürs Publikum. In Graz wiederentdeckt: Johann Joseph Fux "Angelica vincitrice di Alcina" ', *Neue Musikzeitung* 34, Nr. 1 (1985) S.49.

Ruhnke, Martin: 'Francesco Gasparinis Kanonmesse und der Palestrinastil', in *Musicae scientiae collectanea. Festschrift Karl Gustav Fellerer zum siebzigsten Geburtstag am 7. Juli 1972*, hrsg. v. Heinrich Hüschen (Köln, 1973) S.494–511 [*Messa di San Carlo* wird in den Vergleich miteinbezogen].

Rutherford, Charles Leonhard: 'The instrumental music of Johann Joseph Fux (1660–1741)'. Mschr. diss. (Colorado State College, 1967).*

Schenk, Erich: 'Johann Joseph Fux als Klavierkomponist', in *Anzeiger der phil.-hist. Klasse der Österreichischen Akademie der Wissenschaften* Jg. 1947, Nr. 3 (Wien, 1947) S.9–12.

Ders.: *Die Außeritalienische Triosonate* = *Das Musikwerk* 35 (Köln, 1970) [S.12–14, 81].

Schering, Arnold: *Geschichte des Oratoriums* = *Kleine Handbücher der Musikgeschichte nach Gattungen* 3 (Leipzig, 1911) [S.178, 196, 203–7, 209, 212].

Schoenbaum, Camillo: 'Beiträge zur solistischen katholischen Kirchenmusik des Hochbarocks mit besonderer Berücksichtigung J.A. Planiczky's (1691?–1732)'. Mschr. diss. (Wien, 1951) [bes. S.98–136].

Ders.: 'Die "Opella ecclesiastica" des Joseph Anton Plánický (1691?–1732) eine Studie zur Geschichte der katholischen Solomotette im Mittel- und Hochbarock', *Acta musicologica* 25 (1953) S.39–79 [bes. 56–8: Behandlung von Fuxens Solomotetten, 71–3: Notenbeispiele].

S[chönwiese], E[kkehard]: 'In "Angelica" von J. J. Fux ist unentwegt von "glückseligen Inseln" die Rede. Liegen sie im utopischen "Indien"? Wo sonst?', *Postille* 4 (Graz: Jänner, 1985) S. [10].

Schollum, Robert: 'Zur Fux-Gesamtausgabe', *ÖMZ* 17 (1962) S.595.

Scholz, Rudolf: 'Ein Thementypus der Empfindsamen Zeit. Ein Beitrag zur Tonsymbolik', *AfMw* 24 (1967) S.178–98 [180–1].

Schwarz, Johann: *Die kaiserliche Sommerresidenz Favorita auf der Wieden in Wien 1615–1746* (Wien-Prag, 1898) [Opernaufführungen werden erwähnt].

Seifert, Herbert: 'Die Aufführungen der Opern und Serenate mit Musik von Johann Joseph Fux', *StMw* 29 (Tutzing, 1978) S.9–27.

Ders.: *Die Oper am Wiener Kaiserhof im 17. Jahrhundert* = *Wiener Veröffentlichungen zur Musikgeschichte* 25 (Tutzing, 1985) [S.9, 112 u. ö.].

Smither, Howard E.: 'The Baroque Oratorio. A Report on Research Since 1945', *Acta musicologica* 48 (1976) S.50–76 [S.63–4, 76].

Ders.: *A history of the oratorio. I: The oratorio in the Baroque era: Italy, Vienna, Paris* (Chapel Hill, 1977) [bes. S.407–15, mit Abbildung: Gemälde von Buck].

Spielmann, Markus: 'Der Zink im Instrumentarium des süddeutsch-österreichischen Raumes 1650 bis 1750', *Alta Musica* 9 (Tutzing, 1987) S.121–55.

Stieger, Franz: *Opernlexikon*, Teil II: *Komponisten*, Bd. 1 (Tutzing, 1977) S.371.

Suppan, Wolfgang: 'Fuxens Oper "Psiche" in Brünn', *Mitteilungen des Steirischen Tonkünstlerbundes* 42 (1969) S.14.

Ders.: 'Bach und Fux – zur Funktion und Semantik barocker Musik', in *Johann Sebastian Bach und Johann Joseph Fux. Bericht über das Symposion anläßlich des 58. Bachfestes der Neuen Bachgesellschaft 24.-29. Mai 1983 in Graz*, hrsg. v. Johann Trummer und Rudolf Flotzinger (Kassel etc., 1985) S.61–74.

Ders.: 'Zum Jahr der Musik 1985: Bach, Fux, Händel: Zur Funktion und Semantik barocker Musik', *Die Blasmusik* 35 (1985) S.65–7 [Auszüge aus dem gleichnamigen Aufsatz].

Ders.: 'Johann Joseph Fux und die barocke Bläsermusik', *Musikerziehung* 39 (1985/86) S.134–5. – auch in *Musica* 40 (1986) S.54–5. – auch in *Das Orchester. Zeitschrift für Orchesterkultur und Rundfunk-Chorwesen* 34 (1986) S.311–12. – auch in *Österreichische Blasmusik. Fach- und Verbandszeitschrift des Österreichischen Blasmusikverbandes* 34, 1 (1986) S.8–9.

Ders.: 'Möglichkeiten und Chancen einer Fux-Renaissance – vor allem im Bereich der Bläsermusik,' *Alta Musica* 9 (Tutzing, 1987) S.201–12.

Tyler, James: 'The italian mandolin and mandola 1589–1800', *Early Music* 9 (1981) S.438–46.*

Tintelnot, Hans: *Barocktheater und barocke Kunst* (Berlin, 1939) [S.76–7: *Alcina-* und *Costanza*-Aufführungen mit Abbildung].

Tittel, Ernst: *Österreichische Kirchenmusik. Werden – Wachsen – Wirken* (Wien, 1961) [S.133, 140–1 u. ö.].

Tomek, Otto: 'Das Strukturphänomen des verkappten Satzes a tre in der Musik des 16. und 17. Jahrhunderts', *Studien zur Musikwissenschaft* 27 (1966) S.18–71 [69].

Vogl, Hertha: 'Das Oratorium in Wien, von 1725 bis zum Tode Karls VI. 1740'. Mschr. diss. (Wien, 1926) [bes. S.16–21].

Walther, Lothar: *Die Ostinato-Technik in den Chaconne- und Arien-Formen des 17. und 18. Jahrhunderts = Schriftenreihe des Musikwissenschaftlichen Seminars der Universität München. Studien zur musikalischen Kultur- und Stilgeschichte* 6 (Würzburg–Aumühle, 1940) [S.42–5].

Wangemann, Otto: *Geschichte des Oratoriums von den ersten Anfängen bis zur Gegenwart* (Leipzig, 3/1882) [S.109–15].

Weilen, Alexander von: *Zur Wiener Theatergeschichte. Die vom Jahre 1629 bis zum Jahre 1740 am Wiener Hofe zur Aufführung gelangten Werke theatralischen Charakters und Oratorien = Schriften des Österr. Vereins für Bibliothekswesen* (Wien, 1901).

Wellesz, Egon: *Musikalisches Barock und Anfänge der Oper in Wien = Theater und Kultur* 6 (Wien, 1922) [S.75–77: Aufführung von *Costanza e Fortezza*].

Werner, Hildegard: 'Die Sinfonien von Ignaz Holzbauer (1711–1783). Ein Beitrag zur Entwicklung der vorklassischen Sinfonie!' Mschr. Diss. (München, 1942) [S.3, 11, 22–3: Thementypen in den Triosonaten von Fux werden mit jenen von Holzbauer verglichen].

Wessely, Othmar: *Pietro Pariatis Libretto zu Johann Joseph Fuxens 'Costanza e fortezza'* = *Jahresgabe 1967 der Johann-Joseph-Fux-Gesellschaft* 8 (Graz, 1969).

White, Harry M.: 'The Oratorios of Johann Joseph Fux'. Diss. (University of Dublin, 1986).

Ders.: 'An Irish Saint in Eighteenth-Century Vienna: Johann Fux and the Oratorio Volgare', *The Maynooth Review* 12 (1985) S.51–7.

Ders.: 'La Fede Sacrilega und die Oratorien von Fux: Eine Einführung', in *Capella Piccola programme booklet* (Düsseldorf, 1989) S.1–7.

Willnauer, Franz: 'Salome Anno 1714. Drei Opernerstlinge', *NZfM* 121 (1960) S.266–8 [S.266–7: Aufführung von *La Fede sacrilega*].

Winkler, Klaus: 'Die Bedeutung der Posaune im Schaffen von Johann Joseph Fux', *Alta Musica* 9 (Tutzing, 1987) S.177–99.

VI Ausgaben (incl. Bearbeitungen)

1. *Denkmäler der Tonkunst in Österreich* (Wien 1894ff.):

I, 1 [Bd. 1]: *Messen. 1. Missa SS. Trinitatis* [E 113], 2. *Missa S. Caroli (Canonica)* [K 7], 3. *Missa Quadragesimalis* [K 29], 4. *Missa Purificationis* [K 28], hrsg. v. Johannes Evangelist Habert und Gustav Adolf Glossner (Wien: Artaria & Co, 1894; ND, Graz: ADEVA, 1959).†

II, 1 [Bd. 3]: *Motetten. Erste Abtheilung. 27 Motetten für 4 oder 5 Singstimmen allein, oder mit Orgel und Instrumentalbegleitung a capella* [K 54, 137, 139–43, 146–7, 149–58, 204,3, 204,6, 253, 282, 284–7], hrsg. v. Johannes Evangelist Habert (Wien: Artaria & Co, 1895; ND, Graz: ADEVA, 1959).†

IX, 2 [Bd.19]: *Mehrfach besetzte Instrumentalwerke. Zwei Kirchensonaten* [K347, 342] *und zwei Ouverturen* [E109, 110], hrsg. v. Guido Adler (Wien: Artaria & Co, 1902; ND, Graz: ADEVA, 1959).†

XVII [Bd. 34/35]: *Costanza e Fortezza. Festa teatrale in drei Akten.* [K 315]. Dichtung von Pietro Pariati. Die Tänze von Nicola Matheis, bearb. v. Egon Wellesz (Wien: Artaria & Co; Leipzig: Breitkopf & Härtel, 1910; ND Graz: ADEVA, 1959).†

Bd. 47: *Concentus musico-instrumentalis. Enthaltend sieben Partiten und zwar: vier Ouverturen, zwei Sinfonien, eine Serenade* [K 352–358], bearb. v. Heinrich Rietsch (Wien: Artaria; Leipzig: Breitkopf & Härtel, 1916; ND Graz: ADEVA, 1960).†

Bd. 84: *Arie des Orfeo aus 'Orfeo et Euridice'* [K 309], in *Wiener Lautenmusik im 18. Jahrhundert,* hrsg. v. Karl Schnürl (Graz/Wien: ADEVA, 1966).†

Bd. 85: *Werke für Tasteninstrumente* [K 379, 398–403, 405, E 114–28], bearb. v. Erich Schenk (Wien: Österreichischer Bundesverlag, 1947).†

Bd. 101/102: *Laudate pueri* [K 84], *Alma Redemptoris* [K 190], *Ecce nunc benedicite* [K 132], *Isti qui amicisti sunt* [K 182], *Plaudite, sonat tuba* [K 165], in *Geistliche Solomotetten des 18. Jahrhunderts,* hrsg. v. Camillo Schoenbaum (Graz/Wien: ADEVA, 1962) S.77–146.†

2. Sämtliche Werke [= *GA*] (Kassel: Bärenreiter – Graz: ADEVA, 1959ff.):

Serie I, Messen und Requiem:
1. *Missa Corporis Christi.* K 10. Entstanden 1713, hrsg. v. Hellmut Federhofer (1959).†
2. *Missa Lachrymantis Virginis* E 12, hrsg. v. Hellmut Federhofer, Continuobearbeitung v. Franz Eibner (1971).†
3. *Missa brevis solennitatis* K 5, hrsg. v. Josef-Horst Lederer (1974).†
4. *Missa Gratiarum actionis* K 27, vorgelegt v. Wolfgang Fürlinger (1981).†
5. *Requiem* K 55, vorgelegt von Klaus Winkler (1989).†

Serie II, Litaneien, Vespern und Kompletorien:
1. *Te Deum.* E 37, hrsg. v. István Kecskeméti (1963).†
2. *Te Deum.* K 270, hrsg. v. Ingrid Schubert und Gösta Neuwirth (1980).†
3. *Laudate Dominum- und Magnificat-Kompositionen* [K 91, 92, E 29, K 94, 97–101], vorgelegt v. Walter Gleißner (1989).†

Serie III, Kleinere Kirchenmusikwerke:
1. *Motetten und Antiphonen für Sopran und Instrumentalbegleitung* [K 162, 167, 173, 176, 185-7, 205–8, E 80], hrsg. v. Hellmut Federhofer und Renate Federhofer-Königs, Continuobearbeitung v. Karl Trötzmüller (1961).†

Serie IV, Oratorien:
1. *La fede sacrilega nella morte del Precursor S. Giovanni Battista.* Text v. Pietro Pariati. K 291. Entstanden 1714 in Wien, hrsg. v. Hugo Zelzer. Textrevision u. literarhistorische Einleitung von Leopold Ergens. Deutsche Übersetzung v. L. Ergens u. Margarete Gruber (1959).†
2. *La donna forte nella madre de'sette Maccabei.* Text von Pietro Pariati. K 292, hrsg. v. Othmar Wessely. Textrevision u. literarhistorische Einleitung v. Erika Kanduth.†

Serie V, Opern:
1. *Julo Ascanio, Re d'Alba.* Text v. Pietro Antonio Bernardoni. K 304, hrsg. v. Hellmut Federhofer, Textrevision u. literarhistorische Einleitung v. Leopold Ergens, deutsche Übersetzung v. E. Maria Ghezzi, Continuobearbeitung v. Eta Harich-Schneider (1962).†
2. *Pulcheria.* Text v. Pietro Antonio Bernardoni. K 303, hrsg. v. Hellmut

Federhofer und Wolfgang Suppan. Textrevision u. literarhistorische Einleitung von Leopold Ergens, Continuobearbeitung v. Rudolf Steglich (1967).†

Serie VI, Instrumentalmusik:
1. *Werke für Tasteninstrumente*, [K 403,2, 404, 405, E 70, 114–28], hrsg. v. Friedrich Wilhelm Riedel (1964).†
2. *Triopartiten* [K 319–29, 331, E 64], hrsg. v. Erich Schenk + und Theophil Antonicek (1979).†

Serie VII, Theoretische und pädagogische Werke:
1. *Gradus ad Parnassum* [= Faksimile der Ausgabe Wien, 1725], hrsg. v. Alfred Mann (1967).†

3. Wissenschaftliche und praktische Ausgaben (incl. Bearbeitungen) geordnet nach K- und E-Nummern:

K 5: s. *GA* I,3.

K 7: s. *DTÖ* I, 1.

K 7: *Messa Canonica/a/Canto, Alto, Tenore/e Basso.*, hrsg. v. Giovanni Gottfredo Schicht (Leipzig: A. Kühnel, Pl.-Nr. 1096, [1812/13]). – auch Leipzig: C. F. Peters, Pl.-Nr. 1096 [1815].

K 7: [*Missa canonica*], hrsg. v. Hermann Bäuerle = *Meisterwerke Deutscher Tonkunst. Erlesene Meisterwerke zum praktischen Gebrauch* (Leipzig, Brüssel etc.: Breitkopf & Härtel [um 1906].*

K 7: *Missa in honorem S. Caroli. 4-vocum inaequalium.* Verzorgd door: drs. J. A. Bank. (Amsterdam: Annie Bank, 1950).†

K 7: *Christe eleison*, in Fr. W. Marpurg, *Abhandlungen von der Fuge* (s. d.) Tab XLIII, XLIV.

K 7: *Christe eleison, Benedictus*, in A. Choron, *Principes de composition* (s. d.) Bd. 2, Buch 5, S. 57–8.

K 7: *Kyrie eleison, Christe eleison*, in *Auswahl vorzüglicher Musik-Werke in gebundener Schreibart von Meistern alter und neuer Zeit*. Lieferung 4 (Berlin: T. Trautwein, 1836) Nr. 10, S.5–9.

K 7: *Christe eleison* aus der *Missa canonica*, in L. R. v. Köchel, *Fux* (s. d.) S.470–3.

K 7: *Benedictus, Sanctus, Osanna*, in *Der Kanon. Ein Singbuch für Alle*, hrsg. v. Fritz Jöde: Teil 1 (Wolfenbüttel/Berlin: Kallmeyer 1943) S.82–3.

K 7: *Kyrie* aus *Missa S. Caroli*, in A. Liess, *Wiener Barockmusik* (s. d.) S.195–6.

K 10: s. *GA* I,1.

K 11: *Amen* aus der *Missa a 4. Credo in unum*, in J.J. Fux, *Gradus ad*

Parnassum (s. d.) S.268–71.

K 12: *Missa Dies mei sicut umbra* für Soli, vierstimmigen gemischten Chor, 2 Violinen und Continuo (Alt- und Tenorposaune ad libitum) (Erstdruck), hrsg. v. Wolfgang Fürlinger = *Süddeutsche Kirchenmusik des Barock* 21 (Altötting: Alfred Coppenrath, 1985).†

K 18: *Kyrie, Christe eleison* aus der *Missa In fletu solatium*, in J.J. Fux, *Gradus ad Parnassum* (s. d.) S.263-7.

K 20: *Missa Matutina*, für 4 Singstimmen und Orgel (Erstdruck), hrsg. v. Wolfgang Fürlinger = *Denkmäler liturgischer Tonkunst zum praktischen Gebrauch* (Augsburg: Anton Böhm & Sohn, 1979).†

K 27: s. *GA* I,4.

K 28: s. *DTÖ*, I,1.

K 28: *Missa Purificationis* für Soli, gemischter Chor, 2 Violinen, Baß und Orgel, bearb. v. Richard Moder = *Gloria Dei* (Wien: Doblinger, 1958).†

K 29: s. *DTÖ* I,1.

K 29: [*Missa Quadragesimalis*], hrsg. v. Hermann Bäuerle = *Meisterwerke Deutscher Tonkunst. Erlesene Meisterwerke zum praktischen Gebrauch* (Leipzig, Brüssel etc.: Breitkopf & Härtel [um 1906].

K 32: *Missa Sancti Antonii* für 4 Singstimmen, 2 Violinen, Baß und Orgel (Erstdruck), hrsg. v. Wolfgang Fürlinger = *Denkmäler liturgischer Tonkunst zum praktischen Gebrauch* (Augsburg: Anton Böhm & Sohn, 1978).†

K 34: *Missa Sancti Joannis* für 4 gemischte Stimmen, Orgel ad libitum, hrsg, v. Jack H. van der Meer = *Musica Divina* 12 (Regensburg: Pustet, 1956).†

K 43: *Missa 'Velociter currit' (octavi toni)* für Soli, vierstimmigen gemischten Chor, 2 Violinen und Continuo (Erstdruck), hrsg. v. Wolfgang Fürlinger = *Süddeutsche Kirchenmusik des Barock* 8 (Altötting: Coppenrath, 1979).†

K 44: *Kyrie* aus der *Missa Vicissitudinis*, in J. J. Fux, *Gradus ad Parnassum* (s. d.) S.244-6.

K 44: *Kyrie* aus der *Missa Vicissitudinis*, in L. R. v. Köchel, *Fux* (s. d.) S.469-70.

K 46: *Missa in C* für Sopran, Alt, Tenor, Baß, vierstimmigen Chor, 2-4 Trompeten, Pauken, 2 Violinen u. Generalbaß, hrsg. v. Wolfgang Fürlinger = *Die Kantate*. Hänssler Edition 10.275 (Stuttgart: Hänssler, 1977); [1973 ist Vorwort datiert].†

K 54: s. *DTÖ* II,1.

K 54: [*Libera ad 4 voces con Organo*], hrsg. v. Ignaz Mitterer = *Meisterwerke Deutscher Tonkunst. Erlesene Meisterwerke zum praktischen Gebrauch* (Leipzig, Brüssel etc.: Breitkopf & Härtel [um 1906].

K 55: s. *GA* I, 5.

K 55: *Domine, Jesu Christe*, in F[riedrich] Rochlitz, *Sammlung vorzüglicher Gesangstücke*, 3 Bde. (Mainz, Paris, Antwerpen: Schott's Söhne [1837–1842]) Bd. 2, S.144–8.

K 68: *Vespero con l'Hinno* 1: *Nisi Dominus*, 2: *Beati omnes*, 4: *De profundis*, 7: *Magnificat*, in Carolus Proske, *Musica Divina. Sive Thesaurus Concentum Selectissimorum*. Bd. 3 (Regensburg, 1859) S.205–22, 337–44.

K 84: s. *DTÖ* 101/102.

K 91, 92, 94: s. *GA* II,3.

K 95 = K 68,7.

K 97–101: s. *GA* II,3.

K 108 = K 68,1.

K 132: s. *DTÖ* 101/102.

K 136 = K 68,4.

K 137: s. *DTÖ* II,1.

K 137, 139–141: *Graduale*, in: V. Goller, *Die wechselnden Messgesänge für die Adventsonntage für gemischten Chor*. Für den praktischen liturgischen Chorgebrauch eingerichtet v. V. Goller = *Meisterwerke kirchlicher Tonkunst in Österreich* III (Wien–Leipzig: UE, 1913) S.6–8, 17–18, 27–9, 37–9.

K 139–143: s. *DTÖ* II,1.

K 143: *Angelis suis*, in *Florilegium canticum sacrorum. 52 lateinische, klassische, leicht ausführbare Motetten für vierstimmigen, gemischten Chor*, hrsg. v. J. Kromolicki (Augsburg: Anton Böhm & Sohn o.J.) S.20.†

K 146, 147: s. *DTÖ* II,1.

K 149–150, 153: *Offertorium*, in V. Goller, *Die wechselnden Messgesänge für die Adventsonntage für gemischten Chor*. Für den praktischen liturgischen Chorgebrauch. . . S.19–21, 30–2, 9–12.

K 149–158: s. *DTÖ* II,1.

K 151: *Offertorium. Ave Maria gratia plena*, in J. J. Fux, *Gradus ad Parnassum* (s. d.) S.256–61.

K 152: *Tollite portas [für 4 Singstimmen]. Geistliche Chormusik* 113 [Einzelpartitur] und in *Advent und Weihnacht* 2 [Heftausgabe] (Wien: Doblinger, 1956).†

K 153: *Offertorium. Ad te Domine levavi*, in J.J. Fux, *Gradus ad Parnassum* (s. d.) S.247–54.

K 153: *Ad te Domine levavi*, in C. Proske, *Musica Divina*. Bd. 2 (Regensburg, 1855) S.1–6.

K 153: *Ad te Domine levavi*, in L.R. v. Köchel, *Fux* (s. d.) S.473–9.

K 162: s. *GA* III, 1.

K 165: s. *DTÖ* 101/102.

K 167, 173, 176: s. *GA* III, 1.

K 182: s. *DTÖ* 101/102.

K 185–187: s. *GA* III, 1.

K 190: s. *DTÖ* 101/102.

K 204,3, 204,6: s. *DTÖ* II,1.

K 204,3, 204,6: [*Asperges me ad 4 voces con Organo, Asperges me ad 5 voces con Organo*], hrsg. v. Ignaz Mitterer = *Meisterwerke Deutscher Tonkunst. Erlesene Meisterwerke zum praktischen Gebrauch* (Leipzig, Brüssel etc.: Breitkopf & Härtel [um 1906].

K 205–208: s. *GA* III,1.

K 221: *Ave Regina. Marianische Antiphon* [für Sopran, Alt, Tenor, Bass]. Erstdruck, hrsg. v. Otto Biba (Stuttgart: Carus-Verlag, 1981).†

K 222: *Ave Regina Coelorum*, in C. Proske, *Musica Divina*. Bd. 3 S.517–20.

K 227 = K 68,2.

K 253: s. *DTÖ* II,1.

K 270: s. *GA* II,2.

K 282: s. *DTÖ* II,1.

K 284–287: s. *DTÖ* II,1.

K 285–287: *Communiones*, in V. Goller, *Die wechselnden Messgesänge für die Adventsonntage für gemischten Chor*. Für den praktischen liturgischen Chorgebrauch. . . S.13, 33–4, 41–2.

K 286: *Dicite pusillanimes*, in C. Proske, *Musica Divina*. Bd. 2 S.15–18.

K 286: *Dicite pusillanimes (Communio vom 3. Adventsonntag)*, hrsg. v. F. J. Löffler = *Die Chor-Sammlung* A 27 (Regensburg: Friedrich Pustet [1954].

K 287: *Ecce virgo concipiet* = *Geistliche Chormusik* 112 [Einzelpartitur] und in *Advent und Weihnacht* 2 [Heftausgabe] (Wien: Doblinger, 1956).†

K 291, 292: s. *GA* IV,1,2.

K 300: *Tremo la terra* aus *La deposizione dalla Croce di Gesù Cristo*, in F[riedrich] Rochlitz, *Sammlung vorzüglicher Gesangstücke*, 3 Bde. (Mainz, Paris, Antwerpen: Schott's Söhne [1837–1843]) Bd. 2, S.149–52.

K 303: s. *GA* V,2.

K 303: Arie 8 des Marciano aus *Pulcheria*, in van der Meer, *Johann Josef Fux*, Bd. Notenbeispiele (s. d.) S.25–6.

K 304: s. *GA* V,1.

K 304: Arie 15 und 16 der Carmenta aus *Julo Ascanio*, in van der Meer, *Johann Josef Fux*, Bd. Notenbeispiele (s. d.) S.15–24.

K 305: Arie 8 des Sonno aus *Gli ossequi della Notte*, in van der Meer, *Johann Josef Fux*, Bd. Notenbeispiele (s. d.) S.29–32.

K 306: Schlußquartett 12 aus *Il mese di Marzo consecrata a Marte*, in: van der Meer, *Johann Josef Fux*, Bd. Notenbeispiele (s. d.) S.27–8.

K 307: Arie der Mirene *Amor è un bel desir* aus *La decima fatica d'Ercole*, in A. Liess, *Wiener Barockmusik* (s. d.) S.197–201.

K 307: Anfangschor 1 und Arie 7 des Amalteo aus *La decima fatica d'Ercole*, in van der Meer, *Johann Josef Fux*, Bd. Notenbeispiele (s. d.) S.33–41.

K 308: *Dafne in Lauro: Recitativo accompagnato*, Arie 12 der Dafne, Duett 16 Dafne–Apollo, Arie 19 der Diana, in van der Meer, *Johann Josef Fux*, Bd. Notenbeispiele (s. d.) S.9–10, 41–51.

K 309: s. *DTÖ* 84

K 309: *Orfeo, ed Euridice. Componimento da Camera per Musica . . . 1715. Poesia del Dottor Pietro Pariati*, hrgs. v. Howard Mayer Brown (Faksimile-druck) = *Italien Opera 1640-1770* [19] (New York & London: Garland Publishing, 1978).†

K 309: Arie 5 der Proserpina und Arie 8 des Plutone aus *Orfeo ed Euridice*, in van der Meer, *Johann Josef Fux*, Bd. Notenbeispiele (s. d.) S.52–7.

K 310: *Angelica vincitrice di Alcina: Recitativo accompagnato*, Arie 10 der *Alcina*, in van der Meer, *Johann Josef Fux*, Bd. Notenbeispiele (s. d.) S.10–12, 58–60.

K 311: *Diana placata: Recitativo accompagnato*, Arie 1 des Agamemnone, Arie 20 der Ifigenia, in van der Meer, *Johann Josef Fux*, Bd. Notenbeispiele (s. d.) S.8–9, 60–8.

K 312: *Elisa. Festa theatrale per musica; rappressentata nel giardino dell' imperale favorita per il felicissimo giorno natalizio della sacra cesarea e cattolica reale maestà di Elisabetta Cristina* (Amsterdam: Jeanne Roger, No. 482 [1719]).

K 312: Arie 12 des Enea und Arie 26 der Elisa aus *Elisa*, in van der Meer, *Johann Josef Fux*, Bd. Notenbeispiele (s. d.) S.68–73.

K 313: *Psiche: Halb-Accompagnato*, Arioso 16 der Psyche, Arie 22 des Giove, in van der Meer, *Johann Josef Fux*, Bd. Notenbeispiele (s. d.) S.12–13, 73–9.

K 314: Arie 12 der Diana, Arie 20 des Titione, Arie 21 des Amore, Arie 24 der Aurora und Arie 26 der Diana aus *Le nozze di Aurora*, in van der Meer, *Johann Josef Fux*, Bd. Notenbeispiele (s. d.) S.79–106.

K 315: s. *DTÖ* XVII.

K 315: *Costanza e fortezza. An Opera in Three Acts Adapted for modern performance and ed.* by *Gertrude Parker Smith* = Smith College Music Archives, 11 (Northampton, Mass.: Smith College c.1936) [Klavierauszug mit englischem Text].

K 315: Einleitungschor *Ceda Roma*, in A. Liess, *Wiener Barockmusik* (s. d.) S.202–7.

K 315: *Friedens-Hymne* ['Freu dich Rom'] aus der Oper *Costanza e Fortezze*. Text v. Karl Etti (Wien: Doblinger, 1967).

K 316: Arie 10 des Giove aus *Giunone placata*, in van der Meer, *Johann Josef Fux*, Bd. Notenbeispiele (s. d.) S.107–10.

K 317: Arie 32 des Bacco aus *La corona d'Arianna*, in van der Meer, *Johann Josef Fux*, Bd. Notenbeispiele (s. d.) S.111–14.

K 318: Arie 14 der Eternita aus *Enea negli Elisi*, in van der Meer, *Johann Josef Fux*, Bd. Notenbeispiele (s. d.) S.115–16.

K 319–329: s. *GA* VI,2.

K 320: *Triopartita K 320 für 2 Violinen, Basso continuo.* Ausgabe in Partitur und Stimme auf der Basis von Johann Joseph Fux-Sämtliche Werke VI/2. Für die Praxis eingerichtet vom Verlag. Continuobearbeitung Erich Erich Schenk. (Graz: ADEVA, 1980).†

K 320: *Andante* aus der *Partita a 3*, in L.R. v. Köchel, *Fux* (s. d.) S.461–3.

K 320: II. Satz aus *Partita a 3*, in A. Liess, *Triosonate* (s. d.) Beil. S.15–18.

K 321: *Entrata und Siciliane* aus der *Partita a 3*, in L.R. v. Köchel, *Fux*, (s. d.) S.463–8.

K 321, 328: *Partiten G-Dur und F-Dur für zwei Violinen und Bass*, hrsg. v. Andreas Liess = *Hortus Musicus* 51 (Kassel: Bärenreiter, 1950).†

K 322: *Partita a tre per due Violini e Basso continuo*, g-Moll, hrsg. v. Erich Schenk = *Hausmusik* 159 (Wien: Österreichischer Bundesverlag, 1954). – Erstdruck, hrsg. v. Erich Schenk = *Diletto musicale* 440 (Wien: Doblinger, 1973).†

K 322: *Siciliana* und *Giga* aus der *Partita a tre* g-Moll für zwei Violinen und Basso continuo, in: *Weihnachtliche Instrumentalmusik aus alter Zeit*, hrsg. v. Ursula Herrmann (Berlin: Evangelische Verlagsanstalt 1979) Nr.4, 5, S. 12–15.

K 326 = 379.

K 327: *Triopartita K 327 für 2 Violinen & Basso continuo.* Ausgabe in Partitur & Stimmen auf der Basis von Johann Joseph Fux – Sämtliche Werke VI/2. Für die Praxis eingerichtet vom Verlag. Continuobearbeitung von Erich Schenk (Graz: ADEVA, 1980).†

K 328: *Menuett* aus der *Partita* Nr.10 in A. Liess, *Wiener Barockmusik* (s. d.) S.218–20.

K 330: *Sonate für 2 Violinen und Cembalo*, unter dem Namen G. Ph. Telemann hrsg. v. Günter Hausswald (Heidelberg: Süddeutscher Musikverlag W. Müller, 1955).

K 330: *Sinfonia a tre per due Violini e Basso continuo*, D-Dur, hrsg. v. Erich Schenk = *Hausmusik* 164 (Wien: Österreichischer Bundesverlag, 1954). - Erstdruck, hrsg. v. Erich Schenk = *Diletto Musicale* 436 (Wien: Doblinger, 1973).†

K 331: s. *GA* VI,2.

K 336 = 403.

K 339: Allegro aus *Sonata a 3*, in A. Liess, *Triosonaten* (s. d.) Beil. S.1-3.

K 339: *Adagio* aus *Kirchensonate C dur*, in A. Liess, *Wiener Barockmusik* (s. d.) S.214-15.

K 342: s. *DTÖ* IX,2.

K 342: *Kirchensonate für Streichinstrumente* (2 Violinen, Violoncello und ad libitum Kontrabaß) in einfacher oder mehrfacher Besetzung, hrsg. v. Gustav Lenzewski sen. = *Musikschätze der Vergangenheit* (Berlin-Lichterfelde: Vieweg [1927]).

K 342: *Sonata a tre d-moll für Violine I <Querflöte, Oboe>, Violine II, Violoncello und B.c.*, hrsg. v. Willie Hillemann = *Pegasus-Ausgabe* (Wilhelmshaven: Noetzel, 1962).†

K 347: s. *DTÖ* IX,2.

K 351: *Fuge* aus der *Kirchensonate a moll*, in A. Liess, *Wiener Barockmusik* (s. d.) S.210-13.

K 351: *Allegro* aus *Sonata a 3* in A. Liess, *Triosonaten* (s. d.) Beil. S.4-6.

K 351, 377: *Zwei Triosonaten: A-moll, G-moll*, für zwei Violinen, Violoncello (Kontrabaß, Fagott) und Continuo, hrsg. v. Andreas Liess (Continuo-Einrichtung v. Josef Mertin) = *Continuo* (Wien: UE, 1941 und 1957).†

K 352-358: *Concentus musico-instrumentalis in septem partitas, ut vulgo dicimus, divisus: dedicatus Iosepho primo Romanorum Regi* (Norimbergae: Felsecker, 1701).

K 352-358: s. *DTÖ* 47.

K 352: *Menuett*, in A. Liess, *Wiener Barockmusik*, (s. d.) S.208-9.

K 352: *Serenata [Marche, Menuett, Aria, Rigaudon, Intrada, Gigue, Finale]* für zwei Solo-Trompeten und Blasorchester. Aus dem 'Concentus musico-instrumentalis' von 1701. Bearb. v. William A. Schaefer = *Für Blasinstrumente* 5 (Freiburg-Tiengen: Blasmusikverlag Schulz Nr. 1014, 1989).†

K 352, 356: *Suite B^b-Dur.* Blechbläserquintett I. *Bourrée Première*, II. *Bourrée Seconde* [K 352], III *Air* (Sostenuto), IV. *Gigue* [K 356], bearb. v.

Klaus Winkler = *Die Musizierstunde. Bläsermusik für kleine Gruppen* 89 (Rot an der Rot: Rundel, 1986).†

K 352, 353, 354: *Suite C-Dur* für Holzbläserquintett. Flöte, Oboe, Klarinette, Horn, Fagott. I. *Entrée* [K 353], II. *Menuett* [K 352], III. *Follie-Allegro* [K 354], IV. *Gigue-Presto* [K 352], bearb. v. Klaus Winkler = *Die Musizierstunde. Bläsermusik für kleine Gruppen* 111 (Rot an der Rot: Rundel, 1988).†.

K 352, 355: *Quintett* für zwei Klarinetten, Trompete (3. Klarinette), Horn (Tenorhorn) und Fagott. Aus dem *'Concentus musico-instrumentalis'* von 1701 [K 352: *Ouverture, Menuett, Gigue*; K 355: *Rigaudon, Aire la Double*]. Im Bläsersatz v. Wolfgang Suppan = *Für Blasinstrumente* 1 (Freiburg–Tiengen: Blasmusikverlag Schulz Nr. 1010, 1987).†

K 352, 353: *Fünf Tänze für Blechbläserquartett.* Zwei Trompeten, Horn, Posaune/Tuba. Aus dem *'Concentus musico-instrumentalis'* von 1701 [K 353: *Passepied, Menuett*; K 352: *Menuett, Bourrée, Gigue*]. In Bläsersatz v. Friedrich Körner = *Für Blasinstrumente* 2 (Freiburg–Tiengen: Blasmusikverlag Schulz Nr. 1011, 1987).†

K 352, 354, 356: *Johann Joseph Fux-Suite für Blasorchester.* Aus dem *'Concentus musico-instrumentalis'* von 1701 [K 352: *Bourrée, Final*; 354: *Air, Follie*; 356: *Marche des Ecurieus*] von Armin Suppan = *Für Blasinstrumente* 3 (Freiburg–Tiengen: Blasmusikverlag Schulz Nr. 1012, 1987).†

K 352, 354, 355, 356: *Zwei Ouvertüren* [K 355, 356] *und eine Suite* [K 352: *Rigaudon, Gigue*, 354: *Bourrée*, 356: *Menuett*] *für Saxophon-Quartett.* Aus dem *'Concentus musico-instrumentalis'* von 1701. In Bläsersatz von Klaus Winkler = *Für Blasinstrumente* 4 (Freiburg–Tiengen: Blasmusikverlag Schulz Nr. 1013, 1988).†

K 353: Menuett aus dem *'Concentus Musico-instrumentalis'*, in *Wir lernen Hausmusik* von Viktor Korda, Folge II = *Hausmusik* 58[b] (Wien: Österr. Bundesverlag, 1949).

K 353, 355, 356: *Suite F-Dur.* Blechbläserquintett, I. *Marche des Ecurieus* [K 356], II. *Menuett* [K 353], III. *Rigaudon* [K 355], IV. *Passepied* [K 353], bearb. v. Klaus Winkler = *Die Musizierstunde. Bläsermusik für kleine Gruppen* 87 (Rot an der Rot: Rundel, 1986).†

K 354: *Ouverture in F-Dur* aus *'Concentus musico-instrumenentalis'*, für 4 Streicher und basso continuo. Praktische Ausgabe in Partitur und Einzelstimmen nach Bd. 47 der *DTÖ*, hrsg. v. Wolfgang Gamerith, Continuobearbeitung v. Franz Zebinger (Graz: ADEVA, 1980).†

K 355: *Aire la Double, Aria in Canone*, in *Von Händel bis Haydn. Dreistimmige Spielstücke für C-Flöte und Gitarre oder 3 Melodie-Instrumente*, hrsg. v. Helmut Mönkemeyer (Rodenkirchen: P. J. Tonger, 1963) S.10–11.

K 355: *Aria in Canone*, in *Werke für Streicher und Generalbaß* (z. T. mit *Flöte, Oboen*), hrsg. v. Adolf Hoffmann = *Ars canonica* 4 = *Corona.*

Werkreihe für Kammerorchester 104 (Wolfenbüttel: Möseler, 1970) S.23–4.†

K 356: *Ouverture in C-Dur für Streichorchester* aus *'Concentus musico-instrumentalis'*, hrsg. v. Paul Angerer = *Diletto musicale* 110 (Wien: Doblinger, 1964).†

K 356: *Marche des Ecurieus* [u. d. T. *Marsch*], in *16 Märsche für 2 Violinen, Viola (oder 3. Violine), Violoncello und Klavier (z. T. Generalbaß)*, hrsg. v. Adolf Hoffmann = *Deutsche Instrumentalmusik für Fest und Feier* 11 (Wolfenbüttel–Berlin : Kallmeyer, 1938) S.12. – auch als *Deutsche Instrumentalmusik. Werkreihe für Kammerorchester* 11 (Wolfenbüttel: Möseler, 1950) S.12.

K 356: *Marche des Ecurieus* [u. d. T. *Aufzug*], hrsg. v. Willy Schneider, in *Kleine Vortragsstücke alter Meister für Trompete in B und Klavier* = *Edition Schott* 4717 (Mainz: Schott, 1961) S.10.†

K 356: *Marche des Ecurieus* [u. d. T. *Bourrée (Marsch)*], *Sarabande* [nicht identifiziert] aus dem *'Concentus musico-instrumentalis'* hrsg. v. Willi Hillemann, in *Spiel zu Dreien für zwei Sopranblockflöten und eine Altblockflöte oder andere Melodie-Instrumente* = *Edition Nagel* 512 (Kassel: Nagel, 1965) S.12–13.

K 356: *Marche des Ecurieus* [u. d. T. *Marschweise*], hrsg. v. Willy Schneider, in *Ein dutzend Triosätze nach alten Meistern für Holz-oder Blechbläser* = *Das Bläserwerk* 8 = *Aulos* 168 (Wolfenbüttel: Möseler, 1974) S.7.†

K 356: *Marche des Ecurieus* [u. d. T. *Marschartig*], hrsg. v. Wolfgang Suppan, in *Etüden und Vortragsstücke* (Freiburg–Tiengen: Fritz Schulz, 1981) Nr. 3.†

K 356: *Marche des Ecurieus* [u. d. T. *Bourrée*], hrsg. v. Herbert Frei, in *3 Barock-Stücke, dreistimmig.* = *Bläser Ensemble* 3 (Friedrichshafen: Studio-Verlag Rudi Seifert, o.J.) S.3.†

K 357: *Suite in D-Moll aus dem 'Concentus musico-instrumentalis' für kleines Streichorchester und Cembalo (Klavier).* Für den praktischen Gebrauch eingerichtet von Hilmar Höckner (Continuo-Bearbeitung v. Friedrich Wilhelm Lothar) = *Musikschätze der Vergangenheit* (Berlin-Lichterfelde: Friedrich Vieweg, 1937).

K 357: *Ouverture in d-moll* aus *'Concentus musico-instrumentalis'* für 4 Streicher und basso continuo. Praktische Ausgabe in Partitur und Einzelstimmen nach Bd. 47 der *DTÖ*, hrsg. v. Wolfgang Gamerith. Continuobearbeitung v. Franz Zebinger (Graz: ADEVA, 1980).†

K 357: *Suite g-Dorisch.* Blechbläserquintett. I. *Menuett*, II. *Gavotte*, III. *Sarabande*, IV. *Gigue*, bearb. v. Klaus Winkler = *Die Musizierstunde. Bläsermusik für kleine Gruppen* 88 (Rot an der Rot: Rundel, 1986).†

K 358: *Sinfonia für Flauto, Hautbois et Basso (Cembalo)* (Auch für 2

Blockflöten in f' und Cembalo), hrsg. v. Leo Kuntner = *Nagels Musik-Archiv* 146 (Hannover: Nagel, 1938).

K 358: *Nürnberger Partita 1701 für Flöte, Oboe oder 2f-Alt-Blockflöten (Violinen) und Cembalo (Klavier) Violoncello, Gambe nach Belieben,* hrsg. v. Adolf Hoffmann = *Deutsche Instrumentalmusik für Fest und Feier* 18 (Wolfenbüttel–Berlin: Kallmeyer, 1939) auch als *Deutsche Instrumentalmusik. Werkreihe für Kammerorchester* 18 (Wolfenbüttel: Möseler, 1950).†

K 358,2: *La joye des fidels sujets,* in *Der Geigenchor. Stücke alter Meister,* 2. Folge, hrsg. u. bearb. für 3 Geigen oder 3 stimmigen Geigenchor v. Willy Schneider (Zürich: Hug & Co., 1951) S.6–7.

K 361 = 379

K 362 = 368

K 365: *Allegro* aus *Sonata a tre,* in A. Liess, *Triosonaten* (s. d.) Beil. S.7–10.

K 367 = 402

K 368: II. Satz aus *Sonata a tre,* in A. Liess, *Triosonaten* (s. d.) Beil. S.11–13.

K 369: Schlußsatz aus *Sonata a tre,* in A. Liess, *Triosonaten* (s. d.) Beil. S.14.

K 370 = 320

K 375 = 402

K 376: *Adagio* aus *Kirchensonate d moll,* in A. Liess, *Wiener Barockmusik* (s. d.) S.216–17, sowie in ders., *Triosonaten* (s. d.) Beil. S.19.

K 377: *Passacaglia* [= K 320] aus *Sonata a tre,* in A. Liess, *Triosonaten* (s. d.) Beil, S.20–4.

K 377: s. K 351

K 379: s. *DTÖ* 85.

K 379: I., III. Satz aus *Sonata a tre,* in A. Liess, *Triosonaten (s. d.) Beil. S.25–31.*

K 381 = 400

K 386 = 398

K 387 = 399

K 396: Letzter Satz aus *Sonata pastorale a tre,* in A. Liess, *Triosonaten* (s. d.) Beil. S.32–3.

K 397: *Sonata pastorale a tre per due Violini e Basso continuo,* hrsg. v. Erich Schenk = *Hausmusik* 158 (Wien: Österreichischer Bundesverlag, 1954). – Erstdruck. Verbesserte Auflage, hrsg. v. Erich Schenk = *Diletto Musicale* 420 (Wien: Doblinger, 1969).†

K 398 – 403: s. *DTÖ* 85.

K 398: *Presto*, in *Die alten Meister. Eine Sammlung alter Meisterstücke für Klavier zu zwei Händen*, hrsg. v. Emil von Sauer (Wien: UE, 1936) S.38–9.

K 399, 403: *Sonata seconda* und *Sonata sexta*, hrsg. v. Eberhard Kraus, in *Cantantibus Organis* 13 (Regensburg: Pustet, 1965) Nr. 10, S.31–4; Nr. 11, S.35–40 [ohne *Ciacone*].†

K 401: *Sonata*, in *Festliches Orgelspiel*, arr. v. Alexander Kirchner (Wien: Efi-Ton-Verlag, 1949) S.17–19.

K 401: *Sonata quarta*, in *Klaviermusik aus Österreich*, hrsg. v. Hans Kann (Wien: UE, 1965) S.10–13.†

K 403,2, 404, 405: s. *GA* VI,1.

K 403, E 114: *Drei Einzelstücke für Klavier* [*Ciacona, Harpeggio e Fuga, Aria passegiata*], hrsg. v. Erich Schenk = *Hausmusik* 22 (Wien: Österreichischer Bundesverlag, 1949).†

K 404: *Capriccio und Fuge für Cembalo*, Erstdruck, hrsg. v. Isolde Ahlgrimm = *Diletto Musicale* 106 (Wien: Doblinger, 1962).†

K 404, E 115–120: *Ausgewählte Werke für Tasteninstrumente*. Nach Bd. VI/1 der *Fux-GA*, hrsg. v. Friedrich Wilhelm Riedel = *Nagels Musik-Archiv* 234 (Kassel: Nagel, 1972).†

K 404: *Fuge* [Einzelnes Blatt aus einem Sammelband]. (H.M. 1310). O.O., o.J. vgl. Herrmann-Schneider (II).

K 405: s. *DTÖ* 85.

E 12: s. *GA* I,2.

E 12: *Missa in C (Klosterneuburger Messe) für gemischten Chor und Orgel, für den praktischen liturgischen Chorgebrauch* bearb. v. Vinzenz Goller = *Meisterwerke kirchlicher Tonkunst in Österreich* I (Wien–Leipzig: UE, 1913. Weitere Ausgaben 1914, 1954).†

E 12: *Klosterneuburger Messe* für gem. Chor (Soli), 2 Violinen, Violoncello, Kontrabaß, 2 Posaunen und Continuo, hrsg. v. Ernst Tittel (Wien–Graz–Köln: Styria, 1954).†

E 29: s. *GA* II,3.

E 37: s. *GA* II,1.

E 64: s. *GA* VI,2.

E 66: *Sonate (Kanon) für zwei Gamben (Bratschen) und Basso Continuo*, hrsg. v. Helmuth Christian Wolff = *Hortus Musicus* 30 (Kassel etc.: Bärenreiter-Ausgabe 2044 [1950]).

E 66: *Canon (Sonata à 3) d-moll für 2 Violinen (Sopran-oder Tenorflöte in c, Flöten, Oboen) und Generalbaß*, hrsg. v. Adolf Hoffman = *Ars canonica* 2 = *Corona. Werkreihe für Kammerorchester* 102 (Wolfenbüttel: Möseler, 1969).†

E 67: *Sonate für drei Geigen; aus Mus. mscr. 1607 der hess. Landesbibliothek zu Darmstadt* (HS. von Christoph Graupner), in *Kurmainzer Musik und Trio von Fux*, hrsg. v. Adam Gottron = *Veröffentlichung der neudeutschen Musikscharen* III, Folge 2 (Würzburg: St. Rita-Verlag, 1926) S.11–17.

E 67: *Sonata à 3* für drei Violinen, hrsg. v. Wilhelm Friedrich. Erstdruck (Mainz: Schott's Söhne, 1941).

E 67: *Sonata a tre* für drei Violinen, hrsg. v. Wilhelm Friedrich = *Antiqua. Eine Sammlung alter Musik* = *Edition Schott* 3707 (Mainz: Schott's Söhne, 1941).

E 70: s. *GA* VI,1.

E 80: s. *GA* III,1.

E 109: s. *DTÖ* IX,2.

E 109: *Aria*, in *Die alte Geige. Vergessene Weisen großer Meister für Geige und Klavier* (Wien: UE 10582, o.J.) S.18.†

E 109: *Menuett*, in *festliche barockmusik für spielmusikgruppen*, hrsg. v. Franz Blasl = *rote reihe* 2 (Wien: UE 20002, 1969) S.26–7.†

E 110: s. *DTÖ* IX,2.

E 110: *Ouverture (Suite) für Schülerorchester.* Besetzung: Cembalo (Klavier), Violine I, II, Bratsche (Violine III) Violoncello, Kontrabaß ad lib., hrsg. v. Heinrich Lemacher und Paul Mies = *Das Kleine Orchester. Werkreihe des Reichsverbandes für Volksmusik in der Reichsmusikkammer* = *Edition Tonger* 828 (Köln: Tonger, 1929). – auch in *Tonger-Reihe. Werkreihe für kleines Orchester* (Rodenkirchen: P. J. Tonger [1959–1961]).

E 110: *Kleine Kammersonate für Sopran und Altblockflöte mit Basso continuo*, hrsg. v. Willi Hillemann (Wilhelmshaven: Noetzel, 1963).†

E 110: *Passepied 'Der Schmied'*, in *Alte Meister. Erste Reihe. Deutsche Tonwerke des 17. und 18. Jhs.* Neu hrsg.u. für den modernen Flügel bearb. v. Felix Günther. H.2 = *Hausmusik.* Herausgegeben vom Kunstwart Nr. 39–43 (München: Callwey [1907]) S.14.

E 110: *Passepied 'Der Schmied'*, in *Kleine Tänze alter Meister für Sopran-oder Tenorblockflöte (Violine) und Klavier (Cembalo)*, hrsg. v. Hans Georg Weiler = ED 3895 (Mainz: Schott, 1950) S.12.†.

E 110: *Der Schmied*, in *Alte Meister. Spielstücke*, bearb. v. Hugo Herrmann und Alfons Schmid = *Hohner-Album* 225 (Trossingen: Hohner, 1949). – NA in *Das Große Barockbuch für Akkordeon* bearb. v. Hugo Herrmann und Alfons Schmid = *Das Große Akkordeonbuch* (Trossingen: Hohner AG, 1989) S.5.†

E 110: *Menuett*, in *Alte Tänze für zwei Blockflöten im Quintabstand (c" und f')*, hrsg. v. Ruth Kaestner (Halle/Saale: Mitteldeutsche Verlags-

Gesellschaft [1948] S.6.

E 113: s. *DTÖ* I,1.

E 114: s. K 403.

E 114: *Aria passeggiata*, in *Der Weg zur Orgel*, hrsg. v. Viktor Dostal = *Hausmusik* 52 (Wien: Österreichischer Bundesverlag, 1952) S.5.

E 114–128: s. *DTÖ* 85. – *GA* VI,1.

E 115–120: s. K 404.

E 115,5, 118, 119, 121, 122, 124, 126, 127: *Acht Menuette* für ein Melodieinstrument (Sopran-c"-Blockflöte) und Tasteninstrument, hrsg. v. Leopold Kuntner = *Zeitschrift für Spielmusik* 146 (Celle: Moeck, 1950).

E 118–128: *Zwölf Menuette* für Klavier, hrsg. v. Erich Schenk = *Hausmusik* 23 (Wien: Österreichischer Bundesverlag, 1949).

E 118–128: *12 Menuette*. Für kleines Orchester (Schulorchester) mit variabler Besetzung instrumentiert v. Herwig Knaus (Wien: Doblinger, 1955).

Ohne K-, L- oder E-Nummer:
Pastorella/Canto. Alto. Tenore. Basso./Violinis 2bus Violis 2bus/Tuba Pastorica Ex G./Con Organo, in G. Chew, *The Christmas pastorelle* (s. d.) Anhang S.26–54.

Messe in C (Kyrie und Gloria) für Soli, gemischter Chor, Streicher, Bläser, Pauken und Orgel, bearb. u. hrsg. v. Armin Suppan = *Für Blasinstrumente* 7 (Freiburg-Tiengen: Blasmusikverlag Schulz, 1990.†

Drei- und vierstimmige Fugen aus dem *Gradus* in *Orgelstücke in den alten Kirchentonarten*, hrsg. v. B[ernhard] Kothe (Regensburg: Friedrich Pustet, 1870) S.11 (*Gradus* S.190–2), S.14 (*Gradus* S.159–60), S.37 (*Gradus* S.161–2), S.39–40 (*Gradus* S.163–4), S.52–3 (*Gradus* S.166–7), S.63 (*Gradus* S.167–8).

Vierstimmige Fuge aus dem *Gradus* (S.190–2) in einem bis jetzt noch nicht identifizierten Orgelheft verschiedene Autoren beinhaltend, da Titelblatt fehlt (Prag: Marco Berra 'M. B. 139') S.30, Nr. 52.

Zahlreiche Beispiele aus dem *Gradus* und *Singfundament* finden sich auch in den diversen Kompositionslehren – s. VII Musiktheorie.

4. Bearbeitungen, deren Herkunft nicht eruierbar war:

4 vierstimmige Fugen in *Museum für Orgel-Spieler. Sammlung gediegener und effectvoller Orgel-Compositionen älterer und neuerer Zeit*. 2 Bde. (Prag: Marco Berra, o. J., Pl. Nr. 550, 551). Bd. 1: S.65–6; Bd. 2: S.51–2, 74–5, 84–7 [s. a. *Der Orgel-Freund*].

2 vierstimmige Fugen in *Der Orgel-Freund. Ein praktisches Hand-und*

Muster-Buch, hrsg. v. G[otthilf] W[ilhelm] Körner und A[ugust] G[ott-fried] Ritter, Bd. 7 (Erfurt-Leipzig: Gotth. Wilh. Körner's Verlag, o. J.) S.50 Nr. 49, S.51 Nr. 50 [dieselbe auch in *Museum für Orgel-Spieler* Bd. 1, S.65-6 und *Orgel-Brevier* S.36-8].

Vierstimmige Fuge in *Orgel-Brevier. Werke berühmter deutscher und österreichischer Meister aus der Zeit um J. S. Bach.* Für den praktischen Gebrauch bearb. u. hrsg. v. Louis Dité (Wien–London: Josef Weinberger, 1950) S.36-8† [s. a. *Der Orgel-Freund*].

Sarabande in Willy Schneider, *30 Duette für zwei Trompeten = Das Bläserwerk* 3 = *Aulos. Werkreihe für Blasmusik* 163 (Wolfenbüttel–Zürich: Möseler, 1973) S.4. – auch in *Spiel zu Dreien* (s. K 356).

Aufzug in *Zwölf Vortragsstücke für Posaune und Piano* (auch für Tenorhorn, Bariton, Tenor-Saxophon und Trompete spielbar), bearb. v. Gerbert Mutter und Hermann Egner (Rot a. d. Rot: Rundel [1984] S.8-10.†

Menuett in *Aus der Zeit um Bach. Leichte Spielstücke für zwei Blockflöten in gleicher Stimmung (c) oder andere Melodieinstrumente*, bearb. v. Hans Fischer = *Frankfurter Blockflötenhefte* 1 (Frankfurt/Oder: Georg Bratfisch [1948] S.13. – auch in *Triostücke des Barock*, hrsg. v. Willi Hillemann (Hannover: Adolf Nagel [1951]) S.16.

VII Musiktheorie

a) Ausgaben und Bearbeitungen

Gradus ad Parnassum, Sive manuductio ad compositionem musicae regularem, Methodo novâ, ac certâ, nondum antè tam exacto ordine in lucem edita . . . (Wien: Johann Peter van Ghelen, 1725).

Gradus ad Parnassum. A Facsimile of the 1725 Vienna Edition = Monuments of Music and Music Literature in Facsimile. Second Series – *Music Literature* 24 (New York: Broude Brothers, 1966).

Gradus ad Parnassum [Faksimilie der Ausgabe Wien 1725], hrsg. v. Alfred Mann = *Fux-GA*, VII, 1 (Graz: ADEVA, 1967).

Die Lehre vom Kontrapunkt (Gradus ad Parnassum, 2. Buch, 1-3. Uebung) [Übersetzt u. erläutert von Alfred Mann]. (Celle: Moeck, 1938).

Gradus ad Parnassum oder Anführung zur Regelmässigen Musikalischen Composition . . . *Aus dem Lateinischen ins Teutsche übersetzt, mit nöthigen und nützlichen Anmerckungen versehen und herausgegeben von Lorenz Mizlern* (Leipzig: Mizlerischer Bücherverlag, 1742, sowie Leipzig: Johann Samuel Heinsius, 1797; Nachdruck Hildesheim, 1974).

The Study of Counterpoint from J. J. Fux's Gradus ad Parnassum. Übersetzt u. hrsg. v. A. Mann (mit J. Edmunds) = Neuausgabe von *Steps to Parnassus*, New York, 1943 (London: Dent – New York: Norton, 1965).

Salita al parnasso, o sia guida alla regolare composizione della musica . . . fedelmento trasportata dal Latino nell'Idioma Italiano dal sacerdote Alessandro Manfredi (Carpi: Carmignani, 1761).

Salita al Parnasso. Facsimile dell'ed. di Carpi del 1761 = Bibliotheca musica Bononiensis, Sez. II, 46 (Bologna, 1972).

Practical rules for learning composition, translated from a work intitled Gradus ad Parnassum, written originally in Latin by Johann Joseph Fux (London: J. Welcker [ca. 1768]). – London: John Preston [zw. 1778–1797.].*

Ière [-3è] partie du traité de composition musicale fait par le célèbre Fux . . . traduit en francais par le sieur Pietro Denis 3 Bde. (Paris: adresses ordinaires [1773–1775]). – Paris: Bignon, 3 Bde. [c.1780].*

On peut en l'étudiant avec attention parvenir à bien composer en très peu de temps. . . (Paris: Boyer [1788]). – Paris, Lobry [c.1800] – Paris, Nadermann [c.1800] – Paris, Jouve [c.1800].*

The study of the Fugue: a dialogue. By Johann Joseph Fux. Übersetzt u. hrsg. v. A. Mann, in *MQ* 36 (1950) S.525–39 und 37 (1951) S.28–44, 203–219, 376–93.

Exempla dissonantiarum ligatarum et non ligatarum, abgedruckt bei Federhofer, H.: *Drei hanschriftliche Quellen* (s.d.) S.148–50 [die Beispiele stammen nicht von Fux, sondern G. M. Bononcini].

Gründlicher zur Gesanglehre unumgänglich nothwendiger Unterricht in der Solmisation für den Sopran [= *Singfundament*] (Wien: A. Diabelli Nr. 4160 [um 1832].

b) Erwähnungen

Abert, Hermann: *W.A. Mozart. Neubearbeitete und erweiterte Ausgabe v. Otto Jahns Mozart.* 2 Bde. (Leipzig, 7 1955) [Bd. 1: S.32, 80, 119, 250f., 561, 746; Bd. 2: S.73, 115, 124, 303, 676].

Albrechtsberger, Johann Georg: *Anweisung zur Composition* (Leipzig, 1790) [mit Beispielen von J.J. Fux].

Anonym: ' "Harmony" versus "Counterpoint" in teaching', *Zeitschrift der Internationalen Musikgesellschaft* 9 (1907–1908) S.108–18 [109–12].

Arnold, Denis: 'Haydn's Counterpoint and Fux's "Gradus" ', *The Monthly Musical Record* 87 (1957) 58–8.

Badura, Eva: 'Beiträge zur Geschichte des Musikunterrichtes im 16., 17. und 18. Jahrhundert'. Mschr. Diss. (Innsbruck, 1953) [bes. S.70–95, 121–42: Besprechung des *Singfundament*; mit zahlreichen Notenbeispielen].

Bellerman, Heinrich: *Der Contrapunct* (Berlin 2/1877, 4/1901) [seine Beispiele bezieht er größtenteils aus dem *Gradus*].

Benary, Peter: *Die deutsche Kompositionslehre des 18. Jahrhunderts* =

Jernaer Beiträge zur Musikforschung 3 (Leipzig, 1960) [S.74–81].

Birtner, Herbert: 'Johann Joseph Fux und der musikalische Historismus', *Deutsche Musikkultur* 7 (1942) S.1–14.

Cherubini, Luigi: [*Cours de Contre-point et de Fugue* (Paris, 1835)]. *Theorie des Kontrapunktes und der Fuge. In neuer Übersetzung*, hrsg. v. Richard Heuberger (Leipzig, 1911) [bes. S.76–8 mit Beispielen aus dem *Gradus*].

Choron, Alexandre: *Principes de composition des Ecoles d'Italie*, Bd. 2, Buch 5 (Paris, 1808) [S.57–8: *Christe eleison, Benedictus* aus K 7]

Dahlhaus, Carl: 'Hermann von Helmholtz und der Wissenschaftscharakter der Musiktheorie', in *Über Musiktheorie. Referate der Arbeitstagung 1970 in Berlin*, hrsg. v. Frieder Zaminer = *Veröffentlichungen des Staatlichen Instituts für Musikforschung Preussischer Kulturbesitz* 5 (Köln, 1970) S.49–58 [53–4].

Dehn, S. W[ilhelm]: *Lehre vom Contrapunkt, dem Canon und der Fuge*, bearb. v. Bernhard Scholz (Berlin, 1859).

Eggebrecht, Hans Heinrich: 'Über Bachs geschichtlichen Ort', *Deutsche Vierteljahrsschrift für Literaturwissenschaft und Geistesgeschichte* 31 (1957) S.527–56 [548–9, 554: Abhandlung über *Stilus ecclesiasticus*; *Gradus ad Parnassum* ist aus der italienisch-süddeutsch-katholischen Tradition der Musik und Musiklehre hervorgegangen; das Kapitel *De Stylo Rezitativo* wird abgehandelt].

Federhofer, Hellmut: 'Der Gradus ad Parnassum von Johann Joseph Fux und seine Vorläufer in Österreich', *Musikerziehung* 11 (1957/58) S.31–5.

Ders.: 'Zur handschriftlichen Überlieferung der Musiktheorie in Österreich in der zweiten Hälfte des 17. Jahrhunderts', *Mf* 11 (1958) S.264–79 [276–9].

Ders.: 'Johann Joseph Fux als Musiktheoretiker', in *Hans Albrecht in memoriam*, hrsg. v. Wilfried Brennecke und Hans Haase (Kassel, 1962) S.109–15. = *Jahresgabe 1962 der Johann-Joseph-Fux-Gesellschaft* [4].

Ders.: 'Drei handschriftliche Quellen zur Musiktheorie in Österreich um 1700', in *Musa-Mens-Musici. Im Gedenken an Walther Vetter* (Leipzig, 1969) S.139–51 [die auf S.148–50 angeführten Beispiele stammen nicht von Fux, sondern von G.M. Bononcini].

Ders.: 'Mozart als Schüler und Lehrer in der Musiktheorie', in *Mozart-Jahrbuch 1971/2* (Salzburg, 1973) S.89–106.

Ders.: ' "Stylus antiquus" und "modernus" im Verhältnis zum strengen und freien Satz', in *Ars musica – musica scientia. Festschrift Heinrich Hüschen zum fünfundsechzigsten Geburtstag am 2. März 1980*, hrsg. v. Detlef Altenburg (Köln, 1980) S.112–17.

Ders.: 'Fux's Gradus ad Parnassum as viewed by Heinrich Schenker', *Music Theory Spectrum* 4 (1982) S.66–75.

Ders.: 'Johann Joseph Fux. Choral Styles and the "Gradus ad Parnassum" ', *American Choral Review* 24 (1982) als Festschrift für Alfred Mann u. d. T. *From Schütz to Schubert*, S.14–26.

Ders.: 'Georg Reuter d.J. als Mittler zwischen Johann Joseph Fux und Wolfgang Amadeus Mozart', *KmJb* 66 (1982) S.83–8 – auch in *Anzeiger der phil.-hist. Klasse der österreichischen Akademie der Wissenschaft* 120 = *Mitteilungen der Kommission für Musikforschung* 35 (Wien, 1983) S.51–8.

Ders.: 'Johann Joseph Fux und die gleichschwebende Temperatur', *Mf* 41 (1988) S.9–15.

Feil, Arnold: 'Zum Gradus ad Parnassum von J. J. Fux', *AfMw* 14 (1957) S.184–92.

Fellerer, Karl Gustav: 'Vom "Stylo theatrali" in der Musiktheorie des 18. Jahrhunderts', in *Minus und Logos. Eine Festgabe für Carl Nissen* (Emsdetten, 1952) S.55–61.

Frank, Paul L.: 'Kontrapunkt im Lehrplan der amerikanischen Konservatorien', *ÖMZ* 7 (1952) S.262–4.

Friedlaender, Max: *Beiträge zur Biographie Franz Schubert's* (Berlin [1887]) [S.22: die 4 cantus firmi, die Salieri Schubert zur Bearbeitung übergab, stammen von Fux].

Gardner, John: 'The Slopes of Parnassus' *Composer* 21, Autumn (1966) S.11–12.

Gerbert, Martin: *De cantu et musica sacra a prima ecclesiae aetate usque ad praesens tempus*, Bd.2 (St. Blasien, 1774;- ND hrsg. v. Othmar Wessely = *Die großen Darstellungen der Musikgeschichte in Barock und Aufklärung* 4, Graz 1968) [S.283, 293–5, 305, 355, 364–5, 370–2].

Haller, Michael: *Kompositionslehre für polyphonen Kirchengesang mit besonderer Rücksicht auf die Meisterwerke des 16. Jahrhunderts* (Regensburg: 1891) [S.5, 18, 29, 149–50, 240; er folgt in Anlage und Behandung des Stoffes im ersten Teil dem *Gradus*].

Hansell, Sven Hostrup: 'The cadence in 18th-century recitative', *MQ* 54 (1968) S.228–48 (234–6).

Thomas Attwoods Theorie- und Kompositionsstudien bei Mozart. Vorgelegt v. Erich Hertzmann + und Cecil B. Oldman, fertiggestellt von Daniel Heartz und Alfred Mann = *Wolfgang Amadeus Mozart, Neue Ausgabe sämtlicher Werke* X, 30, 1 (Kassel etc., 1965). – Dazu Kritische Berichte (D. Heartz und A. Mann), ebenda 1969.†

Holler, Karl Heinz: *Giovanni Maria Bononcini's musico prattico in seiner Bedeutung für die musikalische Satzlehre des 17. Jahrhunderts* = *Sammlung musikwissenschaftlicher Abhandlungen* 44 (Strasbourg: 1963) (bes. S.139–50).

Holschneider, Andreas: 'Zu Mozarts Bearbeitungen Bachscher Fugen', *Mf*

17 (1964) S.51–6 [51: Kontrapunktische Übung Mozarts über einen Cantus firmus aus dem *Gradus ad Parnassum*].

Jeppesen, Knud: *Der Palestrinastil und die Dissonanz* (Leipzig, 1925).

Ders.: 'Johann-Joseph Fux und die moderne Kontrapunkttheorie', in *Bericht über den I. Musikwissenschaftlichen Kongreß der Deutschen Musikgesellschaft in Leipzig von 4. bis 8. Juni 1925* (Leipzig, 1926) S.187–8.

Ders., *Kontrapunkt. Lehrbuch der klassischen Vokalpolyphonie* (Leipzig, 2/1956) S VIII, IX u. ö.

Kier, Herfried: 'Musikalischer Historismus im vormärzlichen Wien', in *Die Ausbreitung des Historismus über die Musik*, hrsg. v. Walter Wiora = *Studien zur Musikgeschichte des 19. Jahrhunderts* 14 (Regensburg, 1969) S.55–72 (56, 57, 67–9).

Kirnberger, Johann Philipp: *Gedanken über die verschiedenen Lehrarten in der Komposition, als Vorbereitung zur Fugenkenntniß* (Wien, 1793) [S.3–8, wo Kirnberger mehrmals zum *Gradus* kritisch Stellung nimmt].

Kraft, Leo: 'A New Approach to Species Counterpoint', *College Music Symposium* 21 (1981) S.60–6.

Krause, Frieda: 'Der Gradus ad Parnassum', Diss. (Königsberg, 1944) [in der Literatur immer angeführt, jedoch nich greifbar, da nie fertig gestellt].

Krenek, Ernst: 'New Methods in teaching Counterpoint', in *Music Book. Vol. VII of Hinrichsen's Musical Year Book* (London, 1952) S.116–28.

Kurth Ernst: *Grundlagen des Linearen Kontrapunkts. Einführung in Stil und Technik von Bach's melodischer Polyphonie* (Bern, 1917) [S.103–16, 127–45 ad *Das Problem des Kontrapunkts*].

Lester, Joel: 'The recognition of major and minor keys in German theory: 1680–1730', *Journal of Music Theory* 22 (1978) S.65–103 [92–4].

Ders.: 'Simultaneity structures and harmonic functions in tonal music, *In theory only* 5 (1981) S.3–28.*

Mann, Alfred: *The Study of the Fugue* (New Brunswick/New Jersey, 1958; New York, 1965).

Ders.: 'Eine Textrevision von der Hand Joseph Haydns', in *Musik und Verlag. Karl Vötterle zum 65. Geburtstag am 12. April 1968*, hrsg. v. Richard Baum und Wolfgang Rehm (Kassel, 1968) [S.433–7 es handelt sich um den *Gradus*].

Ders.: 'Haydns Kontrapunktlehre und Beethovens Studien', in *Bericht über den internationalen musikwissenschaftlichen Kongress Bonn 1970*, hrsg. v. C. Dahlhaus u. a. (Kassel etc., 1970) S.70–4.

Ders.: 'Beethoven's Contrapunctal Studies with Haydn', *MQ* 56 (1970) S.711–26. – auch in *The Creative World of Beethoven*, hrsg. v. Paul Henry Lang (New York, 1971) S.209–24.

Ders.: 'Haydn's Elementarbuch. A document of classic counterpoint instruction', *The Music Forum* 3 (1973) S.197–237 [Das *Elementarbuch* in Beziehung zum *Gradus*].

Ders.: 'Zur Kontrapunktlehre Haydns und Mozarts', in *Mozart-Jahrbuch 1978/79* (Kassel etc., 1979) S.195–9.

Ders.: 'Ist Komponieren lehrbar? Zur klassischen Fugenlehre', *Musica* 35 (1981) S.335–9 [335–6].

Ders.: 'Haydn's Relationship to the "stile antico" ', in *Haydn Studies. Proceedings of the International Haydn Conference Washington, D.C., 1975*, hrsg. v. Jens Peter Larsen u.a. (New York/London, 1981) S.374–6.

Ders.: 'Bach und die Fuxsche Lehre: Theorie und Kompositionspraxis', in *Johann Sebastian Bach und Johann Joseph Fux. Bericht über das Symposion anläßlich des 58. Bachfestes der Neuen Bachgesellschaft 24.–29 Mai 1983 in Graz*, hrsg. v. Johann Trummer und Rudolf Flotzinger (Kassel etc., 1985) S.82–6.

Schuberts Studien, vorgelegt v. Alfred Mann = *Franz Schubert. Neue Ausgabe sämtlicher Werke*, Serie VIII: Supplement, Bd. 2 (Kassel etc., 1986) [S.3–6, 15–17, 32–4, 149, 226–8, 238].

Ders.: *Theory and Practice. The Great Composer as Student and Teacher* (New York, 1987).

Marpurg, Friedrich Wilhelm: *Abhandlung von der Fuge zweyter Theil* (Berlin, 1754) [Tab. XLIII–XLIV: *Christe eleison* aus K 7].

Mattheson, Johann: *Grosse General-Baß-Schule* (Hamburg, 2/1731) [u. a. S.181: weist auf eine von G.Ph. Telemann geplante Übersetzung des *Gradus* hin, die nie zustande kam].

Mazzola, Guerino – Wieser, Heinz-Gregor: 'Musik, Gehirn und Gefühl. Wie sich Konsonanzen und Dissonanzen im Hirnstrombild des Meschen unterscheiden, *NZfM* 146, 2 (1985) S.10–14 [die Konsonaz-Dissonanz-Aufteilung von Fux dient als Ausgangsbasis].

Van der Meer, John Henry: 'Johann Josef Fux en zijn "Gradus ad Parnassum" ', *Mededelingen Gemeentemuseum Den Haag* 11,1 (1956) S.15–24.

Mizler, Lorenz: *Musikalische Bibliothek* [Nur der 1. Band trägt den Titel *Neu eröffnete Musikalische Bibliothek*], 4 Bde. (Leipzig 1739–1754) [Bd. 2/IV S.118–22; Bd. 3 S.281, 500, 564 Anmk.].

Müller, Hans: 'Wilhelm Heinse als Musikschriftsteller', *VfMw* 3 (1887) S.561–605 [S.593: Heinse über *Elisa*].

Nelson, R.B. – Boomgaarden, D.R.: 'Kirnberger's Thoughts on the Different Methods of Teaching Composition as Preparation for Understanding Fugue', *Journal of Music Theory* 30 (1986) S.71–94 [enthält eine kommentierte englische Übersetzung von J. Ph. Kirnbergers *Gedanken* (s. d.)].

Neumann, Friedrich: 'Physikalismus in der Musiktheorie', *Acta musicologica* 41 (1969) S.85–106 [101].

Nottebohm, Gustav: 'Beethovens theoretische Studien', *Allgemeine Musikalische Zeitung*, Neue Folge I (1863) Sp. 685–91, 701–8, 717–22, 749–54, 770–5, 784–9, 810–15, 825–9, 839–43 [u. a. Sp. 769–75, 784–9: die Kontrapunktlehre von Fux, soweit sie in der Handschrift Beethovens vorliegt, wird abgedruckt].

Ders.: 'Generalbass und Compositionslehre betreffende Handschriften Beethoven's und J. R. v. Seyfried's Buch "Ludwig van Beethovens's Studien im Generalbasse, Contrapuncte" u. sw.', in G. Nottebohm, *Beethoveniana. Aufsätze und Mittheilungen* (Leipzig–Winterthur, 1872) S.154–203 [die dem *Gradus* entnommenen Vorlagen sind angeführt].

Oldman, C[ecil] B[ernard]: 'Th. Attwood's studies with Mozart' in *Gedenkboek aangeboden Dr. D. F. Scheurleer op zijn 70. verjaardag*, (Gravenhagen, 1925) [S.235].

Palm, Albert, *Jérôme-Joseph de Momigny Leben und Werk. Ein Beitrag zur Geschichte der Musiktheorie im 19. Jahrhundert* (Köln, 1969) [S.201–5 u. ö.; hält den *Gradus* für veraltet].

Paolucci, Giuseppe Fr.: *Arte pratica di Contrappunto dimostrata con Esempj di varj Autori e con osservazioni*. Tom 2 (Venezia, 1766) [S.3–5: 4 stimmige Fuge aus dem *Gradus* S.190–2].

Rasch, Rudolf: 'Aspects of the perception and performance of polyphonic music'. Diss. Groningen (Utrecht, 1981) S.79–80.

Riemann, Hugo: 'Der sogenannte strenge Stil', in *Präludien und Studien. Gesammelte Aufsätze zu Aestethik, Theorie und Geschichte der Musik* II (Leipzig [1901]) S.121–39.

Ders.: *Geschichte der Musiktheorie im IX.–XIX. Jh.* (Berlin, 2/1920) [S.413–15, 465–6, 487, 496, 498, 508].

Riepel, Joseph: *Anfangsgründe der musicalischen Setzkunst* (Regensburg, 1752).

Rietsch Heinrich: 'Der "Concentus" von Johann Josef Fux', *Studien zur Musikwissenschaft* 4 (1916) S.46–57 (zugleich Einleitung zu Bd. 47 der *DTÖ*).

Roth, Herman: *Elemente der Stimmführung (der strenge Satz)* (Stuttgart, 1926) [mit Beispielen von J. J. Fux].

Schenk, Erich: 'Ein "Singfundament" von Heinrich Ignaz Franz Biber', in *Speculum musicae artis. Festgabe für Heinrich Husmann zum 60. Geburtstag am 16. Dezember 1968*, hrsg. v. Heinz Becker und Reinhard Gerlach (München, 1970) S.277–83 [277].

Schenk, Johann Baptist: 'Autobiographische Skizze', *StMw* 11 (1924) S.75–85 [77: Studium nach Fuxens Methode].

Schenker, Heinrich: *Neue musikalische Theorien und Phantasien* Bd. 2,1: *Kontrapunkt: Cantus firmus und zweistimmiger Satz* (Stuttgart/Berlin, 1910) [S.XXVIIf. u. ö.].

Sovik, Thomas Jon: 'Gradus ad Parnassum: A Manual of sixteenth-century fundamentals', *Journal of the Graduate Music Students of the Ohio State University* 7 (1978) S.17–35.

Stephan, Rudolf: 'Schönbergs Entwurf über "Das Komponieren mit selbständigen Stimmen" ', *AfMw* 29 (1972) S.239–56 [241–4].

Stockhausen, Julius: *Gesangs-Methode* (Leipzig, 1884) [mit zahlreichen Beispielen aus dem *Singfundament* und dem *Gradus*].

Stöhr, Richard: *Praktischer Leitfaden des Kontrapunkts* (Hamburg, 1911) [S.111, 115, 128: Fugenbeispiele aus dem *Gradus* 149, 153, 169, 179].

Sumner, Floyd: 'Haydn and Kirnberger: A Documentary Report', *JAMS* 28 (1975) S530–9 [mit Einbeziehung des *Gradus ad Parnassum*].

Tittel, Ernst: *Der neue Gradus, Lehrbuch des strengen Satzes nach Johann Joseph Fux* 2 Bde. (Wien, 1959).

Ders.: 'J. J. Fux und sein "Gradus ad Parnassum". Zum 300. Geburtstag des 'österreichischen Palestrina" ', *ÖMZ* 15 (1960) S.129–31.

Ders.: 'Bononcini und Fux', *ÖMZ* 17 (1963/64) S.173–4.

Ders.: 'Wiener Musiktheorie von Fux bis Schönberg', in *Beiträge zur Musiktheorie des 19. Jahrhunderts*, hrsg. v. Martin Vogel = *Studien zur Musikgeschichte des 19. Jahrhunderts* 4 (Regensburg, 1966) S.163–201 [163–72].

Vogler, [Georg Joseph]: *Abt Vogler's Choral-System* (Kopenhagen, 1800) [mit kritischen Anmerkungen zum *Gradus*].

Wagner, Udo: *Franz Nekes und der Cäcilianismus im Rheinland = Beiträge zur Rheinischen Musikgeschichte* 81 (Köln, 1969) [bes. S.106–10].

Weiss, Günther, '57 unbekannte Instrumentalstücke (15 Sonaten) von Attilo Ariosti in einer Abschrift von Johann Helmich Roman', *Mf* 23 (1970) S.127–38 [128–9 eine Abschrift des *Gradus ad Parnassum* wird erwähnt].

Wessely, Othmar: 'Johann Joseph Fuxens "Singfundament" als Violinschule', in *40 Jahre Steirischer Tonkünstlerbund. Festschrift* (Graz, 1967) S.24–32.

Wollenberg, Susan: 'The Unknown "Gradus" ', *Music & Letters* 51 (1970) S.423–4.

Dies.: 'Haydn's baryton trios and the "Gradus" ', *Music & Letters* 54 (1973). S.170–8.

Dies.: 'The Jupiter theme: new light on its creation', *The Musical Times* 116 (1975) S.781–3.

VIII Ikonographie

Ölgemälde von Nicolaus Buck (1717, Gr. 48 × 62 cm). Original Wien, Gesellschaft der Musikfreunde. – Abgedruckt u. a. in *Tagespost* Nr. 44 v. 13.2.1941, S.3; A. Liess, *Johann Joseph Fux*; *Weststeirische Volkszeitung* 22.4.1950; *Die Musik in Geschichte und Gegenwart*, hrsg. v. Friedrich Blume Bd. 4 (1955) Sp. 1162; *NZfM* 118 (1957) S.286; *ÖMZ* 15 (1960) S.131; *Musica* 14 (1960) S.187; *Deutsche Sängerschaft* 65 (1960) S.47; *Steirisches Musiklexikon*, hrsg. v. Wolfgang Suppan (Graz 1962–1966) Tafel XII; *Musik in Österreich. Notring-Jahrbuch 1971* (Wien, 1971) S.66; H.E. Smither, *Oratorium* S.408; I. Schubert, Steirische Musiker in der Welt S.208; *The New Grove Dictionary of Music and Musicians*, hrsg. v. Stanley Sadie Bd. 7 (London, 1980) S.44; *ÖMZ* 45 (1990) S.71.

Karrikatur 'Fuchs am Cembalo' (ein am Cembalo sitzendes Tier, daneben eine Sängerin – vermutlich Anspielung auf Fux und Faustina Hasse-Bordoni): Porzellangruppe von Johann Joachim Kaendler [1. Hälfte 18. Jahrhundert]. Residenzmuseum München. Abgebildet in: *Deutsche Tagespost* No. 47 (Würzburg, 1980) S.9.

Zeichnung von Luigi Scotti, Profil links [Ende 18. Jahrhundert], gestochen im Studio Raimondi zu Florenz. Es ist dies ein großes Tableau mit 42 Tonkünstlern in Medaillons gruppiert. In der Mitte findet sich Fux gemeinsam in einem Medaillon mit Puccini, Iomelli und Sacchini. Bildarchiv der ÖNB Wien (NB 513.117–C).

Lithographie von Heinrich Ernst v. Wint(t)er (1821), Brust, Rechtsprofil [nach L. Scotti] mit der Unterschrift 'Fuchs.' Bildarchiv der ÖNB Wien (NB 501.208). Abgedruckt in *Die Musik* 14 1/2 (1914/15) [Bildbeilage an Jg. 14, H. 10] nach S.192; *Geschichte der Musik in Bildern*, hrsg. v. Georg Kinsky (Leipzig, 1929; auch als *A history of music in pictures*, New York, 1951) S.254/3.

Brust halb links nach N. Buck, mit faksimiliertem Namenszug Fux, lithographiert von A. G. [1. Hälfte 19 Jahrhundert]. Bildarchiv der ÖNB Wien (NB 501.211). Abgedruckt in: Schnabl, *Fux (Jahrbuch der Leo-Gesellschaft 1895*); *Österreichisches Liederblatt* 1 (1955/56) S.2.

Ölgemälde ohne Rahmen nach N. Buck (*c.*1840, Gr. 50 × 63,5 cm). Stadtmuseum Graz (E.Pr.835).

Zeichnung von Ludwig Mayer nach N. Buck [um 1871], in L.R. v. Köchel, *J.J.Fux*.

Brust halb links [nach N. Buck], vermutlich Lithographie, als Foto wiedergegeben. Bildarchiv der ÖNB Wien (NB 522.316/BRF).

Brust halb links [nach N. Buck], mit Namenszug 'Johann Joseph Fuchs.' Bildarchiv der ÖNB Wien (NB 501.210). Abgedruckt: auf dem Johann Joseph Fux-Prospekt der ADEVA; in *Sonate. Steirisches Musikjournal* 0 (1990) S.11.

Feder-(Tusch)zeichnung von Gustav Frank [Ende 19. Jahrhundert] nach der Lithographie von A.G. Bildarchiv der ÖNB Wien (NB 522.414/BRF).

Büste von Otmar Clemencic (1959) Graz, kleiner Burghof, Fotographie in W. Suppan, *Tonkünstler des Barocks* S.17.

Sonderpostmarke '*Europa-Cept 1985 (325. Geburtstag von Johann Joseph Fux - Europäisches Musikjahr 1985)'*. Entwurf Adalbert Pilch [nach L. Scotti], Stich Kurt Leitgeb, Druck Österreichische Staatsdruckerei. Ausgabe 3. Mai 1985.

7 Reproduktionen von Kupfertafeln in *DTÖ* XVII [Bd. 34/35], *Costanza e Fortezza* – danach mehrmals in den Publikationen nachgedruckt.

IX Discographie

1962
Suite III: Alois Forer, Orgel (Elec. E 60743).

1963
Costanza e Fortezza
– *Orchestersuite* aus der Oper: Prager Kammerorchester ohne Dirigenten (Sup.SUA 10385; ST Sup.SUA 50385).
Ein Tag in Versailles: Bernhard Wahl, Kammerorchester Versailles (Pop.CBM 60031–30).
Nürnberger Partita für Flöte, Oboe und Continuo: Berliner Camerata Musicale, Rolf-Julius Koch (Cam.CM 17041 EP; ST Cam.CMS 17017 EP).
Ouverture für 2 Oboen, 2 Violinen, Viola, Fagott und Violoncello: Concentus Musicus, Ensemble für alte Musik (AM AVRS 6305)
Sonata für 2 Viole da gamba und B.c.: Concentus Musicus, Ensemble für alte Musik (AM AVRS 6005)
Serenata für 2 Trompeten, 2 Oboen, Fagott, Streichorchester und Cembalo C-dur: Jean-Francois Paillard, Instrumental-Ensemble Jean-Marie Leclair (Chr.CGLP 75736); Bernhard Wahl, Kammerorchester Versailles (Cotp.MC 20156); R. Poeschl, Solo-Clarine, Mitglieder des Orchesters der Wiener Staatsoper, Sayard Stone (Hel.479056; ST Hel. 429 056).

1964
Sinfonia II: Concentus Musicus, Wien (Col.C 91115, ST Col.STC 91115).
Sinfonia VII: Concentus Musicus, Wien (Col.C 91115, ST Col.STC 91115).

1965
Sinfonia F-dur für Flöte, Oboe, Violoncello und Cembalo: Wiener Barockspieler (ST AM AVRS 6339).

1966
Ouverture für 2 Oboen, 2 Violinen, Viola, Fagott und Violoncello: Concentus Musicus, Ensemble für alte Musik (ST AM AVRS 6305)

Partita Nr. 7 für Blockflöte, Oboe, Cembalo und Viola da gamba (Nürnberger Partita): Ernst Kölz, Blockflöte, Alfred Hertel, Oboe, Eta Harich-Schneider, Cembalo, Hubert Koller, Viola da gamba (SM AM AVRS 6356).
Sonata für 2 viole da gamba und B.c.: Concentus Musicus, Ensemble für alte Musik (ST AM AVRS 6305).

1967
Ouverture G-dur: Marga Scheurich, Cembalo (SM DaCa 92802).
Parthie A-dur: Marga Scheurich, Cembalo (SM DaCa 92802).
Partita a tre für 2 Violinen und B.c.: Jörg Wolfgang Jahn, Gutrun Kehrmann, Violine, Jürgen Wolf, Violoncello, Marga Scheurich, Cembalo (SM DaCa 92802).
Sinfonia F-dur für Flöte, Oboe, Violoncello und Cembalo: Manfred Peters, Blockflöte, Adolf Meidhof, Oboe, Ernst Prappacher, Fagott, Marga Scheurich, Cembalo (SM DaCa 92802)
Sonata für Orgel: Ernst Günthert, Orgel (ST AM AVRS 5054)

1968
Concerto (Parthia) a 4: Musica da camera (Flauto dolce, Barockvioline, Corno di caccia, Violone, Cembalo (ST AM AVRS 5059).
Costantino
- Ouverture: Musica da camera (2 Barockviolinen, Viola, Kontrabaß, Orgelpositiv (ST AM AVRS 5059).
Psiche
- Arie der Psiche: Annelies Hückl Sopran, Musica da camera (2 Barockviolinen, Flauto dolce, Kontrabaß) (ST AM AVRS 5059).
- Arie der Orgia: Annelies Hückl Sopran, Musica da camera (2 Barockviolinen, Viola, Kontrabaß, Cembalo) (ST AM AVRS 5059)
Sinfonia a 3: Musica da camera (Barockvioline, Flauto dolce, Cembalo) (ST AM AVRS 5059)
Sonata a 3: Musica da camera (Barockvioline, Viola, Violone, Orgelpositiv) (ST AM AVRS 5059)
Suite Nr. 2 für Cembalo: Vera Schwarz, Cembalo (ST AM AVRS 5059)
Il Testamento di nostro Signor Gesù Christo
- Arie: Annelies Hückl, Sopran, Musica da camera (Barockvioline, Kontrabaß, Orgelpositiv) (ST AM AVRS 5059)

1969
Nürnberger Partita (s. Partita Nr. 7)
Partita Nr.7 für Blockflöte, Oboe, Cembalo und Viola da gamba (Nürnberger Partita): Ernst Kölz, Blockflöte, Alfred Hertel, Oboe, Eta Harich-Schneider, Cembalo, Hubert Koller, Viola da gamba (SM AM AVRS 130012); Rolf-Julius Koch, Berliner Camerata Musicale (Cam.CM 17017 EP; ST Cam.CMS 17017 EP).

Sinfonia II: Concentus Musicus, Wien, (ST Col.STC 91115; SM Elec. SME 91 688).

1971

Capriccio g-moll K 404: Isolde Ahlgrimm, Cembalo (Euro LK 80 604)
Costanza e fortezza: Prager Kammerorchester (Euro LK 80 738)
Rondeau à 7: Nikolaus Harnoncourt, Concentus musicus Wien (Orig.-Instr.). (Tel SAWT 9563/63-B)
Serenada à 8: Nikolaus Harnoncourt, Concentus musicus Wien (Orig.-Instr.). (Tel SAWT 9563/63-B)
Sonata prima für Orgel: Alois Forer, Orgel (Elite PLPS 30 094).
Sonata a 4: Musica da camera (Barockvioline, Viola, Violone, Orgelpositiv). (ST AM AVRS 5059)
Sonata à 4: Nikolaus Harnoncourt, Concentus musicus Wien (Orig.- Instr.). (Tel SAWT 9563/63-B)

1973

Ad te Domine levavi: Offertorium zu 4 Stimmen; Pohl, Aachener Domchor (HM 2021 4435)

1975

Ad te Domine levavi: Offertorium zu 4 Stimmen; Pohl, Aachener Domchor (BASF DC 214 435)
Aria passeggiata C-dur: Haselböck (Psal PET 127/180 872)
Harpeggio e fuga G-dur: Haselböck (Psal PET 127/180 872)
Ouvertüre G-dur für Cembalo: Scheurich (DaCa 192 802)
Parthie A-dur für Cembalo: Peters (DaCa 192 802)
Partita Nr. 7 (Nürnberger Partita) f. Blockflöte, Oboe, Viola da gamba und Cembalo: Camerata Musicale Berlin (Cam LP 30 021)
Partita a tre für 2 Violinen und B.c.: Jörg Wolfgang Jahn, Gutrun Kehrmann, Violine, Jürgen Wolf, Violoncello, Marga Scheurich, Cembalo (DaCa 192 802)
Rondeau à 7 für Violoncello piccolo, Fagott, Violine, 3 Violen und B.c.: Harnoncourt, Concentus musicus Wien (Tel 6.41 271AW)
Serenada à 8 für 3 Clarinen, 2 Oboen, Fagott, 2 Violinen, Viola und B.c.: Harnoncourt, Concentus Musicus Wien (Tel 6. 41 271 AW).
Sinfonia F-dur für Flöte, Oboe, Violoncello und Cembalo: Manfred Peters, Blockflöte, Adolf Meidhof, Oboe, Ernst Prappacher, Fagott, Marga Scheurich, Cembalo (DaCa 192 802)
Sonata à 4 für Violine, Zink, Posaune, Dulzian und Orgel: Harnoncourt, Concentus musicus Wien (Tel 6.41 271AW)
Sonata Nr.1: Forer (DAU PLPS 30094); Leonhardt (Ph 6775 006)
Suiten für Orgel
– *Nr.2 F-dur*: Haselböck (Psal PET 127/180872)

1976

Rondeau à 7 für Violoncello piccolo, Fagott, Violine, 3 Violen und B.c.: Harnoncourt, Concentus musicus Wien (Tel 6.35 013 ER, Tel 6.41 271 AW)
Serenada a 8 für 3 Clarinen, 2 Oboen, Fagott, 2 Violinen, Viola und B.c.: Harnoncourt, Concentus Musicus Wien (Tel 6.35 013 ER, Tel 6.41 271 AW)
Sonata a 4 für Violine, Zink, Posaune, Dulzian und Orgel: Harnoncourt, Concentus musicus Wien (Tel 6.35 013 ER, Tel 6.41 271AW)
*Sonata Nr.*7: Knitl (Pelca PSR 40 577)

1977

Ad te Domine levavi: Offertorium zu 4 Stimmen: Pohl, Aachener Domchor (EMI 1C 065-99 601)
Sinfonia F-dur für Flöte, Oboe, Violoncello und Cembalo: Parnassus-Ensemble (MXT DB 248)

1978

Messe von Klosterneuburg: Pirenne, Schola Cantorum d. St. Jans-Kath. Hertogenbosch, Instr. – Ensemble (MXT Es 46 258)
Parthie g-moll für Cembalo: Tracey (FSM 53 6 26)

1979

Aria passeggiata C-dur: Knitl (Pelca PSR 40 615)
Costanza e Fortezza
– Suite: Kammerorchester Prag (BM 1413)
Menuette
– *Nr.1 in G*: Knitl (Pelca PSR 40 615)
– *Nr.4 in G*: Knitl (Pelca PSR 40 615)
– *Nr.12 in G*: Knitl (Pelca PSR 40 615)
Pastorella a 7 für Soli, Tuba pastorica, Str. u. B.c.: Koch, Bondi, Eder, Reichardt, Krattinger, Einecke, Unisono-Kammerorchester (UNS 22 779/80)
Sinfonia 2 aus Concentus musico instrumentalis (1701): Harnoncourt, Concentus musicus Wien (EMI 1 C 037–45 574)
Sinfonia 7 aus Concentus musico instrumentalis (1701): Harnoncourt, Concentus musicus Wien (EMI 1C 037–45 574)

1980

Parthie g-moll für Cembalo: Tracey (Tel 6.35 488 EK)
*Partita Nr.*7 F-dür (Nurnberger Partita): Harras, Hünteler, Friedrich, Gmünder (BM 1921)
Sonata Nr.5 Adagio/Allegro/Adagio: Leonhardt (RCA RL 30 381 DX)

1981
Kanon-Sonate für 2 Viole da gamba u. B.c.: Weber, Spengler, Shimbor (Chr SCGLX 73 943)

1982
Ciaconna in D: Kohnen (Acc 7 805)
Plaudite, sonat tuba Kantate: Lajovic, Wohlers, Touvron, Rias-Sinfonietta Berlin (Schw 3 532)
Sinfonia Nr.7 F-dur aus Concentus musico instrumentalis: Parnassus-Ensemble (MXT DB 248)
Sonaten
– *a 4*: Musicalische Compagney (Tel 6.42 825 AZ)
Suiten für Orgel
– *in a*: Allemd./Cour/Sarabd./Aria/Gigue/Menuet: Kohnen (Acc 7 805)

1983
Alma redemptoris Mater: Motette für Tenor u. Instr.; Knothe, Schreier, Capella Sagittariana (Del 27 029 C)
Serenada à 8 für 3 Clarinen, 2 Oboen, Fagott, 2 Violinen, Viola u. B.c.: Harnoncourt, Concentus musicus Wien (Tel 6.41 271 AQ)
Sonaten
– *a 4*: Allegro/Adagio/Allegro; Harnoncourt, Concentus musicus Wien (Tel 6.41 271 AQ)

1984
Aria passeggiata C-dur: Knitl (DC Pel PSR 40615)
Sonaten
– *in g a 4*: Dickey, Concerto Castello (EMI 069–146697–1 T)

1985
Alma redemptoris Mater: Motette für Tenor u. Instr.; Knothe, Schreier, Capella Sagittariana (Del CD 10 059)
Costanza e Fortezza
– Suite: Kammerorchester Prag (DC Bmu 1413)

1986
Suiten für Orgel (Cembalo)
– *Nr. 3*: Allemd./Cour./Bourrée/Menuet/Aria/Gigue: Haselböck (Schw PVW 20 438)
Il Fonte della salute (1716) Kantate:
– *Vedi che il Redentor* f. Sopran u. Instr.: Hofmann, Schola Cantorum Basiliensis (EMI 065–169 568–1)

1987
Menuette
- *Nr.1 in G*: Knitl (DC Pel PSR 40 615); Ullmann (Mdg 0 1261/62, 2 LP)
- *Nr.4 in G*: Knitl (DC Pel PSR 40 615); Ullmann (Mdg 0 1261/62, 2 LP)
- *in B*: Ullmann (Mdg 0 1261/62, 2 LP)

1988
Sonaten
- *a. 4*: Allegro/Adagio/Allegro; Musical. Compagney (Tel 8.44 010 ZS)

1989
Ad te Domine levavi: Offertorium zu 4 Stimmen; Roth, Aachener Domchor
(Aul 53 603)
Parthies für Cembalo
- *Nr.1*: Allemd./Cour./Sarabd./Aria/Menuet/Gigue; Melchersson (Chr CD
74 554)
Plaudite, sonat tuba Kantate: Güttler, Schreier, Virtuosi Saxoniae (Del 10
221)

1990
Harpeggio e fuga G-dur: Kohnen (Acc 7 805)
Johannes der Täufer [*La fede sacrilega nella morte del Precursor S. Gioy.
Battista*]: Reuber/Koslowsky, Lins, Helling, Calaminus, Schwarz u. a. /
Capella Piccola Neuss/Instr.-Ensbl. (ThoCTH 2071/2 – 2 CD)
Rondeau à 7 für Violoncello piccolo, Fagott, Violine, 3 Violen u. B.c.:
Harnoncourt, Concentus musicus Wien (Tel 244 290–2XH)
Serenada à 8 für 3 Clarinen, 2 Oboen, Fagott, 2 Violinen, Viola u. B.c.:
Harnoncourt, Concentus musicus Wien (Tel 244 290–2XH)
Sonaten
- *a 4*: Allegro/Adagio/Allegro; Harnoncourt, Concentus musicus Wien (Tel
244 290–2XH)
Suiten für Orgel (Cembalo)
- *Nr.3*: Allemd./Cour./Bourrée/Menuet/Aria/Gigue: Haselböck (Schw 120
438)

Addenda

Flotzinger, Rudolf – Wellesz, Egon: *Johann Joseph Fux. Musiker – Lehrer – Komponist für Kirche und Kaiser* (Graz 1991).

Krombach, Gabriela: *Die Vertonungen liturgischer Sonntagsoffertorien am Wiener Hof. Ein Beitrag zur Geschichte der katholischen Kirchen-musik im 18. und 19. Jahrhundert* = *Studien zur Landes- und Sozialgeschichte der Musik* 7 (München, 1986) [bes. S. 331–6).

Sämtliche Werke
Serie IV, 3: *Il trionfo della fede*, K 294, hrsg. v. Harry White
Serie VI, 3: *Triosonaten* [K 365, 366=363, 367=375, 368=362, 369, 371, 372, 373=364, 374, 376], hrsg. v. Josef-Horst Lederer (1991).

Schubert, Ingrid: 'Zur Datierung des Erstdruckes der Messe K7 von Johann Joseph Fux', *Mitteilungen der Österreichischen Gesellschaft für Musikwissenschaft* 22 (1990) S.38–39.

Index

Index of works by Johann Joseph Fux cited in the text

*The catalogue numbers in this section, for items 301–306 inclusive, differ by one digit from the catalogue numbers given in the article on Fux by Hellmut Federhofer in *The New Grove*, Vol.5, pp.45–6. These differences derive from the more exact chronology provided in Federhofer's *Grove* work-list by comparison with the original listing in Köchel. Given that the *Fux-Gesamtausgabe* retains the old numbering, however, it is also used here. The Grove digit is given after each of the numbers in question.